QUMRAN CAVE 4

V

QUMRAN CAVE 4

V

MIQṢAT MAʿAŚE HA-TORAH

BY

ELISHA QIMRON
BEN-GURION UNIVERSITY OF THE NEGEV

AND

JOHN STRUGNELL
HARVARD UNIVERSITY

IN CONSULTATION WITH
Y. SUSSMANN

AND WITH CONTRIBUTIONS BY
Y. SUSSMANN
AND
A. YARDENI

CLARENDON PRESS · OXFORD

1994

Oxford University Press, Walton Street, Oxford OX2 6DP
Oxford New York Toronto
Delhi Bombay Calcutta Madras Karachi
Kuala Lumpur Singapore Hong Kong Tokyo
Nairobi Dar es Salaam Cape Town
Melbourne Auckland Madrid
and associated companies in
Berlin Ibadan

Oxford is a trade mark of Oxford University Press

Published in the United States by
Oxford University Press Inc., New York

British Library Cataloguing in Publication Data
Data available

Library of Congress Cataloging in Publication Data
Data available

ISBN 0-19-826344-9

1 3 5 7 9 10 8 6 4 2

Printed in Great Britain
on acid-free paper by
St. Edmundsbury Press, Bury St. Edmunds

CONTENTS

FOREWORD

THE numerous fragments from Cave 4 at Qumran were found by or purchased for the Palestine Archaeological Museum between 1953 and 1959. By 1959, the six manuscripts of MMT had been identified, transcribed, materially reconstructed and partly combined into a common text, but how were such odd fragments to be understood?

Obviously we were dealing with a work containing, *inter alia*, a collection of laws, probably laws governing the conduct of the Qumran sect; but certain major questions of introduction had to be solved from the start. First, who was their author?—the Holy Angels (cf. *Jubilees*—so Milik and myself at first—cf. *DJD* III, p. 222) or some group of humans? The texts could be read, or nearly so, in either way, and various friends tried to win me over to one or the other position. Next, from what group did these laws originate, and how did they relate to other known collections? Finally, what was the historical and theological setting of the homiletic conclusion?

While these weighty questions began to be studied at Harvard and in Jerusalem, and while I started on the composition of the commentary, a ten-year slowdown ensued in my studies, caused by the 1967 war, by its consequences for the work of editing the documents that had been entrusted to the *DJD* team, and by the almost total lack of funds to support their study. Only modest progress was made until one day in January 1979; I was spending a month in Jerusalem, planning the photographing of our card concordance to the texts from Caves 2–10 and exploring the possibilities of a further year's study in Jerusalem, as a fellow of the Hebrew University's Institute of Advanced Studies. One rainy and cold day a young Israeli scholar was brought up to my room with the seemingly predestined name of Qimron. He presented me with his Hebrew University thesis on the language of Qumran, and fixed a date when we might discuss it and related matters.

The thesis was convincing and in many points his views and mine agreed; I wished I had written it myself. When he returned, Qimron asked to see the text of "4QMishn" (as it was then called). He next offered to help my publication of 4QMishn by studying the linguistic side of the text; that offer of collaboration I gladly accepted. As Qimron left I sanguinely thought that in these new circumstances the edition could probably be published quickly, after my next year in Jerusalem—though the sabbatical I was envisaging had to be postponed from 1979–80 to 1981–82.

After spasmodic correspondence between Qimron and myself before the start of my sabbatical in 1981 (a sabbatical where I promised the National Endowment for the Humanities to finish 4QMishn within the year!), our work began in renewed earnest. The material description of the manuscripts was almost finished, and Qimron finished the linguistic discussion; we also came to an agreement on the outlines of the historical understanding of the work, which we now began to call *Miqṣat Maʿaśe Ha-Torah* (MMT).

But what to do with the commentary on the major part of MMT, the legal pronouncements? Although Qimron's specialisation lay in other areas, he did agree to take on this responsibility. This decision was taken after consulting Y. Sussmann who had kindly agreed to act as our advisor on halakhic matters.

Up to that time, little public discussion of MMT had taken place, here a paragraph in 1956 in *RB*, there a paragraph on the grammar in *DJD* III; but now MMT was to receive wider attention. In 1984

we accepted an invitation to give a lecture at the Convention for the 70th Anniversary of the Israel Exploration Society. After this paper (*Biblical Archaeology Today*, pp. 400–407), and a second paper (*The Israel Museum Journal* 4 [1985], pp. 9–12), both of us continued to work each summer in Jerusalem. Next, Qimron was offered a sabbatical year in 1985–86 to be spent at Harvard—thus we thought sanguinely we would continue to work together, and advance the edition even during the academic terms. This sabbatical was made possible by help from Dean George W. Macrae, shortly before his death (in 1985) and by a generous gift to Qimron from the late Mrs. Elizabeth Hay Bechtel. Work continued over that sabbatical year, and Qimron especially advanced our historical and halakhic studies. When both of us returned to Jerusalem there were at least three years further work awaiting us.

A further delay was caused by the retirement in September 1986, and the death shortly thereafter in the spring of 1987, of P. Benoit, O.P., the editor-in-chief of the *Discoveries in the Judaean Desert* project. I had already been appointed Benoit's deputy; from September 1986 my time was much preoccupied by negotiations leading to governmental ratification of my nomination as editor-in-chief of *DJD*. In these negotiations I drew up, in agreement with each of my colleagues, a timetable with target dates for the submitting of each manuscript to the editor-in-chief. Qimron and I agreed that MMT could be ready for the press by the end of 1988.

I would like to express almost all the thanks due to friends, donors, and helpers. At the museum, first called the Palestinian Archaeological Museum, and later known as the Rockefeller Museum, we were helped by Y. Saʿad, administrator of the museum in the Jordanian period, and especially the museum's skilled photographer, the late N. Albina. At the Israel Department of Antiquities and Museums, now called the Israel Antiquities Authority, we were helped by M. Broshi, R. Peled, M. Sharabani, A. Sussmann, J. Zias, and Ṣ. Sagiv, Albina's successor as photographer. E. Puech and H. Stegemann gave generous help in matters of palaeography and reconstruction. In legal questions our councillor was above all Y. Sussmann of the Hebrew University. We have also been helped by J. Baumgarten (Baltimore Hebrew University), M. Kister (the Hebrew University), J. Milgrom (the University of California, Berkeley) and P. Segal.

Special resources have been granted to the one or the other of us by the following: the late Mr. J. D. Rockefeller, and his special grant to the Palestine Archaeological Museum to fund work on the 4Q manuscripts between 1954–60 (J. S.); Duke University Research Council (J. S.) 1962, 1965; American Philosophical Society (J. S.); American Council of Learned Societies (J. S.) 1968–69, 1974–75; the Restoration Council of Los Angeles, and the late Mrs. Elizabeth Hay Bechtel (J. S. and E. Q.) 1985–86; National Endowment for the Humanities (for J. S. as Fellow at the Albright Institute 1981–82); the Memorial Foundation for Jewish Culture (E. Q.) 1986; and *DJD* funds provided through Yarnton Manor, Oxford (J. S. and E. Q.) 1987–90.

Y. Bentolila and C. Greenberg served as typesetters of this book. F. Stewart improved the English.

Cambridge, MA.   JOHN STRUGNELL
June 1993

J. Strugnell retired in 1990 before having completed his contribution to this work. The descriptions of the scripts of 4Q397 and 4Q398 were therefore written by Dr. A. Yardeni. Strugnell has added an appendix containing other possible interpretations of various points concerning which his opinion differed from that presented in this volume. I have also added a short appendix which discusses some points of disagreement concerning the text. The historical discussion (chap. 4) was composed by both Strugnell and myself. The finishing touches were, however, Strugnell's responsibility alone. This explains the disagreement which exists between this chapter and other chapters prepared exclusively by me. The major discrepancy involves the problem of establishing the identity of the Zadokites and their halakha (compare §§ 4.2.6.1/2 with § 5.8). For assistance and advice I am indebted to Professor Y. Sussmann, who generously helped me in solving halakhic problems and corrected many drafts of the halakhic discussion.

Beer Sheba   ELISHA QIMRON
August 1993

We would like to express our sincere gratitude to the Qumran Project of the Oxford Centre for Postgraduate Hebrew Studies, whose continued generous support enables the publication of this volume and the entire series *Discoveries in the Judaean Desert*.

The manuscript was copy-edited by V. Carr-Zakovitch and C. Pfann. The camera-ready copy and the arrangement of the composite text were produced by A. Tov.

Jerusalem   EMANUEL TOV
August 1993

ABBREVIATIONS

1QapGen	The Genesis Apocryphon from Qumran Cave 1.
1QHª	The Thanksgiving Psalms from Qumran Cave 1.
1QIsaª	The Isaiah Scroll from Qumran Cave 1, MSª.
1QpHab	Pesher Habakkuk from Qumran Cave 1.
1QS	The Manual of Discipline from Qumran Cave 1.
1QSa	The Rule of the Community from Qumran Cave 1 (*DJD* I, pp. 107–118).
11QTª	The Temple Scroll.
Alon	G. Alon, *Jews, Judaism and the Classical World*, Jerusalem, 1977. (We cite the Hebrew edition מחקרים בתולדות ישראל, Tel-Aviv, 1969).
Archaeology and History	*Archaeology and History in the Dead Sea Scrolls, The New York University Conference in Memory of Yigael Yadin*, ed. L. H. Schiffman, Sheffield, 1990.
Avigad	N. Avigad, 'The Palaeography of the Dead Sea Scrolls and Related Documents', *Scripta Hierosolymitana* 4 (1958).
Bar-Asher	M. Bar-Asher, 'The Different Traditions of Mishnaic Hebrew', *Tarbiz* 53 (1984), pp. 187–220.
Bar-Ilan	M. Bar-Ilan, הפולמוס בין חכמים לכהנים, Ph.D. Dissertation, Bar-Ilan University, Ramat-Gan, 1982.
Bauer and Leander	H. Bauer and P. Leander, *Historische Grammatik der hebräischen Sprache*, Halle a/S, 1922.
Baumgarten, *Qumran Law*	J. M. Baumgarten, *Studies in Qumran Law*, Leiden, 1977.
Baumgarten, Controversies	J. M. Baumgarten, 'The Pharisaic-Sadducean Controversies about Purity, and the Qumran Texts', *JJS* 31 (1980), pp. 157–170.
Baumgarten, Polemics	J. M. Baumgarten, 'Halakhic Polemics in New Fragments from Qumran Cave 4', in *Biblical Archaeology Today*, Jerusalem, 1984, pp. 390–399.
Baumgarten, Review	J. M. Baumgarten, 'Review of *Megillat ha-Miqdaš*', *JBL* 97 (1978), pp. 584–589.
BDB	F. Brown, S. R. Driver, Ch. A. Briggs, *A Hebrew and English Lexicon of the Old Testament*, Oxford, 1907.
Bendavid	A. Bendavid, *Biblical Hebrew and Mishnaic Hebrew*, I-II, Tel-Aviv, 1967, 1971 (in Hebrew).
Ben-Ḥayyim, *SHG*	Z. Ben-Ḥayyim, *The Literary and Oral Tradition of Hebrew and Aramaic amongst the Samaritans*, V, Jerusalem, 1977 (in Hebrew).
Ben-Ḥayyim, *Traditions*	Z. Ben-Ḥayyim, *Studies in the Traditions of the Hebrew Language*, Madrid-Barcelona, 1954.
Bergsträsser	G. Bergsträsser, *Hebräische Grammatik*, I-II, Leipzig, 1918, 1929.
Beyer	K. Beyer, *Die Aramäischen Texte vom Toten Meer*, Göttingen, 1984.
BH	Biblical Hebrew.

Bickerman   E. Bickerman, *Studies in Jewish and Christian History*, II, Leiden, 1980.

Bresciani   E. Bresciani, 'Un papiro aramaico di eta tolemaica', *Atti della Accademia Nazionale dei Lincei. Rendiconti. Classe di Scienze morali*, Ser. VIII, XVII, 1962.

Brin   G. Brin, 'The Bible as Reflected in the Temple Scroll', *Shnaton: An Annual for Biblical and Ancient Near Eastern Studies* 4, ed. M. Weinfeld, Jerusalem, 1980, pp. 193–224.

Burrows   M. Burrows with J. C. Trever and W. H. Brownlee, *The Dead Sea Scrolls of St. Mark's Monastery*, I, New Haven, CT, 1950.

CBH   Classical Biblical Hebrew.

CD   The Cairo manuscripts of the Damascus Covenant. See E. Qimron, 'The Text of CDC' in *The Damascus Document Reconsidered*, ed. M. Broshi, Jerusalem, 1992, pp. 9–49.

Copper Scroll   J. T. Milik, Le rouleau de cuivre provenant de la grotte 3Q (3Q15), in *DJD* III, Oxford, 1962, pp. 199–302.

Cowley   A. Cowley, *Aramaic Papyri of the Fifth Century B.C.*, Oxford, 1923.

Cross, Development   F. M. Cross, Jr., 'The Development of the Jewish Scripts', in *The Bible and the Ancient Near East*, ed. G. E. Wright, Garden City, NY, 1961.

Cross, Discovery   F. M. Cross, Jr., 'The Discovery of the Samaria Papyri', *Biblical Archaeologist* 26 (1963), pp. 110–121.

DJD   Discoveries in the Judaean Desert.

DSS   Dead Sea Scrolls.

Epstein   J. N. Epstein, *Introduction to the Text of the Mishna*, Jerusalem, 1964 (in Hebrew).

Forty Years   *The Dead Sea Scrolls: Forty Years of Research*, ed. D. Dimant and U. Rappaport, Leiden and Jerusalem, 1992.

Geiger, *Studies*   *A. Geiger's Gesammelte Abhandlungen in hebräischer Sprache*, ed. S. Poznanski, Warsaw, 1910.

Geiger, *Urschrift*   A. Geiger, *Urschrift und Übersetzungen der Bibel*. (We cite the Hebrew translation המקרא ותרגומיו, Jerusalem, 1972).

Gesenius   E. Kautzsch (A. E. Cowley), *Gesenius' Hebrew Grammar*, Oxford, 1910.

Ginzberg   L. Ginzberg, *An Unknown Jewish Sect*, New York, 1976.

Halivni   D. W. Halivni, *Midrash, Mishna, and Gemara: The Jewish Predilection for Justified Law*, Cambridge, Mass., 1986.

HDSS   E. Qimron, *The Hebrew of the Dead Sea Scrolls*, Harvard Semitic Studies 29, Atlanta, GA, 1986.

Haneman   G. Haneman, *A Morphology of Mishnaic Hebrew According to the Tradition of the Parma Manuscript (De Rossi 138)*, Tel Aviv, 1980 (in Hebrew).

Hurvitz, *LBH*   A. Hurvitz, *The Transition Period in Biblical Hebrew*, Jerusalem, 1972 (in Hebrew).

Hurvitz, *P Source*   A. Hurvitz, *A Linguistic Study of the Relationship between the Priestly Source and the Book of Ezekiel*, Paris, 1982.

Joüon   P. Joüon, S.J., *Grammaire de l'Hébreu Biblique*, Rome, 1923.

Kuhn   K. G. Kuhn, *Konkordanz zu den Qumran Texten*, Göttingen, 1960.

Kutscher, *Isaiah*	E. Y. Kutscher, *The Language and Linguistic Background of the Isaiah Scroll (1QIsᵃ)*, Leiden, 1974.
Kutscher, *Studies*	E. Y. Kutscher, *Hebrew and Aramaic Studies*, Jerusalem, 1977.
Kutscher, *Words*	E. Y. Kutscher, *Words and their History*, Jerusalem, 1969 (in Hebrew).
LBH	Late Biblical Hebrew.
Licht, *Srakhim*	J. Licht, *The Rule Scroll*, Jerusalem, 1965 (in Hebrew).
Lieberman	S. Lieberman, *Tosepta Ki-Fshuta*, I-VIII, New York, 1955–1973.
L-S	H. G. Liddell and R. Scott, *A Greek-English Lexicon*, 9th ed., Oxford, 1976.
Mahler	R. Mahler, *Karaites — A Mediaeval Jewish Movement for Deliverance*, 1949 (in Hebrew).
Mandelkern	S. Mandelkern, *Veteris Testamenti Concordantiae Hebraicae atque Chaldaicae*. Lipsiae, 1896.
MH	Mishnaic Hebrew.
Milgrom, *Studies 1*	J. Milgrom, 'Studies in the Temple Scroll', *JBL* 97 (1978), pp. 501–523.
Milgrom, *Studies 2*	J. Milgrom, 'Further Studies in the Temple Scroll', *JQR* 71 (1980), pp. 1–17, 89–106.
Milik, *Enoch*	J. T. Milik, *The Book of Enoch: Aramaic Fragments of Qumran Cave 4*, Oxford, 1976.
Milik, *Tefillin*	J. T. Milik, *Qumran Grotte 4, II* [= DJD VI], Oxford, 1977.
MMT	*Miqṣat Maʿaśe Ha-Torah.*
MS	Manuscript.
MT	Masoretic Text.
Nathan	H. Nathan, *The Linguistic Tradition of Codex Erfurt of the Tosefta*, Ph.D. Dissertation, the Hebrew University of Jerusalem, 1984.
Nöldeke	Th. Nöldeke, *Compendious Syriac Grammar*, London, 1904.
PAM	Palestine Archaeological Museum (now the Rockefeller Museum).
Polzin	R. Polzin, *Late Biblical Hebrew — Toward Historical Typology of Biblical Hebrew Prose*, Missoula, MT, 1976.
QH	Qumran Hebrew.
Qimron, *ʾal Yitʿarev*	E. Qimron, 'אל יתערב איש מרצונו בשבת (CD 11:4)', *Proceedings of the Ninth World Congress of Jewish Studies*, Division D, vol. 1, pp. 9–16.
Qimron, Diphtongs	E. Qimron, 'Diphtongs and Glides in the Dead Sea Scrolls', *Language Studies*, II-III, ed. M. Bar-Asher, Jerusalem, 1987, pp. 259–278 (in Hebrew).
Qimron, *Gram.*	E. Qimron, *A Grammar of the Hebrew Language of the Dead Sea Scrolls*, Ph.D. Dissertation, the Hebrew University of Jerusalem, 1976 (in Hebrew).
Qimron, Observations	E. Qimron, 'Observations on the History of Early Hebrew (1000 B.C.E. – 200 C.E.) in the Light of the Dead Sea Documents', in *The Dead Sea Scrolls: Forty Years of Research*, ed. D. Dimant and U. Rappaport, Leiden and Jerusalem, 1992, pp. 349–361.
Qimron, *Terms*	E. Qimron, 'Halakhic Terms in the Dead Sea Scrolls and their Contribution to the History of Early Halakha', in *The Scrolls of the Judaean Desert: Forty Years of Research*, eds. M. Broshi et al., Jerusalem, 1992, pp. 128–138 (in Hebrew).

Qimron, *TSG*	E. Qimron, 'The Language of the Temple Scroll', *Leshonenu* 42 (1978), pp. 83–98 (in Hebrew).
Qimron, *TSL*	E. Qimron, 'The Vocabulary of the Temple Scroll', *Shnaton: An Annual for Biblical and Ancient Near Eastern Studies* 4, ed. M. Weinfeld, Jerusalem, 1980, pp. 239–262 (in Hebrew).
Qoveṣ	M. Bar-Asher (ed.), קובץ מאמרים בלשון חז״ל, 1–2, Jerusalem, 1972, 1980.
Rabin	C. Rabin, 'The Historical Background of Qumran Hebrew', *Scripta Hierosolymitana* 4, Jerusalem, 1958, pp. 144–161.
Revel	B. Revel, *The Karaite Halakha*, Philadelphia, 1913.
Rosenthal	D. Rosenthal, *Mishna Aboda Zara: A Critical Edition with Introduction*, Ph.D. Dissertation, the Hebrew University of Jerusalem, 1980 (in Hebrew).
Schiffman, *Halakha*	L. H. Schiffman, *The Halakhah at Qumran*, Leiden, 1975.
Schiffman, *Sectarian*	L. H. Schiffman, *Sectarian Law in the Dead Sea Scrolls: Courts, Testimony and the Penal Code*, Brown Judaic Studies 33, Chico, CA, 1983.
Segal	M. H. Segal, *A Grammar of Mishnaic Hebrew*, Oxford, 1927.
Sharvit, *Text and Language*	S. Sharvit, *The Text and Language of Mishna Avot,* Ph.D. Dissertation, Bar-Ilan University, 1976.
Sussmann	Y. Sussmann, 'The History of *Halakha* and the Dead Sea Scrolls: A Preliminary to the Publication of 4QMMT', *Tarbiz* 59 (1990), pp. 11–76 (in Hebrew).
Temple Scroll Studies	*Temple Scroll Studies,* ed. G. Brooke, JSPS 7, Sheffield, 1989.
Wernberg-Møller	P. Wernberg-Møller, *The Manual of Discipline*, Leiden, 1957.
Yadin, *TS*	Y. Yadin, *The Temple Scroll*, I-III, Jerusalem, 1983.
Yadin and Naveh	Y. Yadin and J. Naveh, *Masada I: The Yigael Yadin Excavations 1963–1965*, Jerusalem, 1989.
Yalon, *Scrolls*	H. Yalon, *Studies in the Dead Sea Scrolls: Philological Essays*, Jerusalem, 1967 (in Hebrew).
Yalon, *Studies*	H. Yalon, *Studies in the Hebrew Language*, Jerusalem, 1971 (in Hebrew).

INTRODUCTION

MIQṢAT MAʿAŚE HA-TORAH [= MMT] is a sectarian polemical document. Six manuscripts, all incomplete, were discovered in Qumran cave 4, and taken together they provide a text of about 130 lines. The surviving text, which probably covers about two-thirds of the original, comes from the middle and the end of the work; the beginning is completely lost. The document appears to be in the form of a letter and is unique in language, style and content.

It appears that MMT consisted originally of four sections: (1) an opening formula, now completely lost; (2) an exposition of a calendar of 364 days; (3) a list of more than twenty halakhot, most of which are peculiar to the sect; and (4) an epilogue which discusses the separation of the sect from the multitude of the people and attempts to persuade the addressee to adopt their legal views. The halakhot are the core of the letter, and the rest is merely a framework. (The calendar, although constituting a separate section, may have been related also to the area of halakha.) Most of these halakhot concern the Temple and deal with its purity, its sacrifices and its festivals. The author states that disagreement about these matters is what caused the sect to secede. He here uses the verb פרש, which derives from the same root as the word פרושים 'Pharisees'.

Since the beginning of the text is lost, we do not know for certain who the author and the addressee were, we cannot identify the groups referred to in the letter, and we do not know the name of the work. We have, however, other Qumranic evidence which suggests that the sender may be identified with the Teacher of Righteousness, and the addressee with the Wicked Priest. The name given by us to the work, *Miqṣat Maʿaśe Ha-Torah*, is taken from the epilogue, and means 'some precepts of the Torah' (C 27).

The Text (including Sigla)

The text of MMT is given here in two forms: in chap. 1 we present the text of each manuscript separately, and in chap. 2 we present a composite text based on the evidence of all six manuscripts. (In the concordance and in the general discussions we cite the composite text, without specifying the manuscript on which the text is based in each case; text that is not within square brackets exists in at least one manuscript.) The editing signs in the text are the same as those used elsewhere in the *DJD* series, except that we use two different signs to indicate two different types of lacuna. [ ] marks a lacuna in the text of a single fragment; the size of such lacunae is precisely reproduced in the transcription. ⌊⌋ marks a lacuna between the text of two different fragments or manuscripts when the size of the lacuna is not exactly known. In the case of long restorations, the restored text has been printed in small letters. This occurs in the calendar and in 4Q397 6–13. A horizontal line over a *waw* or *yod* indicates that either of these letters is possible. A horizontal line over an open or a closed *mem* indicates that either of these forms is possible. Note that ( ) marks a deletion by the scribe and { } marks a deletion by the editors.

In the edition of each individual manuscript, lacunae are filled either with the help of text preserved in one or more of the other manuscripts, or according to the context. In the former case the restored text is underlined. The composite text follows at each point the most complete manuscript,

the other manuscripts being used to complete its lacunae, or to provide, in the apparatus, variants to its text.

Each section of the composite text has a heading giving the siglum of the basic manuscript, and next to it, in parentheses, the sigla of any other manuscripts that witness to the text of that section. Each of the sigla in parentheses is underlined or outlined, and text in the composite text which is supported by, or supplemented from, a manuscript represented by a siglum in parentheses is underlined or outlined in the same way. Thus, if the heading reads a (+ $\underline{b}$ + ⊂), then a supplement taken from MS^b will be underlined in the text with a solid line, and one from MS^c will be outlined. When we change the basic manuscript on which the text rests, then a new heading is given, e.g., c (+ $\underline{a}$ + ⅆ).

Each line of the composite text contains exactly the same words as the corresponding line of whatever is the basic manuscript for the section in question. The numbers given to the lines, however, have nothing to do with the manuscript. Instead, each of the three main sections of the document which survive, A (the calendar), B (the halakhot) and C (the epilogue), has its own series of line numbers (B 1, B 2, B 3, and so on). When there is a gap in the text, we have tried to indicate, as far as possible, the number of lines that are missing. Lines may be missing either in the basic manuscript, or between a section of the text coming from one basic manuscript and an immediately following section that comes from another. We have also indicated in the composite text the points at which columns in the various manuscripts begin and end. The composite text follows the original order of MMT as far as we have been able to reconstruct it. Only in one place did Strugnell and Qimron disagree with each other concerning the order of the lines. Strugnell thinks that ll. 18–24 in C should follow l. 9 (see Appendix 2). The composite text is accompanied by an apparatus which includes various materials relating to the text, in particular all variant readings and remarks on emendations by the scribes.

Translation and Commentary

We give a translation and commentary only for the composite text. The commentary is brief, and gives references to the discussions that follow it in chapters 3 to 5. The translation attempts to convey the exact meaning of the original but is by no means literal. (In the discussion of the individual halakhot the relevant text is accompanied by an English translation. This translation is more paraphrastic in nature.)

Discussion and Tools for Further Research

The discussions on MMT deal with three topics: the language, the historical background, and the halakhot. There are other topics which demand treatment—for instance, the theology of MMT—but in order to prevent further delay in publication, we have not discussed them at any length, though we have dealt with some relevant points in the commentary. For similar reasons, we have not provided any indices. A concordance is found at the back of the volume.

1. THE TEXTS

1.2 4Q394

THESE fragments, on fairly thin leather, form two groups. One is in colour a light buff ranging to grey (red where stained) with its back a coarse grey; the other is a light brown which stains to a darker or reddish brown, with a glossy back, bluish to light brown in colour. In both groups the surface is glossy; all fragments have a tendency to lose the topmost layer of surface, leaving apparently uninscribed spaces which in fact once bore writing. There are both horizontal and vertical dry lines; the writing, though irregular in its relation to the horizontal lines, is most frequently suspended from them.

We may note the following dimensions: Height of roll: 16.6 cm, with twenty lines of writing. Width of column between dry lines: 11.2 cm; width of column (by corrected letter spaces): 35–42; intercolumnar space between dry lines: 12–16 mm. Top margin: 11–12 mm; bottom margin (from lowest inscribed dry line): 21–26 mm. Distance between lines: 5.5 mm (4.8 mm in the calendaric fragment); height of average letter (*šin*): 3–3.5 mm (2.5–3 mm in the calendaric fragments). Photos: PAM 40.618*, 41.372*, 41.375*, 41.462*, 41.594*, 41.760*, 41.780*, 42.056*, 42.472, 42.815*, 43.477, 43.492, 43.521.

1.2.1 Script

The script merits somewhat extended attention. Although the scribe's tendency to curve whatever can be curved gives an initial impression that this hand is a member of the rustic semiformal series, closer inspection shows that it does not fit into that fairly constant group of hands but rather stands in the series of Herodian vulgar semiformals (cf. the second and third hands of 1QH^a, and the discussion of 3Q15 in *DJD* III pp. 217–21). The following description will suggest that it is an early Herodian representative of this type of script, whereas 1QH^a represents a middle Herodian, and 4QCant^b and 3Q15 represent even later examples of that family. Many of the features that separate the early from the middle Herodian forms of the rustic semiformal are also found in this hand. There are almost no true apices or *keraiai* (for some possible examples cf. *ʾalep* and once in *reš*) though thickening and rounding at the end of strokes is less rare, occurring frequently in *ʾalep*, sometimes in *lamed*, sometimes in *nun*, and regularly in the *samek*; this feature, however, was found already in Hasmonean semiformals, cf. 4QH^b. The ticks (e.g., in *reš*, *bet*, *dalet*) and bent ends (in *ʿayin*, *ṣade* and *šin*, cf. also some specimens of *zayin* and *gimel*) which are so characteristic of the late Hasmonean and early Herodian periods, are well developed in this manuscript.

ʾAlep is in almost every case a three-stroke letter (as it still is in a few of 1QH^a's specimens and in the early rustic semiformal hands) and the ends of all its strokes show curving and thickening loops, or even true *keraiai*. Two particular forms deserve noting, (*a*) one where the lower left and upper right strokes are drawn in a continuous, though bent, stroke (cf. ראש in 8 iv 11) and (*b*) one where the thickening at the lower right of the diagonal is so close to the right upstroke as to give a (false) impression that the latter loops out of the former.

Bet is drawn with a separate base running from the left, as the pseudo-ligatures show.

The forms of *dalet* stand generally in the formal tradition: many specimens have the box-headed form, imitating the shape of the late Hasmonean and early Herodian formal *dalet* (the form persists in vulgar semiformals until late, cf. 1QH[a] and 3Q15); but the semiformal looped head is also found.

One form of the *he* is frequent and most peculiar, cf., e.g., the second *he* in הטהר 3–7 i 19. While the thickness of the crossbar imitates that of the rustic semiformal, the letter is drawn in a very different way: it consists of an up-stroke which at the top turns down sharply to the left in a narrow inverted V, with a thick cross stroke either drawn from slightly below the peak, or drawn from left to right and then back again to the left! This cross stroke sometimes ends in a hook, imitating very roughly the way in which the rustic semiformal's cross stroke moves up in an angle at its end before coming down into the left downstroke, but in 4Q394 the stroke often has nothing to do with the left downstroke. (Less frequently we find in this hand true specimens both of the formal and of the rustic semiformal *he*.) This peculiar form may be an imitation of the shape of *he* found in the cursive, although drawn in a different manner. To my knowledge, it is not found in other vulgar semiformal hands.

The distinctive forms of *waw* are made by a long line with a round dot or short hook at its head, while the distinctive form of *yod* has a heavy triangle at, or often slightly below, the top of the vertical; there is however an epicene form, with a large non-curling hook, which does duty for both letters (cf. כי in 3–7 i 19 or בין in 8 iv 6 with שמעו in 8 iv 2 or המוצקות in 8 iv 5).

The *zayin* is totally devoid of decoration save for an occasional curl at its base.

Similarly straight lines characterise the three-stroke H form of *het*, a form which derives from older formal models, but remains at home (though mixed with other forms) in the vulgar semiformal at all times, cf. 1QH[a] and 3Q15.

The *tet* is made with two strokes in the late Hasmonean and later style (probably even in טהורים 3–7 i 18) although the letter shows a great variety of shapes, the base varying from the horizontal to a 45° upward angle. A characteristic of *tet* in this hand is the presence of thickening, or of a hook, to the left side of the left stroke. This feature might seem to provide an argument for dating this hand late, especially in view of its systematic use, but it should be noted that the thickening occurs on the left, not the right, of the stroke; it is only a decorative development of the curve from the left found at this point in Hasmonean semiformals like 4QH[b], which can also be seen in the late Hasmonean (and early Herodian) cursive and semicursive. As an idiosyncrasy of the hand it should certainly not be compared with the *keraiai* on the right of the same stroke in the rustic semiformal, the late Herodian formal, or in late vulgar scripts like 1QH[a], nor be used as an indication of late date.

Medial *kap*, whether narrow or broad, is still a long letter, as indeed it tends to stay at all times in semiformal hands. Only rarely does 4Q394 have squat examples. Its down-stroke sometimes starts in conservative style above the topstroke, but sometimes continues from it at a sharp angle. One should note this sharp angle, found at this point also in *mem*, and also the sharp angle at the bottom of *kap*, *mem* and *pe*.[1] The sharp angles of *kap* and *mem* which characterise the present hand probably imitate (in appearance) those of a figure-3 shaped *kap*. Note that no specimen of final *kap* survives.

The large hook of *lamed* is common to all Herodian hands. The thickening or hook at the top left is found in rustic semiformals, and spasmodically in vulgar semiformals (so occasionally in 1QH[a]); here it is fairly regular.

---

[1] In the case of some instances of *pe* this sharp angle is caused by the drawing of the base from left to right in the style of *bet* (so occasionally in 1QH[a]) and derives probably from the cursive hands. There is no trace of such a change of direction in clear cases of *kap* (and so we are often spared confusing the two letters when they are of like height), nor in many of the other specimens of *pe*.

The first feature of *mem* that one notices is the epicene use of medial and final forms in either position.[2] In *mem* itself, most important is the order of strokes, with the leftward diagonal drawn last. In the rustic semiformal the shift from this form takes place at some time in the first half of the Herodian period; in the vulgar semiformal, 1QH[a], 4QCant[b] and 3Q15 all regularly show the later form. Other characteristics are the sharp angles at the right top and bottom, and the flat base line, both typical of late hands such as that of 1QH[a]. The final *mem*, in whatever position it is used, is distinct from many specimens in the rustic tradition by its horizontal top and (occasionally) bottom strokes; the start of the final closing stroke shows no tendency to the newer positions that it adopts in later vulgar hands like that of 1QH[a].

Nothing in either *nun* or final *nun* is surprising within the semiformal tradition of the Herodian period (or even of the Hasmonean for that matter); the thickening and bending of the ends have not yet become *keraiai* or sharp hooks.

Samek we find in both the 'triangular' and 'square' shapes, but in each case with the upstroke looping heavily into the horizontal.

ʿ*Ayin* maintains its archaic upright stance, as generally in semiformals and semicursives (so 3Q15 but contrast 1QH[a]). Characteristic of this hand is the way in which the two tops are curved in towards each other, in the style of the *ṣade* and of the three tops of *šin*, but apart from the unornamented nature of these curves the feature is of no significance for dating.

Medial *pe* (sometimes used even in final position) has, in addition to the separately drawn base found in some specimens (to which attention has already been drawn), a very little-developed head which is early in origin, though it survives late in some vulgar semiformals such as 1QH[a]. The final form has heads showing various degrees of involution, but nothing that warrants surprise at any point in the Herodian period.

The head of the *ṣade* was probably the model for the head of the ʿ*ayin*; in the case of *ṣade*, this curve of the left top to the right is frequent in the semiformal tradition.

Qop remains in many specimens a remarkably small letter, though in later vulgar semiformals it follows the general Herodian tendency to elongate the tail. In most specimens the upstroke loops into the cross stroke (as in the rustic semiformal, and, among vulgar specimens, in 1QH[a] and 4QCant[b]). Even those without a loop seem to be drawn with the same order of strokes.

Reš occasionally has a sharp angle at the shoulder (cf. the sharp angled shoulders of *mem* and *kap*). Its initial tick, although in only a few specimens, is so elaborate that it resembles a triangular *keraia* (cf. תערובת 8 iii 19).

In the *šin* the projection of the left stroke below the right is characteristic of the semiformal at all times. The curved arms, on the other hand, are unusual in vulgar semiformals, and idiosyncratic here, but were characteristic both of the rustic semiformal and of that Hasmonean semiformal (of the type of 4QH[b]) which was probably the common ancestor of the traditions of the rustic semiformal and of the present hand.

Although there is no looped *taw*, the strokes seem still drawn in that same order; the peculiar flourish or hook at the end of the cross stroke may however be seeking to imitate the appearance of the later *taw* with its looped top. The old order of strokes in *taw*, which had been replaced in semiformal hands already in Hasmonean times (cf. 4QH[b]), has a checkered history in the Herodian rustic semiformal. In many cases, though, *taw* is still found in association with the three-stroked ʾ*alep*, which might suggest that it belonged to these hands in an earlier stage than 4QNum[b]. However

---

[2] The lack of a final form of *ṣade* is also generally characteristic of the vulgar semiformal, although here we have no surviving specimen of *ṣade*, whether medial or final position; in the present manuscript one can see some cases of medial *pe* in final position. All these cases should be considered as being in accord with a tendency (visible in 3Q15 and also on the ossuaries) of the vulgar semiformal to use final and non-final forms freely in both positions.

this may be, it survives late in many of the vulgar semiformals (cf. 1QH^a, 4QCant^b), doubtless under the influence of the order of strokes in the cursive.

  To sum up, if we dismiss the scribe's idiosyncracies (to curve whatever can be curved and to accentuate right-angled changes of direction, as, e.g., in *mem*), we may still rely on certain features for dating the hand. The relative lack of *apices* or *keraiai* is no strong indication of an early Herodian date since some vulgar semiformals avoid these flourishes; but, among the individual letter forms, the three-stroked *ʾalep*, the *mem*, the head of the *pe* and the size of the *qop* are probably the most reliable elements, typologically speaking, for dating, and they too tend to support a date no later than the early Herodian period.

1.2.2 Orthography

The orthography of the present scribe is not very consistent. The indications of non-historical orthography are the use of מחני once for the construct singular מחנה (8 iv 8), הטמה once for הטמא (3–7 i 19), להבי for להביא (8 iv 8), ושלושא for ושלושה (1–2 iv), מסיא[י]ם once for משיאים (3–7 i 16), בשש עשר אשר for בששה עשר אשר (1–2 iv).

  Note the alternation of the independent שא with the bound form, e.g in שהם (3–7 i 4), בשל שא (3–7 i 19). As for the forms ראואי and ראו for ראוי, see § 3.2.2.4.

  Passing beyond these vulgarisms and other oddities, note how *ū* and *ō<aw* are recorded regularly; *ō<ā* is recorded in almost all cases (but מאת 3–7 i 2). Short *u* is regularly recorded, except in קרב[ן] (?; 1–2 v) and הקדש (8 iv 10; the reading is not certain; cf. § 3.1.1). The word ראש (8 iv 11) is spelled historically, and there is one case of לא against five of לוא. On טהר and טהרה, see § 3.1.1.2; on ז[ב]חם see the commentary to B 11. As for *yod*, it serves to indicate *ī*; the only exception is בעשרם in 1–2 iv (note that we find כיא, never כי). *Yod* also indicates *ē<ay*, in plural constructs, plural suffixed forms and other internal diphthongs, and once in the singular construct in מחני (8 iv 8).

  In the forms of the pronouns, the alternation between long and short forms seems random. Pronominal suffixes are always of the short form, e.g. עליהם (8 iii 13), זבחם (3–7 i 11), but הוא and היא interchange with הואה and היאה, and הם interchanges with the longer forms והמה, מהמה; the variation does not seem to be conditioned by the position of the word in the sentence.

1.2.3 4Q394

1.2.3.1 4Q394 1–2 i–v

v	iv	iii	ii	i	
בו שבת	בתשעה	בֿו[שבת]	[ו]אֿחֿ[ד]	[בששה]	
בעשרים	בו[שבת]	בע[שתיעשר]	בֿ׳ שֿבת	עשר	
ושנים	בֿשש אֿשר	בו שבת	[ב]עֿשרים	[בו שבת]	
בו מועד	בו שבת	בשמונה	ושמונה	בֿעֿשרים	
השמן	בעשרם	עשר בו שבת	בו שבת	ושלושה	5
אֿחֿ[ר הש]בֿת	ושלושא	בעשרים	עליו אחר	בו שבֿת	
אֿחֿ[רין]	בֿו שבת	וחמשה	השבת	[ב]שלֿ[ושי]ם	
קרבֿ[ן]	בש[לו]שים	בו שבת	ו[יו]ם השנֿי	[בו שבת	
[העצים]	[בו שבת	בשנים	[השלישי נוסף	בשבעה	
בשבעה		בחמ[י]שֿ[י]	ושלמה	בשלישי	10
בששי		ש[ב]ֿ[ת]	התקופה	שבת	
שבת		[בשלושה	תשעים	בארבעה	
בארבעה		בו מועד	ואחד יום	עשר	
עשר		היין אחר	באחד	בו שבת	
בו שבת		השבת	ברביעי	בחמשה	15
בעשרים			יום זכרון	עשר בו חג	
[ואחד]			[בארבעה]	שבועות	
				[בעשרים]	

1.2.3.1.1 Notes on the Reading

L. 1 Part of the uniscribed top margin is seen over this line in col. v.

L. 3 בֿשש אֿשר An alternative reading בששה עשר is unlikely for several reasons: (a) the vertical line before the last šin can hardly be a bottom of ʿayin of the calendar; it fits, however, a type of ʿayin found in the other column of this manuscript; (b) the traces before this line are not characteristic of he; (c) there is no sign of any scraping in the space between the two words which would suggest that he had stood there.

1.2.3.2 4Q394 3–7 i

[ושמונה בו]שבת על[י]ו אחר [ה]ש[ב]ת ויום השני השלישי]

[נו]סף ושלמה השנה שלוש מאת וש[ש]ים וארבעה]

יֹום

‏[ל שהם מ]קצת דברי]   אלה מקצת דברינו [

 5   [[ה]מֹעשים שא אֹ[נ]חֹ[נ]ו חושבים וכו]לֹם על]

וטהרת [הרֹ]ת [ועל תרומת ד]גֹן ה[גוים שהם מ . . ים]

ומֹגיעֹ[י]ֹם בה אֹ[ת]ֹהם וסמטֹ[מאים אותה ואין לאכול]

מדֹגֹן [הגֹו]ֹיֹם] ואין [לבוֹא למקֹ[ש] ועל זֹבֹח החטאת]

שהם מבֹשלֹים [אות]ֹה בכלי [נחושת ומ . . ים בֹה את]

 10   בשר זבחיהֹם ומֹ[ ]ֹם בעֹזֹרֹ]ה ומ . . ים אוֹתֹה]

במֹרק זבחֹם ועל זֹבֹח הגוים [אנחנו חושבים שהם זֹובחֹים]

אל הֹ[ן [שא הֹיֹא] כ]ֹמי שזֹנת אליו [ואף על מנחת זֹבֹח]

השל[מים] שמניחיֹם אותה מיום ליום וֹאֹף [כֹתוב [

שהמנֹ[חה נאכֹלֹת] עֹל הֹחלבים והבשר ביוֹם זֹֹ[בֹ]חם כי לבני]

 15   הכוהנֹ[ים] רֹֹאו להֹזֹהֹ[יֹ]ר בדבר הזה בשל שלוֹא יֹ[היו]

מֹסיאֹ[י]ֹם את העֹם עוון ואף על טהרֹת פרת החטאֹת

השוחֹט אותה והסורף אותה והאוסֹף [א]ֹת אפרה והמזה אֹת [מי]

החטאת לכול אלה להעריֹ[בוֹ]ֹת השמש להֹיֹות טהורים

בשל שא יהיה הטהר מזה על הטמה כי לבני

bottom margin

1.2.3.2.1 NOTES ON THE READING

L.1 After ʿayin only lamed is a letter high enough to have been written in the space without leaving traces on the surviving leather. Our further supplement is modelled on the text of frg. 1–2 ii עליו אחר השבת אֹ[חד] והשנֹ[י]; but we must almost certainly, in view of the lack of additional traces such as yod would have left, postulate a phonetic orthography עליו = עלו. In [ה]ש[בת, the trace on the separate fragment is not especially characteristic of any letter, and if the fragment should be moved further to the left, it will instead give the base of one of the letters after השבת.

L. 2 Note the short, but final, pe. We read שלוש assuming a direct join between frg. 3 and frg. 4. This is supported by the possible identification of the base of the letter in l. 1 (frg. 4) as the base of the śin of [ה]ש[בת]. There remains nothing of the space above the word מאת, so it is not known whether an interlinear waw stood there.

As for וֹשִׁים[, the theoretically possible alternates וחמשים, וחמש or וארבע are to be excluded on material grounds, and with them the calendars that go with them, while *šin* fits the trace.

L. 3 יוֹם Materially nothing excludes the alternative reading of הם.

L. 4 דבֿרינו The *bet* is damaged but almost certain; the hole where the surface has been lost follows the line of the missing parts of the *bet*.

L. 5 In view of the space, a broad letter (*he, bet, mem, kap*), not a *waw*, must have stood before סֹעשים. As for א[ֹנ[ֹחֹ]נו, after שא and a blank space, *ʾalep* would fit the traces, thus is should probably be reconstructed as we have done, as also the style of the document suggests. In לֹם[, the leather is split apart, but the traces fit final *mem* perhaps slightly better than the alternative final *kap* (if indeed such a form were to be found in this hand).

L. 6 After וטהרת one or two letters are almost completely lost, either by accident and damage to the surface or, more probably, by deletion, cf. the shape of the damage and the following *he*. Of the letters after *he*, so much has been lost that no further reading is possible.

L. 7 ומֹגיעׁ[י]ֹם Before the certain *gimel* the trace could be of *yod, he* or *mem* (though perhaps *mem* would be too broad); between *ʿayin* and final *mem*, there could be *waw/yod* or nothing. After בה the trace is clearly of *ʾalep* rather than *šin*; a diagonal continues below the upstroke toward the lower right corner.

L. 11 זבֿ Materially *kap* or *pe* are better readings of the traces of the second letter. זבֿ would be a contextually appropriate *ad sensum* reading; but in themselves these traces allow numerous other alternatives, e.g. זפֿ, זכֿר.

L. 12 The trace after אל ה is easiest read *waw* or *yod*, but *mem* or *kap* would not be impossible. The top of the *lamed* from השלמים of the line below appears at the left of this *waw/yod*, at the edge of the fragment. The following traces can be read הׁיׁא; the first letter has two descending strokes and a topstroke with a curve upwards at its left tip; for a *he* of this shape, cf. those in הטהר (1. 19) and והבשר (1. 14). The following trace must be of *pe, waw* or *yod* rather than of a letter like *bet, kap*, etc.; the two points seen at the end are not inconsistent with *ʾalep* (though other letters are possible). In שׁנֹת some of the surface has been lost. There is no space between מי and שׁנֹת. Materially, several other readings could fit the traces, for example: כמושבת, כמושכת, [כ]מי שזפת. In אליו the size of the hole is not so great as to require any additional letter between *ʾalep* and *lamed* (cf. אלה in l. 18).

L. 13 One of the traces before אותה comes from the tip of the *lamed* in החלבים *infra*. The other is a projection above the line, not inconsistent with final *mem*. The word שמניחםֹ was found on a small fragment. The placement of this fragment here is certain. In ואפ, the change of a stroke at the base of the last letter, and its angle, both require *pe* or *bet*.

L. 15 רֹאו It is impossible to read רא[ו]י.

L. 18 Note the points above and below the *ṭet* in להֹיׁות טהורים; do they serve to correct the lack of separation between the two words?

1.2.3.3 4Q394 3–7 ii

top margin

ואﬠ]   אהרן]ראואי [להיות מ[

[על ﬠﬡ]רות הבק]ר והצאן שהם מ . . ים מן[אין[

[עורות]יהם כלי]ם   אין[

[להביא]ם למקד]ש   [

                                                                5

                                                               10

הכו]הנים ראואי[ן להש]מ]ר בכול הדﬠ]ברﬡ[ים האלה בשל שלוא יהיו[

משיאים את העﬦ עוון [ועﬡ]ל שא כתוב] איש כי ישחט במחנה או[

[ישחט]מחוץ למחנה שור וכשב ועז כי ◦[בצפון המחנה]   15

ואנﬡנו חושבים שהמקדש]ו משכן אוהל מועד הוא ויﬧ]רושלי]ם[

מחנה היא וחו]צה[לﬨחנה[ﬥ הוא חוצה לירושלים הﬡ[וא מחﬡנה

עריﬥ]הם חוץ ממ]חנה[ﬧﬡﬧ ﬡ[ו   החטאת וﬡ]מוציאים את דשא

[ה]מﬦזבח ושוﬧ]פים שם את החטאתכי ירושלים הﬡ[יא המקום אשר

bottom margin

1.2.3.3.1 NOTES ON THE READING

L. 13 ראואי Seems to have been followed at a short distance by a final *mem*, but in view of this manuscript's irregular use of final letters, one may read [להש]מ]ר].

L. 14 Before שא the two points of ink best fit the two tips of the hook of *lamed* (unless the surface is damaged at this point).

L. 15 After כי there are traces of *mem*, *ʾalep* or *gimel*. The letters וכש of וכשב were found on a small fragment.

L. 17 Again note the points above and below the *mem* of מחנה, which perhaps indicate that the division between words had been inadequately indicated.

L. 18 In the first word at the start of the line, the second letter could be *waw/yod*, but it could also have had a projection to the left suggesting, e.g., *reš, bet, mem*. Note the isolated points above

mem in מ[חנה]; perhaps they signal a failure to indicate the space between words. Of the letters after מ[חנה], *ʾalep* is certain, and it stood above *reš* (rather than *ʿayin* or final *mem*). The following trace, if the letter started from the line, could only be *lamed*, but perhaps it is an interlinear *waw*.

1.2.3.4 4Q394 8 iii

] ב[יום] [

] ועל האוכל אנחנו חושבים שיאכל את] הולד

[שבמעי אמו לאחר שחיטתו ואתם יודעים שהוא כן ו]הדבר כתוב

ועל העמו]ני והמואבי   *vacat*   [עברה]

10   [והממזר ופצוע הדכה וכרות השפכת שהם באים] בקהל

] ונשים] לוקחים

[להיותם עצם אחת]   טמאות ואף חוש[בים אנחנו

[שאין]   ואין לבו]א עליהם

] ואין לה]תיכם [ו]לעשותם

15   [עצם אחת]   ואין להבי]אם

[למקדש]   ואתם יודעים שמקצת] העם

] מתוכ]כים

[כי לכול בני ישראל ראוי להזהר מכול ת]ערובת [ה]גבר

[ולהיות יראים מהמקדש]   ואף ע[ל הסומ]י[ם

[שאינם רואים להזהר מכל תערו]בת] ותערובת

bottom margin

1.2.3.4.1 NOTES ON THE READING

L. 9 On an earlier photo (PAM 40.618) the ני זה was clear, but now the ink has left the surface, leaving only vague traces behind.

L. 13 The traces before עליהם are not characteristic; *ʾalep* is the most likely reading.

L. 15 Can a *he* be vaguely made out, directly before אם, on PAM 40.618? Before that, very vague traces of a final *nun* preceded by others (more certain) of *yod/waw* can be made out.

L. 18 Before בר read either *ʿayin* or, better, *gimel*. Is the spot before that the remains of another letter, e.g. *he*, or is it accidental?

L. 19 הסומ]י[ם The loop at the top left of the fourth letter is found on some examples of *mem*; the traces after the expanse of damaged surface (one letter space broad) almost certainly represent another *mem*.

1.2.3.5   4Q394 8 iv

top margin

שמ אינם רואימ[א]   *vacat*

[וא]ף על החרשים שלוא שמעו חוק [ומ]שפט וטהרה ולא

[ש]מעו משפטי ישראל כי שלוא ראה ולוא שמע לוא

[י]דע לעשות והמה באימ לטה[ר]ת המקדש   *vacat*

[ו]אף על המוצקות אנחנו אומר[ים] שהם שאין בהם   5

[ט]הרה ואף המוצקות אינמ מבדילות בין הטמא

[ל]טהור כי לחת המוצקות והמקבל מהמה כהם

לחה אחת ואין להבי למחני הק[ו]דש כלבים שהם

אוכלים מקצת [ע]צמות המ[ק]דש ו[ה]בשר עליהם כי

ירושלים היאה מחנה הקדש והיא המקומ   10

שבחר בו מכל שבטי [ישראל כי] ירושלים היא ראש

מ[ח]נות ישראל   ואף על מטע[ו]ת עצי המאכל [הנ]טע

[בא]רץ ישראל כראשית הוא לכוה]נימ ומעשר[הבקר]

[והצון לכוהנימ הוא   ואף על הצ]רועימ א[נחנו]

[אומרים שלוא יבואו עם טהרת הקו]דש כי [בדד]   15

[יהיו מחוץ לבית ואף כתוב שמעת שיג]לח[וכבס]

1.2.3.5.1 NOTES ON THE READING

L. 1 Since the spot after בהמ (not a damaged בהמה) in l. 5 is accidental, the spot some distance after רואימ should probably be considered accidental also, and not a mark of punctuation.

L. 5 Trace of the *ʾalep* of [וא]ף is seen on PAM 41.760.

L. 6 The second and third letters of מבדילות are still vaguely discernable.

L. 7 Note the top left corner, and the discontinuity between the strokes, characteristic of *qop*. For the difficult first *mem* in מהמה, we postulate that its second stroke followed the line of the fold and is now lost; a *kap* would be plausible materially but the sense would then require emending it to *mem*. In כהם the *he* has lost much of its surface.

L. 9 Is the *waw* of אוכלים written over a corrected *kap*, the scribe having begun to spell the word defectively?

L. 9 The apparent traces before those of the *mem* of מקצת is nothing but a hole. The first two letters of [ע]צמות are badly damaged, and 4Q397 is not helpful; although the traces here are easily completed as a *ṣade*, the base of the *ʿayin* seems remarkably near the horizontal for this hand, and *kap* or *mem* could be, materially speaking, the best reading; our reconstruction is, however, contextually the most plausible. In the following word, our המ[ק]דש, after *he*, a *pe* or *bet* seems more likely in

view of the apparent change of stroke for the base; one could further object to the *qop* in הַמֹּ[דש] that the interlinear letter resembles rather a *samek*.

L. 10 The apparent traces after המקוֹם are only holes in the leather. Note, however, that the head of the letter after the *qop* fits *dalet* better than *waw*.

L. 12 מֹ[חֹנוֹת The initial letter seems best explained as the top of a final *mem*, and not *šin*, once allowance is made for the twisting of the fragment from its true alignment. At the end of the line המאכֹל is the reading of 4Q396; here *lamed* is very difficult unless we assume that most of the ink has been lost in the corner of the hook.

L. 14 After הצ[רועים, 4Q396 shows that the text read אֹנֹחנו; here however the trace seems best explained as the corner of a thin cartouche drawn around the next word (such as is found round the divine name on an unidentified fragment from Cave IV); after the traces of the cartouche, the remaining marks fit with the *ᵓalep* of אֹנֹחנו.

1.2.3.6 4Q394 8 v

```
                                                                    ]∘      10
                                                                    ]ה
                                                                    ]כֹ
                                                                    ]ה
```

1.2.3.7 4Q394 9

```
                        ]∘[          ]עֹלֹ[
           ]היה ]∘ [ ∘ ∘∘ [ העם]
          [∘כפר על[יה]ֹם כי על ]
              ]לֹ[ ]∘[ ]כֹ∘∘[
```

1.2.3.7.1 NOTES ON THE READING

It is not certain whether a column ended (on a line drawn after כפר על) and another started with כי or whether the text is continuous, with traces of damaged letters in the intervening space. If we take the two dots in l. 2, after היה[, as the scribe's device for correcting the lack of separation between words, as elsewhere in this manuscript, the alternative of continuous text will be preferable. If instead we see the fragment as containing two columns, the intercolumnar space would be slightly narrower than that between the columns of frg. 8. [In fact, frg. 9 is a join of two fragments (see PAM 41.760 and 41.780). In my opinion, there is no basis for this join. E. Q.]

1.2.3.8 4Q394 10

```
                        [ ∘ ]ועל [
```

1.3   4Q395

The leather is brittle of slightly less than medium thickness, in colour ranging from buff to light brown, with a sub-glossy surface which has a tendency to lose its topmost stratum together with the traces of writing. The back is red when stained and grey when not. No trace of either vertical or horizontal dry lines can be detected; if the lines were horizontal then the margin was very uneven. The width of the uninscribed margin (17.5 mm) suggests that possibly in this manuscript the section אלה מקצת דברינו represented the incipit of the whole work, not being preceded by the calendaric discussion which probably preceded this section in 4Q394. Height of the average letter (*bet*): 3 mm. Space between lines: 5–7 mm. Width of column: 42–44 corrected letter spaces. Photos: PAM 41.762, 43.477.

1.3.1   Script

The hand offers a strange mixture of early Herodian and of late Hasmonean letters, usually formal in style. A certain number of letters do not yet show the changes that they experience in late Hasmonean or Herodian times. Thus *ʾalep* is a three-stroke letter; *bet* is a one-stroke letter, in which the thickening of the middle of the base stroke is reminiscent of the archaic semiformal hand; *dalet* is an unornamented two-stroke letter. The *he* is archaic in appearance—the left downstroke usually does not proceed from the cross stroke but is a distinct stroke, and indeed in some examples the top stroke is drawn from left to right in cursive style, turning into the left downstroke. The head of *waw*—a hook, sometimes drawn tightly against the upstroke, so creating a triangular appearance—is distinct from that of *yod*. *Lamed* has a hook of a typical late Hasmonean form. *Taw* is still drawn with its left stroke a descender (with a sharply-angled base) rather than an ascender, as in the later order of strokes.

Some other letters, however, have clearly undergone their Herodian or later Hasmonean change in structure. So the *ṭet* is drawn with the right portion of the letter as a separate stroke. One of the forms of *ḥet* shows the influence of the continuous stroke of the Herodian form, while another shows an earlier treatment of the right top. *Zayin* in some specimens is slightly bent at the top of the stroke, but one example is only an unadorned vertical line. The order of strokes in *mem* is not clear. One of the heads of *pe* curls inward, though the others are earlier in appearance—the base is drawn from left to right (presumably under semicursive influence, though it is peculiar to find this form of *pe* side by side with the earlier form of *bet*). In one of the two damaged examples of *śin* the middle arm fails to join the left stroke, a feature usually found only in late hands. Of the remaining letters, the final *nun* has a form typical of both the late Hasmonean and early Herodian periods, with a bent head, not a thickening of the stroke. *ʿAyin* is problematic in that its short tail is remarkably archaic in appearance, although the stance of the letter is rather that of the Herodian hands. *Reš* is a two-stroke letter—a most odd form.

In general the absence of decorations and *keraiai* shows that the hand is, at the least, of early Herodian date. The mixture of forms (sometimes of the same letter) which have undergone their major late Hasmonean or early Herodian shift with those that have not renders precise dating difficult. The mixture will perhaps have to be explained by postulating an Herodian scribe who attempts to write in an archaising Hasmonean style, which he constructs by borrowings both from the formal and the semiformal hands. Attention should be drawn to an idiosyncracy of this scribe which is rare in the formal hand, the attempt to utilize a distinction between thick and thin strokes.

1.3.2 Orthography

The text is too short, and the vowels that it contains too few, for reliable extrapolation about the orthographic practices of the scribe and their regularity. The vowels *i*, *o* and *u* are always recorded, except in אהרן (l. 11). For טהרת see § 3.1.1.2.

1.3.3.1 4Q395 1

[זֹבֹ]ח החטאת שהם מבשליֹם אותֹה בכֹלי

[בה] את בשר זבחיהם וֹמֹ

[אֹותֹ]ה במרק זבחֹם ועל זבֹח הגויים

[זובחֹ]ים אֹל

[זבח הֹ]שלֹמים שמניחים אותה מיום ליום וֹאֹף כתוב   5

שהמ[נֹחה נא]כֹלֹת [על הֹחלבים והבשר ביום זֹובֹחם כי לבני הכוהנֹים]

ראוי לה[הֹ]זֹהֹר בדבֹר [הזה בשל שלוא יהיו מסיאֹים את העם עוון]

                                                                                פרת
ואֹף על טהרת החֹטֹ[את השוחֹט אותה והסורף אותה והאוסֹףֹ]

את אפ[רה] והמזה אֹתֹ] מי החטאת לכול אלה להעריבות השמש]

להיות טהור[יֹ]ם בֹשל שא יהיה הטהר מזה על הטמה כי לבני]   10

[אהרן ראוי להיו[ת] מֹ]

[עֹורֹות הֹ]בֹקֹר

1.3.3.1.1 NOTES ON THE READING

L. 2 The first letter is almost certainly a *bet* (although unfortunately there is no certain and complete example of *kap* in this hand which we might compare). As for our *he*, it is not implausible palaeographically, but one could alternatively divide these traces between two letters and read, e.g., בזר[.

L. 8 The interlinear פרת has been added by the original scribe.

1.4 4Q396

The thin leather, with a sub-glossy surface, is usually light grey in colour, though when stained it becomes brown, and the surface appears glossy. In occasional patches the surface has been lost. The back is coarse, with the same colours as the front. No vertical dry lines are apparent; although the right margin is fairly regular, the left is very far from being so. There are horizontal dry lines, but the writing follows these very lackadaisically, the letters sometimes being suspended from the lines, sometimes standing free well below them (cf. 1–2 iv 5). Height of column: 11 lines, 9 cm. Width of column (from right margin to right margin, the left margin being so irregular): 10.5 cm (col. ii), 12 cm (col. iii). Space between lines: 5–8.5 mm (average 7 mm). Height of average letter (*bet*, *šin*, *taw*): 2–3 mm. Top margin: 10–12 mm. Bottom margin (from lowest ruled line): 10.5 mm. Width of

inscribed column: col. i, about 50 corrected letter spaces; col. ii, 29–36 corrected letter spaces; col. iii, 32–39 corrected letter spaces. Photos: PAM 40.619, 41.286, 41.638, 42.602, 42.631, 43.490.

1.4.1 Script

In general the hand stands within the semiformal tradition of Herodian times, not however in the rustic subdivision of that tradition, but in the vulgar. It is noteworthy that, for several letters, formal and semiformal, typologically early and late forms exist side by side.

In *ʾalep* we only rarely find specimens of the inverted V form; a type with three distinct strokes is more common. In only a few forms does the right stroke have any thickening, but occasionally (e.g., באים 1–2 i 5, or טמאתם 1–2 iii 7) this will be a full *keraiai*. The diagonal is customarily a doubly-curved stroke, again without *keraiai*. In the left leg the stroke curves sometimes, in cursive style, almost back to the diagonal; this can scarcely indicate that this stroke was the first to be drawn, and must be considered as a decorative element comparable to that which we find in 1QM.

Bet must be discussed with *kap*. Of *bet* we find two principal forms, one where the base is drawn from left to right, the other made with a sharp angle at the base but with only one stroke. The right shoulder of both of these forms will sometimes be drawn with a slight projection upwards; in most specimens, however, this sharp angle extends rather to the right of the downstroke, in the same style as the angle at the base. This treatment of the right shoulder, and the sharply angled base, is also characteristic of *kap* in most examples, although that letter tends to have a narrower head. When *bet* is less deep a letter than usual, it is not clearly distinguishable from *kap* (except when *bet* has a separately drawn base), cf. בין (1–2 ii 8), בוזה (1–2 iii 10) and בתוך (1–2 iv 4). At the same time there are some specimens of the typical formal *bet*, e.g. כתוב (1–2 iv 6).

In *gimel* the left leg is very high on the diagonal, a trait that would be archaic in formal hands but is to be expected in the semiformal at all times. The main stroke is bent either singly or doubly, but unornamented at its top.

Again, *dalet* presents itself in two forms, a two-stroked box-headed form typical of the Herodian formal hand (and of the vulgar semiformal?), and the round rustic semiformal type in which the cross stroke loops into the descender. Attention should be paid to the hook at the left, at the start of the cross stroke; it is remarkably developed, sometimes starting so low that the topstroke crosses it midway along its length. A similar form is found in final *mem* and perhaps in *he*. Another semiformal characteristic is the curve at the base of the *dalet*, cf. הקודש (1–2 iii 5), קודש (1–2 iv 5).

One of the several forms of *he* is made in a single line, the right upstroke looping into the crossbar and the latter into the left downstroke (cf. especially היא 1–2 iii 3); the form (cf. especially the style of these loops) is that of the vulgar semiformal of later Herodian times. Beside this, we find a form closely similar in general appearance, but in which the left downstroke is drawn in a separate stroke after the completion of the hook at the left of the cross stroke, cf. שהמה (1–2 iv 8). The analogy of *dalet* and final *mem* might suggest that in fact the cross stroke here was drawn from left to right, moving into the right downstroke, and with the left downstroke drawn last. A third form of *he* shows a different treatment of the right shoulder, which is drawn with two distinct strokes as in השפכת (1–2 i 5), הולד (1–2 i 3), שהם (1–2 ii 10). A fourth *he* (הטמא 1–2 ii 8) is the true cursive, with left to right crossbar then moving into the left downstroke.

Waw has a hook at the top, but unfortunately so also do some forms of *yod*, although the scribe also has several three-stroke forms of *yod* in his repertory (as well as, once, a lambda-shaped specimen, cf. השמיני 1–2 iv 1). The survival or revival of three-stroked forms of *yod* in the Herodian period, and indeed the fact that they never completely fell out of use in semiformals even in late Hasmonean times (when the formal had lost them), deprives this form of significance for dating.

Zayin usually has a very slight bend at the top, but in one case (final, in שעטנז 1–2 iv 7) there is a deep hook backwards.

As with *he*, there are several types of *ḥet*. One is the typical rustic semiformal letter, where the right stroke curves and loops into the crossbar, which itself joins the left slightly below the shoulder. Together with this we find the H form, drawn with three distinct strokes.

Ṭet is the expected late-Hasmonean and Herodian form, with a tendency for the left tip to curve to its left, and in some specimens with a very developed curl at the right. This feature, and the breadth of the letter, suggest lateness.

For *kap* see the discussion of *bet* above. The final *kap* has a broad head, and its shoulder is looped in semiformal style, a form which penetrates the formal hand very late.

Medial *mem* in most cases is drawn with the tick on top drawn last, and with the base alternatively inclined or horizontal. The diagonal joins the upper shoulder and the base joins the lower shoulder in sharp angles in the style of *bet*. In some cases, where the tick is also drawn at the shoulder, one may suspect that the letter was drawn in the old style, or even with an outline in the form of *bet* with a figure-3 downstroke, and with the diagonal then drawn last (cf. שמע 1–2 ii 5, מגדף 1–2 iii 10). But unfortunately there are no true ligatures to confirm this suspicion. In final *mem* note that the initial tick sometimes forms a semicircle crossing the top line (as in האדם 1–2 iv 2); cf. *dalet* above. The left downstroke, in rare cases, is separate from its tick (cf. עם 1–2 iii 5). Though in certain cases the downstroke seems continuous with the semicircular hook at the top (cf. 1–2 i 1), this cannot indicate that the letter was drawn in one movement as in *samek*.

Samek, as far as one can see, has the looped form of the formal and the rustic semiformal, rather than the crossed form more frequent in vulgar semiformal hands. That it is occasionally slightly open at the bottom is of dubious significance for the dating of the hand.

The Hasmonean vertical stance of *ʿayin* remains at home in the semiformal hands until a late date. Note that in this hand there is a slight bend inward, or thickening, of the top right, and an exceedingly short base.

The head of *pe* is not very developed, but again such involutions are not a regular feature of the vulgar semiformal. At the end of some words a form is found which appears medial, but is distinct from the normal medial form in having a base line leaving the vertical in a curve, not a sharp angle— a curve which at a later date is chiefly characteristic of vulgar semiformals, cf. 1–2 ii 3, iii 4. There are also regular examples of final *pe*, as in מגדף (1–2 iii 10).

There are two types of *ṣade*: in one the tip of the right stroke is merely thickened; in the other the tip is a clearly independent stroke starting below the cross stroke, probably imitating in shape, though not in manner of writing, the heavy end of the round semiformal *ṣade*. The curved left tip is standard in the semiformal, as is the very irregular use of final *ṣade*.

Qop shows not only the Hasmonean two-stroke form (surviving late in the vulgar semiformal) but probably also looped one-stroke specimens. Both these types are sometimes long, sometimes very short.

Reš is very broad.

In some specimens of *šin* the middle or right stroke fails to reach the left downstroke, and in others the left stroke sometimes breaks through a little at the bottom; the former trait is perhaps an indicator of lateness (but cf., e.g., 4Q395), the latter is common in the semiformals. The tips of the strokes are however very little developed, cf. 4QCant^b.

We find, as we expect in the vulgar semiformal, *taw* drawn with the old order of strokes, maintained under cursive influence (cf. a rare looped specimen in 1 iii 3 כראשית).

The vulgar semiformal tradition is represented at Qumran by several widely different styles (in contrast to the fairly consistent rustic semiformal group). Relative or absolute dating of its

representatives is hard. In general the occasional *keraiai* and like flourishes in this manuscript show the influence of early or mid-Herodian formal hands, and even the latest forms (e.g., *he*) do not require a date typologically later than that of, e.g., 1QH^a.

1.4.2 Orthography

כי is regularly so spelt, and we find לוא five times against לא once. Quiescent *ʾalep* is written historically in ראש, יאכל and ראשית, but phonetically in צון (1–2 iii 4; = צאן). The vowels *u/o* are recorded in all cases but twice: הכהנים (1–2 iv 9); מכל (1–2 ii 2). For the form טהרה, see § 3.1.1.2.

1.4.3.1   4Q396 1–2 i

top margin

אי]נם שוחטים במקדש	]
אנ̇ח̇נו חו̇שבים שאין לזבוח א[ת האם ואת הולד ביום אחד	]
ועל האוכ̇ל אנח]נו חושבים שאיאכל את הולד	]
א̇ כן ו̇הדבר כתוב עברה *vacat* [	]
[ועל העמוני̇ והמואבי והממזר ופ̇צוע הדכה וכרו]ת השפכת שהם באים	5
בקהל] ונשים]ל̇ו̇ק̇ח̇י̇ם להיו]תם̇ עצם	

1.4.3.1.1   NOTES ON THE READING

L. 1 Before final *mem* there is a ligating base of a letter, e.g., *nun, taw vel sim*. In במקד̇ש, *qop* is certain; though we read *šin*, its right hand curved stroke seems not to touch the left hand stroke, and this, together with the 'break through' at the bottom of the left stroke, creates the impression of לו.

L. 3 שאיאכל is written without word division.

L. 4 Before כן, *ʾalep* or *ḥet* (not *zayin*) can be read. After כן there is a faint but clear *yod/waw* before הדבר.

L. 5 Before השפכת, a *taw* can be clearly seen on later photos, e.g. PAM 43.490, although it was folded over when the earlier photos were made.

L. 6 The trace after ל̇ו̇ק̇ is not characteristic enough for any materially certain identification, but is consistent with 4Q394's לוקחים. In להיו]תם̇ the final *mem* is badly damaged by a crack, but the right end of its top is decisive for its being a final *mem*, not a *he*.

1.4.3.2   4Q396 1–2 ii

top margin

ולהיות יראים מהמקדש [ואף על̇ הסומ̇י̇ם̇] שאינם	
רואים להזהר מכל תערו̇]בת ותערובת אי̇]ש̇ם̇ אינם	
רו̇א̇י̇ם̇ ואף על החרו̇]שים שלוא ו̇]שמעו חוק	
ומשפט̇ וטהרה ולא שמ̇עו מש̇]פטי̇ ישראל	
כי שלוא ראה ולוא שמע לוא יו̇דע ו̇ל̇עשות והמה	5

באים לטהרת המקדש ואף על המוצקו֯ת אנח֯נ֯ו֯

אומרים שהם שאין בהם טהרה ואף המוצקות

אינם מבדילות בין הטמא לט֯הור כי לחת המוצקות

וה֯מ֯קבל מהמה כהם ל֯חה אחת ואין לה֯בי למחני ה֯ק֯ודש

כלבים שהם אוכל֯ים מקצת עצמות ה֯מ֯קדש והבשר   10

עלי֯ה֯ם כי ירו֯ש֯ל֯ים היא֯ה מחנה הקודש והיא המקו֯ם

bottom margin

1.4.3.2.1 NOTES ON THE READING

L. 2 להזהר On the photo that we print, the top of the second *he* is still covered by an incrustation, and this, together with a fold after *zayin*, creates the impression of לההיר; after the surface has been cleaned, however, PAM 43.490 is decisive for the reading להזהר. After תער the trace is inadequate for a decision between תערב֯ת and תערו֯בת. Before אינם, the *šin* (so 4Q394) is clear on PAM 43.490, though it is twisted badly out of position. When earlier photos were made it was still covered in part with incrustations, and could hardly be identified as *šin*. As for the final *mem*, its top has suffered accidental damage, but no other reading is possible.

L. 3 There is a clear trace of *waw* before אף, though most of it has gone with the loss of the surface.

L. 5 The *lamed* of לעשות has now been lost; for traces of it cf. PAM 41.286 or 41.638.

L. 6 In ואף the *pe* was probably medial, as, e.g., in l. 3 above. A text to fill the lacuna at the end of the line is provided by 4Q394 with על המוצקות אנח֯נ֯ו. It is hard to see with what from this text the trace in 396 can be identified (perhaps *waw*—either preceded by a word division, or a supralinear correction to restore מוצקות?).

L. 9 וה֯מ֯קבל וה seems grammatically necessary, but it is hard to identify the surviving damaged and twisted traces with parts of those letters.

1.4.3.3 4Q396 1–2 iii

top margin

שבחר בו מכל שבטי י֯שראל כי יר֯ו֯שלים היא ראש

מ֯ח֯נ֯ות ישראל ואף ע֯ו֯ל מ֯ט֯עת עצ֯י֯ ה֯מאכל הנטע

בא֯רץ ישראל כראשית הוא לכוהנים ומעשר הבקר

והצון לכוה֯נים הוא ואף על הצרועים א֯נ֯ח֯נו

א֯ומרים שלוא י֯בואו (לט) עם טהרת הקוד֯ש כי בדד   5

י֯ה֯י֯ו מחוץ לבית ו֯אף כתוב ש(ב)מ֯עת שיגלח וכבס י֯שב מחו֯ץ

לאוהלו שבעת י֯מ֯ים ועתה בהיות טמאתם עמהם

הצרועים באים ע֯ם֯ טהרת הקודש לבית ואתם יודעים

שעל השוגג שלוא יעשה את המצוה ונעלה ממנו להביא (ח)

[חטאת ועל] העושה ביד רמה כת[וֹב שהואה בוזה ומג[דֹ]דֹּ֮ף   10

[ואף בהיות להמֹה טמאות נגע] אין להאכילם מהקו[ד]שים

bottom margin

1.4.3.3.1 NOTES ON THE READING

L. 2 Of the first word only *taw* is certain. The traces on each side of the tear are not in their true relative positions.

L. 5 Note the form of correction. The scribe first intended לטהרת, but in midcourse decided to write עם טהרת. In הקודש, the *dalet* has a peculiar curve at the base, and only faint traces of the tail of the *qop* are visible. For such a curved tail in *dalet* (though slightly less developed), cf. iv 5 below. The surface where the *šin* would have stood has been lost.

L. 6 The *yod* of [יֹ]שב was scraped. The surviving traces show that the final *ṣade* of מחוׄץ was final; contrast בֹּאׄרץ in l. 3.

L. 8 The trace before טֹהרת is not identifiable, though it would fit with עֹ[ם or עׄ[ד.

L. 9 In ממנו, although the second *mem* is damaged, the traces cannot be divided in any other way. The last letter in the line is either *ḥet* or *he*. The dots around it indicate deletion. It appears that this is the first letter of the word חטאת which was written at the beginning of the following line. Cf. 1QIsaᵃ ii 11–12 where the וה of והוכיח is written at the end of l. 11. Such practice is known from medieval manuscripts.

L. 10 [וֹב The reading of the first letter as *waw* is preferable to the few other possibilities (e.g., *yod*, *pe*). In ומג[ד]דֹף note that the *pe* is final.

L. 11 מהקו[ד]שים Enough of the *waw* survives to exclude *dalet*, and consequently מהקד[שים].

1.4.3.4   4Q396 1–2 iv

top margin

עד בוא השמש ביום השמיני ועלׄ [טמאת נפשׄ]

האדם אנחנו אומרים שכול עצם ש[היא חסרה]

ושלמה כמשפט המת או החלל הֹוֹאׄ֯ [*vacat*]

ועל הזונות הנעסה בתוך העם והמה ב[ני זרע]

קדש משכתוב קודש ישראל ועל בה[מתו הטהורֹהֹ]   5

כתוב שלוא לרבעה כלאים ועל לבושֹ[ו כתוב שלוא]

יהיה שעטנז ושלוא לזרוע שדו וכֹ[רמו כלאיׄם]

[בֹ]גלל שהמה קדושים ובני אהרון ק[דושי קדושים]

[ואׄ]תֹּׄם יודעים שמקצת הֹכהֹנים והֹ[עם מתערבים]

[והם]מֹתוככים ומטמאיֹ[ם]את זרֹעֹ[הקודשֹ ואף]   10

את [זרע]ֹׄם עֹׄם הזוׄנֹות כֹׄי לבני אהרון   [

1.4.3.4.1 NOTES ON THE READING

L. 1 A point, whose function is uncertain, is found in the manuscript after השמיני?

L. 5 ‎בה The top right of the *he* is uncharacteristic, and the top left damaged, but *ḥet* would be an even more difficult reading.

L. 9 At the end of the line, after *waw* (damaged, but materially preferable to *yod*), there are traces which cannot be characterised: *he* is not impossible.

L. 10 Syntactically ‎ומטמא[ם is probably needed; the trace at first glance seems too inclined for *yod*, having rather the angle of *ʾalep* or *gimel*, but in fact the leather is slightly detached and twisted and could be straightened enough to be reconcilable with *yod*, a letter which is itself, too, slightly inclined.

L. 11 After ‎הזונות the surviving trace certainly does not favour *waw/yod*; the letter has lost some of its surface to the left, and we should rather read *kap* or *bet* (or even perhaps *ḥet*). Cf. the angle at the right shoulder.

1.5 4Q397

The leather is in colour a light buff with a bluish tinge, turning to a brown or light red when stained. It is of medium thickness, with a fairly smooth bluish-grey back. The inscribed surface is matt but smooth, becoming glossy when stained. In general, this surface is much wrinkled; at numerous spots the top layer has peeled off, carrying away the writing with it. Horizontal dry lines can be seen clearly; the writing sometimes hangs from these lines, at others it lies with the top strokes of the letter on the lines, and at others is written so that the dry line crosses even lower down on the letters. Vertical dry lines cannot be seen. Average height and breadth of the medium-sized letter (e.g., *he*): 3 mm x 3 mm. Space between dry lines: 7–9 mm. Space between columns: above 8 mm., cf. frg. 14. Column width: 60–75 corrected letter-spaces, but in the last column diminishing to only 35 corrected letter-spaces. Column height: uncertain, but over 15 lines. Photos: PAM 41.412*, 41.517*, 41.582*, 41.583*, 41.593*, 41.762, 41.780*, 41.809*, 41.811*, 41.891*, 42.246*, 42.472, 42.499*, 42.557*, 42.577*, 42.717*, 43.476, 43.489 (and 41.805, 42.623, 43.383, etc., with other plates of mixed rustic fragments).

1.5.1 Script

These fragments seem to belong to the early Herodian group of scrolls, i.e., from about the end of the first century BCE to the beginning of the first century CE. Their script seems to fit into the group defined by F. M. Cross as 'round semiformal'.[3] In the fragments, all letters except *gimel* are represented.

The letters are shaped with a thin calamus, the edge of which was somewhat rubbed away. The thickness of the strokes is generally homogeneous. The tops and the bases of the letters ascend at a slight slant to the right, and the downstrokes slope down to the right. The script therefore seems to bend forward. This feature is characteristic of the Jewish book hand from the Herodian period onward. There are a few groups of letters which share common graphic elements, especially the following: (*a*) The letters *bet*, *dalet*, *reš* and *qop* have large serifs (inherited from the official Aramaic script) which slant towards the left edge of the tops and join them in a sharp angle. (*b*) *Waw* and *yod* are very similar in form. At their top they have a large and straight hook, slanting down to the left, or a big triangular loop (similar loops are characteristic of a certain type of letters inscribed on some

---

[3] Cross, *Development*, p. 173.

ossuaries from the Herodian period[4] and still appearing in non-calligraphic script in a letter from the year 134 CE).[5] (c) In *zayin*, *ṭet*, *nun*, *ṣade*, *šin* and sometimes *ʿayin* (*gimel* is absent here), the top of the left downstroke bends backwards (this is a stage towards the crystallization, apparently in the post-Herodian period, of the group of letters שעטנ״ז ג״ץ which had a similar ornament at the top of their left downstrokes). The absence of an additional short stroke on the right side of the tops of *zayin* and *nun*, characteristic of the Jewish book hand from about the middle of the Herodian period, is one of the criteria for the early dating of the script, although this extra stroke may still be absent in later non-calligraphic types of the Jewish script. (d) In *ʿayin* and *šin*, the top of the right stroke bends to the left, a feature which appears already in the late Hasmonean period. (e) *Kap*, *pe* and *ṣade* are relatively long, their bases slanting down below the imaginary base line. *Kap* and *pe* show an early feature (which also may appear in later non-calligraphic types of script) in that a medial form occurs in final position (ואפ, בתוכ; *ṣade* in final position is absent in these fragments).

ʾAlep has a somewhat wavy diagonal. Its right stroke, which starts at the line's height, descends almost vertically until it meets the lower half of the diagonal. In quick writing it may be wavy and its top bent backwards. The left stroke starts below the top of the diagonal, slopes down to the left and curves back to the right where it terminates at the imaginary base line. This form of the letter appears, for example, in 4QNum[b].[6]

Bet is broad and short, with a long horizontal base, apparently drawn from left to right but without going beyond its meeting point with the downstroke. In 4Q409, written in a very similar script, a *bet* appears with a long base drawn from left to right and extending far beyond its meeting point with the downstroke.[7]

Dalet (also *he*) has a wavy downstroke, starting above the line and slanting down to the right edge of the top, creating a right serif. At the meeting point it turns a little and slopes down to the right and at the bottom it curves somewhat back to the left.

He has a double-stroke top resembling an obtuse-angled triangle and is therefore thicker than the other strokes. The double-stroke top is an inheritance from a certain type of the 4th century BCE Official Aramaic script.[8] It continued to exist in the 'proto-Jewish' script of 4QSam[b][9] and in a certain type of the Jewish book hand (for example 4QSam[a][10] and 1QIsa[b]).[11] The occurrences of the letter *he* with a double-stroke top in an ossuary inscription from the Qidron Valley[12] and in another unpublished ossuary inscription, testifies to this practice in the Herodian period.

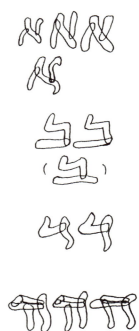

---

[4] See the alphabetic chart in Avigad, following p. 80, col. xxvii.

[5] See Avigad, p. 83, cols. xxix and xxx.

[6] See Cross, Development, fig. 2, l. 5.

[7] 4Q409, col. i, l. 10.

[8] This type of *he* is documented, for example, in a contract from Samaria dated to the year 335 BCE. See F. M. Cross Jr., 'The Discovery of the Samaria Papyri', *Biblical Archaeologist* 26 (1963), pp. 110–121; it appears also in a document from Ketef Yeriho from about the same period or a little later. See H. Eshel and H. Misgav, 'A Fourth Century B.C.E. Document from Ketef Yeriho', *IEJ* 38 (1988), pp. 162 and 173.

[9] F. M. Cross Jr., 'The Oldest Manuscripts from Qumran', *JBL* 74 (1955), fig. 2, l. 2.

[10] See Cross, Development, fig. 2, l. 3.

[11] See Avigad, p. 75, col. ix.

[12] The ossuary, which bears the inscription מתיה, belongs to the collection of the Institute for Archaeology of the Hebrew University of Jerusalem (no. 1463).

Waw is a straight downstroke with a long and straight hook, slanting down from its top to the left, or with a triangular loop to the left of its top.

Zayin is a somewhat wavy downstroke. About the middle of the Herodian period the letter usually appears in the book hand with a thickening at the right side of its top made by an extra short stroke (probably in analogy to *nun*).

The downstrokes of *het* start above the crossbar and the right downstroke is sometimes wavy in a similar form as in *dalet* and in *he*. In the late Herodian period an extra short stroke appears at the top of the right downstroke in those letters (probably in analogy to *zayin*).

Tet has a broad base which ascends at a slight slant to the right. Already in the Hasmonean period the base of *tet* is occasionally straight, but usually it is round or pointed at its bottom. The broad base of *tet* became standard from the Herodian period on. In careless writing the right stroke sometimes goes beyond its meeting point with the base (this happens already occasionally in 1QIsaᵃ).[13] This is the first stage in the evolution of the cursive form of the letter which appears in many variants in the post-Herodian period.

Yod is similar to *waw*, but is sometimes shorter. The two letters became gradually similar in form during the Hasmonean period. Only in the Byzantine period do they gradually become different in length; it took another few centuries (until about the 9th or 10th century) before they became different also in their form.

Kap is somewhat longer than *bet* and its top is perhaps narrower. Otherwise the two letters are shaped very similarly. During the Herodian period, when *bet* started to develop its tail at the lower right corner, *kap* gradually became shorter. Here the medial form appears also in final position but it seems that its base is drawn from right to left and sharpens to a point at its left edge (in 4Q409 a medial *kap* appears at the end of the word וברכ).

Lamed has a curved body open to the left, creating a long base. The body is low and is not hanging on the line (a similar form appears in 4QNumᵇ). The curved form of *lamed* is common in semi-cursive types of the Jewish script. In the calligraphic book hand of this period the letter usually lacks a base, its body is small and narrow and the right diagonal is straight and short.[14] At the top of the mast it has a small triangular loop or a thickening created by an extra stroke, a remnant of the long hook that appeared in a certain type of the 3rd century official Aramaic script[15] and continued to appear in the Hasmonean book hand. It appears later on in many variant forms in different styles of the Hebrew script.

Mem has a medial and a final form. The medial form has a small top which ascends aslant to the right. Its left stroke slopes down to the left, starting at the vertical serif. The serif, which was part of the top of *mem* in

---

[13] M. Burrows (with the assistance of J. C. Trever and W. H. Brownlee), *The Dead Sea Scrolls of St. Mark's Monastery*, I, New Haven, 1950, pl. iii, l. 26 (והנטפות).

[14] Cross, *Development*, fig. 2, ll. 3, 4.

[15] E. Bresciani, pp. 258–264.

the official Aramaic script and in the proto-Jewish and Hasmonean book hand, became gradually an independent stroke from the Herodian period on.

Final *mem* is extremely short for this period, but the left downstroke is characteristic of the first half of the Herodian period. It starts above the right half of the long top and descends aslant to the left, crossing the top at its centre and turning down vertically until it meets the long base. The base slants down to the left and occasionally goes beyond its meeting point with the left downstroke.

Nun inherited the backwards-bent top from the official Aramaic script and was followed by other letters such as *zayin, ṣade, ʿayin, ṭet, gimel* and *šin*. Here *nun* is shaped without the extra stroke to the right of its top (see also the description of *zayin*, above). It has a medial and a final form. The medial *nun* has a long and slanting base and the final *nun* is a long and wavy downstroke with an emphasized bent-to-the-right top.

Samek is closed. The left downstroke crosses the top at its left half and descends towards the base, occasionally crossing it. Sometimes the base goes beyond the meeting point. The letter appears in a similar form already at the beginning of the Herodian period.

ʿAyin curves the top of its right stroke to the left. The straight left stroke slopes down to the right. The letter is bigger than the Hasmonean *ʿayin* and has a fairly long base, but still lacks the extra strokes that develop in the Herodian period.

Pe has a pointed top and a broad slanting base, similar to the base of *kap*. It has a curved 'nose'. The letter is still relatively long. No final form of *pe* occurs in these fragments.

Ṣade is quite developed with both tops curved towards each other (especially the right top is curved to the left, a feature characteristic of the beginning of the Herodian period). Apparently it is shaped on the analogy of *ʿayin* and *šin*. The wavy downstroke bends to the left and creates a short slanting base. No final form of *ṣade* is documented here.

Qop has a relatively short leg which starts at the serif near the left edge of the top. The right stroke sometimes touches the leg and closes the letter. The short *qop* is typical of the Hasmonean book hand. During the Herodian period its leg became longer.

Reš differs from *dalet* in that it lacks the right serif. Its body is formed like a right-angle, bending forwards. Its top is broad and a long and straight serif slants down to its left edge.

Šin, with its outer tops curved towards each other, appears, in this form, in a certain type of the Hasmonean book hand,[16] and later in non-calligraphic scripts of the post-Herodian period.[17] The middle stroke is curved and is almost parallel to the right stroke, and it meets the left downstroke near its centre. The left downstroke occasionally descends beyond its meeting point with the right outer stroke.

---

[16] See Avigad, p. 67, col. viii; p. 75, col. ix.
[17] Ibid., p. 83, col. xxx.

Taw has parallel downstrokes which slope down to the right. The right stroke is somewhat longer than the left one as a result of the letter bending forward. The left downstroke bends at its bottom at an angle to the left and creates an almost horizontal short base. The right shoulder is curved. Similar forms of *taw* appear in the Hasmonean and in the Herodian book hand.[18]

In conclusion, the script of 4Q397 fits into the group of scrolls from the first half of the Herodian period. Early and late features are found together. Among the late features, we may cite: the short final *mem*, the thick and straight serifs which slant down to the left edge of the tops, the bending forward of the letters, the triangular loops at the left tops of *waw*, *yod* and sometimes *lamed*, which resemble the loops in certain Herodian ossuary-inscriptions, and the double-stroke at the top of *he*, common in the Herodian period. All these features are characteristic of the middle and second half of the Herodian period. There are two prominent early features: the absence of an extra stroke at the right top of *nun* and *zayin*, and the occurrence of the medial forms of *kap* and *pe* in final position. Even though these also may appear in certain later non-calligraphic types of the Jewish script, they must be taken into account for an early dating since the scribe was especially careful to emphasize the graphic elements characteristic of the style of script he was using. The style and the stage of evolution of the script in the fragments generally resemble those of the script in 4QNum[b]. On the basis of all these observations we may date the fragments of 4Q397 to the first half of the Herodian period.

ADA YARDENI

1.5.2 Orthography

The *yod* indicates all cases of long *i*, e.g., הנ[ב]ביאים] (14–21 10), בדברים (14–21 8). Note the historical orthography employed in כי (14–21 5), המת (6–13 11), מחנה (6–13 3), and כראשית (6–13 5). *Waw* is used more extensively and it records every case of *u/o* whether long or short, final or internal, e.g., מכול (3 5), קודש (6–13 12), חושבים (5 3), כתוב (14–21 12), או (6–13 11). For pronouns and pronominal suffixes the incomplete paradigm runs אתם, בידנו, כתבנו, אנחנו, היאה, ממנו, בו, הואה, -כה, עמהם, להאכילמה, לעשותמה, אתמה.

1.5.3.1 4Q397 1–2

[   ] ‏]ה ואף על עור[ו]ת ועצמות הבהמה הטמאה אין לעשות[

[מן עצמותמה] ומן ע[ו]ר[ו]ות]מה ידות כ[ל]ים   ואף על עור נבלת[

[הבהמה] הטהורה [והנוש]א א[ו]{ו}ת(ה) נבלתה [לוא יגש לטהרת המקדש]

[   ] ‏ו[ת שהמ]ה   וא[פ על הע]ו

1.5.3.1.1 NOTES ON THE READING

L. 3 (את){ו}א   It is possible that a deleting dot stood above the *waw* where there is now a hole.

---

[18] Ibid., p. 67, col. viii; p. 75, col. ix.

1.5.3.2   4Q397   3

ראוי להשמר ב[כ]ול הד̇בר[ים האלה

בצ[פ]ו̇ן המחנה̇[

וירושלים הי[א] מחנה וחוצה ל[מחנה הוא

[החט]א̇ת [ומוצי]א̇ים [את דשא המ̇זבח

5   המקום אש̇ר בחר בו[מ̇כול שב̇[טי ישראל

ה[

1.5.3.3   4Q397   4

א[נח̇נו חו[שבים

[האוכל̇[

1.5.3.4   4Q397   5

ועל העמונ̇י והמואב̇י ו[ה]ממזר ופ̇[צוע הדכה

ונשים לוקחים להיו[ת]מ̇ה עצם אחת [

[טמאות ואף חושבים] אנחנו

וא[י̇ן להתיכמה ולעש[ותתמ̇ה עצם אחת

5   שמק̇[צת העם̇[

להזהר]מ̇כ̇ול ת̇[ערובת הג̇בר

1.5.3.1.1   NOTES ON THE READING

L. 3 חושבים The last two letters are clearly visible on PAM 43.476.

L. 6 The stroke before כ̇ול has no thickening or hook at its head. It is not clear whether the letter after מ̇כ̇ול stood in a new word or not.

1.5.3.5   4Q397   6–13

top margin (?)

[אנח̇נ̇ו̇ אומרים שהם שאין בהם טהרה ואף המוצקות אינם מבדילות בין ה[טמא לט[הור]

[כי לחת המוצקות והמ̇קבל מהמה כהם לחה אחת ואין להב̇י למחני הק̇[ודש כלבים]

[שהם אוכלים מקצת ע[צ]מות המ̇[ק]דש וי̇[הבשר ע[ע]ליהם כי ירושלים היאה̇ ו[מחנה הקודש ו[היא]

[המקום שבחר] בו מכ̇ול [שבטי̇ ו]ישראל כי ירושלים ראש מ̇חנ̇ו̇ת ישראל וֿהיאה ואף על מטע̇[ת]

[עצי המאכל הנטע בֿאֿרץ ישראל]ל כֿרֿאֿשֿיֿת [הוא לכוהנים ומעשר הבקר]וֿהצֿ[ון ל]כֿוהנים [הוא]   5

[ואף על הצרועים אֿנֿחֿנו אומרים שלוא יבואו עם טהרת הקֿודש כי בדד יֿהֿיו]

[מחוץ לבית וא]ֿף כֿ[י]ֿף שֿמעת שיגלֿ[וֿ]חֿ וֿ[כבס ישֿ]ֿחֿ מחוֿ[ץֿ למחנה וֿהֿלֿוֿ אוהלו שבעת ימֿ[יֿם ועתה]

[בהיות טמאתם עֿ]ֿמֿהם הצֿ[ר]ֿועים באים עֿמֿ[ ]ֿשֿ טהרת הֿ[קֿוֿדֿ]ֿשֿ לבית [ואתם יודעים שעל השוגג שלוא]

[יעשה את המצוה וֿנֿעֿלֿ]ֿם ממנוֿ [לֿהֿבֿיֿא] חֿטאת ועֿ[ל] העושה ביד רמה כתוֿב שֿהֿוֿ[אֿ]אֿ בֿ[ו]ֿזֿה וֿ[מֿגֿדֿ]ֿף

[ואף בהיות לה]ֿמֿ[ה ט]ֿמֿאות נֿ[גֿעֿ אֿיֿן] להאכילם [מֿהֿקוֿדֿשים עד בוא השמש ביום הֿ]ֿשֿמֿי[נֿי ועל]   10

[טמאת נפש]האדם שאנחנו אוֿ[מֿ]ֿרֿים שכולֿ[וֿ]עצם שֿהֿיֿא חֿסֿרֿה וֿשֿלֿמֿה כֿמֿ[שֿ]ֿפֿ[ט]ֿט המת או החלֿ[לֿ]

[הוֿאֿ]   ועל הזנות הנֿעֿ[שֿ]ֿסֿה בתוך העֿ[וֿם וֿהֿמֿה בני זרע קדֿשֿ] כֿשֿכתוב קודש [ישֿראל]

[ועל בֿהֿמֿתו הטהוֿ]ֿרֿה כתוב שלוֿ[אֿ]ֿ לֿהֿרֿבֿיֿעֿ[וֿ]ֿה כלאים ועל לבושוֿ שלוֿא יֿהֿיה [כלאים ולֿא לזרוֿעֿ]

[שדו וֿבֿרֿמו כלאיֿ[ם] בֿ[גֿ]ֿלֿל שֿהֿ[מֿה קדושים ובני אהרון קֿדֿושים ואתֿ[ם יֿוֿדֿ]ֿעֿים]

[שֿמֿקֿצֿת הֿכֿהֿנֿים וֿהֿעֿם מתערבים והם מֿתֿוֿכֿכֿים וֿמֿטֿמֿאֿ[ים את זרֿעֿ הֿקֿוֿדֿ]ֿשֿ [ואֿף את זרעֿם]   15

1.5.3.5.1 NOTES ON THE READING

L. 3 Note the traces of a letter before מחנה.
L. 9 שהו]אֿה and not שהו]אֿ.

1.5.3.6 4Q397 14–21

top margin (?)

[ ]ֿשֿמֿ[ ]ֿ[ ]   [

נֿעֿותֿ[ו]   וֿ[יֿשֿיֿבוֿאֿ]ֿו   [

וֿמֿי ישֿנֿ[וֿ]   [יֿהיה מתֿ]   [

ועל הנשיֿ[ם   החמֿ[וֿ]ֿס והמעלֿ]   [

כי באלהֿ[בגלל וֿ]ֿהֿחֿמס והזנות אבֿדֿ[ו   מקצת]   5

מקומות [ואֿף] כתוֿ[וֿב בספר מושה שלוֿ[אֿ]ֿא תבֿיֿא תועבה אֿ[ל ביתכה כי]

התועבה שנואה הֿיֿאֿהֿ [ואתם יודעים שֿ]ֿפֿרֿישנו מרוֿב העֿ[ם ומכול טמאתם]

[וֿ]ֿמֿהתערב בדברים האלה ומֿלֿבוא עֿמֿהם עֿ[מֿהם]ֿלֿגֿב אלה וֿאֿתם יֿ[וֿדֿעים שלוֿא]

[יֿ]ֿמֿצא בידנו מעל ושקר ורעֿהֿ כי על [אֿלֿה]ֿאֿנֿחֿנֿו נותנים אֿ[ת   ואֿף]

[כֿתֿבֿנֿ]ֿו אליכה שתבין בספר מוֿשֿֿהֿ [וֿ]ֿבֿסֿפֿרֿ[יֿ] הנֿ[בֿ]ֿיאים ובדוֿ[יֿ]ֿד   [10

[במעשיֿ] דור ודור ובספר כתוב וֿ[וֿלֿ]ֿו   וֿיֿ[ם לֿ]ֿוֿ לואֿ

וֿקֿדֿמֿנֿיֿוֿתֿ לֿ[וֿ]ֿה ואף כתוב שֿ[וֿ]ֿתֿסֿורֿ[וֿ] מהֿדֿ[וֿ]ֿרֿ[וֿ]ֿך וקרתֿ[וֿ]ֿכֿה הרעֿה וֿ[כתֿ]ֿוֿב וֿהֿיֿא

[כי יבוא עֿלֿיֿכֿה כוֿ]ֿל הדברוֿ[י]ֿם הֿאֿלֿה בֿאֿחֿ[רֿית הימֿ[י]ֿם הֿבֿ[רֿ]ֿכֿה וֿ[הֿ]ֿקֿללה

והשיבותֿהֿ אל לבב]ֿכה ושבתֿ]ֿה אלו בכֿ]ֿל לבבכה ובֿ]ֿכוֿ]ֿל נֿפשֿ]ֿכה]ֿבֿאחריתֿ[

15   ]ֿוכתוב בספר]ֿמושה ובֿסֿ]ֿפרי הנביאיֿ]ֿם שיבואֿ]ֿו   ]ֿ שלֿ]ֿו   [

     ]ֿ   הברכֿ]ֿות שֿ]ֿבֿאֿוֿ   בֿיֿ]ֿמֿ]ֿי [שלומוה בן דויד ואֿף הֿקֿללותֿ]

1.5.3.6.1 Notes on the Reading

L. 5 Before כי we read]ֿ◦ֿו; this belongs to the preceding column.

L. 7 It is not clear whether there was an intentional *vacat* after הֿיֿאֿהֿ or whether the absence of traces of writing is caused by the loss of the surface.

L. 8 The *waw* would completely fill out the line to the margin. In]ֿלֿגֿב it is not clear whether the *lamed* belonged to the word גב or to another word.

L. 9 על [אלה According to Strugnell, part of the fragment with traces of the *ʾalep* has been lost. In אֿנחנו, a very small fragment, completing the traces of the first three letters, has now become detached from the larger fragment, but it can be seen on an early photograph (41.762).

1.5.3.7 4Q397 22

שבֿ]ֿאֿוֿ]ֿמֿיומֿ]ֿי ירוֿבֿעֿםֿ

]ֿשֿיובאֿ]ֿו

בֿסֿפר מוֿשֿ]ֿה וזֿ]ֿה

1.5.3.8 4Q397 23

עצתֿ]ֿכה והֿ]ֿרחיק

]ֿבֿשל שתֿ]ֿשֿמֿח

]ֿמקצֿ]ֿת דברינו

1.6 4Q398

The papyrus is coarse (ranging in colour from a dark yellow to a light buff) and the surface layer has partly gone at numerous places, both large and small. The manuscript at first glance appears to be only some ten lines in height, but in fact we have neither top nor bottom margin in frg. 2. In frg. 1 there are 15 mm from the top of the last inscribed line to the bottom of the fragment. Yet if, as is probable, frgs. 1 and 2 were preserved superimposed on one another, then the considerations that apply to frg. 2 also apply to this fragment, and the apparent base would be only a *vacat*. There are, as is customary with papyri from Qumran, no dry lines, whether horizontal or vertical, to guide the scribe. The writing is somewhat irregular with regard to an ideal horizontal line; the right margin is well observed, the left far more irregularly. The width of the columns is about 11 cm; frgs. 11–13 had 45–55 corrected letter spaces, frgs. 14–17 i had about 45 corrected letter spaces, and frgs. 14–17 ii had 40–48 corrected letter spaces. The average space betwen lines was 8.5 mm for frgs. 1 and 2, 7 mm for the remaining fragments; the average letter's height (e.g., ח, ש) is 4 mm in frgs. 1–2, and 3.5

Palaeographic Comparative Chart

4Q448

4Q398 (MMT)

4Q212 (En⁵)

Masada 556

in the other fragments. Photos: PAM 41.992*, 42.067*, 42.071*, 42.183, 42.368, 42.557*, 43.489 and 43.491.

1.6.1 Script

The script of 4Q398 belongs to the group of semi-cursive Jewish scripts. In general the letters have no serifs except for those inherited from the Aramaic mother script. At first glance, one notices the thick horizontal strokes as against the relatively thin down strokes that are caused by the use of a calamus-pen, the broad edge of which was held perpendicular to the line. This feature does not usually characterize the early Jewish book hand and it appears only in a few documents in semi-cursive script, as, for example, in a liturgical poem from Qumran dating to about the middle of the first century BCE (4Q448; unpublished). Another feature these two documents share, together with still another document in semi-cursive script from Masada (Masada 556),[19] is the similar relative size of the letters inside the alphabetic system, which points to a closer relation to the Hasmonean period than to a later stage of evolution of the Jewish script. An uncommon feature in 4Q398 is the tendency of the scribe to pose a final *he* and final *kap* lower than the line or the previous letter (e.g., לך, אלה, ונחשבה).

A comparison of the skeleton forms[20] of the letters in 4Q398 to the skeleton forms of the letters in the different stages of development of the cursive and semi-cursive Jewish scripts suggests that the script of 4Q398 belongs to the period of transition from the Hasmonean to the Herodian styles.

Only a few letters are actually cursive: *taw* is cursive in all its occurrences; final and medial *nun* ; a few occurrences of *waw* and *yod* without the hook; a cursive *mem* occurs once, as does a cursive *ʾalep* . The other letters are in different stages of evolution towards cursiveness. *Nun*, *pe* and *ṣade* have a concave base stroke; *bet*, *tet* and *samek* are in a stage of transition towards their typical cursive form. It seems that the script of 4Q398 reflects a period in which the cursive forms of most of the letters, as they are attested from about the middle of the Herodian period, have not yet crystallized. What follows is a detailed description of the main characteristics of each letter of the alphabet according to the structure of the skeleton of the letter in question.

ʾAlep is written with three strokes. A similar form of the letter appears in documents written in the semi-cursive script of the late Hasmonean period (e.g., 4QEn[g])[21] and also in the round semi-formal (e.g., 4QIsa[b] and 4QNum[b]).[22] The diagonal descends to the right and sharpens to a point at its bottom, while a thin straight stroke slopes down on its right and joins it below its centre. On its left, from below its top, a thin, convex-to-left stroke slopes down until it reaches a common imaginary base line. The letter stands upright or inclines backwards somewhat. A cursive form of *ʾalep*, which appears only once, belongs to the type which is made with two strokes. The upper slant stroke bends its top down to the right as a remnant of an ornamental extra stroke, characteristic of the Herodian book hand *ʾalep*. This form of cursive *ʾalep* appears often as the final form of the letter in the Herodian and post-Herodian periods.

Bet is made with two strokes and has a convex top without the inherited serif. This semi-cursive form appears, along with another variant of a more

---

[19] Y. Yadin and J. Naveh, *Masada I: The Yigael Yadin Excavations 1963–1965*, Jerusalem, 1989, pl. 45, no. 556.
[20] The skeleton of a letter is its inner structure, built of the centre lines of its strokes.
[21] For the script, see Cross, Development, p. 149, fig. 4, l. 5.
[22] Ibid., p. 138, fig. 2, l. 5.

cursive form made with one stroke, in a list of names on a lid of a sarcophagus from Beth Phage[23] and occasionally in ossuary inscriptions, but is rare in documents written in ink. Nevertheless it appears in 4Q448 (mentioned above). In a few occurrences of the letter the base stroke extends to the right beyond its meeting point with the downstroke. This reflects a transitional stage towards the appearence, at about the beginning of the first century CE, of the cursive form made with one stroke and resembling the numeral 2. The form without the extended base stroke resembles the medial *kap*, except for its height (*bet* is shorter).

Only remnants of the letter *gimel* appear, thus precluding a description of its form.

Dalet is made with two strokes. The downstroke starts above the roof and descends vertically while the roof is drawn horizontally or somewhat slanting upwards to the right. The inherited serif is a straight stroke which slopes down to the left edge of the roof. The extension of the down-stroke at the right shoulder of *dalet* distinguishes it from *reš*.

He appears in two variant forms: a medial form that resembles the archaic tripod-form, inherited from the Aramaic mother-script, and a final form with a horizontal, short and fat top, lacking the serifs which appear in the Herodian book hand. A vertical left downstroke starts near the left edge of the top and descends parallel to the right downstroke. The distinction between medial and final forms of *he* is well attested in the few known documents written in cursive script of the early Hasmonean period (the Nash papyrus[24] and ostracon no. 72 from Murabbaʿat[25]). It does not appear regularly in the cursive script of the Herodian and post-Herodian periods.

Waw is sometimes made without the typical hook. Its length varies, and occasionally it is very short. There is no clear distinction between the forms of *waw* and of *yod*. The identification in form of these two letters started in the Jewish book hand in the early Hasmonean period (their form is already almost identical in 1QIsaᵃ).[26]

Zayin is a straight vertical downstroke. It resembles *waw* and *yod* when these letters appear without the hook but is somewhat longer.

Ḥet is made with three strokes: a narrow horizontal cross stroke between two vertical downstrokes of equal length. The downstrokes usually start above the cross stroke but occasionally the left one starts from the left edge of the cross stroke. The form of *ḥet* in 4Q398 resembles the form of the letter in the early Hasmonean book hand as well as in the late Hasmonean and Herodian semi-cursive (e.g., 4Q448 and 4QEnᵍ).

Ṭet deserves special attention as it may help to establish an approximate date for our document. It is made with either one or two strokes and in four movements. The cursive form of *ṭet*, which appears in documents from the middle of the first century CE onwards, has developed from a similar form.

---

[23] J. T. Milik, 'Le couvercle de Bethphage', *Hommage à [Andre] Dupont-Sommer*, Paris, 1971, pp. 75–94.

[24] W. A. Albright, 'A Biblical Fragment from the Maccabaean Age: The Nash Papyrus', *JBL* 56 (1937), pp. 145–176.

[25] P. Benoit, J. T. Milik, R. de Vaux, *Les grottes de Murabbaʿat*, DJD II, Oxford, 1961.

[26] For the script of 1QIsaᵃ, see Avigad, p. 67, col. vii.

Here it is in transition towards its cursive form. Its mother-form is already attested in 1QIsa^a [27]where the right downstroke starts to extend beyond its meeting point with the base stroke which slants upwards. A similar *ṭet* appears in 4QEng , and a more developed form appears in an undated ostracon in cursive script[28] which may be assigned to the beginning of the first century CE or somewhat earlier. A semi-cursive form, very similar to that in 4Q398, still appears in the date formula of a document from the year 134 CE (NH 47b) .[29] Given these data we may say that the form of *ṭet* in 4Q398 should not be assigned to a date earlier than the middle of the first century BCE.

Yod resembles *waw* and appears sometimes with the typical hook and sometimes without it.

Kap has both a medial and a final form and the distinction between them is regular (unlike the *kap* in 4Q448 that has only a single form—the middle one—which serves also at the final position in the word).[30] Both forms lack the inherited serif. The medial form is made with two strokes in three movements and is still long and narrow, extending below the imaginary base line. As already said, it differs from *bet* mainly in its height. *Kap* became shorter during the Herodian period, when the tail of *bet* had already fully developed.

The final form is made with two strokes—a straight horizontal stroke from left to right joins a long downstroke below its top. A similar form of final *kap* appears occasionally in late Herodian book hand (e.g., 1QH^a). A similar final *kap*, without the left serif, appears also in the above-mentioned ostracon from Masada (556) and already occasionally in documents from the post-Herodian period (e.g., the above-mentioned document NH 47b).

Lamed appears in two main forms. The long flag which descends from the top of the mast to the right in one of the variants is uncommon in the tradition of the Jewish script, but already appears in a document in Aramaic script from about the middle of the 3rd century BCE that was found in Egypt.[31]

In 4Q397,[32] which is written in a semi-formal script, a similar ornament, although somewhat shorter, descends from the top of the mast of *lamed* to the right. In a cursive form of *lamed* from the post-Herodian period (NH 8),[33] where the letter is made with a single vertical downstroke, a similar ornament descends from its top to the right. In the more common form of *lamed* which appears in 4Q398 a short hook, similar to the hook of *waw* and *yod*, descends from the top of the mast to the left.

---

[27] See, for example, Burrows, pl. iii, 4th line from the bottom.

[28] A. Yardeni, 'New Jewish Aramaic Ostraca', *IEJ* 18 (1990), fig. 2, l. 5.

[29] The documents from Naḥal Hever are to be published soon.

[30] Medial *kap* in final position is attested already in 1QIsa^a. This phenomenon seems to have existed for only a short time until the distinction between medial and final forms of *kap* became regular during the Herodian period.

[31] Bresciani, pp. 258–264.

[32] See above, 4Q397, pp. 21–25.

[33] See above, n. 29.

Mem has both a medial and a final form. The medial form is still relatively large and it extends below the imaginary base line. During the Herodian period the medial *mem* was shortened to the average height of the letters. Here it is in a transition period during which the inherited serif became an independent short stroke. It is difficult to tell if here it is an independent stroke or made in one stroke with the top, as in the early *mem*, or, perhaps, with the left diagonal, as for example in the *mem* of 1QpHab.[34] The short high diagonal is typical of the middle of the Herodian period (the scroll of Thanksgiving Hymns) but it is already attested earlier (the Nash papyrus and Mur 72). A similar form of medial *mem* appears, along with other variants, in ostracon 556 from Masada, and as the final form of the letter in 4Q448. A cursive form of *mem* is also attested (in the words ולעמך, עמך). A cursive form of *mem* already appears in Mur 72 (in a supra-linear addition). In the semi-cursive script of 4QEn^g a similar form of cursive *mem* appears regularly in medial position. Its form did not change significantly during the Herodian and post-Herodian periods.

Final *mem* also is still very long. The left downstroke starts above the middle of the broad top, crosses it and descends vertically until it touches the base stroke and continues down. This form of final *mem* is typical of the late Hasmonean and the early Herodian periods. It became shorter during the Herodian period.

Nun appears in medial and final forms. The medial *nun* lacks the thickening or the bending backwards of its top that are characteristic of the book hand *nun*. It appears here in a cursive form (e.g., in the word ונחשבה) and in a semi-cursive form (e.g., in the word והתבנן).

Final *nun* appears in an extreme cursive form, as a straight downstroke (e.g. in the words הבן, והתבנן). This form of cursive *nun* already appears occasionally in the Aramaic cursive script in the 5th century BCE (e.g., Cowley 46).[35]

Samek is already closed. The letter becomes closed during the late Hasmonean period, when the right downstroke bends to the left in the direction of the left downstroke (in 1QIsa^a and in Mur 72 it still is open). In the cursive script it is sometimes made with one continuous stroke and perhaps it is thus made here also (e.g., in the word ונסלוח).

'Ayin is here a small letter in an upright position, made of two short straight diagonals, very much like the late Aramaic *'ayin* (e.g., in SP 1 from 335 BCE)[36] as well as the early Hasmonean *'ayin* (1QIsa^a and Mur 72). It lacks the thickening or the bending of the tops of the strokes, and especially of the right stroke, which is typical to the letter in the Herodian and post-Herodian periods. The letter already became bigger during the Hasmonean period.

Pe appears in both a medial and a final form. The medial form is made with two strokes and is a narrow letter. In contrast to its form in the book

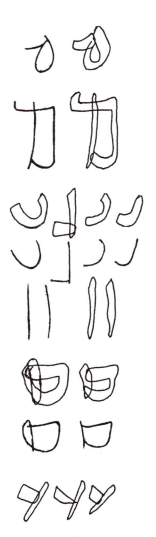

---

[34] For the script of 1QpHab, see Avigad, p. 75, col. xii.

[35] See, for example, E. Sachau, *Aramäische Papyrus und Ostraka*, Leipzig, 1911, Tafel 31, Papyrus 31, l. 10, in the word באבני.

[36] Cross, Discovery, pp. 110–121.

hand, its base stroke is concave and is drawn toward the next letter. Its top is sharp and the characteristic hook is relatively long but does not bend back into the letter as it occasionally does in the Herodian period. Final *pe* also is made with two strokes, as a short extra stroke is added at the left edge of the convex top (in the word ואף it is made from left to right). It reflects the development of the letter in the Herodian period (a similar form appears in 4QNum[b]).

Ṣade appears only in medial position. It is made with two strokes. Its right arm is drawn from left to right in an almost horizontal, straight or somewhat convex stroke. This rare form of *ṣade* appears in a certain type of the cursive script and is already attested in Mur 72. In the common form of the letter the right arm is a slanted, somewhat curved stroke which descends from right to left until it touches the left downstroke near its centre. In the cursive script the right arm is drawn first and the letter is sometimes made with one continuous stroke. Here the letter is of medium height and does not extend below the imaginary baseline. The left downstroke resembles *nun* and curves at its bottom to the left in the direction of the next letter.

Qop is made with three strokes. Sometimes the right stroke is very short (e.g., in the word לצדקה) so that the letter occasionally disappears altogether (e.g., in the word וצדקיה) and resembles a certain type of cursive *qop* (4QEn[g]). The long downstroke became common in the early Herodian period.

Reš is distinct from *dalet* and is made with one stroke. In 4Q398 it also is shorter than *dalet*, but this is not a stylistic feature.

Šin is made with three strokes. The two right arms are parallel to each other and descend at a slight slant to the left until they meet the left downstroke. The letter is of medium size and lacks the bending or thickening at the top of its strokes which is characteristic of the Herodian book hand. On the other hand it differs from the main cursive form which is made with one continuous stroke. The almost vertical left downstroke extends below its meeting point with the lower right arm. The form of the letter is typical of the late Hasmonean and early Herodian semi-cursive script. A similar, though somewhat more cursive form, appears in 4QEn[g].

Taw is made with either one or two strokes, starting with the left downstroke. The history of the looped *taw* already begins in the Aramaic script and it first appears in documents from the 5th century BCE. In the Aramaic script it remained a secondary form, but in the Jewish cursive it became the main form. It is the main form of the letter in the Nash papyrus and it appears also in scrolls from Qumran written in semi-cursive script (e.g., 4QXII[a][37] and 4QEn[g]). In the Herodian and post-Herodian periods it appears in many variant forms, sometimes with a huge loop and sometimes with a long right downstroke. Its form in 4Q398 is the usual one in the cursive script, and since a similar form still appears in documents of the

---

[37] See Cross, Development, p. 149, fig. 4, l. 1.

second century CE (cf. Mur 30),[38] it does not allow a precise dating of the script.

Summary

4Q398 belongs to a small group of documents written in semi-cursive script. The significant differences in the sizes of the letters is reminiscent of the late Aramaic and early Jewish scripts. Ornamental elements, which usually leave some impression even in the cursive and semi-cursive scripts, are almost completely lacking (except for those inherited from the Aramaic mother-script, and a remnant of an ornamental element in a single occurrence of a cursive *'alep*), and this may suggest a connection with the Hasmonean script. The letters *ṭet* and *samek*, however, are more developed, and first appear in this form in documents from the Herodian period. This fact, and the occurrence of the developed cursive *'alep*, force us to assign these fragments to a somewhat later date. In 4Q398 only a few letter forms are actually cursive. These are *taw* (in all occurrences), final and medial *nun* and occasionally *waw* and *yod*. In addition to the cursive *'alep* there is one occurrence of a cursive *mem*. The forms of the following letters can be distinguished as semi-cursive: *'alep*, *bet*, *he*, *ḥet*, *ṭet*, *kap*, *samek pe*, *ṣade*, *šin*. The script reflects a period before the full crystallization of the cursive script as it is attested in documents from the first half of the first century CE. It thus seems that the script of 4Q398 fits well into the early Herodian period.

ADA YARDENI

1.6.2 Orthography

The manuscript presents some irregularities, as indeed we expect in the semi-cursive tradition (cf. J. T. Milik in *DJD* III pp. 223–30), but not very many. The pronouns and pronominal suffixes are generally spelt as in the Masoretic tradition, e.g., אליך, לבבך, הוא, מהם ,והם; exceptions are מלפנו ,אלו, השיבותה and במעשיהמֹה. *Yod* marks all occurrences of long *i*, whether final or internal, e.g., מי, כי, איש, והרחיק (for מכירים 11–13 3, see § 1.6.3.9.1). *Waw* marks almost all occurrences of *u/o* vowels whether long or short, internal or final, e.g., זכור (14–17 ii 1), תערובת (5 3). Exceptions are והתבנן (11–13 6), וקדמניות (14–17 i 4), בכל (14–17 ii 4; cf. also § 1.6.3.11 1—n. on l. 4). On ערמה, טהרה and במצאך, see § 3.1.1.2; on עונות, see § 3.1.1. The occurrences of היא for היה (cf. היה in 11–13 7) and הקללא are both vulgar. For the peculiar form באוו, see § 3.2.1. For ירושלם, see *HDSS*, p. 91.

1.6.3.1   4Q398 1–3

ואף על ע[וֹ]ר נבלת [וֹהבהמה[וֹ] הטהורה [והוֹ]נושה

את נבלתֹהֹ לוֹא י[וֹ]גשֿ לטהרת הֹ[וֹ]קודש

[על]

1.6.3.1.1   NOTES ON THE READING

L. 1 The word [ה]נושה (= הַנּוֹשֵׂא) cannot be seen on any photograph, but Strugnell said that it did exist.

1.6.3.2   4Q398 4

י]בֿואֿו[
ל תעֿ]רובת[
ארץ[

1.6.3.3   4Q398 5

י תמֿ∘[
שֿר עשו הֿ]
תערובת[
הֿ]אשה ב[

1.6.3.4   4Q398 6

הא[
כל[

1.6.3.5   4Q398 7

דֿש והעֿ]
לֿ]טהרת הקֿ]
לֿ[

1.6.3.6   4Q398 8

ש א[
זֿ רֿ[

1.6.3.7   4Q398 9

הֿ ∘[
קד]שֿ קֿ]דשים

1.6.3.8   4Q398 10

רֿצה מֿ]

1.6.3.9   4Q398 11–13

[הבר]כֹֿוֿת שֶׁ[בָּ]אֿ[וֿ]וֿ   ⵔ[ ]∘   ]בֿימי שלומוה בן דויד וֿאֿף הֿקֿללות

[שֶׁ]בָּאֿוֿוֿ בימי [ירֿ]וֿבעֿםֿ בן נבט ועד גֿל[וֿ]ת ירושלם וצדקיה מלך יֿהֿוֿ[ד]ה

[שֶׁ]יֿבֿ[יֿ]אֿם בֿ[ֿ]   ]וֿאֿנחנו מכירֿיֿםֿ שבאוו מקצֿת הברכות והקללוֿֿת

שֶׁכֿתֿוֿב בסֿ[וֿ]פר מוֿ[]שֿה וזה הֿוֿא אחרֿיֿת הימים שישובו בישראל

5   לתֿ[ו]מיד   וֿ]ולוֿא ישובו אֿחֿוֿ[ר]וֿהֿרֿשעים יֿרֿשֿ[יֿע]וֿֿ וֿאֿ[ם] [ ]

וֿהֿ[∘∘   ]ֿזֿכֿוֿֿ את מלכי ישרא[ל] והתבנן במעשיהֿמֿֿהֿ שמי מהם

שהיא יראֿ[וֿ] את   התוֿ[ו]רה היה מצוֿ[ל]מצרות והם מֿבֿ[ק]שֿי תורה

1.6.3.9.1 Notes on the Reading

On the disagreement over the placement of these fragments, see Appendix 2.

There has been considerable loss of minute particles of the surface all along the left edge of the fragment. The smudging in ll. 4–5 seems to be accidental, and not an attempt at erasure.

L. 1 We read בֿימי (and not כימי or מֿימי) because of the height of the base line.

L. 2 ירֿ]וֿבעֿםֿ The small trace of ink, at half the height of the writing, must come from *waw* and not *reš* (unless we dismiss it as an accident) and the resultant orthography is fully consonant with our scribe's habits. In גֿל[וֿ]ת the first two letters and the last are certain despite damage. It is possible that *waw* was tucked in the hook of *lamed* as, e.g., in אלו (frgs. 14–17 i 7). The word יֿהֿוֿ[דה] seems to have been added between the lines, or at least to have been placed in the margin, where it droops below the line of the writing. The writing is smaller (perhaps the work of a corrector?), but the hand is not necessarily a different one: most traces have been carried away with the loss of most of the surface at this point.

L. 3 In מכירֿיֿםֿ there are certainly traces of ink between *kap* and *reš*, but it is difficult to see in them a regular *yod*. It could be that the ink from *reš* has run back along the fibres, or we could have a corrector's *yod* inserted to regularise the orthography. שֿבאוו The breadth of the hook of the last letter best fits *yod*; the hook of the preceding letter is tighter, but the forms of the two letters are the epicene ones. The *waw* of הברכות is damaged by a hole but clearly was of the tightly hooked form, the hook being almost as long as the rest of the letter. In והקללוֿֿת the last two letters drop below the line (as was the case with יהודה in the preceding line), and can only be discerned in view of the needs of the context.

L. 4 Rather than [כ]שֿכֿתֿוֿב בסֿ[פר]. For *samek* only *qop* or *lamed* would be possible alternatives. בישראֿל Only to the left of the *qop* in the line above can we see any trace of the ink from the *lamed*, but the last two letters are still materially highly likely.

L. 5 Of the traces before ולוא only the upper one is composed of ink (the apparent trace at the bottom being just the shadow cast by a hole), and it cannot be identified with certainty; *waw*, *yod* and *he* are all plausible. וֿאֿ[ם] The last letter may be a *pe*; *bet* is materially unlikely.

L. 6 The first letter is either *waw* or (a remote possibility) *zayin*, but scarcely *yod*. The third letter had a descender with no base. The four letters of זֿכֿוֿֿ are held in their original place by one fibre. Despite the damage, the first three letters can be identified with a fair degree of certainty, even without considerations of context. The reading במעשיהֿמֿֿהֿ is positive, במעשיהם being ruled out by the traces at the left of the split in the papyrus.

L. 7 Above יֹרא there is a trace of writing. It is best understood as a descender from a letter in the line above (such as *qop*, final *kap* or final *nun*). The traces below מצול] belong to a superimposed layer of papyrus. The words מצרות והם can be read as one word מצרותיהם (cf. Ps 34:18).

1.6.3.10   4Q398 14–17 i

[בידנו מעל ושקר ורעה כי על כול אלה אֲנחנו נוֹת]נׁים את

כתב]נוׁם [שתבין בס]פֿׁר מוֹשׁה   ]

[ובסׁפרי הנביאים ובדוׁיׁד ובמעשי דור ו]דור [וב]סׁפֿׁר כתוׁב

יֹם לֹ• לוֹא ל]ך וקדׁמׁנׁיוֹת •מׁ•   ]

[כתוׁ]בׁ שׁתֹ[סור מהדׁרך וקֹ]רׁ[אֹ]תֹךׁ [הרעׁ]ה וׁכתוב והיא כי   5

יבוׁ]א עׁליׁך [כוׁל הדברים] האׁלה בֹּאחרי[ת] הׁימים הבׁרכה

[וה]קללׁא [והשיבותׁ]ה אל לׁ[בב]ך ושׁבֹתֹה אלו בכל לבבך

[ובׁכוׁ]ל נפשׁ[ך בַּאחריׁ]ת [העׁת] וׁחׁ[ ]•[[

1.6.3.10.1   NOTES ON THE READING

L. 4 After the word •מׁ• and a space there is a clear sign which looks like a cursive *ʾalep* (see § 1.6.1 above).

1.6.3.11   4Q398 14–17 ii

top margin

[נשוׁ]אֹי עונׁות זכור [את] דוֹיֹד שהיא איש חסדים [ו]אֹף

הׁיׁא [נׁ]צׁל מצׁרות רבות ונסלוח לוֹ ואף אנחנו כתבנו אליך

מקצת מעשי התורה שחשבנו לטוב לך ולעמך שׁרֹ[א]יֹנֹוׁ

עמך ערמה ומדע תורה הבן בכל אלה ובקש מלפנו שׁיׁתׁקׁן

את עצתך והרחיק ממך מחשב(ו)ת רעה ועצֹת בלׁיׁעׁל   5

בשל שתשמח באחרית העת במצאך מקצׁת דברינו כׁן

ונחשבה לך לצדקה בעשותך הישר והטוב לפנו לטוב לך

ולישראל
vacat

1.6.3.11.1   NOTES ON THE READING

L. 1 There is no trace of writing above the line; materially this could be the top line. עונׁות So we must read, and not עתות. For the decisive form of the ligature of נו, cf. חשבנו in l. 3; note both the curved base of *nun* and the form of *waw* that the ligature necessitates. In שהיא the right and centre of the *ʾalep* are partly covered by a fold. אֹף Although there is a small lacuna in the papyrus before

אַ֯, there survives enough uninscribed surface before that word, and too little space in the lacuna, to allow us to restore this document's characteristic וְאַף (J. S.).

L. 2 הִיא וְ[נ]צל After הִיא the gap is a little wider than appears, the lacuna corresponding to the prolongation of a fold at this spot. It is also not clear whether an interlinear *waw* exists before the *lamed* or whether it is only the curved banner descending from the head of the *lamed*. The reading וְ[מ]צ֯יל (cf. § 1.7.3.1.1) is not impossible. In מצֹרות רבות, the impression of two *dalets* is an illusion created by two holes.

L. 3 שֹׁ[א]נֹ֯יֹ The faint traces are best read thus (giving a text identical with that of 4Q399).

L. 4 בכל It is hard to decide whether an interlinear cursive *waw* stands after the *kap* or whether it is part of the flag of the *lamed*; cf. וְ[נ]צל in l. 2 and ולישראל in l. 8. שִׁיתֹּקֹן Two long descenders can clearly be seen reaching down into the following line, so that our reading is suggested. Materially both שׁ[ת]יֹקֹן and שׁיתֹקֹן are possible readings of the traces. The small detached fragment above should be moved to the left, so that its leftmost descender joins with the leftmost stroke of the main papyrus to make the final *nun* .

L. 5 מחשב(ו)ת The *waw* is certainly blurred. Probably it was deleted intentionally to give the regular מחשבת רעה.

L. 6 דבֹרינו Loss of fibres has carried away the characteristic right shoulder of the *dalet* and left the letter looking like a *reš*. Was there an additional word after דברינו, i.e., כן? It all depends on the analysis of the head of the *lamed* of לך in the following line, and whether we see it as a flagged *lamed* or not. Certainly there is a trace of ink where the top of the putative *kap* would have stood, and one could then interpret the other traces as the base of *kap* ligating with the head of final *nun* which would come down from that base line, and which itself would run down parallel to a *lamed* at its right; cf. בן in frgs. 13–15 l. 1. This is perhaps easier than interpreting both strokes as parts of *lamed* with its descending flag as in ולישראל in l. 8 below, because one would still be forced to explain as accidental the horizontal stroke above it at the top of *lamed* which is materially one of the more certain traces.

L. 7 It is hard to decide between בעשותך and כעשותך; the breadth of the head favours perhaps *kap* (cf. our introductory remarks on the script—the left-to-right direction of the base line spreads from *bet* to *kaf* and *pe* in many semi-cursive hands).

1.7   4Q399

The leather is of medium thickness, in colour a dark buff-grey which becomes light brown when stained. The surface is fine, smooth but scarcely glossy. The back is poorly smoothed, and greyish-brown in colour. The long tear to the right, probably made in antiquity, has carried off with it a portion of the surface along the edge. The scribe seems only to have ruled one vertical dry line between columns, the one marking the start of the lines, instead of two. He even made one more line than he needed, in that such a vertical has been made for the start of an uninscribed third column. The horizontal dry lines are clear, and the letters stand free below the lines. Height of column: 7.2 cm. The text is written on eleven lines, though twelve have been ruled. Top margin: 1 cm. Bottom margin (from the lowest dry line): 1.25 cm. Average space between lines: 4.5 mm. Height of average letter (*bet*, *reš* or *mem*): 2 mm. The width of col. i is 35 corrected letter spaces and of col. ii 32 corrected letter-spaces (8.4 cm between the vertical dry lines). Photos: PAM 41.823, 43.491.

1.7.1   Script

The script is a regular Herodian formal. The two-stroked *dalet*, the *waw/yod*, and the *reš* are typical of all periods of the Herodian formal. In *lamed, nun, pe, ṣade and šin*, the degree of ornamentation

curves and bent arms (only rarely *keraiai*) suggests a date not too late among the Herodian formals, as does the survival of the old sequence of strokes in *taw* and the transitional stance of the ʿ*ayin*. Note further that in *he* the left downstroke is a separate third stroke, while the cross stroke emerges (in a loop) from the right upstroke, a mixture of early and late features. Other letters show the coexistence of two forms in this hand; thus the ʾ*alep* in שראינו (i 11) is formed with three strokes, but that in במצאך (ii 3) with only two, in later style. Again we find the semiformal final *kap* (with no independent downstroke) in לך (i 11) side by side with a formal type (with its separate strokes) in במצאך (ii 3). Because the script has generally been carefully drawn, it is sometimes difficult to decide in what order the strokes were made from the few specimens of certain letters. (This could have been important as an indicator of relative date within the Herodian formal series.) Thus it is unclear whether *bet* was drawn with a base from left to right (it probably was), and whether *mem* had its tick added last, as in the later style (it probably did).

These indicators, some suggesting earliness and others lateness, together with the general style of ornamentation of these and other letters, suggest a mid-Herodian date in the formal series, approximately contemporary with 1QM.

1.7.2 Orthography

The spelling follows the standard of MT, with none of either the fuller or the unhistoric phonetic spellings of QH. In pronouns and their suffixes, we find without exception ־ך and ־יו. On במצאך, see § 3.1.1.2.

1.7.3.1 4Q399 i

1–8

[זכור את דו֯י֯ד שהיא איש חסדים ואף֯ הי֯א֯] מ֯צ֯ו֯ל   9

[מצרות רבות ונסלוח לו ואף כתב]נ֯ו֯ אנחנו אליך   10

[מקצת מעשי התורה שחשבנו לטו]ב֯ לך שראינו   11

bottom margin

1.7.3.1.1 Notes on the Reading

L. 9 מ֯צ֯ו֯ל[The traces of the first two letters are materially indecisive. The third letter, materially considered, could as easily be a *yod* as a *waw*.

L. 10 Although there is no specimen of final *mem* on this fragment, it is unlikely that the surviving traces could come from the bottom left of a final *mem* and so attest כותבים; the traces in fact fit nicely with a ligature of נו, i.e., כתב]נ֯ו֯ אנחנו, reversing the order of the words found in 4Q398.

1.7.3.2 4Q399 ii

top margin

[עמך ערמה ומדע תורה הבן באלה ובקש] מלפניו   1

[שיתקן את עצתך והרחיק ממך] מ֯ח֯שבת רע   2

[בשל שתשמח באחרית העת] במצאך מדברינו   3

4   [כן ונחשבה לך לצדקה בע]שׂותך הישר   לפניו

5   [לטוב לך ול]יׂשראל   *vacat*

vacat 6–11

1.7.3.2.1 NOTES ON THE READING

L. 5 ולישראל Both the traces belong to the *yod* and not to לי.

1.7.3.3   4Q399 iii

vacat   1–4

1.8 The Variant Readings

The following are all the variant readings attested in the manuscripts.

a	b	c	d	e	f
רֽאֽו	ראוי				
להזה'ר	לה[ז]הֿר				
פרת החטאֿת	פרת החטֿ[את]				
ראואי	ראוי				
			[הנוש]א	[ה]נושה	
[וי]רושלי[ם] מחנה היא			[וירושלים הי]א מחנה	(§ 1.6.3.1)	
		[להיו]תֿםֿ	[להיו]תֿם		
[לה]תֿיֹכֿםֿ			להתיכמה		
הקֿדש			הקודש		
ירושלים היֿא רֿאש מֿ[חנות ישראל]		[יר]וֿשלים היא ראש [מֿ]חֿנֿוֿת ישראל	י[רושלים ראש מחנות ישראל]הֿיאה		
		אנחנו	שאנחנו		
		הזונות	הזנות		
		משכתוב	כשכתוב		
		לרבעה	[לֿהֿרביע]ה		
		[וא]תֿםֿ	[ואת]מה		
		[כתב]נֿו אליכה	[כתב]נֿום (?)		
		[ו]הֿקֿללֿה	[וה]קֿללא		
		[לבב]כֿה	ל[בב]ך		
		לבבכה	לבבך		
		(?) מֿיומֿ[י]	בֿימי		
		(?) שֿיובא[ו]	[ש]יֿבֿיֿ[א]ֿם		
			ל[נ]צֿל (?)		מֿצול
			אנחנו כתבנו	[כתב]נֿוֿ אנחנו	
			ולעמֿך		missing
			בכל אלה		[באלה] (?)
			מלפנו	מלפניו	
		[עצת]כֿה	עצתך		
			מחשב(ו)ת		מֿחֿשבת
			רעה	רע	
		מקצ[ת דברינו]	מקצת דברינו	מדברינו	
			והטוב		missing
			לפנו		לפניו

1.8.1 NOTES TO THE TABLE

1.   Most of the variants are purely linguistic. They include four main types:

(*a*)   Defective spelling typical of BH in one manuscript in contrast to plene spelling typical of Qumran manuscripts in another; for instance, לבבה/לבבך (see § 3.1.2), הקודש/הקדש (see § 3.1.1). There is also vulgar spelling with final ʾalep (characteristic of MS^e) in contrast to the usual spelling with final he:]ו[הקללה/]וה[קללא.

(*b*)   Unique phonetic spellings illustrate the pronunciation of QH: ראו/ראוי/ראואי (see § 3.2.2.4); זנות/זונות (see § 3.2.4); מלפניו/מלפנו (see § 3.2.2.1).

(*c*)   Morphological variants: for instance, we find short pronouns and pronominal suffixes in most of the manuscripts (see § 3.3.1.1); the long forms, היא, אתמה and the like, are characteristic of MS^d. Other morphological variants are להזהיר/להזהר (see § 3.5.2.6a); לרבעה/להרביעה (see § 3.5.4.11); בימי/מיומ]י[ן (see § 3.5.1.23); רעה/רע (see § 3.5.2.13); נצל/מצול (see § 3.3.3.4).

(*d*)   Syntactical or lexical variants, most of them involving word order (see §§ 3.4.7 and 3.4.8). On אנחנו/שאנחנו, see § 3.5.2.30; on כשכתוב/משכתוב, see § 3.5.4.5.

2.   There are several cases where one manuscript has a shorter text than another. Thus MS^f has shorter text than MS^e. This involves no more than one word in each case. Sometimes MS^f has a lacuna in a passage for which we have the text in MS^e. In such cases, the length of the lacuna in MS^f on occasion indicates that the lost text in MS^f was shorter than the (preserved) text in MS^e. (On פרת החטאת, see § 5.3.3.2; on the classical מדברינו compared with מקצת דברינו, see § 3.5.2.23.)

3.   Although there is a considerable overlap in the texts preserved by MS^a and MS^c, there are no differences between their readings.

4.   Only in B 60–61 and in C 30 do we have a variant attested by more than two manuscripts, such as could be significant for classical stemmatic criticism.

2. THE COMPOSITE TEXT

A

a (= 4Q394 1–2 i–v)

v	iv	iii	ii	i	
בו שבת	בתשעה	בו[שבת]	[ו]א̇ח̇[ד]	[בששה]	1
בעשרים	בו שבת]	בע[שתי עשר]	ב̇' שֿבת	עשר	2
ושנים	ב̇שֿשֿ אשר	בו שבת	[ב]ע̇שריֹם̇	בו שבת]	3
בו מועד	בו שבת	בשמונה	ושמונה	ב̇עשרים	4
השמן	בעשרם	עשר בו שבת	בו̇ שבת	ושלושה	5
אֿח̇]ר הש[ב̇ת	ושלושא	בעשרים	עליו אחר	בו שבת	6
אֿח̇]ריו	ב̇ו שבת	וחמשה	השבת	[ב]שֿל[ושיֹ]ם	7
קרב̇[ן]	בש[לֿוֹשֿיֹם̇	בו שבת	ו̇[יוֹ]ם̇ השנ̇[י]	בו שבת	8
העצים]	[בו שבת	בשנים	[השלישי נוסף	בשבעה	9
	בשבעה	בחמ̇[י]שֿ[י]	ושלמה	בשלישי	10
	בששי	[שֿ]ב̇[ת]	התקופה	שבת	11
	שבת	[בשלושה]	תשעים	בארבעה	12
	בארבעה	בו מועד	ואחד יום	עשר	13
	עשר	היין אחר	באחד	בו שבת	14
	בו שבת	השבת]	ברביעי	בחמשה	15
	בעשרים		יום זכרון	עשר בו חג	16
	ואחד]		בארבעה]	שבועות	17
				בעשרים]	18

a (= 4Q394 3–7 i)

[ושמונה בו]שבת עלֹ[ו]ו אחר [ה]שֿ[ב̇ת ויום השני השלישי השלישי]	19
[נוֹ]ס̇ף ושלמה השנה שלוש מאת ושֿ[שים וארבעה]	20
יֹום	21

---

i 4–6 בעשרים ושלושה בו שבת The calendar lists, in order, the Sabbaths, the feasts and the epagomenal thirty-first day at the end of each quarter. The suffix in the regularly recurring word בו 'on it' refers to the (e.g., second) 'month'.

ii 6–9 עליו אחר השבת ו[יו]ם השנ[י] השלישי נוסף] The restoration is based on the structure of the Qumran calendar and on A 19–20. The formula denotes the twenty-ninth, the thirtieth and the thirty-first days of each third, sixth, ninth and twelfth month. The words עליו and אחר (ה)שבת occur in other calendaric works from Qumran. The most relevant passage is 4QMishd 1:2–3: בעשרים וחמשה בו שבת על ידעיה ועלו [מועד] השעורים בעשרים וששה בו אחר שבת 'The twenty-fifth of it (i.e., the first month) is a Sabbath in (the week of service) of Yedaʿaya and next to it (comes) the festival of the barley on the twenty-sixth of it on Sunday'. We translated the terms עליו and אחר השבת in MMT according to their meaning in 4QMishd. For על with the meaning 'next, immediately after', see the commentary on B 11. The word עליו can, however, refer (at least in MMT) to the specific month. על may also be taken as a substitute for ב (see Yalon, *Studies*, pp. 341–345, 431–433.) Similar usages of על occur in translation of Greek phrases על הפטית 'in the consularship of' in pYadin 7, l. 1 from Naḥal Ḥever. (I am indebted to Dr. I. Knohl and Prof. J. Greenfield for this example.) In Nabatean we find על שני חרתת 'in the years of Haratat' (J. Cantineau, *Le Nabatéen*, I, Paris, 1930, p. 45); and perhaps also in Neh 12:22 על מלכות דריוש הפרסי. The restoration is tentative and alternative restorations are possible (e.g., והשלישי הנוסף). In any case, the occurrence of the formula here after the last Sabbath of the third and the twelfth months suggests that what stood here is a reference to the epagomental thirty-first day.

i   [The sixteenth (day) of it (i.e. the second month) is a Sabbath]. The twenty third of it is a Sabbath. The thirtieth [of it is a Sabbath. The seventh of the third (month) is a Sabbath. The fourteenth of it is a Sabbath. The fifteenth of it is the Festival of Weeks. The twenty-

ii   fi]rst of it is a Sabbath. The twenty-eighth of it is a Sabbath. After it (i.e. the Sabbath), Sunday and Monday, [Tuesday is to be added (to this month). And the season terminates—ninety-one days. The first of the fourth (month) is a Memorial Day. The fourth]

iii   of it [is a Sabbath]. The el[eventh] of it is a Sabbath. The eighteenth of it is a Sabbath. The twenty-fifth of it is a Sabbath. The second of the fif[th (month) is a Sabbath. The third of it is the Festival of the (New) Wine ...

iv   The ninth of it is a Sabbath]. The sixteenth of it is a Sabbath. The twenty-third of it is a Sabbath. The thirtieth [of it is a Sabbath. The seventh of the sixth (month) is a Sabbath. The fourteenth of it is a Sabbath. The twenty-first]

v   of it is a Sabbath. The twenty-second of it is the Festival of the (New) Oil, on the day af[ter the Sab]bath. Af[ter it] is [the Wood] Offer[ing ...

19   [... The twenty-eighth of it (i.e. the twelfth month)] is a Sabbath. Unto it (i.e. the twelfth month), after [the] Sab[bath, Sunday and Monday, a day]

20   [is to be ad]ded. And the year is complete—three hundred and [sixty-four]

21   days

iii 2 [בע]שתי עשר   This form of the number appears in BH and in QH, but not in MH (see § 3.5.1.20a).

iii 9–11 [בשנים בחמ]י[ש]י ש[ב]ת   Months are referred to by ordinal numbers.

iv 3 בשש אשר   For the reading, see § 1.2.3.1.1. This is a phonetic spelling for בששה עשר (pronounced *bešiššasar*). It results from the weak pronunciation of the gutturals (see § 3.2.1).

iv 6 ושלושא   Written with final *'alep* (contrast i 5; see § 3.1.4.2).

v 2-5 בעשרים ושנים בו מועד השמן   This feast is described in 11QT^a 21:12ff (see Yadin, *TS*, I, pp. 111–122).

v 8 [קרב]ן   If we are right in restoring the word here as קרבן, then the next word was probably העצים. The six days of the wood-offering, which began on the twenty-third of the sixth month, were also regarded as a feast in the calendar of the Temple Scroll (see Yadin, *TS*, I,

pp. 122–128).

19-20 ע[ל]ו אחר [ה]ש[ב]ת ויום השני השלישי נו[ס]ף   See the commentary on ll. ii 6–9. For the phonetic spelling ע[ל]ו (rather than [עלי]ו), see §§ 1.2.3.2.1 and 3.2.2.1. To judge from the word order, נו[ס]ף is a participle rather than a perfect. If so, all the sentences in the calendar are nominal.

20 ושלמה   A participle rather than perfect (see § 3.4.1.1), there being no verbal clauses in the calendar.   מאת   In all likelihood, this form represents a defective spelling of ō, though it is untypical of the DSS. It is less likely that the *'alep* represents the ō (as in ראש), since, according to MT, the *mem* is first followed by the vowel *e* (see *HDSS*, § 200.133).   וש[שים] [וארבעה   Restored according to the sectarian calendar.

1   Five or six columns of calendar are missing here.

B

a(+ b) (= 4Q394 3–7 i)

1	ל שהם מ[קצת דברי]	אלה מקצת דברינו
2	[	[ה]מעשים שא א[נ]ח[נ]ו חושבים וכו[ל]ם על[
3	2-[ים . . מ 2-שהם ה[גוים ד]גן ועל תרומת	וטהרת [ ]הר[ו]
4	[הם ומט]מאים אותה ואין לאכול]	ומגיע[י]ם בה א[ת
5	ועל זֹבח החטאת]	[לבוא למק]ש ואין מדגן [הג[ו]ים]
6	[	שהם מבשלים [אות]ה בכלי [נחושת ומ . . ים בה3 את
7	]ים בעז[ר]ה ומ . . ים אותה]	בשר זבחיהם ומ[
8	במרק זבחם ועל זב[ה4 הגוים [אנחנו חושבים שהם זובחים]
9	[שֹא ה[א] כ-5-]מ[שֹונת-5 אליו [ואף על מנחת זבח6]	אל ה[ן
10	[	ה[של]מים] שמניחים7 אותה מיום ליום א[ף [כתוב
11	שהמנ[חה נאבלת] על החלבים והבשר ביום זֹ[ב]חם כי לבני]
12	הכוהנ[ים] ראו8 להז[ה]ר9 בדבר הזה בשל שלוא י[היו]

1 **אלה מקצת דברינו** This is a heading for a list of rulings, like אלו מן ההלכות שאמרו in t. Šabb. 1:16; אלו הדברים in m. ʿEd. 4:1; אלה הדברים in Deut 1:1 (see Nachmanides). In accordance with the heading of Deuteronomy, one may restore [... ישרא]ל after דברינו. (Note that both MMT and Deuteronomy end with ישראל.) Yet other restorations such as [בתורת א]ל are equally possible. QH uses the biblical form אלה, and not the MH אלו. אלה is also attested in the later Hebrew dialect of the Bar-Kokhba documents (see §§ 3.3.1.3 and 3.7.3). מקצת is an Aramaism (see § 3.5.2.23). C 31 MSᶠ has מדברינו instead of מקצת דברינו (cf. Dan 2:42 where מקצת and מן interchange, and t. Šabb. cited above). For דברינו 'our rulings', see § 5.3.2.3 and m. ʿEd. cited above. **שהם** On ש- see §§ 3.3.1.4 and 3.5.2.30.

2 **[ה]מעשים** A synonym of דברים. The terms occur together also in 1QS 6:18. For the exact meaning and history of this term, see § 5.3.2.2. **שא** The spelling with ʾalep occurs several times in MMT (see § 3.1.4.4).

3 **וטהרת** This is not a defective spelling of the BH form (טָהֳרָה), but rather the MH form (טַהֲרָה; see §§ 3.1.1.2 and 3.5.2.11). **[ד]גן ה[גוים]** Introduces the first halakha; it deals with the grains of the gentiles. The expression דגן הגוים occurs again in l. 5. These grains may not be eaten or brought into the Temple (see § 5.7.1). **[מ .. ים]** A restoration of a participle plural form.

4 **ומגיע[י]ם בה** Elsewhere in QH נגע ב means 'touching (or eating) pure things' (see HDSS, p. 111 and Lev 12:4). Does the hipʿil here mean 'to let do' (see § 3.5.3.1)?

The feminine suffix in בה implies that דגן is not the subject; this, and the mention of the Temple, suggests the restoration [תרומת].

5 **לבוא למק־ש** Materially either לבוא (qal) or לביא (hipʿil) is possible. The hipʿil, however, suits neither the morphology (having no he) nor the syntax (having no accusative complement). The qal of בוא fits better, having a passive sense 'be entered'. A similar problem in the reading and understanding of יביאו/יבואו occurs in TS 47:8, 9 (see E. Qimron, 'New Readings of the Temple Scroll', IEJ 28 [1978], p. 170). The expression בוא ל- (+ adverb of place) is typical of the Hebrew of the Second Temple period (see § 3.5.2.2). **זב]ח החטאת** Introduces another halakha. The text is very fragmentary and can be interpreted in various ways (see § 5.2.7). If the reading זב[ח] is correct, it should be taken as designating all kinds of sacrifices, as it does in MH.

6 **שהם מבשלים [אות]ה** The plural participle with the third person pronoun describes the custom of the opponents. On the use of the participle in MMT, see § 3.4.1.5. Does the feminine suffix in [אות]ה and בה refer to the word חטאת (see the commentary to l. 57)?

7 **בעז[ר]ה** If the reading is correct, then this is the first known occurrence in Hebrew of עֲזָרָה with the meaning 'court' (see § 5.7.2d).

8 **במרק** 'Broth' On the connection between this noun and the verb מרק in Lev 6:21, see § 5.7.2 n. 3a. **ועל זבח הגוים** This begins a halakha about accepting the sacrifices of gentiles (see § 5.7.3). The preposition ועל intro-

1 These are some of our rulings [...] which are [some of the rulings according to]
2 [the] precepts (of the Torah) in accordance with [our opinion, and] all of them concern [...]
3 and the purity of [the ... And concerning the sowed gifts of the] new wheat grains of the [gentiles which
    they ...]
4 and let their [...] touch it and de[file it, and no one should eat]
5 any of the new wheat grains of t[he gen]tiles, [nor] should it be brought into the sanctuary. [And con-
    cerning the sacrifice of the purification-offering]
6 that they cook in a [copper] vessel [and that they ...] in it
7 the flesh of their sacrifices, and that they [...] in the Temple court (?) [and that they ...] it
8 with the broth of their sacrifices. And concerning the sacrifice of the gentiles: [we are of the opinion that
    they] sacrifice
9 to the [...] that it is like (a woman) who whored with him. [And concerning the cereal-offering] of the
    sacrifice
10 of well-being which they (the opponents) leave over from one day to the following one: but [it is writ-
    ten]
11 that the cereal-offer[ing is to be ea]ten after the suet and the flesh (are sacrificed), on the day when they
    are sacri[ficed (i.e. before sunset). For the sons of]
12 the priest[s] should take care concerning this practice so as not to

---

duces the subject (see § 5.2.4). The noun זבח is used collectively; in l. 7 the plural form occurs. On the defective
spelling of the word גוים, see § 3.2.3. אל [זובח]ים.
The usual expression is זבח לפני or זבח ל- (note that the
qal, not *piʿel*, is used).

9 [כ]מי שזנת   We can neither give a satisfactory explanation of these words nor explain the other possible readings (מושבת or מושלת). [ואף על מנחת] זבח השל[מי]ם.
Begins a new halakha about the cereal offering (see
§ 5.7.4).

10 שמניחים   Equivalent to שהם מניחים (cf. Nathan, pp.
315-318). It refers to the opponents.   מיום ליום   From
one to the other (i.e., after sunset), cf. Rashi on Num
30:15 (ביום שמעו followed by מיום אל יום), and the long
discussion in § 5.7.4.

11 על החלבים   The preposition על denotes time. This
phrase is a biblical technical term used in regulations concerning sacrifices (see E. Qimron, 'Biblical Philology and
the Dead Sea Scrolls', *Tarbiz* 58 [1989], pp. 300-302, and
§ 5.7.4, n. 90). ביום ז[ב]חם   Cf. Lev 19:16 ביום
זבחכם יאכל; the corrected reading may represent either an
assimilation of the vowel to the labial or an inflected
infinitive of *qal* with passive meaning.   [כי לבני]
הכוהנ[י]ם ראו להזהר   This formula occurs several
times in MMT. It establishes the responsibility of the
priests (and their chief) for the purity of the Temple, and is
based on Num 18:1: ... ויאמר ה' אל אהרן אתה ובניך ובית
(Num 18:1). *Tg. Pseudo-*
Jonathan adds here (and also in verse 23) אין לא מזדהרין.

See also Rashi on these verses. (In Num 18:7 the verb
שמר, which is the equivalent of זהר [see below], occurs;
see Lieberman, V, 1325.) In MMT, however, the point is
that the priests let the laymen suffer punishment rather
than suffer the punishment themselves (as in the biblical
source).

12 ראו   (= ראוי) The word occurs only in post-classical
Hebrew. Its collocation with a prepositional phrase is
peculiar (see §§ 3.5.3.10 and 3.4.2.3). On the alternative
spellings ראואי and ראו, and the pronunciation they
reflect, see §§ 3.2.2.3 and 3.2.2.4. להזה'ר   Originally
להזהר (*nipʿal*); the *yod* is interlinear. In l. 26 the classical
parallel להשמר occurs (see § 3.5.2.6). בדבר   'In this
precept' (see § 5.3.2.3). בשל ש-   Cf. בדיל ד- in
Aramaic (§ 3.5.2.5).

---

1   Erasure before הר, perhaps of וט.
2-2 The restoration מ..ים means that a verb in participle plural may
     have stood here.
3   Or בה].
4   This reading is materially uncertain, yet it seems to be the most
     plausible one. See § 1.2.3.2.1.
5-5 The reading is uncertain. See § 1.2.3.2.1.
6   The trace of the letter after the word זבח in b is that of ה rather
     than ת.
7   Found on a small fragment. See § 1.2.3.2.1.
8   ראוי b.
9   לה[ז]הר b, or (less possible) לה[ז]ה'ר.

מסיא[י]ם את העם עוון ואף על טהרׄת פרתׄ¹ החטאׄת 13

השוחֵׄט אותה והסורף אותה והאוסֵף [אׄ]ׄת אפרה והמזה אׄת [מי] 14

החטאת   לכול אלה להעריׄ[בון]ׄת השמש לׄהׄיׄות טהורים 15

בׄשל שא יהיה הטהר מזה על הטמה כי לבני 16

a (+ b) (= 4Q394 3–7 ii)

ואף] [אהרן]ׄ[ראואי²] [להיות מׄ 17

מן] [על עׄוׄרׄות הבקׄ]ר והצאן שהם מ . . ים 18

אין] [עורות]יהם כלי[ם 19

[[להביא]ם למקדׄ[ש³ 20

d (+ e) (= 4Q397 1–2)

[ה ואף על עורׄ]ות ועצמות הבהמה הטמאה אין לעשות] 21

[מן עצמותמה] ומן עׄ[ו]רׄ[ו]תׄ[מה]ומה ידות כׄ]לים   ואף על עׄוׄר נבלׄת] 22

[הבהמה] הׄטׄהׄורׄה [ׄהנושׄׄאׄ⁴ אׄׄ[ו]ׄ{ה}⁵ נבלתׄהׄ [לוא יגׄשׄ לטהרת הקודש] 23

[ ]ׄת[שהמׄ]ה מ . . ים⁶   וא[וׄף על העׄ[24

a (+ d) (= 4Q394 3–7 ii)

[ ] כי לבני [25

הכׄו[הנׄ]יׄם ראואי] להש[מ]ׄור ⁷-בׄכׄׄוׄל הדׄ[י]בׄרׄי[ם] האלה בשל שלוא יהיו] 26

משיאׄים את העמׄ עוון [ועׄ]ׄל שא כתוב] איש כי ישחט במחנה או] 27

[ישחט]מׄחוץ למחׄנה שׄׄוׄר וכשב ועז כי °[בצפׄ[ון המחנה·⁷-] 28

ואׄנׄחׄנו חושבים שהמקדשׄ[משכן אוהל מועד הוא וי[רׄושלׄי[ם] 29

---

13 מסיא[י]ם את העם עוון   The original š in מסיאים is here spelt with a *samek* (see § 3.1.6). The expression השיא עוון is classical (see § 3.5.17). The *hipʿil* here means 'let (do)' (see § 3.5.3.1). It appears that MMT took the suffix in והשיאו אותם עוון אשמה (Lev 22:16) as referring to the laymen, unlike Rabbi Yishmael who took it as reflexive (see Geiger, *Studies*, pp. 140–143). On the history of the word העם 'the public', see § 3.5.1.17. ואף על טהרת פרת החטאת   Here begins a halakha on the purity of those preparing the ashes of the red cow (see § 5.7.5). The opening ואף על is an alternate of ועל (see § 5.2.4). On the attestation of אף in Hebrew, see § 3.5.3.3. On the term טהרה, see §§ 3.1.1.2 and 3.5.2.11. On the new term פרת החטאת, see §§ 3.5.3.8 and 3.5.3.2.

14 השוחט אותה ...   A periphrastic construction with את; MH prefers the enclitic construction, e.g: הגוזז את הצמר המלבנו והמנפסו והצובעו והטווהו ... הצד צבי השוחטו והמפשיטו והמולחו והמעבדו והמוחקו והמחתכו (*m. Šabb.* 7:2; cf. § 3.4.4). והסורף   Original š spelt with *samek* (see § 3.1.6). [מי] החטאת   This MH term (which occurs once in BH) is.the equivalent of the usual BH term מי נדה (see § 5.3.3.2). The sprinkling of the purifying water is, of course, a separate ritual (see at § 5.7.5). The restoration of [מי] is required by the content; materially the reading והמזה את החטאת is equally possible (את is the last word of the line). We prefer to restore the word מי since חטאת is not an equivalent of מי חטאת, but see *t. Para* 4:12, 11:3, and S. Lieberman, *Tosefeth Rishonim*, III, Jerusalem, 1939, pp. 228–229 and 250.

15 לכול אלה   In apposition to the long inclusive subject; cf. 1QM 7:4-5: וכול פסח או עור או חגר ... כול אלה לוא ילכו אתם למלחמה; cf. also 1QSa 2:8 and 1QM 9:5. להעריׄ[בון]ׄת השמש   Equivalent of BH כבוא השמש and MH הַעֲרֵב שמש. On the form and history of this term, see §§ 3.3.3.5 and 3.5.4.2. Cf. 11QTª 49:20, ויטהרו לערב and ibid. 50:8–9. וטהר לערב. לׄהׄיׄות טהורים   Infinitive instead of finite verb (see §§ 3.4.2.1 and 3.4.2.2).

16 בׄשל שא יהיה הטהר מזה על הטמה   Paraphrasing Num 19:19: והזה הטהר על הטמא. On -בשל ש-, see the commentary to l. 12. On the periphrastic tense, see § 3.4.1.3. הטהר is a *qatel* form rather than defective spelling of הטהור (see §§ 3.1.1.2 and 3.5.2.10). For הטמה with *he* instead of *ʾalep*, see § 3.1.4.1. כי לבני אהרן On the possible significance of this statement, see § 5.7.5f.

17 ראואי   A phonetic spelling of ראוי; see the remarks and references in the commentary on l. 12 above.

17–18 [ואף על עׄו]רׄות   For the reconstruction of the following lines, which contained several halakhot concerning the purity of skins, see §§ 5.7.6, 5.7.7 and 5.7.8.

13 cause the people to bear punishment. And concerning the purity-regulations of the cow of the purification-offering (i.e. the red cow):

14 he who slaughters it and he who burns it and he who gathers its ashes and he who sprinkles the [water of]

15 purification—it is at sun[se]t that all these become pure

16 so that the pure man may sprinkle upon the impure one. For the sons of

17 Aaron should [... ... ... And]

18 [concerning] the hides of cattle [and sheep that they ... ... from]

19 their [hides] vessels [... ... ... to]

20 [bring] them to the sanctuary [... ... ...]

21 [... ... ...] And concerning the hi[des and the bones of unclean animals: it is forbidden to make]

22 handles of [vessels from their bones] and hides. [And concerning] the hide of the carcass

23 of a clean [animal]: he who carries such a carcass [shall not] have access to the sacred food ... ...

24 [...] And concerning the [... ... ...] that they [use to ... ...]

25 [... ... ... for the sons]

26 of the priests should [take care] concerning all [these] practices, [so as not to]

27 cause the people to bear punishment. [And concerning] that it is written: [if a person slaughters inside the camp, or]

28 [slaughters] outside the camp cattle or sheep or goat: for [... in] the northern part of the camp.

29 And we are of the opinion that the sanctuary [is the 'tent of meeting'] and that Jerusalem

---

22 ‏ידות‎   In MH, ‏ידות‎ is the plural of ‏יד‎ 'handle' (see § 3.5.3.4a). The text is, however, too broken to establish the meaning of the word here.

23 ‏[י]גש לטהרת ה[קודש]‎   The equivalent of BH ‏נגש אל‎ ‏הקדש‎. Cf. ‏באים לטהרת המקדש‎ (B 54).

25–26 ‏[כי לבני] הכו[הנ]ים‎   Cf. the commentary on l. 11 above.

26 ‏[להש[מ]ר בכול הד]ברים‎   Cf. l. 12 above. The word ‏להשמר‎ is the classical equivalent of ‏להזהר‎ (see above). The plural in ‏הדברים‎ refers to the halakhot about skins.

27 ‏[וע[ל שא כתוב‎   Here begins a halakha about slaughtering clean animals; on the reconstruction and interpretation of the text in ll. 27–34, see §§ 5.4.1 and 5.7.7.

28 ‏מחוץ למחנה‎   'Outside Jerusalem' (see § 5.4.2). This is the BH expression; on l. 30 the QH equivalent is used (cf. § 3.5.2.8). ‏[בצ]פון המחנה]‎   'To the north of Jerusalem' (see § 5.7.7). ‏שור וכשב ועז‎ Cf. Lev 17:3. All three nouns are used collectively. The word ‏כשב‎ is a rare metathesized equivalent of ‏כבש‎. It is attested twelve times in MT (all of them in the Torah), and fourteen times in the Samaritan Version. In QH the form ‏כבש‎ predominates (but ‏[ו]כשב ועז‎ ‏שור‎ also occurs in 4QTah^a). MH occasionally uses the form ‏כשב‎. In both BH and MH, ‏כשב‎ is collocated with ‏עז‎ while ‏כבש‎ is often collocated with

‏איל‎.

29 ‏ואנחנו‎   This BH pronoun was in use also in post-BH (alongside ‏אנו‎—see § 3.3.1.1.2). ‏חושבים שהמקדש‎   Variant of ‏אומרים ש‎- 'decide on halakhic matters'; both the meaning and the syntax are peculiar, see § 3.5.4.3. ‏[וי]רושלי[ם] מחנה היא‎   The variant reading of MS^d ‏[הי]אה מחנה]‎ shows that the copula can come after either the subject or the predicate (see § 3.4.8). In BH, the word ‏מחנה‎, when referring to the encampment which surrounds the tabernacle, is always determined. Here, as sometimes in MH, it has no formal determination. In fact, being a technical term, it is determined by itself. On the spelling of ‏ירושלים‎ (with *yod*), see Kutscher, *Isaiah*, pp. 5, 106.

---

1   ‏פרת‎ is supralinear in b.

2   ‏ראוי‎ b.

3   One or two lines are missing here.

4   f ‏[ה]נושה‎; see § 1.6.3.1.1.

5   See § 1.5.3.1.1.

6   About four lines are missing here.

7-7   MS^d must have had a shorter text here.

מַחֲנֶה הִיאֹ¹ וְחוֹ(צָה) לַמַחֲנֶ[ה] הוא חוצה לירושלים]הֹוֹאֹ² מֹחֹנֹה   30

עֹרֹ[י]הֹם חוץ ממֹ[חנה [ ]אֹרֹ ¹]³ אֹ החטֹאֹת וֹ[מֹוֹצִיאִים את דשא   31

[הֹ]מֹזבח ושורֹ]פים שם את החטאת כי ירושלים]הֹיא המקום אשר   32

[בחר בו מֹכול שֹבֹטי ישראל   [33

[הֹ⁴   ]   34

c (+ <u>a</u> + d) (= 4Q396 1–2 i)

אי]נֹם שוחטים במקדש   ]   35

[ועל העברות אַנֹחֹנֹו חֹוֹשבים שאין לזבוח אֹ[ת האם ואת הולד בֹיום אחד   36

ועל האֹוֹכֹל אנח]נֹו חושבים שאיאכל את הֹוֹלד   ]   37

[שבמעי אמו לאחר שחיטתו ואתם יודעים שהו]אֹ כן וֹהֹדבר כתוב עברה   38

[ועל העמונֹיֹ והמואבי והֹמֹמֹזר ופֹצוע הדכה וכרו]ת השפכת שהם באים   39

[בקהל   ונשים]לֹ[וֹ]קֹחֹים להיו]תֹ⁵ עֹצֹם עצֹם   40

[אֹחֹת ובאים למקדש   [41

a (+ <u>c</u> + d) (= 4Q394 8 iii)

טמאות ואף חושֹ]בֹים אנחנו   ]   42

ואין לבו]אֹ עליהם   [שאין   43

ואיֹן לֹהֹ[ת]יֹכֹם⁶ [וֹ]לעֹשֹותֹם   ]   44

ואין להבי]אֹם   [עצם אחת   45

ואתם יודעים שמקצֹת הֹעֹם   [למקדש   46

מֹ . . ים   מתוכ]כים   [וה . .   47

[כי לכול בני ישראל ראוי להזהר מֹכֹוֹל תֹ[ע]רובת [ה]גֹבר   48

[ולהיות יראים מהמקדש ואף ע]ל הסומֹ[י]ם   49

30–31   וחוצה למחנה ... הוא מחנה ער]י]הם   The fact that the phrase וחוצה למחנה comes first implies that it is the subject of the passage on which the controversy centers (see § 5.4.2b). On the form and attestation of the combination ל- חוצה, see §§ 3.2.2.1 and 3.5.2.8 (cf. חוצה לארץ in MH).

31   חוץ ממ[חנה]   Another late variant of BH מחוץ למחנה (see § 3.5.2.8). We cannot offer a plausible restoration of the text that is missing after these words. דשא [ה]מזבח The word דשא is a misspelling of דשן, the product of phonological causes (see § 3.2.7); in the biblical source of this passage (Lev 4:12, 6:4), דשן is mentioned in connection with 'outside the camp'.

32–33   המקום אשר [בחר]   This is a biblical phrase (cf. Deut 12:5), a fact which explains the use of the biblical relative pronoun אשר; cf. המקום שבחר in ll. 60–61. On the relative pronoun in MMT and elsewhere, see § 3.5.1.2.

35   אי]נם שוחטים במקדש   Refers to the practice of the opponents (see § 5.7.7).

36   ועל העברות]   Here begins a halakha about slaughtering pregnant animals (see § 5.7.8). א]ת האם ואת הולד This is an exegetical replacement of the biblical expression אותו ואת בנו (Lev 22:28; see § 5.7.8). The reading

הולד is more likely than הילד (see the discussion in § 3.5.3.4).

37   ... ועל] האוכל [אנח]נו חושבים שאיאכל   The verb אכל implies that eating the fetus was discussed here. On אנח]נו חושבים ש-, see above l. 29. On the spelling שא-, see § 3.1.4.4. For orthographical and grammatical reasons we take the verb as nip'al rather than qal. The use of the passive verb to express the indefinite personal (logical) subject is characteristic of BH. It is also found in QH, but not in MH (see Kutscher, Isaiah, pp. 44 and 402; Y. Wertheimer, Leshonenu 34 [1970], pp. 155–156). For the use of את after a passive verb in BH, see BDB, p. 851; Yokheved Oron, 'Nominative את in Mishnaic Hebrew', Studies in Hebrew Language and the Talmudic Literature Dedicated to the Memory of Dr. Menahem Moreshet, Ramat-Gan 1989, pp. 27–34. In QH there is a single case of a somewhat similar usage: ונענשו את רביעית לחמו 1QS 6:25.

38   שהו]א כן   If the restoration is correct, this may be compared to the phrase תדע לך שהוא כן and the like which occur (though rarely) in MH. והדבר כתוב עברה This phrase may be in apposition to שהוא כן. The word דבר means 'ruling' (see l. 1 above). For the term כתוב, see

30 is the 'camp', and that 'outside the camp' [is outside Jerusalem], that is, the encampment of

31 their settlements. It is 'ouside the c[amp' where one should ... the purification-offering and] take out the ashes of

32 [the] altar and bu[rn the purification-offering. For Jerusalem] is the place which

33 [He has chosen] from among all the tribes [of Israel ... ...]

34 [   ]

35 [... ... ...] they do [not] slaughter in the sanctuary.

36 [And concerning pregnant (animals)] we are of the opin[ion that] the mother and its fetus [may not be sacrificed] on the same day

37 [... ... ... And concerning] eating (a fetus): we are of the opinion that the fetus

38 [found in its (dead) mother's womb may be eaten (only) after it has been ritually slaughtered. And you know that it is] so, namely that the ruling refers (to) a pregnant animal.

39 [And concerning the Ammonite] and the Moabite and the mamzer [and him whose testicles] have been crushed [and him] whose male member [has been cut off], who (nevertheless) enter

40 the congregation [and ... ... and] take [wives to be]come one bone

41 [and enter the sanctuary ... ...]

42 [... ... ...] impurities. And we are of the opinion

43 [that one must not ... ... and one must not coha]bit with them,

44 [... ... ... and] one must not let them be united (with an Israelite) and make them

45 [one bone ... ... and one must not] let them en[ter]

46 [the sanctuary. And you know that] some of the people

47 [... ... ...] and become uni[ted.]

48 [For all the sons of Israel should beware] of any forbidden unions

49 and be full of reverence for the sanctuary. [And concerning] the blind

---

§ 5.3.2.6. The word עברה 'pregnant' occurs also in 4QDᵉ (see § 5.7.9, n. 117), and is known from MH (see § 3.5.3.6). The syntax here is awkward and the phrase is difficult to translate; was an original כתוב בעברה written by haplography as כתוב עברה? Cf. ולהשיב ענוה 1QS 11:1; Wernberg-Møller, p. 150; and perhaps כתבידה (for כתב בידה; Y. Yadin and J. Naveh, *Masada*, I, Jerusalem 1985, p. 44).

39 ... [ועל העמו]ני והמואבי   Here begins a halakha concerning those forbidden to enter the congregation (see § 5.7.9).   השפכת   Instead of the שִׁפְכָה of the MT (Deut 23:2). The form in MMT resembles that of the Samaritan tradition (see § 3.5.4.12).   שהם באים בקהל Instead of הבאים. Here the subject refers to the antecedent. In such cases BH generally uses the definite article rather than the relative אשר (or ־ש). In certain traditions of MH, as well as in the documents of Bar-Kokhba, the participle may be preceded by ־ש with or without the third person pronoun (see § 3.4.5).

40 לוקחים   עצם אחת 'Marry' (see § 3.5.2.17a). Based on Gen 2:21–24 (see § 5.7.9, n. 122).

42 טמאות = טְמֵאוֹת or טַמְאוֹת.   ואף חושבים אנחנו When preceded by an adverb the pronoun follows the par-

ticiple (see § 3.4.7, n. 88). On the expression, see the commentary to l. 29.

43 עליהם   Instead of עליהן (cf. להתיכמה, לעשותם in the following line, and § 3.3.1.2.1).

44 להתיכמה   This *hipʿil* form, as well as the *hitpolel* מתוככים in ll. 47 and 81, is derived from the root תוך. The meaning of this verb in MMT is apparently 'to cohere' (see § 3.5.4.12). On the use of the infinitive, see § 3.4.2.1.

48 תערובת ה[ג]בר   Refers to illegal marriages (see §§ 3.5.2.32 and 3.5.2.4). Cf. ביאה in MH.

49 ולהיות יראים מהמקדש   The injunction to be full of

1-1 d מחנה הי[א].

2 Or הה[ו]א.

3 See § 1.2.3.31.

4 Perhaps one line is missing here.

5 d להיו[תמה]; the top of the lamed is invisible in c and the lacuna before seems to be too small.

6 d להתיכמה.

[שאינם רואים להזהר מכל תערו]בת] ותערובת   50

a (+ c + d) (= 4Q394 8 iv)

[א]שם אינם רואים   51

[וא]ף על החרשים שלוא שמעו חוק [ומ]שפט וטהרה ולא   52

[ש]מעו משפטי ישראל כי שלוא ראה ולוא שמע לוא   53

[י]דע לעשות והמה באי]ם לטה[ר]ת המקדש   54

[ו]אף על המוצקות אנחנ[ו אומר]ים] שהם שאין בהם   55

[ט]הרה ואף המוצקות אינם מבדילות בין הטמא   56

[לט]הור כי לחת המוצקות והמקבל מהמה כהם   57

לחה אחת ואין להבי למחני הק[ו]דש בלבים שהם   58

אוכלים מקצת [ע]צמות המ[ק]דש ו[ה]בשר עליהם כי   59

ירושלים היאה מחנה הקדש¹ והיא המקום   60

c (+ a + d) (= 4Q396 1–2 iii)

שבחר בן מכל² שבטי ¹[שראל כי ³־²יר]ושלים היא ראש   61

[מ]חנות ישראל־³ ו[א]ף ע[ל מ]טעת עצי[המאכל הנטע   62

---

reverence for the Temple is based on Lev 19:30 and 26:2 ומקדשי תיראו; it is also found in 11QTª 46:11 (see Yadin's commentary) and in rabbinic halakha (see Talmudic Encyclopedia [in Hebrew], 17, pp. 495 ff.). The combination היה + ירא is a substitute for the ancient stative ירא (see § 3.4.1.4). On the use of the infinitive, see § 3.4.2.1, and on מן, see § 3.2.6. ואף ע]ל הסומ[י]ם]. See the detailed discussion of this halakha in § 5.7.10. On the forms of the MH verb סמי, see § 3.5.3.5.

50 שאינם רואים   I.e., blind in both eyes. The construction is typical of MH (see § 3.4.1.5). להזהר מכול [תערו]בת The infinitive is either the complement of רואים or the predicate of the whole sentence (see § 5.7.10). ותערובת [א]שם The word ותערובת seems to be the subject of a new sentence rather than a repetition in a distributive construction such as בכול יום ויום. This, however, is based on our restoration and interpretation of [א]שם. It is unclear why תערובת אשם is referred to as something that should be seen.

52 ואף על החרשים   Written on a new line. שלוא שמעו In the perfect, meaning 'who have never heard' (unlike the case of the blind). חוק ומשפט וטהרה These are three kinds of law (see §§ 5.3.2.5 and 3.5.1.16).

53 משפטי ישראל   Unattested elsewhere in the scrolls. כי שלוא ראה The particle -ש serves here as an indeterminate pronoun (see § 3.5.2.30).

54 לעשות   'To perform the laws of the Torah' (see § 3.5.3.8). והמה באים לטהרת המקדש The combination בוא + ל- is characteristic of post-classical Hebrew (see § 3.4.2.2). The expression בא לטהרה is peculiar (cf. נגש לטהרה on l. 23, and the discussion at § 3.5.2.2a). On the

term טהרת המקדש, see § 5.3.2.1.

55 ואף על המוצקות   Here begins a halakha on the purity of the streams (see § 5.7.11). The word מוצקות is a *hupʿal* participle of the verb יצק (or צוק). It is the equivalent of the term נצוק, the *nipʿal* participle of צוק in MH (for further discussion see § 3.5.4.4). Note, however, that the term in MMT is in the plural (is it an abbreviation of הלחות המוצקות ?) whereas the one in MH is in the singular. For ואף על, see the commentary on l. 13. אנחנו אומרים The verb אמר refers to polemical law, as in MH (see § 3.5.3.2). שהם שאין בהם [ט]הרה The word שהם seems to be redundant; we therefore take it as meaning 'themselves' (see § 5.7.13). The pronoun is feminine, as are the following suffixes in the passage (see § 3.3.1.1.4). The repetition of -ש in שאין can be explained as an attraction. Note the combination טהרה + ב + אין, meaning 'impure'.

56 ואף המוצקות אינם מבדילות   Another halakha concerning the streams of liquid (see n. 31 and § 5.7.11). מבדיל is apparently a technical term, the antonym of חיבור 'connective' found in the parallel halakha in *m. Tohar.* 8:9 (cf. also Gen 1:6, Exod 26:33). בין הטמא לטהור The construction is typical of post-classical Hebrew (see § 3.4.6).

57 כי לחת המוצקות   The word לחה is not attested in BH (see § 3.5.2.16). והמקבל מהמה The verb קבל is typical of post-classical Hebrew. In MH the participle מקבל can mean 'a receptacle'. The meaning in MMT is close to that in MH (see § 3.5.2.29). The suffix in מהמה refers to the word המוצקות, which is the genitive in the construct לחת המוצקות. The use of the plural pronoun resulted from

50 who cannot see so as to beware of all mixture and cannot see a mixture that incurs

51 [reparation]-offering;

52 and concerning the deaf who have not heard the laws and the judgements and the purity regulations, and have not

53 heard the ordinances of Israel, since he who has not seen or heard

54 does not know how to obey (the law): nevertheless they have access to the sacred food.

55 And concerning liquid streams: we are of the opinion that they are not

56 pure, and that these streams do not act as a separative between impure

57 and pure (liquids). For the liquid of streams and (that) of (the vessel) which receives them are alike, (being)

58 a single liquid. And one must not let dogs enter the holy camp, since they

59 may eat some of the bones of the sanctuary while the flesh is (still) on them. For

60 Jerusalem is the camp of holiness, and is the place

61 which He has chosen from among all the tribes of Israel. For Jerusalem is the capital of the

62 camps of Israel. And concerning (the fruits of) the trees for food planted

attraction. Such an attraction occurs also in l. 62 (הנטע), and elsewhere in the DSS, e.g., כמשפט התורה הזואת (11QT^a 50:7); ... בהדר תשבחות כבוד מלכותו בה (4Q403 1 i 32). It also occurs in BH (Gesenius, § 146a), in MH and elsewhere (see Y. Avineri, *Hekhal Rashi*, 2, Jerusalem, 1985, pp. 173, 179). For other similar cases of attraction in the DSS, see 1QS 5:7, 11QT^a 47:7, 17, 1QM 8:11, 1QH^a 6:34. See also Lev 13:9, 1 Kgs 17:16, Dan 3:19, 27. כהם לחה אחת The function of the word כהם is problematical. Since the words לחת המוצקות והמקבל מהמה are the subject, and the words לחה אחת are the predicate, the word כהם must be a copula. כהם may be either the equivalent of הם (the כ being meaningless) or the equivalent of כ (the הם being meaningless). It is also possible to understand כהם לחה אחת as a transformation of כלחה אחת הם. We were not able to find evidence to support any of these possible explanations. Note, however, the construction of כמו in 2 Sam 18:3 and Haggai 2:3. On the form כהם, see § 3.5.1.10.

58 ואין להבי ... Dogs should not be brought into Jerusalem (see § 5.7.12). On the spelling להבי, see § 3.1.4.1. The infinitive denotes the predicate; the subject is impersonal (see § 3.4.2.1). The *hip'il* may be taken as purely causative, but we preferred to translate it 'let ... enter'; cf. גם אל יבא איש [את בתו ע[ם הקודש (4QD^f [= 4Q270]), and § 3.5.3.1. למחני הקודש Equivalent to המחנה of the Pentateuch. The construct of the pattern מקטה is spelt in QH either with *he* or with *yod* (see § 3.1.2).

59 מקצת See the commentary on l. 1. עצמות המקדש The bones of the sacrifices, cf. טהרת המקדש above l. 54.

60 ירושלים היאה מחנה הקדש This passage is significant for establishing the scope of the laws of purity (see § 5.4.2). On the position of the copula, see § 3.4.8. On the spelling ירושלים, see Kutscher, *Isaiah*, pp. 5, 106. The term מחנה הקודש is unattested elsewhere. והיא המקום שבחר בו ... See the commentary to l. 32. Note that היא and היאה occur side by side in this line.

61–62 ראש מחנות ישראל The cities of Israel are called מחנות, in contradistinction to Jerusalem which is labelled מחנה הקודש (see § 5.4.2d). On the spelling of the word ראש, see § 3.1.4.

62 ואף על מטעת עצי המאכל הנטע ... The fruits of the fourth year of the trees in the Land of Israel (see § 5.7.13). Curiously enough, neither fruits nor the fourth year are explicitly mentioned in this halakha, and the content can be deduced only from the linguistic allusions to Lev 19:23. The word מטעת seems to be superfluous, adding nothing to הנטע. Should one take the expression מטעת עצי המאכל to be a fixed term, like נטע רבעי in MH? In 4QD^e the word המטעת occurs in a list of priestly gifts. In MH the word נטע in this term denotes the fruit rather than planting, and so does the word אילן in, for instance, *m. Roš Haš.* 1:11: ראש השנה לאילן. In BH the word עץ sometimes means 'the fruits of the tree', see, e.g., Gen 3:1, 6, 11 (= פירי אילנא in *Tg. Pseudo-Jonathan*). For ואף על, see the com-

---

1 d הקו[ו]דש; in fact it is not impossible to read הק[ו]דש in a.

2 d מב̇ול.

3-3 d י[רושלים ראש מחנות ישראל]היאה.

בֹּאֶרץ ישראל בֻּרֵאשִׁיֻת הֹוֹא לכוהﬦים וֻמעﬡﬧ הבקר 63

והֹﬠﬣﬨﬣﬡ לﬣﬢﬣﬡﬦﬢ הוא ואף על הﬢﬧﬤﬣﬥﬦ אֻנֹﬡﬣﬧﬤ 64

אﬦﬡﬥﬦﬨﬥ שלוא יֻבואו ﬡﬥﬦﬤﬥ עם טהרﬨﬥﬡ הקﬥﬦﬣﬤﬧﬣ בﬦ בדד 65

ﬦﬥﬤﬣﬨﬥ מחוץ לבית וﬡﬥﬡﬤﬥ כֻﬨﬥﬡ שמעﬨﬡﬥﬧﬤﬣﬨﬥﬡ שﬦﬥﬡﬤﬢﬤ וכבס ﬦﬥﬨﬤﬡﬥ מחֹﬥﬤ 66

לﬡﬥﬦﬣﬤﬥ שבעﬨﬥ יﬦﬤﬦﬥ ועתה בהיות טמאתם עﬤﬦﬥﬦﬥ 67

הﬡﬢﬧﬥﬡﬦﬤﬦﬥ באים עﬤﬦﬥ טﬣﬨﬥﬧﬨﬥ הﬦﬥﬤﬣﬤﬥ לבﬦﬨ ואﬨﬦ יוﬦﬤﬦﬥﬦ 68

שﬨﬥﬡﬣﬥ השוﬨﬤﬨﬤ שלוא יﬧﬤﬣﬦﬤ את המצוה וﬦﬨﬨﬣﬣﬥ מﬦﬦﬨﬤ להביﬡ (ח) 69

ﬦﬨﬡﬨ וﬦﬡﬥ הﬡﬤﬧﬥﬤ ביד רמה כﬨﬥﬡﬤ שהוﬦﬡﬤﬦ בﬥﬦﬤ וﬦﬨﬨﬢﬦﬥﬤﬦ 70

ﬦﬡﬦﬤ בהﬦﬦﬥﬨ להﬦﬦﬣﬥﬤ טﬦﬡﬦﬥﬨ נﬨﬤ אﬦﬦ להﬡﬦﬦﬤﬤﬥﬦ מהﬦﬡﬥﬦﬣﬤﬥﬦﬦ 71

c (+ d) (= 4Q396 1–2 iv)

עד בוא השﬦﬦﬢ ביום השﬦﬦﬤﬦﬦ ועל טﬦﬡﬨ נפﬦﬦ 72

האﬦﬦ אנﬦﬦﬤﬥ אומרﬦﬦﬦ שﬦﬦﬥﬦﬥﬦ עצﬦ שﬦﬦﬦﬦ חﬦﬦﬤﬦ 73

וﬦﬦﬦﬦﬦ כﬦﬦﬦﬦﬦ הﬦﬦﬦ או הﬦﬦﬦﬦ הﬥﬦﬦﬦ 74

וﬡﬦﬦ הﬦﬦﬦﬦ הﬦﬦﬦﬦﬦ בﬦﬦﬥﬦ הﬦﬦﬦ והﬦﬦﬦ בﬦﬦﬦﬦ זﬦﬦﬦﬦﬦ 75

קדﬦ מﬦﬦﬦﬦﬦﬦﬦ קﬦﬦﬦﬦ ישראל ועﬦ בﬦﬦﬦﬦﬦﬦ הﬦﬦﬦﬦﬦﬦ 76

---

mentary to l. 13 above; on the attestation of the word מטעת, see § 3.5.1.19. The expression עץ מאכל is biblical (see § 3.5.2.20). The verb הנטע refers to the genitive מאכל (see the commentary to l. 57 above).

63 בארץ ישראל This is a halakhic, rather than a geopolitical, term (see §§ 5.3.2.1 and 5.3.3.3). כראשית The fruits of the tree in its fourth year are to be treated like ראשית and are not subject to redemption (see § 5.7.13). ומעשר הבקר והצון The cattle tithe should be given to the priests (see § 5.7.14). The terminology here is biblical, in contrast to the mishnaic מעשר בהמה (see § 5.3.1.3). On the spelling of הצון, see § 3.1.4.1.

64 ואף על הצרועים Here begins a detailed halakha about the impurity of lepers (see § 5.7.15). On the distribution of the synonyms צרוע and מצורע, see § 5.3.1.2.

65 שלוא י[בואו עם The expression בא עם does not denote motion, but mixture (as in C 8; cf. Ps 26:4), i.e. the healed lepers should be isolated. In l. 68, however, the syntax of בא עם is different. טהרת הקודש The sacred food (see § 5.3.3.6). כי בדד ... For the reasons for restoring לבית, and for the interpretation of the sentence, see § 5.7.15f.

66 ו]אף כתוב Followed by a paraphrase of Lev 14:8. שמעת שיגלח וכבס The conjunction מעת ש- is postclassical (see § 3.5.2.27). וכבס is an instance of the biblical consecutive perfect. For the lack of complement, cf. Jer 2:22, 4Q514 i 6, 9. This usage is more frequent in MH.

67 ועתה Expressing a contrast to what precedes it.

בהיות טמאתם עמהם Instead of בהיותם טמאים (cf. שאין בהם טהרה on ll. 55–56). On the inflected infinitive in time clauses, see § 3.3.3.1.1. טמאה is of the qitlat pattern (see §§ 3.1.12 and 3.5.2.12). The form עמהם is typical of post-classical Hebrew (contrast the classical עמם, on which see § 3.5.2.26).

68 הצ]רועים באים ע[ם טהרת הקודש לבית In contrast to l. 65. The word לבית replaces the word אהל in l. 67 and in its biblical source (cf. § 5.2.3d). ואתם יודעים Here the reference is to the high priest and his colleagues rather than to the opponents (see §§ 4.2.3 and 4.2.6.3). On the form of the pronoun אתם/אתמה, see § 3.3.1.1.3. Note the use of the participle where BH would use the perfect (ידעתם; see § 3.4.1.5).

69 [שעל השוגג ...] The restoration is based on Lev 5:2. ונעלה ממנו The word ונעלה is a misspelling for ונעלם; the mem was not written in final position before the other two mems (see §§ 3.2.7 and 5.7.15f). Compare למעלן but למעלה מן in MH (M. Bar-Asher, Qovez, 1, p. 171 n. 46; G. Haneman, Qovez, 2, p. 20). Note also the possible elision of mem in Jer 15:1 שלח מעל for שלחם מעל (Z. Ben-Ḥayyim, Leshonenu, 11 [1941], p. 93). להביא חטאת This is the predicate.

70 [ועל העושה ביד רמה כת]וב On the restoration, which is based on Num 15:27-31, see § 5.7.15f. שהואה בוזה ומגדף Paraphrasing Num 15:30 (Kister). For the polemical nuance given to this passage, see the Sipre to this verse and b. Sanh. 99ᵇ. A similar polemical passage

63 in the Land of Israel: they are to be dealt with like first fruits belonging to the priests. And (likewise) the tithe of the herd

64 and the flock should be given to the priests. And concerning (healed) lepers we

65 are [of the opinion that they may not] enter (any place) containing sacred food but should be isolated

66 [(and) outside any house]. And it is (indeed) written that after he (i.e. the leper) shaves and washes he should dwell outside

67 [his tent seven] days; but now while their impurity is (still) with them

68 le[pers enter] into a house containing sacred food. And you know

69 [that if someone violates a prohibitive commandment unintentionally], and the fact escapes him, he should bring

70 a purification offering; [and concerning him who purposely transgresses the precepts it is writ]ten that he 'despises and blasphemes'.

71 [Moreover, since thay have the] impurity of leprosy, one should not let them (the lepers) eat of the sacred food

72 until sunset on the eighth day. And concerning [the impurity] of

73 the [dead] person we are of the opinion that every bone, [whether it]

74 has its flesh on it or [not], should be (treated) according to the law of the dead or the slain.

75 And concerning the practice of illegal marriage that exists among the people: (this practice exists) despite their being so[ns] of holy [seed],

76 as is written, Israel is holy. And concerning his (i.e. Israel's) [clean ani]mal,

---

occurs in 1QS 5:11–12.

71 [מאות נ]גע[ט]   Both the combination and the plural are peculiar. אין להאכילם מהקו[ד]שים The *hipᶜil* here means 'let someone do' (see § 3.5.3.1). On the 'modal' use of the infinitive, see § 3.4.2.1, and on the assimilation of the *nun* in מהקודשים, see § 3.2.6. The term קדשים designates the sacred food eaten in the Temple in BH, QH and MH. Both the rabbis and the sectarians maintained that access to this food required the highest degree of purity (see § 5.7.15).

72 עד בוא השמש ביום השמיני   In contrast to the rabbinic halakha, MMT states here that lepers bear the impurity of leprosy until sunset on the eighth day of their purification process (see § 5.7.15). The language here is biblical (cf. § 3.3.3.1.1). ועל [טמאת נפש] האדם   This introduces a halakha about the impurity of human bones (see § 5.7.16).

73 אנחנו אומרים   See the commentary to l. 55. The reading שאנחנו in MSᵈ implies that what precedes is the heading and not the object of אומרים (cf. § 5.2.4 and n. 32). שכול עצם ש[היא]   If the restoration is correct, this is equivalent to עצם) כל שהיא) in MH, and means 'whatever it may be', i.e. the smallest quantity.

74 ושלמה   See the detailed discussion at § 5.7.16. כמשפט המת או החלל הוא   The preposition *kap* expresses conformity to a rule (BDB, p. 454), as in 11QTᵃ 47:10, 15. The pronoun is used indefinitely, and could be read also היא.

75 ועל הזונות הנעסה בתוך העם   We take this halakha to be a condemnation of intermarriage between priests and laymen (see § 5.7.17). J. M. Baumgarten, however, thinks that it refers to intermarriage between Israelites and aliens, and that the emphasis on the higher degree of sanctity of the sons of Aaron is only by way of *a fortiori*. The word זונות is a variant of זנות (cf. זנות in MSᵈ; see § 3.5.2.7). It denotes illegal marriages (see § 5.7.17, n. 177). The expression עשה זנות is not known to us from any other Hebrew source; cf., however, עבד + זנו in Aramaic (§ 3.5.3.7a). The form of the word הנעסה is biblical (§ 3.3.3.3), but its spelling is late (§ 3.1.6). On the word העם, see § 3.5.1.17.

76 משכתוב קדש ישראל   The form משכתוב is a calque of the Aramaic מדכתיב (see § 3.5.4.5). MSᵈ reads כשכתוב (see § 3.5.2.15). Here the term כתוב can hardly introduce a quotation of Jer 2:3. It states rather that Israel is holy according to the Scripture (see the discussion on כתוב in §

1-1 The scribe first intended לטהרת (see § 1.4.3.3.1).

2 Originally שבעת.

3 See § 1.4.3.3.1.

4 d שאנחנו.

5 d הזנות.

6 d כשכתוב.

77   כתוב שלוא לרבעה֗ו כלאים ועל לבוש]ו כתוב שלוא[

78   יהיה שעטנז ושלוא לזרוע֗ שדו וב]רמו כלאים[

79   ]ב[גלל שהמה קדושים ובני אהרון ק]דושי קדושים[

80   ]וא[ת֗ם֗² יודעים שמקצת הכֹהנים ו]העם מתערבים[

81   ]והם [מתוככים ומטמאי]ם [את זרע֗] הקודש ואף[

82   את]זרע]ם֗ ע֗ם הזונֹות כֹ]י לבני אהרון³   [

5.3.2.6). On ישראל as meaning the laity, see § 3.5.2.14.
ועל בה]מתו הטהור[ה כתוב   The text cites several cases of forbidden mixtures which are analogous to illegal marriages. If our restoration is correct, MMT restricts the law of *kilʾayim* (Lev 19:19) to pure animals; this is in contrast to the rabbinic view (*Sipra*, ed. Finkelstein, p. 401). The comparison of illegal marriages with *kilʾayim* is found in both rabbinic and Karaite sources. The word כתוב introduces the content of the biblical law rather than a quotation (see §§ 3.5.4.5 and 5.3.2.6).

77 שלוא לרבעה כלאים   On the syntax of this infinitive and those following, see § 3.4.2.1. The *piʿel* of רבע in this meaning is peculiar; MS^d uses the *hipʿil* as in BH (see § 3.5.4.11).

78 שעטנז ... ושלוא לזרוע שדו   Cf. Lev 19:19.   This is an independent clause; the particle -ש denotes command (see § 3.4.2.1). Here both שדה and כרם occur, whereas in the Bible שדה occurs in Lev 19:19 and כרם in Deut 22:9. For the form שדו (= שדהו), see § 3.2.2.2.

79 בגלל שהמה קדושים   The conjunction -ש בגלל does not occur elsewhere in early Hebrew sources, but it is found in Aramaic (see § 3.5.4.1). The pronoun המה refers

77 it is written that one must not let it mate with another species; and concerning his clothes [it is written that they should not]

78 be of mixed stuff; and he must not sow his field and vine[yard with mixed specie]s.

79 Because they (Israel) are holy, and the sons of Aaron are [most holy.]

80 But you know that some of the priests and [the laity mingle with each other] [as well as]

81 [And they] unite with each other and pollute the [holy] seed [as well as]

82 their own [seed] with women whom they are forbidden to marry. Since [the sons of Aaron should ...]

to the word העם. [ובני אהרון ק]דושי קדושים]   The epithets קודש קודשים and קדושי קדושים refer in the scrolls either to the priests or to the angels (see § 5.7.17d). Our restoration [ק]דושי קדושים] conforms with קדושים at the beginning of the line, but [ק]ודש קודשים] is equally possible (cf. § 1.6.3.7).

80 [וא]תם יודעים   Refers to the addressee (see the commentary to l. 68). שמקצת   See the commentary to l. 1.

81 מתוככים   'Cohere', *hitpolel* of תוך (see the commentary to l. 14). זרע [הקוד]ש   Cf. Ezra 9:2.

82 עם הזונות   'With women whom they are forbidden to marry' (see § 5.7.17).

---

1   d [לֹהרביעֹ]ה.

2   d ואת[מ]ה].

3   About eighteen wide lines (such as those of MS^d) are missing here (according to the claculation of H. Stegemann).

C

d (+ e̲) (= 4Q397 14–21)

[		[ ]מֹ̇שֵׁ[ ]ֹ[	1
[	וֹ[שִׁ̇יֹבֹ̇וֹאֹ]וֹ	וֹ[עֹותֹ]וֹ	2
[	וֹ[יֹהיה מֹתֹ]	וֹמֹי̇ ישֹנֹ̇וֹ	3
[	החמֹ[סֹ והמעֹל]	ועל הנשֹי[ם	4
בגלל וֹ[החמס והזנות אבדֹ]וֹ מקצת]		כי באלה̇[ו	5

מקומות [ואף] כתוֹ[ב בספר מושה שלֹ]וֹא תביֹא תועבה אֹ[לֹ] ביתכה כיֹ]   6

התועבה שנואה הֹיֹאֹ̇ה [ואתם יודעים שֹ[פֹ]רֹשנו מרוֹב העֹ[ם ומכול טמאתם]   7

[וֹ]מֹהתערבֹי בדברים האֹלֹה ומלבוא עֹ[מֹהם עֹ[ל]גֹב² אלֹה וֹאֹתם יֹ[ודעים שלוא]   8

יֹ[מֹצא בידנו מעל ושקר ורעֹה כי על [ואלה אֹ[נֹחנו נותניֹם אֹתֹ לבנו ואף]   9

[כתבֹ]נֹוֹ³ אליכה שתבין בספר מֹוֹשֹׁהֹ [וֹ]בֹסֹפרֹ[יֹ הנֹ[בֹ]יאים ובדוֹ[יֹ]ד   [10

[במעשי] דור ודור ובספר כתוב וֹ[[וֹ]לֹ[יֹ[ם לֹ· לוֹא   11

[לך וקדֹמניֹוֹת   [ﬧ]הֹי⁴ ואף כתוב שֹ[יֹ]תֹסורֹ[ו] מהדֹ[רֹ]וֹרֹ[ֹ] וקרתֹ[ﬧ]וֹ הרעֹה וֹכֹתֹ[וֹב]   12

e (+ d̲) (= 4Q398 14–17 i)

והיא כי   13

[יבוֹ]א עליך [וכול הדברים] הֹאלה בֹאחריֹ[ת] הימים הבֹרֹכה   14

---

4   ועל הנשׁי[ם]   If the restoration is correct, then the reference here is to the law relating to incest; cf. הזנות on the next line. For על denoting legal matters, see § 5.2.4. החמ]ס והמעל   This pair of words is used to denounce transgressions against the laws of the Torah, as are החמס והזנות on the next line, תועבה on ll. 39 and 40, and מעל ושקר ורעה on l. 42. Such words are frequently found in the admonitions of 1QS and CD, e.g., 1QS 4:10 תועבות שקר; 1QS 4:21 מעשי תועבה ברוח זנות; 1QS 11:11 תועבות נדה—cf. also 1QS 10:19; CD 4:17, 19:17. Note that the word חמסא occurs also in similar combinations in Qumran Aramaic, e.g., 4QEnᵇ 7:8; 4QEnᵉ 2 i 16.

5   אבד]ו החמס והזנות   See the commentary on l. 4. מקצת] מקומות   Cf. Deut 12:2 אבד תאבדון את כל המקמות.

6   [ואף] כתו[ב]   What follows is based on Deut 7:26 ולא תביא תועבה אל ביתך; the restored word ביתכה may refer to the Temple. On the term כתוב, see § 5.3.2.6.

7   התועבה שנואה היאה   This is a sort of interpretation of the biblical word תועבה. M. Kister notes that *Tg. Pseudo-Jonathan* translates the Hebrew תועבה with Aramaic שניאה. תעב and שנא are similar in meaning, and תועבה is used as a synonym for איבה in 1QS 4:17. On other expressions paired with תועבה, see the commentary to l. 4, and 1QH 11:11, 1QpHab 12:6–10. Onkelos translates תועבה with מרחקה; the relation

between רחק and תעב is already evident in 1QHᵃ 14:21 וכרחקך אותו כן אתענבנו. See also § 3.5.1.26. On the form היאה, see § 3.3.1.1.1. On the position of the copula (after the predicate), see § 3.4.8. [פרשנו מרוב הע]ם Here we have the earliest attestation of the use of פרש for 'depart, secede'; the later scrolls use the term סור מדרך העם instead (see § 3.5.3.9). On the significance of the use of the term פרש here, see 4.1.4.2. The separation discussed here is the consequence of the hateful behavior of those who violated the purity laws of the Torah. The word רוב has here its biblical meaning 'multitude' rather than its mishnaic meaning 'majority'; there is no certain attestation of the MH meaning of this word in QH. On the history of the word עם, see § 3.5.1.18.

8   בדברים האלה   The word דברים refers to legal matters; see the commentary on B 4 (where both דברים and אלה occur), and l. 31 below. ומלבוא   With both *lamed* and *mem*; contrast [ו]מהתערב with *mem* but without *lamed* (see § 3.3.3.1.3). The expression בוא עם is parallel here to התערב. לגב אלה (or [ע]ל גב אלה)   The preposition על גב occurs in MH in contexts of the mixing of pure food (see § 3.5.3.7). It is less plausible to take גב here as a noun with the meaning 'sect' (as in Syriac); but cf. 1QSa ii 4). ואתם י[ודעים] אל יבוא בקהל אלה (1QSa ii 4). See the commentary on B 58. Here we witness an appeal to a referee; this is frequent in C; אתם יודעים (always

1 [... ... ...]

2 [... ... ...] that they will come [   ]

3 And who will [... ... ...] he will [   ]

4 And concerning the women [... ... ... the malice] and the treachery [...]

5 for in these [... because of] malice and the fornication [some]

6 places were destroyed. [And it is] written [in the book of Moses] that you should [not] bring any abomination [into your home, since]

7 abomination is a hateful thing. [And you know that] we have separated ourselves from the multitude of
the people [and from all their impurity]

8 and from being involved with these matters and from participating with [them] in these things. And you
[know that no]

9 treachery or deceit or evil can be found in our hand (i.e. in us), since for [these things] we give [... And]

10 we have [written] to you so that you may study (carefully) the book of Moses and the books of the
Prophets and (the writings of) David [and the]

11 [events of] ages past. And in the book (of Moses) it is written [... ... ...] not

12 [...] and former days [...] And it is written that [you will stray] from the path (of the Torah) and that
calamity will meet [you]. And it is written

13 'and it shall come to pass, when

14 all these things [be]fall you', at the end of days, the blessings

---

plural) occurs also in B.

9 [י]מצא בידנו מעל ושקר ורעה   On the biblical
expression נמצא ביד, and on the lack of concord in number, see § 3.5.1.15. On the other words, see the commentary on l. 5 above. כי initiating a causal clause is used as
in BH (unlike MH, which used -ש instead), see § 3.3.1.4.
[א]נחנו   As in BH and not אנו as in MH and QH (see
§ 3.3.1.1.2).

10 כתב[נו   MSᵉ ad loc. has כתב[נום] with a final *mem*.
This *mem* is either a pronominal suffix, referring to
בדברים האלה in l. 8 and to אלה in l. 9, or a case of mima-
tion (see § 3.2.7). The restoration שלח[נו is equally possible. אליכה   Written with final *he* (see § 3.1.2).
שתבין בספר מושה   The expression הבין ב- denotes
here careful study of a written text or the like. It is characteristic of LBH and QH (see § 3.5.2). ספר מושה is the
Pentateuch. The term occurs in CD 7:17. ובדוי[ד]   In
this context דויד probably refers not only to the Psalms of
David, but rather to the Hagiographa. This is a significant
piece of evidence for the history of the tripartite division
of the Canon (see § 4.1.4.2).

11 בינו שנות דור ודור Cf. Deut 32:7   [במעשי] דור ודור,
ובספר. ובהבינכם במעשי דור ודור and especially 4QDᵉ
כתוב   Does ספר refer to the five-book Torah, i.e.,
ספר מושה? We been unable to suggest any restoration for the end of this line.

12 ואף כתוב ש[תסור] מהד[ר]ך   Cf. Deut 31:29 וסרתם
מן הדרך וקראת אתכם הרעה באחרית הימים. The form
מהדרך (rather than the מן הדרך of MT) is typical of MMT
(see § 3.2.6). וקרתך   replaces the periphrastic construction וקראת אתכם of the Bible.

12–14 וכתוב והיא כי יבו[א   The long paraphrase after
וכתוב follows Deut 30:1-3. It represents the biblical
source in an idiosyncratic form that is at the same time
both abbreviated and supplied with explanatory additions
that date the promise in Deuteronomy to the end of days.
On the biblical construction והיה כי, see § 3.4.1.2; on the
spelling here of היא with final *ʾalep*, see § 3.1.4.2.
יבו[א]   The MT reads יבאו, with concord of number
with the subject. באחרית הימים   An addition to the
MT. [ו]הקללא   The words that follow in
Deuteronomy, אשר נתתי לפניך, were omitted. On the
spelling of קללא with final *ʾalep*, see § 3.1.4.2.

---

1 Or מהתערב.

2 Or ע]ל גב].

3 e כתב]נום].

4 There are traces of letters here in both d and e, but we could not
propose any suggested text which would account for all the
traces.

[וה]קֹללֹא¹ [והשיבותֹ]הֹ אל לֹ[בב]ךֹ² וֹשֹׁבֹֹתֹֹהֹ אלו בכל לבבךֹ³   15

[ובכו]ל נפשׁ]ך [ ]ה[ ]°[ ] בֹ]אֹחרי]תֹ]   16

[כתוב בספר מֹ]ושה ובספרי הנביאים שיבואוֹ]   שֹׁלֹ[17

e (+ d̲) (= 4Q398 11–13)

[הבר]כֹֹוֹת שֹׁ]ב]אֹ]ו]וֹ ב[ ]°[ ]]בֹיֹמֹי שלומוה בן דויד ואֹף הֹקללות   18

[ש]באוֹו בֹיֹוֹמֹי⁴ יר]וֹבעֹם בן נבט ועד גל]ו]ת ירושלם וצדקיה מלך יֹֹהֹוֹדֹ]ה]   19

[ש]יֹבֹ]יֹ]אֹם⁵ בוֹ]]וֹאנחנו מכירים⁶ שבאוו מקצת הברכות והקללות   20

שֹׁכֹֹתוב בסֹ]פֹר מוֹ]שֹׁה וֹזֹה הוֹא אחריֹת הימים שישובו בישר]אל]   21

לתֹ]מֹיד   וֹ ולוא ישובו אֹחֹוֹ]ר   ]והרשעים ירשׁ]יעֹ]ו]וֹ וֹאֹמֹ[22

והןֹ]   ]וֹזֹכֹוֹר את מלכי ישרא]ל] והתבנן במעשיהֹמֹ]ה shmï מהם   23

שהיא יראֹ]ו את   התוֹ]רה היה מצֹלֹ]°⁷ ⁸-מצרות והם-⁸ מֹ]בֹ]קֹ]שי תורה   24

15   אל ל[בב]ך   Note the omission of שמה ה' אלהיך הדיחך בכל הגוים אשר. The absence of this important phrase may be accidental or it may be an intentional elimination of a reference to the historical dispersion. ושבתה אלו Rather than ושבתה אלי. Deuteronomy has ושבת עד ה' אלהיך. In BH the use of עד after the verb שוב, though not rare, is less common than the use of אל; עד produces a heightened effect. שוב עד is very rare in Qumran Hebrew; שוב אל is, in contrast, common, and in 1QIsaᵃ 9:12 there is a parallel to what we find here: there the עד that occurs after שוב in MT is replaced by על (frequently confused with אל in 1QIsaᵃ).

18–24   The text of these lines was taken from one of the large frgs. 11–13 of MSᵉ. This text has no parallel in any of the other manuscripts and its placement is somewhat doubtful. In placing it here, we are following a suggestion put forward by M. Kister. The arguments in favour of this placement, as well as the objections to it raised by H. Stegemann, are set out in the Appendix.

18   בימי שלומוה [ ]°[ ]]°[שבא]ו]ו [הבר]כ]ו]ת   From the extant text in ll. 18–21, we learn that the writer believes that some of the blessings of Deuteronomy were fulfilled in the days of Solomon, and that some of the curses were fulfilled in the time of the kings of Judah and Israel. At the end of days, however, the blessings will return, and (if our reconstruction and interpretation of ll. 21–22 are correct) they will last forever and will not be cancelled. The curses will fall upon the wicked and exterminate them. Note, however, that David's days are not

mentioned explicitly in the extant text, though the word בימיו implies a reference to him. On the spelling שלומוה, see § 3.1.3.1, and on the spelling דויד, see Kutscher, *Isaiah*, pp. 5, 99. ואף הקללות On ואף, see § 3.5.3.3. MMT uses the plural (קללות) instead of the classical collective (see *HDSS*, § 330.3b); cf. also הברכות והקללות (l. 20); only in the biblical paraphrase (ll. 14–15) do we find the collective use הברכה והקללא.

19   בימי   For the possible variant [מיומ]י (an Aramaism), see § 3.5.2.13. עד גל[ו]ת Infinitive construct expressing time (see § 3.3.3.1.1). ירושלם Spelt historically without *yod*, in contrast to the plene spelling common in the second half of the Second Temple period (Kutscher, *Isaiah*, pp. 5, 106). וצדקיה rather than וצדקיהו; the יהו- form is typical of the First Temple period, while the shorter יה- form is typical of the Second Temple period (see § 3.5.2.28).

20   שיביאם   The suffix refers to 'the curses' rather than to 'Jerusalem and Zedekiah'. As to the subject, it may be either indefinite or God. If the fragment of MSᵈ with the word שיובאו is not mislocated, the former is preferable. מכירים שבאוו On the special usage of הכיר here, see § 3.5.4.7. The form שבאוו is a phonetic spelling for שבאו (see § 3.2.1). מקצת See the commentary on B 1.

21   שכתוב   The word does not agree, either in number or in gender, with its antecedent (הברכות והקללות). For this reason it cannot be taken as an adjective; it is, rather, an adverb complementing the predicate שבאוו. The absence

15 and the curses, ['then you will take] it to hea[rt] and you will return unto Him with all your heart

16 and with all your soul', at the end [of time, so that you may live ... ...]

17 [It is written in the book] of Moses [and in the books of the Prophets] that there will come [...]

18 [the blessings have (already) befallen in ...] in the days of Solomon the son of David. And the curses

19 [that] have (already) befallen from the days of Jeroboam the son of Nebat and up to when Jerusalem and
Zedekiah King of Judah went into captivity

20 that He will bring them [...]. And we know that some of the blessings and the curses have (already) been
fulfilled

21 as it is written in the bo[ok of Mo]ses. And this is at the end of days when they will return to Isra[el]

22 [forever ...] and not be cancelled, but the wicked will act wickedly, and [...]

23 and [...]. Think of the kings of Israel and contemplate their deeds: whoever among them

24 feared [the To]rah was delivered from troubles; and these were the seekers of the Torah

---

of כמו or כ before שכתוב is known from the Aramaic דכתיב (though כדכתיב also exists) and the MH שנאמר; these terms introduce biblical citations, however, and that is not the case here. בס[ס]פר מו[שה. Cf. Deut 30:1. היא הוא אחרית הימים וזה Materially one could read היא (= היה) rather than הוא or היא and take this as referring to the blessings and the curses which had already arrived (שבאו; in a pesher on Genesis [4Q252 1 iv 1–2] the term אחרית הימים refers to the days of Saul). But then the words that follow, the future שישובו, etc., would make no sense. The phrase וזה הוא אחרית הימים (rather than ובאחרית הימים or the like) is, however, awkward. שישובו בישר[אל] לת[מיד] There are other possible restorations here which would give the sentence quite different meanings. For the meaning of שישובו, see § 3.5.1.24.

22 [ולוא ישובו אחו]ר The expression שוב אחור has two different meanings: (*a*) 'to be defeated', e.g., Ps 9:4 (with a personal subject); (*b*) 'to be cancelled' (with an abstract noun as subject). This second meaning is not found in the Bible (see § 3.5.1.24; *HDSS*, p. 114). Since ישובו אחור would refer to the blessings and the curses rather than to Israel, the second meaning seems to fit better. והרשעים ירש[יע]ו Cf. Dan 11:10 והרשיעו רשעים. The verb הרשיע may have a passive or reflexive meaning, as in Pr 12:3, but any meaning here depends on the restoration, which is uncertain.

23 [זכור את מלכי ישרא]ל The author suggests to the addressee that he should learn from the history of the

kings of Israel, and especially of David. This fits our conjecture that the addressee was a leader of Israel (see § 4.2.6.5). The verb זכר parallels בין, as in Deut 32:7 (זכור ימות עולם בינו שנות דור ודור) and Isa 43:18. For this meaning of זכר, see *BDB*. והתבנן Spelt defectively. On the use of *hitpolel*, see M. Moreshet, 'Polel/Hitpolel in Mishnaic Hebrew and in Aramaic', *Bar-Ilan*, 18–19 (1981), pp. 248–269 (Hebrew). שמי מהם ש- The construction is unique. It is reminiscent of the relative ש- מי in MH, but here מן with a retrospective suffix enters between the two components. An apparently similar construction occurs in Jud 21:8 מי אחד משבטי ישראל אשר לא עלה, but, as elsewhere in the Bible, מי is here interrogative (cf. also Isa 50:1 and other apparently similar constructions in *BDB*, p. 567 § g).

---

1 [ו]הקללה d [.

2 [לבב]כה d [.

3 לבבכה d

4 מיומ[י] d (on a small fragment).

5 שיוב[א]ו d (on a small fragment).

6 See § 1.6.3.9.1.

7 Or [מצול].

8-8 מצרותיהם is syntactically less plausible.

e (+ <u>d</u> + f) (= 4Q398 14–17 ii)

25   [נשו]אׄיׄ עונׄות זכור [את] דוׄיׄד שהיא איש חסדים [וׄ]אׄףׄ

26   היׄא [נׄצׄ]לׄ מצׄרות רבות ונסלוח לו ואף ²אׄנׄחׄנׄו כתבנוׄ² אׄלׄיׄךׄ

27   מקצת מעשי התורה שחשבנו לטובׄ לך ולעמרׄ³ שׄרׄ[א]יׄנׄוׄ

28   עמך ערמה ומדע תורה הבן ⁴בכל אלה⁴ ובקש מלׄפׄנׄוׄ⁵ שׄיׄתׄקׄןׄ

29   את עצתרׄ⁶ וׄהׄרחיק ממך מחׄשׄבׄתׄ⁷ רעׄהׄ⁸ ועצׄת בליׄעׄל

30   בשל שׄתׄשמח באחרית העת בׄמׄצׄאׄך ⁹־מׄקׄצׄת דׄבׄרׄיׄנוׄ־⁹ כֺׄן

31   ונחשבה לך לצדקה בעשׄוׄתׄך הׄיׄשׄר והטוׄבׄ¹⁰ לפׄנׄיׄוׄ¹¹ לטוׄב לך

32   ולישׄראׄל

---

24 שהיא ירא [את התו]רׄה   On the periphrastic construction of היה with a stative verb, see § 3.4.1.4. For the phrase ירא את התורה, cf. וממשפטיך יראתי Ps 119:120; היה מצול מצרות Pr 13:13. A periphrastic tense with passive verb. The form מצול, which replaces the standard נצל (see l. 26 and the apparatus), should be taken as a passive participle on the *maqtūl* pattern (see § 3.3.3.4). The common phrase נצל מצרות is used of David in 1 Sam 26:24 and in Ps 34:18 and 44:9. For another possible reading, see § 1.6.3.9.1. מבׄ[ק]שׄי התורה This expression is found in 4QJubᵃ (= 1:12): ואת מבקשי [ה]תׄורה ירדופׄו] (J. C. Vanderkam and J. T. Milik, 'The First *Jubilees* Manuscript from Qumran Cave 4: A Preliminary Publication', *JBL*, 110 [1991], p. 251).

25 [נשו]אׄי עונות   Restored in accordance with Isa 33:24. זכור See the commentary to l. 23. דויד Spelt with a *yod*, as is usual in texts written in the Second Temple period (Kutscher, *Isaiah*, pp. 5, 99). שהיא (= שהיה) A vulgar and phonetic spelling typical of this manuscript. איש חסדים A post-classical expression (see § 3.5.2.9). .

26 היא נצל מצרות   See the commentary to l. 24. ונסלוח לו An infinitive absolute used as a finite verb (see § 3.4.2.4). ואף אנחנו כתבנו אליך 'We have sent you' (see § 3.5.1.13). On the variant order אנחנו כתבנו, see § 3.4.7, and on אנחנו itself, see § 3.4.7.

27 מקצת מעשי התורה   See the commentary to B 2. שחשבנו The word is hard to translate and its syntactical function is unclear. לטוב לך ולעמך On this biblical expression, see § 3.5.1.9. The addressee may have been a ruler, since his conduct had bearing on the welfare of the people of Israel.

28 עמך Cf. Job 12:16 and *BDB*, p. 768 3b. ערמה Apparently pronounced *ᶜerma* or the like (see § 3.1.1.2). The word is typical of BH (see § 3.5.1.20). ומדע תורה The word מדע is an Aramaic synonym of the original Hebrew דעת; the expression מדע תורה occurs in the Saturday evening prayer (see §§ 3.5.2.18 and 3.5.1.27). 'Knowledge of the Torah' is apparently ascribed to the messianic king in a pesher on Isa 11:2 (4Q161 8–10:18): ואל יסומכנו ב[דעת]תׄורה (the restoration is based on רוח דעת in the biblical verse). הבן בכל אלה On בין ב-, see the commentary to l. 10; כל אלה may well refer to the laws mentioned in section B. ובקש מלפניו A post-classical expression (see § 3.5.2.4). The preposition לפני (as קדם in Aramaic) is used when referring to God or to a king, instead of a 'direct' preposition such as ל-, מן (see § 3.5.2.17). On the spelling of מלפנו (without *yod*), see § 3.2.2.1. שיתקן If our reading is correct, this is a unique instance of תקן in QH (see § 3.5.2.33).

29 את עצתך The word עצה may be translated in several different ways, for instance as 'will' or 'heart'. But, when

25 whose transgressions were [for]given. Think of David who was a man of righteous deeds and

26 who was (therefore) delivered from many troubles and was forgiven. We have (indeed) sent you

27 some of the precepts of the Torah according to our decision, for your welfare and the welfare of your people. For we have seen (that)

28 you have wisdom and knowledge of the Torah. Consider all these things and ask Him that He strengthen

29 your will and remove from you the plans of evil and the device of Belial

30 so that you may rejoice at the end of time, finding that some of our practices are correct.

31 And this will be counted as a virtuous deed of yours, since you will be doing what is righteous and good in His eyes, for your own welfare and

32 for the welfare of Israel.

followed by a second person pronominal suffix, it means nothing more than 'you'; cf. 1QS 1:12–13 לברר דעתם באמת חוקי אל וכוחם לתכן כתם דרכיו וכול הונם כעצת צדקו. Note the conversive *waw* (see § 3.4.1.1). והרחיק. The word רעה, like its variant רע, is used substantively (like רוע; see § 3.5.1.23). מחשבת רעה Cf. 1QHᵃ 2:26, ומזמות בליעל ועצת בליעל מחשבת בליעל 1QHᵃ זמות בליעל 1QHᵃ 4:13, יועץ בליעל 4:13, etc., 6:21; see also 1QM 13:11. For another concurrence of מחשבה and רוע, בליעל see 1QHᵃ 7:3.

30 בשל שתשמח On ש-בשל, see the commentary to B 12. A unique synonym of באחרית העת; cf. 4Q169 2 iii 3, 4Q173 1 5. באחרית הקץ הימים

במצאך מקצת דברינו כן On the form במצאך, see § 3.3.3.1.2; for מקצת דברינו (and its variant מדברינו), see the commentary to B 1. On the use of כן here, see § 3.5.1.12; for the use of מצא, see § 3.5.2.22.

31 ונחשבה לך לצדקה On this phrase, see § 3.5.1.8. The entire concluding formula is perhaps influenced by Deut 6:24-25. בעשותך What type of clause is this? Cf. Deut 12:28: כי תעשה הטוב והישר בעיני ה' אלהיך למען ייטב לך ולבניך ... For the use of the infinitive, see § 3.3.3.1.1. הישר והטוב In 4QTLevi 1 i 16 we find דשפיר ודטב קדמיך. Onkelos renders this Hebrew expression דכשר ודתקין. In both of these Aramaic parallels the *he* is not rendered by the Aramaic definite article, but by

the relative ד. In the sect's view, this formula referred to the perfect performance of God's commandments; see § 5.2.3c. In the historical books of the Bible, the regular formula for evaluating each king of Judah and Israel is ויעש הישר בעיני ה' (vs. ויעש הרע בעיני ה'); but in the formula of 2 Chr 14:1 and 31:20 both ישר and טוב occur. לטוב לך לפנו See the commentary to l. 28. ולישראל Means the same as לטוב לך ולעמך on l. 27—see the commentary there.

1 f מצול.

2-2 f [כתב]נו אנחנו.

3 Missing in f.

4-4 f [באלה] (?).

5 f מלפניו.

6 d [עצת]כה.

7 Originally מחשבות f; מחשבת.

8 f רע.

9-9 f מדברינו.

10 Missing in f.

11 f לפניו.

3. THE LANGUAGE

THE initial impression given by the language of MMT is that it differs from the Hebrew of the other Qumran manuscripts in being closer to MH. But this similarity to MH may be misleading since there are many biblical and Qumran features in MMT which contrast with MH usage. In order to establish the true nature of the language of MMT, we shall describe the distinctive features it presents under the various subdivisions of linguistic analysis (such as orthography, phonology, morphology, syntax and vocabulary), systematically comparing each feature, general or particular, with BH, with QH, with MH and with Aramaic. We shall thus be able to characterise more precisely the nature of the language of MMT, and to determine both its relationship to other phases and traditions of Hebrew and its location in the history of the Hebrew language.[1]

3.1 Spelling

The spelling used in the manuscripts of MMT is, in broad outline, identical with that of other non-biblical Qumran manuscripts, being likewise 'fuller' than that found in the MT. Here we shall note its more prominent features, comparing them with the orthography of the MT. Together with the description of each manuscript (in chap. 1), we have given a detailed description of the spelling in MMT, noting all rules and exceptions. The variety of orthographic practices among the manuscripts of the Mishna and of other Tannaitic writings, witnesses all late in date, precludes us from comparing the orthographic practices of MMT with those of MH. Some early witnesses to MH—for instance, the Bar-Kokhba letters and various funerary and other inscriptions—have not been thoroughly studied, and can only occasionally be drawn on for comparison.

It should be noted, furthermore, that orthographic practices characterise individual scribes, or schools of scribes, or periods, but not necessarily dialects. Two scribes, the one accustomed to writing biblical manuscripts, and the other to writing semiformal documents, will produce orthographically different copies of a work such as MMT, even if they are copying from the same original manuscript.

3.1.1 The *Waw* as Vowel Marker

In the Bible, *waw* usually represents only long vowels and even those not consistently. In many Qumran scrolls *waw* almost always represents all *o/u* vowels, whether short or long (*HDSS*, § 100.2). In this respect, the spelling in MMT is generally identical with that of other Qumran scrolls.

Here are some examples from MMT of the use of *waw* as a vowel-marker (they are arranged according to the historical length of the vowel, as deduced from the concordant evidence of the Tiberian traditions and of comparative Semitics): קודש (B 76); מהקו[ד]שים (B 71); מכול (B 33); חוק (B 52); קודש (B 76); מושה (C 17); הכוהנ[י]ם (B 12); אהרון (B 79). The only exceptions are: מאת (A 20); קרבן[ן] (A v); מכל (B 50, 61); בכל (C 15, 28); אהרן (B 17); הכהנים (B 80); הקדש (B 60; the reading is not certain);

---

[1] For a treatment of the corresponding features of QH, see *HDSS* and Qimron, *Gram.*

והתבנן (C 23); וקדמניות (C 12); and perhaps עונות (C 25 see *HDSS*, § 200.17e), במצאך (in manuscripts e and f, C 30),[2] and זו[ב]חם (B 11). On לא (B 52), see § 3.1.4.3.

3.1.1.1 *Waw* as Vowel Marker Where Other Traditions of Hebrew Attest No *o* Vowel

In the word הזונות (B 75 in Ms^c = הזנות in Ms^d), a *waw* is written where in the Tiberian tradition we find a *shewa* (הַזְּנוּת). This may well indicate an original short *u*. What its length was in the QH tradition is a question of debate; it may represent either a full or a reduced vowel (cf. מהקו[ד]שים B 71 and *HDSS*, § 100.21). For another solution, see M. Bar-Asher, 'A Preliminary Study of Mishnaic Hebrew as Reflected in Codex Vatican 32 of *Sipre*-Bamidbar', *Teʿuda* 3 (1983), p. 156.

3.1.1.2 Illusory Cases of Defective Spelling

The words טמאה and טהרה are written in what looks like a defective form in MMT (e.g., in B 67, 68): the former is always written so in the other Qumran scrolls as well, and the latter almost always so. These can scarcely be consistently defective spellings of *u/o*, but must rather reflect different traditions of pronunciation; the form טמאה being pronounced as טְמָאָה (as in the Babylonian tradition of MH), and טהרה as טַהֲרָה (as in MH; contrast the biblical טָהֳרָה). It is also possible that the word ערמה (C 29), which is always written defectively in the Qumran manuscripts (eight times in Kuhn's concordance, and eight times in the 4Q concordance), may not have been pronounced as it was in BH, i.e., with an *u/o* vowel (see below § 3.5.2.10 on the word טהר [= טָהֵר?] as a possible alternate for טהור, and Qimron, *Gram.*, § 100.21; for ו = יו see § 3.2.2.1).

3.1.2 The *Yod* as Vowel Marker

In the MT, *yod*, when a vowel-marker for *i*, represents only the long vowel *i*, and even that not consistently. In the Qumran Scrolls, the *yod*, when a vowel marker, normally represents the long vowel *i*, and only very exceptionally the short one (*HDSS*, § 100.32). The same is true for MMT; contrast, e.g., טהורים (B 15), השמיני (B 72) and דויד (C 18) with מקצת (B 1), שבטי (B 61) and וכבס (B 66). There is thus no evidence of the short *i* being represented by *yod*, as it frequently is in later Hebrew. The only example of a defective spelling for long *i* is בעשרם (A iv). Concerning the apparently defective spelling in גוים (B 5), see below § 3.2.3. When it represents *e* (< *ay*) inside the word, the *yod* is, historically speaking, a consonant, not a vowel-marker, and is only rarely dropped in the MT. Phonetic rather than historical orthography produces many cases of defective spelling of this vowel in Qumran scrolls other than MMT (*HDSS*, § 100.33). In MMT, however, defective spelling of this vowel does not occur, even in those manuscripts which show some vulgar phonetic traits; cf. אין (B 71), זבחיהם (B 7), עליהם (B 59), אליכה (C 10), אליך (C 26), דברינו (B 1).

In the Qumran manuscripts, *yod*—both medial and final—represents the resolved dipthong *e* < *ay*. When final, it occurs not only in the plural construct (דברי, etc.), as in BH, but sometimes also in singular construct nouns from *lamed-yod* roots, e.g., מעשי (instead of BH's מעשה; see *HDSS*, § 100.34). This spelling also occurs once in MMT, in למחני הקודש (B 58; contrast מחנה הקדש in B 60). It should be noted that *yod* is used here for the *e* (*ṣere*) of the construct, and not for the *e* of the

---

[2] Both witnesses to C 30 attest the spelling במצאך. If this represents the biblical בְּמָצְאֲךָ* (cf. בְּמָצַאֲכֶם Gen 32:20), the defective spelling in both witnesses would be abnormal, though not impossible. It is perhaps worth envisioning the possibility that an *a* by-form of the biblical *o*-infinitive developed in this word, perhaps to bring it into concord with the *a*-form of the imperfect: יִמְצָא. For the possibility of *a*-infinitives, cf. in BH שכב, שפל, and especially מחאז Ezek 25:6 (another *lamed-ʾalep* verb). MH knows many infinitive *qal* forms of the type לִקְטַל (see N. Berggrün, 'Studies in Mishnaic Hebrew', *Leshonenu* 18 [1953], pp. 82–88 and Haneman, §§ 31.256–31.258). Their suffixed forms, however, have the *o* vowel, e.g. לזורעה (Haneman, §§ 31.26–32.133). For such infinitive forms in some *piyyuṭim*, see J. Yahalom, 'The Palestinian Vocalization in Hedwata's Qeduštot', *Leshonenu* 34 (1970), pp. 45–46 (citing also βααφζι of the Hexapla).

absolute (*segol*). The same is true of other Qumran manuscripts: the phonetic spelling of *e* with *yod* rather than *he* in *lamed-yod* nouns occurs almost exclusively in the construct, and not in the absolute (*HDSS*, § 100.34).

3.1.3 *He* as Marker of the Final Vowels *a* and *e*

In BH, when *he* is a mater lectionis and not a consonant, it consistently denotes the final vowels *a* and *e*. An alternative spelling in which *ʾalep* represents these vowels occurs only when a glottal stop was once the final consonant of the root. In the MT a spelling without *he* is usual only for the forms of the perfect with second person afformative and for those pronominal suffixes of the second and third persons singular and plural that end with the vowel *a* (e.g., מלכיה, מלכך, שמרת); in the Qumran manuscripts, in contrast, the plene spelling with a *he* is usual in these categories (e.g., ספרכה, שמרתה; *HDSS*, § 100.7). In MMT, the afformatives of the perfect are written plene, e.g. ושבתה (C 15), והשיבות]ה (C 15); the pronominal suffixes, however, are usually defective, as in MT לבבך (C 15), עליך (C 14), ממך (C 29), etc., although the plene spelling is also found, e.g. אליכה (C 10).[3]

The predominantly defective spelling of this pronominal suffix in the manuscripts of MMT might be taken to reflect a pronunciation without the final vowel, as in Aramaic and, in certain phonological environments, also in MH.[4] The fact that MS[d] uses the full spelling argues against this. It does not, however, rule it out completely, since at Qumran there clearly existed two pronunciations of the pronouns and pronominal suffixes, e.g., *-kemma* and *-kem*, *hemma* and *hem* (cf. *HDSS*, § 322.2). But there is also other evidence against the theory that the defective spelling reflects a pronunciation without the final vowel, and this is that the defective spelling, though unusual at Qumran, is nevertheless used consistently in a few manuscripts, e.g., 1QH[a] (but only in cols. 13–17 written in hand a) and 1Q34. This suggests that the phenomenon reflects a scribal convention rather than a morphological or phonological development.

3.1.3.1 *He* Replacing Radical *ʾAlep* as Vowel Marker for *e*

He indicating final *e* (< *i*; instead of the historically correct *ʾalep*) occurs only once, and that in the non-formal MS[a] in הטמה (B 16); cf. 1QIsa[a] 6:5, 35:9, 52:11. Such spellings occur in other Hebrew sources (*HDSS*, § 100.7).

3.1.3.2 *He* as Marker for Final *o*

In BH *he* occasionally represents final *o*, e.g. כה, שלמה. In pre-exilic times *he* was the standard mater lectionis for final *o*, as we see from the inscriptions; in the Qumran scrolls such a *he* may be preceded by a second mater lectionis, an additional *waw* (*he* no longer being freely used as a mater lectionis for *o*).[5] Most attestations are of the words פוה and כוה, both of which are frequent in biblical manuscripts from Qumran (*HDSS*, §§ 100.51–100.52). In MMT only one example with the extra *waw* occurs, שלומה (C 18); cf. the purely phonetic שלומו in the Copper Scroll (3Q15 v 6, 8–9).

---

[3] The manuscripts of MMT differ from each other in this matter; for example, where MS[e] has לבבך (C 22), MS[d] has לבבכה; each manuscript tends to be consistent, however, in its own practice (see in chap. 1).

[4] For the pronunciation of these suffixes in the various Hebrew phases and traditions, see Ben-Ḥayyim, *Traditions*, pp. 22–39. Note that some phases of Hebrew (e.g., Samaritan) show a similar coexistence of pronominal forms in *-ak* and verbal afformatives in *-ta*.

[5] Only rarely do we find occurances of *he* representing final *o*; most of these are in 4QD[a] (see S. Talmon and I. Knohl, 'A Calendrical Scroll from Qumran Cave IV - Miš Ba (4Q321)', *Tarbiz* 60 [1991], p. 520, n. 34).

3.1.4 ʾAlep

3.1.4.1 ʾAlep in Conservative (Historical) Spellings

In the consonantal text of the Bible, ʾalep is not added to serve as a vowel-marker; in almost all cases where ʾalep designates a vowel, it is a quiescent radical. Quiescent ʾalep is written consistently; there are only very occasional cases of the omission of a radical ʾalep in a position in which it has become quiescent (e.g., רשית for ראשית). In the Qumran manuscripts such omissions of a quiescent ʾalep are more common (*HDSS*, § 100.61).

In MMT, etymological ʾalep is still written, even though it was no longer pronounced: חטאת (B 13, 15, 70; *ā < aʾ*); כראשית (B 63; *e < iʾ*), ראש (B 61; *ō < ā < aʾ*); but להבי (B 58), הטמה (B 16). On ה]נושה, see § 1.6.3.1. Mixed historico-phonetical spellings, such as ראוש or רואש, which are common in other Qumran manuscripts, are not found in MMT; this may, however, be merely a matter of chance, there being so few words of this type in the work. On the other hand, one does find total omission of quiescent ʾalep in the purely phonetic spelling והצון (B 64).[6]

3.1.4.2 Non-radical ʾAlep as a Vowel Marker for *a* in Final Position

ʾAlep in final position is written only when radical, as in תביא, בוא, לבוא, נושא. In MSᵉ, non-radical ʾalep is occasionally found in final position to mark the final vowel (five cases against many of the normal Hebrew *he*): וה]קללא (C 15) and היא (for היה C 13, 24, 25, 26) also ושלושא, in Msᵃ (iv 6). This spelling may reflect the orthography used in Palestine during the post-exilic period (perhaps under the influence of Aramaic). It is the convention still followed in the Copper Scroll (forty examples of א-, versus eight of ה-), and is found, though rarely, in 1QIsaᵃ and other Qumran manuscripts and also in the Bar-Kokhba letters (cf. *HDSS*, § 100.7).

3.1.4.3 לוא, a Combination of Historical and Phonetic Spelling

In the word לא a *waw* is usually added before the ʾalep in MMT, as is usual in the other Qumran scrolls (*HDSS*, § 100.51); so לוא in B 52, B 53, etc., but once ולא (B 52). The origin of this spelling may lie in the desire to indicate that the vowel after *lamed* was *o* (which the now-silent ʾalep would scarcely suggest); it is also consistent with the orthographic conventions of those scrolls where most *u/o* vowels were marked by a *waw*.[7] The frequent occurrence of לוא suggests that it is only by chance that similar combined spellings, such as רואש, צואן, etc. (with *waw* as mater lectionis for *o* added to the historic ʾalep), have not been found in MMT.

3.1.4.4 -ש and שא

A distinct phenomenon is the use of ʾalep in the spelling of the relative -ש (vocalised as שְ, שַ, or שֶ). This word is regularly prefixed to the following one[8] in MMT, i.e., it has the same spelling as is known elsewhere: e.g., -ש as in שהם (B 1), שלוא (B 52). Less frequently one finds שא, either written as a separate word (e.g., B 2, 9, 16) or joined to the next word (B 37).

Other spellings of -ש with the addition of a vowel letter are known: in BH we find -שה in שהשמם (Lam 5:18), שהתקיף (Qoh 6:10), כשהסכל (Qoh 10:3), and in the Copper Scroll -שי in שיבצפון, שיבית, שיבית; but the spelling שא was not previously known from Second Temple sources. In rabbinic manuscripts, and particularly in some Geniza fragments of a *Yelamdenu*-type midraš three spellings (שא, שה, שי)

---

[6] For the development of these spellings and other parallel ones, see Kutscher, *Isaiah*, pp. 20, 163–165, 171.

[7] In Kutscher's opinion, the *waw* served especially to prevent a pronunciation under the influence of Aramaic, cf. idem, *Isaiah*, pp. 171–174.

[8] In Hebrew orthography a word of one letter is never written separately.

can be found.[9] שה is also found in inscriptions at Dabbura and Bet Shearim from the second to fourth centuries (e.g., שהלרבי).[10]

3.1.4.5 כי

We do not find an *'alep* added at the end of the word כי in MMT (see B 53, 57, 59, etc.), though in many of the Qumran manuscripts the spelling כיא is frequent, and in some (1QM, 1QS) even regular (Qimron, *Gram.*, § 100.51).

3.1.5 Representation of *w* and *y*

Consonantal *yod* is written with one *yod*, and consonantal *waw* with one *waw*, e.g., דויד (C 18), היה (C 24). This is a convention common to both BH and QH; in MH, consonantal *waw* and *yod* are frequently doubled in writing (*HDSS*, §§ 100.51–100.9).

3.1.6 ש or ס—The Graphic Representation of Historical *ś*

The phoneme *ś* is occasionally represented by a *samek*: e.g., הנעסה (B 75), מסיא[י]ם (B 13), והסורף (B 14). These instances doubtless reflect the sound change *ś* > *s*. The BH spelling with ש is, however, more common: לעשות (B 44), ולעשותם (B 44), מעשי (C 27), [ה]מעשים (B 2), משיאים (B 27), ומעשר (B 63), [ה]נושה (see C 7), שנואה (C 7), ישראל (B 62, 63), ושור[פים (B 32), [ו]הבשר (B 59), [ו]הבשר (B 11), והבשר (B 54), § 1.6.3.1), עשר, עשרים (seven times in A i–v).

The spelling with ס for ש is very infrequent both in BH and in Hebrew manuscripts from Qumran, but is the rule in the Copper Scroll; it is often found in the Bar-Kokhba letters, and not infrequently in MH texts. It is also frequent in Qumran Aramaic manuscripts, being found in most of the manuscripts of Enoch, and in 11QtgJob (*HDSS*, § 100.8). The contrary spelling change (ס > ש) is not attested in MMT; it exists, though it is rare, in QH, is infrequent in MH, but is fairly common in the Bar-Kokhba letters (*HDSS*, § 200.15).

3.2 Phonology

In a short unvocalized text such as MMT one cannot expect very much evidence for pronunciation, and indeed MMT provides only isolated pieces of evidence for peculiarities of pronunciation. We shall attempt to describe and explain these peculiarities of pronunciation (often attested by special spellings) by a comparison with evidence from other Qumran manuscripts and from other traditions of Hebrew.

3.2.1 Non-Pronunciation, or Weakening, of the Gutturals

In the Qumran Hebrew manuscripts, especially in those written in non-formal hands, there are a number of spelling irregularities involving gutturals. Gutturals may, for instance, be omitted or misplaced, or one guttural may be miswritten for another. We can infer from this that in the pronunciation of Qumran, gutturals were 'weakened',[11] i.e., often so little pronounced as to be imperceptible. It is surprising that MMT shows little clear evidence of this phenomenon. In one non-formal manuscript (MS[a]), in the calendaric section, we find one clear example of this newly developed weakening of the gutturals: בשש אשר (A iv) for בשׁשה עשר. It must have been pronounced *bešišša asar* and then, by crasis, *bešiššasar*; the form in 4Q402 1 i 30, בשש עשר לחודש, was doubtless pronounced in exactly the same way; cf. also אֹסר (4QEn[a] iii 10); שבעשרה (Copper Scroll 1:4).[12]

---

[9] Cf. Epstein, pp. 1235, 1252.

[10] J. Naveh, *On Stone and Mosaic*, Jerusalem, 1978, pp. 25–26.

[11] Kutscher, *Isaiah*, pp. 505–511; *HDSS*, § 200.11.

[12] Cf. also 2:8.

Again, the form שבאו 'which came' (C 18, 19 and 20) in MS[e] (another manuscript written in a non-formal hand) perhaps indicates that the *'alep* was not pronounced between vowels, and survived in writing probably due to tradition, but in pronunciation was replaced by the glide, indicated by *waw*, באו 'came' = ba^wu ($< bau < ba'u$). Cf. also בו 'they came' 4Q141 (= Phyl. N) 12, יבאו 4QD[a] and תהוו 'emptiness' = to^wu 4Q504 1–2 iii 3. In MT we occasionally find a *dagesh* in the *'alep* in forms like this one (e.g., רָאוּ Job 33:21).[13] The purpose of this *dagesh* was probably to ensure the distinct pronunciation of the *'alep* in order to prevent pronunciations like ru^wu, ba^wu (cf. HDSS, § 200.133 and Qimron, *Diphthongs*, pp. 270–271).

On the loss of *'alep* in הטמה (B 16) and צון (B 64), see § 3.1.4.1.

3.2.2 Contraction of Descending Diphthongs

3.2.2.1 $-aw > -\bar{o}$ in Final Position

In the third person singular masculine pronominal suffix, when attached to plural endings, we find (in the vulgar manuscripts a and e) the spelling ו- instead of יו-: אלו (C 15), מלפנו (C 28), לפנו (C 31), עללו (A 19).

Such spellings of ו- where יו- is expected are quite frequent in the Qumran manuscripts, there being over thirty cases in the published texts;[14] there are also reverse instances with יו- instead of the expected ו- in the third person masculine singular suffix of singular nouns, e.g., ברואשיו 'on his head' 1QIsa[a] 59:17.

Such instances of the interchanges between the spellings יו- and ו- lead H. Yalon and Z. Ben-Hayyim to infer that the diphthong *aw* in the suffix יו- was contracted, and that ו- and יו- were pronounced alike, as in the Samaritan oral tradition.[15]

3.2.2.2 The Suffix with *Lamed-Yod* Nouns, e.g., שדו > שדהו

A similar phenomenon must be reflected in the form שדו (B 78; $<$ שדהו $< *\acute{s}adayhu$); cf. שדו in 4QPhyl. L 9 (= שדהו, Deut 5:18). The *he* of the suffix was omitted between the two vowels, just as it was when this same suffix was added to masculine plural nouns or to prepositions (מלכיו אליו; from *'*ilayhu* and *malakayhu*). Such an omission of *he* also takes place, rarely in BH and more frequently in QH, when a suffix is added to a singular noun from a *lamed-yod* root, e.g., מראיו (= מראהו) in the MT (Job 41:1) and in the Qumran manuscripts יבול עליו (= יבול עלהו; 1QH[a] 8:26; cf. HDSS, § 322.141). Cf. also רעו (4QS[e] 1 iii 18 = רעהו 1QS 9:19). The diphthong that evolved after the omission of the *he* was contracted in QH to *o* (§ 3.2.2.1). The form שדו is of great importance, for it is a phonetic spelling which exactly reflects the pronunciation of this type of word at Qumran.

3.2.2.3 Contraction of the Diphthong *-uy*

It was not only the diphthong *aw* in final position that underwent contraction, but also the diphthong *uy*, as can be seen from the spelling ראו (B 12 in MS[a] as against ראוי in MS[b]) . Contraction of the diphthong *uy* to *o* is known to us with certainty only from the Samaritan pronunciation where we find, for instance, גלוי pronounced *galo*. Twice in MT we find $uy > u$: העשו (Job 41:25) and צפו

---

[13] See I. Yeivin, 'The Dageshed Alephs in the Bible', *Studies in Bible and the Ancient Near East Presented to Samuel E. Loewenstamm*, Jerusalem, 1978, pp. 223–226.

[14] From among the unpublished texts, note 4QD[e] in which the spelling ו- for יו- occurs five times while יו- never occurs.

[15] In the Samaritan oral tradition, *debaro* (< *debaraw**) = 'his words', and *debaru* = 'his word'. The spellings יו- and ו- therefore occur interchangeably in Samaritan manuscripts, as they do in Qumran. So Yalon, *Scrolls*, pp. 61–62; Ben-Hayyim, *Traditions*, pp. 79–82; Kutscher, *Isaiah*, pp. 443, 447; HDSS, §§ 200.18, 322.141.

(*Ketib*, Job 15:22). Note also the spelling פניו (= פנוי 'empty') in a letter of Bar-Kokhba (*DJD* II, p. 162). Spellings such as that shown in our form are occasionally found in other Qumran texts: וגלו (= וגלוי; 4Q175 11) and לבליו (1QIsaᵃ 44:17; pronounced *liblo*) as well as the regular בלוי עץ (1QIsaᵃ 44:19; contrast MT's בול; cf. *HDSS*, § 200.18).

3.2.2.4 Resolution of the Diphthong *uy* into Two Vowels with Glide

Together with the form ראו, which attests to the contraction of the diphthong *uy* (§ 3.2.2.3), one finds the form ראואי (B 17, 26), in which the break-up of the diphthong into two vowels (= *ra'ui*) appears. Between the two consecutive vowels a glide has been produced (= *ra'ʷi*), and the *'alep* is merely its graphic marker.[16] This form has parallels in the Samaritan oral tradition, e.g., רצוי pronounced *raṣuwwi*, עשוי pronounced *'asuwwi*, and perhaps also in MH, e.g., כָּרָאוּיִי (*m. Ohalot* 1:10, Kaufman MS; cf. the same form recorded in Babylonian vocalisation as רָאוּ֗י); note also the spellings צפואי (= *ṣabbuwwi*) in a Samaritan manuscript at Exod 38:17, 19 (= MT's צפוי) and נואי = *noʷi* in MH. The correspondence with the Samaritan oral tradition is particularly instructive, for there, too, the diphthong *uy* can be pronounced in two different ways, as *o* or as *uwwi*. The comprehensive explanation offered here is preferable to the possibility that the form ראואי is a backformation from ראואים* (for which see below § 3.2.3). It is, however, surprising that MMT, unlike the Samaritan tradition, has both contraction and resolution of *uy* in the same word and in the same manuscript.

3.2.3 Orthography and Pronunciation of גויים

The spelling גויים (B 8) is not simply a defective one. The forms of this word that occur in the non-biblical scrolls from Qumran are as follows: גואים (thirty-one times), גואי (twice), גוים (sixty-five times), גוי (= גויי; six times), גויים (sixteen times), גויי (once). It would seem that neither *yod* nor *'alep* was pronounced here. These spellings are, in fact, merely devices to represent the two consecutive vowels resulting from the assimilation of the consonantal *yod* to the following vowel (*goyim* > *goim*): in many cases of defective spelling of this word as גוי/גוים the *waw* marks *o*, *yod* marks *e* or *i*, and nothing marks the consonant which has been reduced to a glide between the two consecutive vowels; in the spellings with *'alep*, the purpose of this letter is to mark that glide. Thus we find the sequence of forms *goyim* (גויים) > *go-im* (גוים) > *goʸim* (= גואים!), and similarly with the spellings of the construct.[17]

3.2.4 Pronunciation of זונות

For the form זונות (B 75), which perhaps reflects an original short *u* in the initial vowel (cf. BH's זנות), see § 3.1.1.1.

3.2.5 The Shift *š* > *s*

For the probable shift *š* > *s*, see § 3.1.6.

3.2.6 Assimilation of the *Nun* of מן

A phenomenon that can be viewed as morphophonological is the assimilation of the *nun* of מן to the article. In ancient Hebrew sources the *nun* of מן was usually assimilated to the following consonant

---

[16] For the interpretation of such parallels see, for instance, Ben-Ḥayyim in *Henoch Yalon Jubilee Volume*, Jerusalem, 1963, pp. 158–9; M. Bar-Asher, *The Tradition of Mishnaic Hebrew in the Communities of Italy*, Jerusalem, 1980, pp. 43–44; Qimron, *HDSS*, § 200.18; *Diphthongs*, pp. 259–278.

[17] Cf. *HDSS*, § 200.17 and Qimron, *Diphthongs*.

(even if it was a guttural);[18] generally, however, it was not assimilated to the article.[19] In MMT, in contrast, the *nun* of מן is always assimilated to the article:[20] מהמקדש (B 49), מהקו]ד[שים (B 71), מהד]ר[ך (C 12). Such consistency of usage is known to us in BH only in the description of the Temple in Ezek 40:1–43:17, where the form occurs fourteen times.

3.2.7 Elision of *Nun* in Final Position

In B 31–32 דשא המזבח is written for דשן המזבה. This misspelling resulted from a phonological phenomenon: elision or addition of final *nun* is frequent in Hebrew and Aramaic sources from the Second Temple period onward. Z. Ben-Ḥayyim explains it as resulting from the fact that final vowels became nasalized.[21] It therefore happened that, on the one hand, a *nun* or *mem* was sometimes erroneously added to indicate the nasalization, and, on the other hand, an original *nun* or *mem* was dropped orthographically (for evidence and bibliography, see *HDSS*, § 200.143).

In view of the existence of the phenomenon in MMT, we can explain the form ונעלה (ממנו) (B 69) as ונעלם (see commentary). Here the sequence of *mems* may also account for the elision of one *mem*.[22] The opposite phenomenon may be attested in the form כתב]נ[נום (C 10 MS[e] versus כתבנו in MS[d]); the text of these two manuscripts, however, differs here and the additional *mem* could be taken as a suffix (see commentary).

3.3 Morphology

The following discussion by no means constitutes a full description of all forms found in MMT; forms which are common to all the phases of Hebrew under discussion (BH, QH and MH) are not listed, as they cannot help us locate the language of MMT.

3.3.1 Pronouns

3.3.1.1 Personal Pronouns

3.3.1.1.1 Third Person Singular

In the third person we find not only the regular BH forms הוא (masculine; B 63, 64) and היא (feminine; B 30, 32, 60, 61)—pronounced *hū, hī*—but also the forms with final *he* that are found exclusively in QH: הואה (masculine; B 70) and היאה (feminine; B 60, B 61 MS[d]).[23]

These bisyllabic forms might seem at first glance to have been pronounced *hūʾa, hīʾa*. Since the gutturals were pronounced weakly in QH, however, the pronunciation *hūa, hīa* is more probable, in

---

[18] There are in BH, especially in the later books, some cases of unassimilated *nun* (though not before the article). This feature becomes more common in QH, and very common in the Bar-Kokhba documents (see Kutscher, *Isaiah*, p. 214; Qimron, *Gram.*, § 200.161; Polzin, p. 66).

[19] מן ה- occurs about 700 times in BH as against about a hundred occurrences of מה- (A. Sperber, *Hebrew Grammar—A New Approach*, New York, 1943, pp. 140–143). In QH we have noted six instances of מה-, all of them in 11QT[a] (31:11–12 [four times]; 49:21; 66:5). In MH it is very rare, and at Murabbaʿat we find it once in מהמערב (Mur 30).

[20] In MMT there are, of course, numerous cases of assimilated *nun*, e.g., מכול, and once even] ומן ע[.

[21] M. Bar-Asher has recently demonstrated (in a lecture) that Ben-Ḥayyim's explanation is inconsistent with the accentuation tradition of MH (compare למֹעלה vs. למעלָן).

[22] In reliable manuscripts of MH one finds the opposition למעלה מן vs. למעלן (see the article cited in the commentary).

[23] For the pronunciation and origin of these pronouns, see S. Morag, 'The Pronouns of the Third Person Singular in the Dead Sea Scrolls', *Eretz-Israel* 3 (1954), pp. 166–169; Kutscher, *Isaiah*, pp. 431–440. On the possibility that the ending is a real survival of the proto-Semitic anceps final vowel, see not only Arabic (cf. Old South Arabic), but also Ugaritic (though of course in both these languages, unlike Hebrew, final short vowels survive).

which case a glide may have come into being,[24] with *hūa / hīa* becoming *hūʷa / hīʸa*, the glide being graphically represented by *ʾalep*. הוה (1QIsaᵃ 7:14) and היה (ibid. 30:33, 36:21) are apparently alternative attempts to represent these same forms (*HDSS*, § 321.13).

3.3.1.1.2 First Person Plural

The 'BH' form אנחנו (first person plural; B 29, 36, 37, 42, 55, 64, 73, C 9, 20, 26) is unexpected in this document, since the MH form אנו predominates in the other Qumran texts. The tendency of the Qumran texts to safeguard against vernacular features[25] is rarely evident in MMT, especially in its halakhic parts; we therefore tend to think that אנחנו was a spoken form in MMT's dialect (see § 3.7.2). We have no evidence for a stylistic distinction between אנחנו and אנו, such as exists in the case of אנכי and אני (*HDSS*, § 321.11).

3.3.1.1.3 Second Person Plural

In the second person masculine plural we find both אתם (B 68, 80, C 7, 8) and אתמה (B 80 MSᵈ; with final vowel). The form with a final vowel is characteristic both of written Qumran Hebrew and of Samaritan Hebrew. Many pronouns and pronominal suffixes in Qumran Hebrew have two forms, one with final *he* and one without (*HDSS*, § 322.2).[26]

3.3.1.1.4 Third Person Plural

In the third person plural there are two forms, one with a final vowel and one without: הם (B 1, 6, 39, 55, 58, C 24) and המה (B 54, 75, 79). A feminine הנה is found in BH, but is absent from MH, which used a single monosyllabic form of common gender, הן (occasionally written הם). In MMT the feminine is also written הם (in B 55), a form identical to the masculine. This feature of common gender is characteristic of LBH and QH (*HDSS*, § 321.16; cf. § 3.3.1.2.1, and see how המון is used also as a feminine in biblical Aramaic, Dan 2:34). It is no doubt only by chance that we find no case in MMT of המה as an alternative form of the feminine.

3.3.1.2 Pronominal Suffixes

3.3.1.2.1 Third Person Common Plural

As in the other scrolls, there are two forms: one with a final vowel, (ה)מה- (found once in MT, Ezek 40:16: אליהמה), and one without, (ה)ם-. These forms are used in MMT as suffixes for both third plural masculine (טמאתם [B 67], במעשיהמה [C 23]) and third plural feminine (בהם [B 55], אינם [B 56], עליהם [B 59], מהמה [B 57]).[27] The forms with final vowel are known also from the Samaritan oral tradition.[28]

The use of the third person masculine plural pronominal suffix as both masculine and feminine is the rule in the later books of the Bible, in QH (cf. § 3.3.1.1.4) and indeed in MH. In some Official Aramaic dialects the forms of the third person feminine plural (in pronoun, pronominal suffix and verb) were identical with those of the masculine. This feature, then, is characteristic of Aramaic, LBH, MH and QH. Qumran Aramaic does in fact distinguish generally, but not always, between the

---

[24] *HDSS*, § 200.133.

[25] This is exemplified by the mechanical substitution of אשר for -ש in some phrases.

[26] On the origin of the long forms, see Kutscher, *Isaiah*, pp. 433–451.

[27] See Qimron, *TSG*, pp. 87–90.

[28] Ben-Ḥayyim, *SHG*, pp. 175–176.

masculine, e.g., ‫הון‬-, and the feminine, e.g. ‫הן‬-;[29] it is therefore unlikely that the QH phenomenon can be ascribed to Aramaic influence (*HDSS*, § 322.18).

3.3.1.2.2 Suffixes of other Persons

On the second person masculine singular pronominal suffix, see § 3.1.3, and on that of the third person masculine singular attached to a noun in the plural, see §§ 3.2.2.1–2.

3.3.1.3 Demonstrative Pronoun

The plural demonstrative pronoun is ‫אלה‬ (B 1, 15, C 5, 8 [twice], 14, 28); this is the form current in BH and in QH. The MH form ‫אלו‬ may already have occurred twice in Ben-Sira (51:24) alongside ‫אלה‬.[30] It is possible that the BH form ‫אלה‬ survived also in some dialects of MH, since it occurs in the contracts from the time of Bar-Kokhba;[31] its few occurrences in Tannaitic literature need to be the subject of further research.

Note the use of the demonstrative pronoun with the definite article in ‫בדבר הזה‬ (B 12), ‫בדברים האלה‬ (C 8), and especially ‫]כו[ל הדבר]ים[האלה‬ (C 14). This construction is characteristic of BH and QH, while MH uses both ‫הדבר הזה‬ and ‫דבר זה‬.

3.3.1.4 Relative Pronouns

In MMT, as in MH, the relative pronoun is ‫ש‬- (e.g., B 1, 2, 6, 10, 11, 12 ff.; on its spelling see § 3.1.4.4). The BH form ‫אשר‬ occurs only once, in the phrase ‫המקום אשר]בחר[‬ (B 32–33); contrast in the same manuscript ‫המקום שבחר בו‬ (B 60–61). Is this usage to be explained by the influence of the biblical phrase on the original author or on one of the copyists?

The relative pronoun ‫ש‬- is rarely found in the Bible, and then almost exclusively in the later books. In the earlier books it occurs only a few times, in texts from the northern part of the country, and probably reflects the local dialect.[32]

In QH ‫אשר‬ predominates but, as in LBH, it is in some cases quite probable that ‫אשר‬ is a mechanical substitution for ‫ש‬- in a phrase where, in speech, MH's ‫ש‬- would more naturally have been used.[33] It seems that the QH writers contemporaneous with MMT preferred to use BH's ‫אשר‬, perhaps regarding ‫ש‬- as a vulgarism; cf. § 3.5.2.30.

The predominance of ‫ש‬- is what gives MMT its MH appearance. A closer examination reveals, however, that the use of ‫ש‬- in MMT differs from its use in MH. In MH ‫ש‬- functions as both BH's ‫אשר‬ and BH's ‫כי‬ initiating an object or causal clause. In MMT it functions as ‫אשר‬ and as ‫כי‬ initiating an object clause, but it does not replace ‫כי‬ initiating a causal clause.[34] Since the very existence of ‫ש‬- in

---

[29] For discussion and bibliography see M. Sokoloff, *The Targum to Job from Qumran Cave XI*, Ramat-Gan, 1974, pp. 19–20. It is more probable, however, that the forms in the 11QtgJob (4:9, 31:1, 32:2), which the editors read as examples of orthographically abnormal ‫הין‬-, should be read instead as ‫הון‬- (= masculine used for the feminine; cf. also ‫בינה)ו(ן‬ in 11QtgJob 41:8). Note also the epicene ‫להון‬ (referring to the feminine ‫עיניה‬) in 1QapGen 20:3.

[30] But this is quite uncertain, for the form is found only in one of the mediaeval manuscripts, B, which unfortunately tends to modernize Ben-Sira's language; see also E. Qimron, 'Three Notes on the Text of the Temple Scroll', *Tarbiz* 51 (1982), pp. 136–137.

[31] Murabbaʿat 24 C 16, D 13; but, in a letter from the same site (No 45 l. 7), we find also ‫אלו‬ (which is attested also in the Beth Sheʿarim inscriptions). The form ‫האל>ל<ה‬ that is said to occur on an ostracon from Masada (Yadin and Naveh, *Masada I*, p. 35) is the result of a misreading. Ada Yardeni suggested the reading ‫מאה‬ in a personal communication.

[32] See Ben-Yehuda, s.v.; E. Qimron, 'On the Second Temple Period Hebrew in the Book of Psalms', *Beth Mikra* 73 (1978), pp. 140–141.

[33] C. Rabin, p. 148.

[34] B 16, 28, 53, 57, 59, 61; C 9. The only exception is C 27 (‫שראינו‬). B 58 (‫שהם אוכלים‬) may still be interpreted as a relative clause. ‫שמי מהם‬ (C 23) has a retrospective pronoun which is typical of a relative clause. This disproves G. Brin's view that ‫כי‬ was not in use in the living language of the author of the Temple Scroll (pp. 214–217).

MMT is in contrast with the literary standard of the period, it cannot be assumed that the way it is used in MMT reflects only some, but not all, of the ways it was used in the spoken dialect underlying the document. Why should its author prefer the biblical כי in causal clauses if -ש had replaced it in his spoken language? There is no reason to doubt that the use of -ש in MMT reflects the spoken language underlying this document. The divergence from MH implies that this dialect differed from MH as we know it from the literary sources.[35]

3.3.2 The Noun and its Endings

3.3.2.1 *He* as an Otiose Termination

In CBH the use of the afformative -ה in words denoting place, as in החוצה, שמה, expresses direction (or has some other adverbial function).[36] This -ה is found in MH only in the phrases לארץ חוצה and חוצה לה, where the -ה does not express direction. Nor is it used adverbially unless a preposition is added, as in ואין מוציאין לחוצה לארץ (*m. Šeb.* 6:6), contrast מי שיצא חוץ לתחום (*m. ʿErub.* 4:11).[37]

In MMT we find the phrase וחוצה למחנה (B 30), which is substantival (= 'the outside of the camp'), as is חוצה לארץ in MH. In the other scrolls the -ה occurs frequently in certain words denoting place. This -ה does not, however, express direction. The employment of this -ה is facultative.[38]

The subject demands a historical study. Yet it is clear that the use of this -ה in QH differs from its use in CBH and in MH. In some cases the use of this -ה in QH is similar to its use in LBH, but in others it is not. Thus in the scrolls one finds the form סביבה, while in LBH only סביב is to be found. The word סביבה can never express direction, so the original function of the -ה here (as in other such words) is unknown. We also note that in QH this -ה is especially frequent in nominal constructions such as סביבה ל-, חוצה ל-, which are similar in form and usage to חוצה לארץ in MH.[39] This implies that the -ה represents a new feature and cannot be viewed as a modification in function of the BH *he* of direction.

3.3.2.2 The Plural Ending

The masculine plural ending in MMT is -ים, as in BH and QH[40], e.g., [ה]מעשים (B 2), הגוים (B 8), באים (B 39). By contrast, in MH we find both -ים and -ין. The new form in MH resulted from the fact that *mem* and *nun* in final position became identical in pronunciation. This phenomenon is already found in QH; the scribes, however, preferred the traditional orthography (*HDSS*, § 200.142).

3.3.3 The Verb (Including Infinitive and Participle)

Unfortunately we have no evidence at all for some important parts of the verbal paradigm. No forms occur of the imperfect with afformatives, of the imperfect with objective pronominal suffixes, or of the first person imperfect (whether 'cohortative' or not). In these categories QH has forms distinct

---

[35] The assumption that אשר occurs in this period as a result of the mechanical replacement of MH's -ש (see n. 11) should be re-examined in the light of our observation. One should check where it replaces causal כי and where it does not, thus establishing its origin in each source.

[36] See J. Hoftijzer, *A Search for Method: A Study in the Syntactic Use of H-Locale in Classical Hebrew*, Leiden, 1981.

[37] The treatment of Ḥ. Nathan, pp. 19–20, who failed to see the various functions of such phrases, is misguided.

[38] See Qimron, *TSG*, pp. 95–96, *HDSS*, § 340.

[39] Note the construct in מבֵית לפרכת and the like (Gesenius, p. 421 n. 3).

[40] In the texts published so far there are approximately eight occurrences of -ין (Qimron, *TSG*, 93–94; cf. also Milik, *Tefillin*, M 21).

from those of BH and MH, and it would have been of great interest to know MMT's usage. The forms attested that are not common to BH, QH and MH are treated in the following sections.

3.3.3.1 The Infinitive

3.3.3.1.1 Construct and Suffixed Infinitives

For the forms attested for these, cf. ועד גל[ו]ת ירושלם (B 67), בהיות טמאתם עמהם (B 72), עד בוא השמש (C 19), במצאך (C 30, cf. § 3.1.1 n. 2) and בעשותך (C 31).

These constructions, which contain various prepositions having temporal meaning, and express the subject by a suffix or a *nomen rectum*, are characteristic of BH and QH (cf. *HDSS*, § 400.03). In MH (*a*) the infinitive is only found with the preposition -ל preceding it; (*b*) suffixes used with the infinitive of transitive verbs are always objectival;[41] and (*c*) the temporal constructions with the infinitive that are so frequent in MMT are practically non-existent.[42] In another MH dialect, however, that of the Copper Scroll, we find בבואך לסמול (x 5–6), i.e. the same temporal construction of the infinitive construct with subjective suffixes that we find in MMT. It is also attested, though rarely, in biblical Aramaic: כמקרבה לגבא (Dan 6:21).

3.3.3.1.2 *O*-infinitive > *A*-infinitive

For this possibility, which arises in the case of במצאך, see n. 2 to § 3.1.1.

3.3.3.1.3 The Form מלקטול

In one instance, ומלבוא (C 8), we find a form of the infinitive that is very typical of MH,[43] but which never occurs in BH. Elsewhere in QH it occurs in biblical quotations: מלכסות (4Q166 ii 9 = לכסות Hos 2:11), and ו[מ]לגעור (4Q176 8–11 11).[44] Interestingly, ומלבוא follows an infinitive without *lamed*, מהתערב (ibid.); this is the form proper to BH and QH (but not MH). Infinitives with both a *mem* (necessary for the meaning) and an (otiose) *lamed* appear in MH after verbs of preventing, restraining, and the like;[45] in MMT it may be that the form depends on פרשנו, a verb of similar meaning, or some even more appropriate verb now lost in the lacuna. Aramaic follows the same practice in the Targumim; one can find infinitives with both *mem* and *lamed* translating infinitives which in the Hebrew Bible have only *mem*, e.g. ירא מהביט (Exod 3:6 MT) = Onqelos דחיל מלאסתכלא. The construction with *lamed* is found in 11QtgJob, but in Old Aramaic the construction without *lamed* occurs.[46]

3.3.3.2 The Imperfect of היה

The imperfect of היה is יהיה (B 16, 78, C 3), as in BH and QH, and not yet יהא, as it has become in MH (and is already in the Bar-Kokhba texts).

---

[41] Cf. Segal, §§ 344–350.

[42] The temporal meaning is regularly expressed by כש- followed by a verb; for the few rare exceptions with an infinitive, see M. Mishor, 'On the Use of the Inflected Infinitive and the Verbal Noun in Mishnaic Hebrew', *Leshonenu Laʿam* 31 (1980), pp. 7–11.

[43] It is especially frequent in the Palestinian transmission of MH (Rosenthal, pp. 80–83).

[44] On the reading here, see J. Strugnell, 'Notes en Marge du volume V des *Discoveries in the Judaean Desert of Jordan*', *RQ* 7 (1970), p. 232.

[45] Segal, § 346.

[46] See M. Sokoloff, *The Targum to Job from Qumran Cave XI*, Ramat-Gan, 1974, p. 124.

3.3.3.3 The Feminine of the *Nipᶜal* Participle of *Lamed-Yod* Verbs

In the feminine singular of the *nipᶜal* participle of *lamed-yod* verbs we find הנעסה (B 75 = BH הנעשה). This is the form that is proper to BH and QH, and is to be contrasted with הנעשית, etc., of MH.[47]

3.3.3.4 The *Maqtūl* Pattern

The form מצול (C 24) is, *si vera lectio*,[48] very peculiar. It could be interpreted as a *maqtūl* passive participle (as in Arabic). This form can be found, though rarely, in BH and in QH, e.g. מצפוניו 'his treasures' (Obad 6), 'his hidden things', מסלול 'highway' (Isa 58:7, et al.), מדושתי 'that which is threshed by me' (Isa 21:10), משובים 'those repenting' (1QS 5:2), ממותים 'the slain' (2 Chr 22:11 *Ketib*), and also in MH.[49]

3.3.3.5 העריַ[בו]ַת השמש

The form העריַ[בו]ַת (B 15) belongs to the pattern הקטילה/־ות, which produces verbal nouns of the *hipᶜil* conjugation. There are three types of *hipᶜil* verbal nouns: (1) הֶקְטֵל, the original Hebrew form, (2) הַקְטָלָה/ות, which was borrowed from Aramaic, and (3) הַקְטִילָה/ות, which is a special Hebrew modification of the Aramaic form, maintaining the *i* vowel, perhaps on the analogy of the Hebrew *hipᶜil*.[50]

All three of these verbal nouns are attested in QH: הניפת העומר 11QTᵃ 11:10, 4Q513 4 2, הנף העומר 11QTᵃ 18:10, הכרות 1QIsaᵃ 3:9 (= MT הכרת), להנפה 1QIsaᵃ 30:28 (MT). Note that the pure Aramaic form הקטלה occurs only in a biblical scroll, and that the scroll there agrees with the MT.

In the Aramaic infinitive the construct and suffixed form ends in the feminine -*ut*, e.g., להודעה but להודעותני. Kutscher has shown that such -*ut* construct forms occur also in Hebrew, for example, שתיקותיך [= הכרת פניהם in the MT (Isa 3:9)]; הכרות פניהם in 1QIsaᵃ as שתיקותיך (Ezek 24:26); להשמעות אזנים against שתיקה in MH; and so שפיכות דמים as against שפיכה.[51]

The form הקטילות itself is, however, known to us only from later Hebrew sources: להפיצותם in Daniel Al-Kumissi's *Commentary of the Twelve Prophets*,[52] and להצליחותנו in *Midr. Tanḥuma*.[53] The form הקטילה is rare in standard MH, occurring more commonly in later sources.[54] The fact that הקטילת/ות occurs twice at Qumran in nonbiblical scrolls, here and in 11QTᵃ 18:10 (while הקטלה is never attested in QH except in biblical manuscripts), probably indicates that it was a common form in QH. Since it is also attested in Samaritan Hebrew (*aṣṣiga* = הציגה Deut 28:56, for MT's הצג),[55] and in Sir 14:13 (השיגה), it is to be considered a feature common to various Hebrew dialects of the post-exilic period.

---

[47] Haneman, p. 364. The form הנעשה occurs, however, in some traditions of MH (Rosenthal, pp. 78–79).

[48] In C 24 (MSᵉ) we read מצול, but in C 26 in MSᵉ the reading [נ]צל seems preferable (though it was perhaps then corrected to [מ]צול or [נ]צול, which is MSᶠ's reading).

[49] Yalon, *Scrolls*, pp. 107–108, e.g. מעוקות 'troubles'; מחושי ראש 'headache', cf. also מצוק Sir 43:4 (var מוצק).

[50] These three types also occur in Hebrew with the root ערב (הערב, הערבה, העריבות).

[51] Kutscher, *Studies*, pp. 131–133 (Hebrew).

[52] Daniel Al-Kumissi, *Commentary of the Twelve Prophets*, ed. I. D. Markon, Jerusalem, 1957, p. 56.

[53] Tanḥuma Buber, *Shlaḥ*, I, MS Oxford—cf. M. Zeidel, 'A Note on the Pattern הפעילה', *Leshonenu* 23 (1959), p. 128.

[54] Qimron, *TSG*, p. 94 (and n. 65).

[55] Ben-Ḥayyim, *SHG*, p. 152.

The phrase להעריבות השמש (which is similar to MH's הערב שמש[56] as against בוא השמש in BH) did not originate in MH, since MH generally uses the word חמה rather than שמש. We also see that the phrase הערב שמש was originally used adverbially, exactly like כבוא השמש in BH.

3.3.3.6. The Form זָנַת

The reading שׁזֹנת [כ]מֹי in B 9 fits better from a material point of view than the other possible readings, but the text is too broken for any reading to be certain. If our reading is correct, we have here the MH equivalent of the BH זנתה (as representative of the BH and QH *lamed-yod* pattern in general; cf. הויית 1QIsa[a] 17:1, 19:17).[57]

3.4 Syntax

3.4.1 The Tenses

3.4.1.1 The Consecutive Perfect

BH's consecutive perfect, with future meaning, is still found in MMT:

$$\text{(B 66)} \quad \ldots \text{שמעת שיגלח וכבס}$$
$$\text{(C 13–15)} \quad \text{והיא כי [יבו]א עליך} \ldots \text{ושבתה}$$
$$\text{(C 28–31)} \quad \text{ובקש מלפנו שיתקן} \ldots \text{והרחיק ממך} \ldots \text{ונחשבה לך לצדקה}$$

Note, however, that the first of these occurs in a biblical paraphrase, the second is a direct biblical quotation, and the others are in the archaising language of the homily of section C. In A 20, the form ושלמה (השנה) is apparently a participle. To take it as a perfect with a conjunctive *waw* is less plausible, since וקטל in QH is primarily used for future time (see also the commentary).

In CBH, וקטל normally refers to the future; there are, however, a few cases where it refers to past time. In LBH such cases are more frequent.[58] In MH, the consecutive perfect is not used for the future, and any *waw* standing before a perfect is purely conjunctive.[59] In the DSS, וקטל occurs approximately four hundred times and is mostly used for the future time, although in some cases it refers to the past.[60]

It is a little surprising that there is no case of ויקטל, the consecutive imperfect used as a narrative past tense. This may partially be explained by the prescriptive, and therefore non-narrative, nature of the work, but in C there are sequences of narrative verbs where ויקטל may have been expected. ויקטל scarcely appears in MH except as a result of special stylistic circumstances.[61]

3.4.1.2 והיה כי, etc., Introducing Temporal Clauses

The construction והיא (=והיה) כי [יבו]א (C 13–14) needs further discussion; in it we have one of the consecutive forms of the verb היה before a temporal clause. This construction is almost exclusively

---

[56] For the indefinite form שמש, see G. Ṣarfatti, 'Determination of Fixed Phrases Formed by Means of the Construct State in Mishnaic Hebrew', *Studies in Hebrew and Semitic Languages Dedicated to the Memory of Professor E. Y. Kutscher*, Ramat-Gan, 1980, pp. 140ff; Nathan, pp. 281–283.

[57] See Kutscher, *Isaiah*, p. 343; Haneman, pp. 342–351. (Haneman demonstrates here that הָיָת is a pausal form in MH, and this is not the case in 1QIsa[a].)

[58] Joüon, § 119 z (a usage especially common in Qoheleth).

[59] Segal, § 156; S. Sharvit, *The Text and Language of Mishna Avot,* Ph.D. Dissertation, Bar-Ilan University, 1976, p. 125.

[60] Cf. M. S. Smith, *The Origins and Development of the Waw-Consecutive*, Atlanta, 1991 (and the bibliography there). Examples of unconverted וקטל are: 1QH[a] 11:34, 14:5; 4Q160 7:2, 4; 4Q179 1 i 5; 4Q370 i 4, CD 19:34, 20:23 (see also Kutscher, *Isaiah*, p. 354).

[61] Segal, n. 59 above.

confined to CBH; contrast CBH ויהי ככלות שלמה להתפלל (1 Kgs 8:54) with LBH וככלות שלמה להתפלל (2 Chr 7:1). The phrase in MMT (cf. commentary) is a quotation (though in other aspects modified) of Deut 30:1-2, and the phrase והיה כי is doubtless found here for that reason.

In QH, והיה כי occurs only once, in 1QS 6:4 והיה כי יערוכו השולחן . . . הכוהן ישלח ידו. Furthermore, constructions with temporal כי, frequent in BH, are found in QH only in biblical quotations (or in passages in a biblicising style). In general, the temporal and conditional uses of כי are very rare in QH (only two or three examples are to be found in the 4Q Concordance). An initial והיה of this type, while frequent in BH, is very rare in QH; even when it is in the source from which a passage derives, it is usually dropped: compare בקרבכם למלחמה ועמד הכוהן ודבר . . . (1QM 10:2) with BH's והיה כקרבכם אל המלחמה ונגש הכהן ודבר (Deut 20:2; cf. HDSS, § 400.03).

3.4.1.3 The Periphrastic Tense היה + Participle

והזה הטהר על הטמא (Num 19:19); and perhaps also: בשל שא יהיה הטהר מזה על הטמה (B 16) paraphrases [ ]מת יהיה (C 3); בשל שלוא י[היו] מסיא[י]ם (B 12–13); and ו]אף היא [נ]צל מצרות רבות (C 25–26).[62] This periphrastic tense, usually expressing continuous or habitual action, is very frequent in MH and Aramaic.[63] In BH it is found only occasionally, mostly in the later books;[64] CBH uses the imperfect forms יקטל or וקטל to denote habitual actions. In QH the periphrastic construction is attested approximately fifty times.[65] Our text thus reflects, in this feature, the language of the later periods.

3.4.1.4 היה ירא

The phrases היה ירא in ולהיות יראים מהמקדש (B 49) and שהיא ירא (C 24), which formally belong to § 3.4.1.3, demand a separate discussion. The word ירא is a stative verb, and its perfect form may well represent an imperfect action.[66] There is therefore no real difference between ירא and היה ירא. The periphrastic construction is nevertheless very rare in BH (and may be dialectical): compare 1 Kgs 18:3 (cf. verse 12); 2 Kgs 4:1, 17 32; 33, 41 (contrast verse 28). It is far more frequent in MH[67] (and in Aramaic).[68]

Why was the periphrastic construction preferred in the later language? Stative verbs have a special form in BH: the perfect is קָטֵל (and קָטֹל).[69] In MH the form קָטֵל is not used in the perfect.[70] Stative verbs are therefore generally either expressed by other conjugations[71] or, less frequently, the construction היה + participle is used.[72] This tendency in MH may account for the periphrastic construction in MMT.

---

[62] On grounds of sense, we prefer to read here היא rather than הוא. Although in the Temple Scroll יהיה קוטל is much more frequent than היה קוטל, this is to be explained by nature of the book—where laws are laid down for the future—and not by any linguistic tendency to avoid היה קוטל.

[63] Segal, pp. 156–158. Again, because of the content of MMT, with its many legal prescriptions, the periphrastic construction occurs usually in the imperfect.

[64] Joüon, pp. 340–341.

[65] Most conspicuously in certain sections of the Temple Scroll that are also in other linguistic respects distinct from the rest of that scroll; cf. A. Wilson and L. Wills, 'Literary Sources of the Temple Scroll', HTR 75 (1982), pp. 275–288. Cf. also HDSS, § 400.01.

[66] Gesenius, § 106g.

[67] Also in hitpaʿel היה מתירא.

[68] Cf. הוה דחיל in Aramaic, e.g. in the Palestinian Targum of Exod 3:6, where כי ירא מהביט becomes ארום הוה דחיל מלמסתכי.

[69] Bergsträsser, II, § 14b–d.

[70] Haneman, § 31.12.

[71] Bendavid, II, pp. 482–483.

[72] Segal, § 107.

3.4.1.5   The Use of the Participle

The participle is used as a present tense in phrases where BH uses the imperfect, or, with stative verbs, either the perfect or the imperfect. Thus the numerous cases of אנחנו אומרים; note especially ואתם יודעים (B 68, 80), which is semantically the same as אתם ידעתם, cf. Gen 44:27 and elsewhere; שאינם רואים (B 50; compare, e.g., אשר לא יראון ולא ישמעון Deut 4:28); Onqelos renders these imperfects by participles (cf. also Jer 5:21; Ps 115:5, 135:16).

The participle is frequently used in the plural to denote a customary action. In most cases it appears in references to the incorrect practice of the opponents of the sect (see § 5.2.4). In MH the plural of the participle is used in impersonal prohibitions or commands, as is the infinitive in QH (cf. § 3.4.2.1). This usage may be found in B 31 [ו]מוציאים 'one should take out', but the text is broken and our reconstruction and interpretation are tentative.

3.4.2   The Infinitive

3.4.2.1   Modal Use of the Infinitive

The modal use of the infinitive with -ל (לקטל) is typical of LBH, of QH, and of Aramaic, but is only rarely found in MH.[73] This infinitive generally expresses commands or (with the negative particles אין or לא) prohibitions or statements of impossibility, e.g. כיא כול אשר לוא נחשבו בבריתו להבדיל אותם (1QS 5:17–18), and in the negative ולוא לסור . . . ואין לצעוד (1QS 3:10–11). In such constructions the personal subject is usually not specified (*HDSS*, § 400.02). The infinitive is also used (though rarely) instead of a finite indicative verb, e.g., 1QHᵃ 6:9–10: ובחסדיך תשפטם . . . וכפיכה להורותם וכי'שור אמתכה להכינם בעצתכה (*HDSS*, § 400.02).

In MMT, as in LBH and QH, we find examples of such infinitives with אין or לוא used prohibitively: ועל בה[מתו הטהור]ה (B 58); ואין להבי למחני הקודש כלבים (B 71); אין להאכילם מהקו[ד]שים (B 76–78). Note כתוב שלוא לרבעה כלאים ועל לבוש[ו כתוב שלוא] יהיה שעטנז ושלוא לזרוע שדו ו[כרמו כלאי]ם that here both the infinitive (twice) and the imperfect are used to denote prohibition.

The phrase ושלוא לזרוע . . . is very instructive, since it is certainly an independent clause.[74] The use of -ש (or אשר) in such constructions is very rare and confined almost entirely to Hebrew contemporary with the Qumran sect (e.g., 1QS 9:16 [with אשר], *m. Ḥag.* 2:2). It is more common in contemporary Aramaic: see for instance the formulaic phrases in *Megillat Taʿanit*: (ו)די לא לאתענאה, (ו)די לא למספד. These relative particles occur more commonly with imperfects introducing prohibitions and commands, both in QH and in other contemporaneous Hebrew and Aramaic sources (*HDSS*, §§ 400.11, 400.12).

3.4.2.2   Modal Use of the Infinitive with Prepositional Phrase

In one place we find a prepositional phrase indicating the logical subject before the infinitive: לכול אלה להיות טהורים . . . (B 15). It is difficult in such cases to determine what, grammatically speaking, is the subject and what is the predicate. Similar examples (and also instances with the negative) occur in LBH; in these the negative particle (which usually negates the predicate) is put either before the

---

[73] A. Kropat, *Die Syntax des Autors der Chronik*, Giessen, 1909, pp. 24–25; H. Bauer and P. Leander, *Grammatik des Biblisch-Aramäischen*, Halle, 1927, § 85 e; E. Y. Kutscher, *Encyclopedia Judaica*, 16, p. 1588. This 'modal' usage is not found in ordinary MH, which employs instead the imperfect or the participle.

[74] It might seem at first glance that ושלוא continues the words כתוב שלוא . . ., thus making the clause a dependent one, like those that precede it. But for this to be so the logical subject and the word order would have to be changed. To supply וכתב alone would be inadequate: we would need to read ועל שדו וכרמו כתב שלוא לזורעם כלאים—certainly too much to assume.

infinitive[75] or before the prepositional phrase.[76] Professor E. Rubinstein, whom we consulted about this complicated problem, thinks that in all of these modal-infinitive constructions (even in cases such as ולא למפתח) the infinitive is the subject, and the negative itself functions as a modal predicate.

3.4.2.3 Modal Use of the Infinitive with ראוי

The modal infinitive in MMT is also used with the word ראוי: ראוי להזהר [כי לבני] הכהנ[ים] (B 11–12); כי לבני אהרן ראוי להיות (B 16–17). The word ראוי is an unnecessary element here; if it were omitted, the meaning of the sentence would remain the same; cf. § 3.5.2.29a.

3.4.2.4 Infinitive Absolute Used as Finite Verb

[ו]אף היא [נ]צל מצרות רבות ונסלוח לו (C 25–26). The form ונסלוח in this passage is morphologically a *nipʿal* infinitive absolute rather than a *nipʿal* perfect or a *qal* imperfect.[77] Such infinitive absolutes continuing a finite verb occur approximately sixty times in the Bible.[78] Thus we find: ונשלוח ספרים 'letters were sent' (Esth 3:13), ונהפוך הוא 'but it turned out to the contrary' (Esth 9:1), ונעתור להם 'and He entreated them' (1 Chr 5:20), ונחתום בטבעת המלך 'and it was sealed with the king's ring' (Esth 8:8).

It has been noticed that this phenomenon is especially typical of LBH.[79] Yet while frequent in several late biblical books,[80] it is rare (or absent) in other late Hebrew sources.[81] The fact that it occurs in MMT is very significant for the history of this usage in particular and for the history of the infinitive absolute in general.

3.4.3 Temporal Clauses of the Type בקטלו

Temporal clauses beginning with (ו)ב- followed by a suffixed infinitive are common in QH and BH,[82] but not in MH (nor, usually, in later Aramaic dialects). In MMT we found as many as five examples of such clauses (see above, § 3.3.3.1.1).

3.4.4 Pronominal Direct Objects

In CBH a pronominal direct object may appear either as a suffix of the verb or as a suffix of את; in LBH, QH and MH, however, the former type predominates; the latter is found mainly after the participle (*HDSS*, § 400.08). In MMT, relevant material occurs only with the infinitive: לעשותם (B 44), להתיכם (B 44), להאכילם (B 71), לרבעה (B 77); here the suffixed object is the usual form. With the participle, however, we find again השוחט אותה והסורף אותה (B 14; MH would use השוחטה etc.), and with the plural: מניחים אותה (B 10; as is usual in Hebrew).

---

[75] e.g., 1 Chr 23:26 וגם ללוים אין לשאת את המשכן (here the infinitive seems to be the predicate).

[76] e.g., 2 Chr 26:18 לא לך עזיהו להקטיר לה׳ (here the prepositional phrase seems to be the predicate).

[77] Bergsträsser, II, § 16i; cf., however, a case of the *qal* imperfect of סלח with *o* in אסלוח (*Ketib* Jer 5:7). In the parallel biblical expression (ונסלח לו Lev 4:26, 30, 31, etc.) we have the *nipʿal* consecutive perfect denoting the future.

[78] Bergsträsser, II, § 12 m; A. Rubinstein, 'A Finite Verb Continued by an Infinitive in Biblical Hebrew', *VT* 3 (1953), pp. 362–367.

[79] See Bergsträsser, ibid., and Rubinstein, ibid. The subject has recently been treated in several articles (see E. Qimron, 'Observations on the History of Early Hebrew (1000 B.C.E.-200 C.E.) in the Light of the Dead Sea Documents', in *Forty Years*, pp. 358–359; see the research cited there). Let us add that the usage occurs three times in 4QTob: בכן דבר ונתון לו את בלהה; בא [אליו טובי]ה ואמור לו; טובי וכתוב תהלה בתשבוחות [; and once in 4QTNaph: וסבול אותכה במ[עיה] אמי ותלד... (see the preliminary concordance).

[80] Especially in Esth, but also in Jer, Zech, Dan, and Neh. In some passages this usage should apparently be read according to the biblical text in contrast to the vocalization, e.g., Esth 9:23, 24, 27, 32.

[81] See Rubinstein, ibid.

[82] BH also has the construction with (ו)כ- + infinitives (e.g., (ו)בקטלו)), but with a somewhat different meaning (Joüon, pp. 510–511).

3.4.5 שהם באים

BH and MH rarely employ the construction of relative pronoun + independent personal pronoun + participle. Instead they use constructions of the type exemplified by הבאים. But constructions of the former type do occasionally appear.[83] The manuscripts of MH differ from each other in using הבאים, שהם באים and שבאים. These different constructions probably reflect different dialects.[84] The use of -ש before the participle appears to be normal in the Bar-Kokhba documents. Note that the pronoun הם is missing in שמניחים (B 10). The relevance of such constructions to the study of the dialects of MH has already been demonstrated, but further study is needed (see § 3.5.2.30).

3.4.6 בין X ל-Y

While pre-exilic Hebrew generally uses the construction בין X ובין Y, post-exilic Hebrew (and MH) uses the construction בין X ל-Y.[85] We say 'generally' because, when X = Y (e.g., בין איש לאיש), or when X and Y are antonyms, the construction בין X ל-Y can be found also in classical BH.[86]

In MMT we find: ואף המוצקות אינם מבדילות בין הטמא לטהור (B 56–57). It is true that in this case X and Y are antonyms: nevertheless the historical distribution of the two possible expressions of this idea is very instructive; in Leviticus one finds only בין הטמא ובין הטהור (10:10, 11:47), while in Ezekiel the later form בין הטמא לטהור (22:26) occurs,[87] as it does also in QH, cf. CD 12:19–23, 4Q512 40 3–4. Other typical expressions from 4Q are 4Q375 ושפטתי בין איש לרעהו ובין אב לבנו ובין איש לאשתו and 4Q393 1 5 להבדיל בין אור לחושך 1:6 (compare Gen 1:4 ויבדל אלהים בין האור ובין החשך). Other examples are rare, except in biblical quotations, cf. CD 19:20–21.

3.4.7 כתבנו אנחנו

C 26 MS[e] reads ואף אנחנו כתבנו, but MS[f] reads ואף כתב[נ]ו אנחנו. When the personal pronouns come before the finite verb they seem to have an emphatic nuance.[88] This is not the case in ואף כתבנו אנחנו, where the pronoun follows the verb. Here we have a special construction in which the pronoun has no readily apparent function. This construction (with the verb in the first person followed by the pronoun) is especially common in Qohelet (e.g. 1:10) and in Song of Songs (5:5, 6). Its occurrence here confirms the view of H. L. Ginsberg that it was a feature of the spoken language of a late period.[89] The variation in word order implies that the pronoun has no emphatic nuance in either construction. Nor does the word אף have any emphatic function (see § 3.5.3.3).

3.4.8 The Position of the Copula

Kutscher states[90] that in a defining nominal sentence the copula comes between the subject and the predicate; in a descriptive nominal sentence it comes after the predicate. This, according to him, is the

---

[83] e.g., Deut 20:20, *m. ʿAboda Zara* 4:9.

[84] Rosenthal, pp. 80–81. The phenomenon should be studied in the broader context of the syntax of the third person independent pronoun (cf. Nathan, pp. 315–316).

[85] G. Haneman, 'On the Preposition בֵּין in the Mishna and in the Bible', *Leshonenu* 40 (1976), pp. 35–53; cf. J. Barr, 'Some Notes on *ben* "Between" in Classical Hebrew', *JJS* 23 (1978), pp. 1–12 (Barr does not mention Haneman's work); Hurvitz, *P Source*, pp. 113–115; and *HDSS*, § 400.17.

[86] Haneman, ibid., p. 48.

[87] Cf. also the distribution of the various expressions combining בין with חל and קדש.

[88] The personal pronoun in such cases may be the predicate, the verb being a subject clause. Note the parallel construction with participle ואף חושבים אנחנו in contrast to ואנחנו חושבים. A construction like *ואף אנחנו חושבים would have a special emphasis on the pronoun. Cf. 11QT[a] 36:14 והשערים באים vs. 41:12 ויוצאים השערים.

[89] L. Ginsberg, *Koheleth*, Tel Aviv and Jerusalem, 1961, p. 29. We find this construction also in Pr 24:34 and in Lev 5:5, 26:32; in Leviticus it apparently has a contrasting function.

[90] Kutscher, *Studies*, p. רלד.

case in all ancient Hebrew (and Aramaic) sources. If Kutscher's statement is generally correct,[91] then we have in MMT exceptions to it, since we find that the manuscripts are divided as to the position of the copula: in MSᵃ we find וי[רושלי]ם מחנה היא (B 29–30), in contrast to MSᵈ's reading וירושלים כי י[רושלים ראש מחנות היו]א מחנה (ibid.), and MSᶜ has כי ירושלים היא ראש מחנות ישראל (B 61–62), MSᵈ היא[ה ישראל] (ibid.).

Whether מחנה in B 29–30 is to be taken as definite or indefinite, one of these two clauses is an exception to the rule. We think that the word מחנה, even though without the article, is definite, since it denotes one particular camp (though in CBH that meaning would be expressed by המחנה). In any case, ראש מחנות ישראל (B 61–62) is, formally speaking, certainly definite; the version in MSᶜ is an exception to Kutscher's rule.

3.5 Lexical Elements

MMT's lexical materials will be arranged in four groups:

(*a*) Elements attested in CBH (and sometimes in LBH and QH) which do not appear in MH.

(*b*) Elements attested for the first time in texts from the period of the Second Temple (i.e., the later biblical books, Ben-Sira and the DSS). Some of these appear in MH, others do not.

(*c*) Elements from MH not found in the literature of earlier periods (BH and QH).

(*d*) New elements found neither in earlier texts (BH, QH) nor in later texts (MH).

In the case of common words, we have permitted ourselves to ignore the occasional exceptions. Thus, on the one hand, we have sometimes, on grounds of frequency, viewed a word as late even if it occurs occasionally in pre-exilic Hebrew: for example, the relative pronoun -ש which can be found, though rarely, in early (apparently dialectical) biblical texts. At other times we have classified some particular biblical words as not used in MH, even if they are occasionally found in Tannaitic texts; when they occur there, it is often in connection with biblical verses and the like. We have, however, usually mentioned these exceptions in our discussions of the individual words.

In expressions where the relative pronoun is combined with other elements (prepositions, etc.) we have not been formalistic; viewing -ש and אשר as essentially the same, we classify -בעת ש 'when' as belonging to late BH, though in fact in late BH בעת אשר, not -בעת ש, is the form found.

3.5.1 Classical Biblical Hebrew Elements

3.5.1.1 אַחֲרִית :אחרית הימים (C 14), באחרית העת (C 30)

The word אחרית is common in both BH and in QH, but not in MH, which employs different equivalents, e.g., סוף (see Bendavid, I, p. 336); in Tannaitic literature אחרית is found only in *m. Qidd.* 4:13 and the parallel in *t. Qidd.* 5:16. In QH (cf. also Biblical Aramaic Dan 2:28), its use is generally restricted to the phrase באחרית הימים (frequent in BH and QH), with an occasional אחרית הקץ. MMT's phrase אחרית העת is a hapax legomenon; its biblical ring is of course at home in C.

3.5.1.1a אֵלֶּה: see § 3.3.1.3.

3.5.1.2 אֲשֶׁר: היא המקום אשר [בחר בו] מכול שב[טי ישראל] (B 32–33)

The prevalent relative pronoun in MMT is -ש (or שא, cf. § 3.1.4.4); even the CBH relative אשר, found here in a clearly biblical expression, is replaced with -ש in היא המקום שבחר בו מכל שבטי ישראל,

---

91 Kutscher unfortunately never published the article he promised on this subject.

(B 60–61). It is well known that אשר is the relative pronoun most frequently used in CBH, LBH and QH. (For the distribution of -ש in BH, QH and MH, see § 3.5.2.30.)

3.5.1.3   בָּדָד   כי בדד [י]היו [מחוץ לבית] (B 65–66)

בדד is a biblical word that was not in vernacular use in MH. In QH it is used only three times, all in contexts that are biblicising (e.g., 4Q179 2 4) or liturgical (4Q504 6 9).

3.5.1.3a   בוא השמש: see § 5.3.1.4.

3.5.1.4   בחר: והיא המקום שבחר בו מכל שבטי ישראל (B 60–61)

In MH ברר (rather than CBH's בחר) is used in the *qal* in the sense 'to choose', while for the *nipʿal* 'to be chosen', BH, QH, and even MH use √בחר and not √ברר. Cf. Polzin, p. 131 # 15; Qimron, *TSL*, A 7.

3.5.1.5   בין   *hitpolel*: והתבנן במעשיהמה (C 23)

The word התבונן in particular, and the *hitpolel* conjugation in general, is characteristic of BH and of QH (התבונן occurs five times in Kuhn's concordance, and twenty-five times in 4Q unpublished texts), but not of MH.

3.5.1.6   בְּלִיַּעַל: והרחיק ממך מחשבת רעה ועצת בליעל (C 29)

This word is commonly used in QH in the sense of 'wickedness'. In QH it is also frequent as the name of the Angel of Wickedness, i.e., wickedness personified (a non-biblical usage, but cf. Nah 2:1). In MMT, the parallelism with רעה shows that the meaning is 'wickedness', as it is also in BH (contra the BH Lexica; cf. Ben-Yehuda, *s.v.*). The word is practically not found in Tannaitic literature, though the biblical בליעל 'wickedness' does occur in a story of Yannai and the Pharisees recorded in the Babylonian Talmud (*Qidd.* 66a).

3.5.1.7   חֹק: ואף על החרשים שלוא שמעו חוק ומשפט וטהרה (B 52)

B. de Vries (*Hebrew Encyclopedia*, s.v. 'Halakha', vol. 14, pp. 499–500) states that it is no coincidence that the biblical terms חוקים and משפטים (and even תורה, in its restricted biblical sense of a specific law) were not retained in MH, but only the term מצוה. In our document, as frequently in BH and QH, חוק and משפט are still in use.

3.5.1.8   חשב (in the expression נחשב לצדקה)

Nipʿal (not *qal*, whose form is ונחשובה in QH) is to be found in ונחשבה לך לצדקה (C 31). Cf. the *qal* in והאמין בה' ויחשבה לו צדקה (Gen 15:6), the *nipʿal* in ותחשב לו לצדקה (Ps 106:31) and the *hitpaʿel* in ויתחשב לו לצדקה (cited by Milik, *Copper Scroll*, p. 225). The passive use of the *hitpaʿel* here is a late feature. Note also וצדקה יהוה לך קדם יהו in an Aramaic papyrus from Elephantine (Cowley, № 30:27). The use of the word צדקה as a synonym of צדק is current in BH and QH, but not in MH.

3.5.1.9   טוב in the phrase לטוב לך: לטוב לך ולעמך (C 27), לטוב לך ולישראל (C 31–32)

Cf. לטוב לנו (Deut 6:24); the opposite phrases—לרע לכם Jer 7:6, 25:7 and לרע לו Qoh 8:9—prove that לטוב was taken as an adjective (or noun) rather than as an infinitive (and this is confirmed by the Tiberian vocalisation).

3.5.1.10   כָּהֶם: כי לחת המוצקות והמקבל מהמה כהם לחה אחת (B 57–58)

The inflection of -כ with the pronominal suffixes -כן, -כם, -הם is found in BH in all periods, but not in MH (see under -כ in dictionaries of the Bible); compare also מהם.

כמו and its compounds, כמוך, כמוהו, כמוני (BH, MH), are also found in QH. On the use of the third masculine plural pronominal suffix -הם instead of the third feminine plural -הן, see § 3.3.1.2.1.

3.5.1.11   כִּי: כי ירושלים היאה מחנה הקדש (B 59-60 and elsewhere), כי שלוא ראה ולוא שמע (B 53)

In BH, כי is normally found at the beginning of causal clauses or, less often, at the beginning of conditional clauses (= 'if') and clauses of time (= 'when'). In QH, as in the later biblical books, its use to express time or condition is already archaic (cf. Brin, pp. 214–217); it is, however, still quite frequently used at the beginning of causal clauses. The same causal use is found in MMT (cf. § 3.3.1.4). In the Tannaitic literature, כי is not even used to express cause; only the adversative phrase לא כי אלא 'it is not so, but . . .' (cf. Brin, ibid.), and וכי introducing a question ('It is really . . ?'), are found.

3.5.1.12   כֵּן 'right true': במצאך מקצת דברינו כן (C 30)

The adjective כן (from √כון) is non-existent in MH (only the adverb כן 'thus, so' occurs). In the Bible it is used as substantive (undeclined), as it is in MMT, e.g., דברים אשר לא כן (2 Kgs 17:2; see BDB, p. 467 and Bendavid, I, p. 350); on שהוא[א כן] (B 38), see commentary.

3.5.1.13   כתב אל: ואף אנחנו כתבנו אליך מקצת מעשי התורה שחשבנו (C 26–27)

Post-exilic Hebrew uses the construction כתב על instead of the classical כתב אל (BDB, p. 507, § II). This accords with the general decline in the use of the preposition אל in post-exilic Hebrew. (This decline continues into QH and MH; cf. זעק על, שלח על in QH.) Either of the two CBH meanings of כתב אל, 'send to' or 'write for the benefit of', is possible here. For the use of כתב referring to laws, cf. 2 Kgs 17:37, Esth 8:8, 9:23 and BDB s.v. כתב.

3.5.1.13a   לקח 'marry': ונשים] לוקחים [להיו]תם עצם אחת (B 40–41)

The phrase לקח אשה 'marry' is typical of CBH. In LBH and in QH it is sometimes replaced by its MH equivalent נשא אשה (see E. Y. Kutscher, 'Marginal Notes to the Biblical Lexicon', *Leshonenu* 30 [1966], pp. 22–23 [= *Studies*, pp. 325–353]; S. Japhet, 'Interchanges of Verbal Roots in Parallel Texts in Chronicles', *Leshonenu* 31 [1967], pp. 176–177, n. 50; Polzin, p. 146; Brin, p. 197). It is not clear whether לקח אשה was in use in any spoken post-biblical Hebrew dialect. On the one hand, it is non-existent in MH. On the other hand, it occurs not only in Second Temple period Hebrew, but also in the Babylonian Talmud and in Aramaic. Surprisingly, it is found there not only in *qal*, as in BH, but also in the causative conjugation (הקחת; contrast נתן in BH and השיא in MH; see J. C. Greenfield, 'Papyrus Yadin 18', *IEJ* 37 [1987], pp. 248–250).

3.5.1.14   מַעַל 'unfaithful act' (C 4, 9)

This word is frequently used in all periods of BH and QH, but not in MH.

3.5.1.15   מצא in constructions such as שלוא י]מצא בידינו מעל ושקר ורעה (C 8–9)

Compare in BH: ועולה לא נמצא בשפתיו (Mal 2:6); and in QH: אם נמצא עולתה בך (Ezek 28:15); ושקוצים לא ימצא בה (1QS 10:23). For the expression נמצא ביד, see וכוזבים לא ימצאו בשפתי (1QS 10:22); Exod 21:16. The lack of concord in number between the subject and the verb נמצא can be found elsewhere, as in 1QS 10:23 (cited above); in the two biblical instances there also is a lack of concord

in gender. The quasi-copula מצא (in the masculine singular) frequently does not concord, resembling in this respect היה in BH (cf. J. Blau, 'Studies in the Syntax of Biblical Hebrew', *Tur Sinai Volume*, eds. M. Haran and B. Z. Luria, Jerusalem, 1960, pp. 143–147).

3.5.1.16   מִשְׁפָּט 'law, custom':

(B 52–53) ואף על החרשים שלוא שמעו חוק ומשפט וטהרה ולא שמעו משפטי ישראל

(B 74) כמשפט המת או החלל הוא

In MH the word דין has replaced משפט of BH and QH, and also their חוק (see de Vries on חוק, above § 3.5.1.8).

3.5.1.17   נשא (in the unique BH phrase להשיא את X עוון 'to let someone bear punishment')

This phrase does not occur in MH. In MMT it appears in משיאים (מסיא[י]ם) את העם עוון (B 13, 27), but as a biblical allusion. It is a technical term in BH, and is also used (though rarely) in QH: cf. והשיאו אותם עון אשמה (Lev 22:16); פן ישיאנו עוון אשמה (1QS 5:14).

3.5.1.18   עַם meaning 'the people of Israel', as in the biblicising מסיא[י]ם את העם עוון (B 13, 27)

Cf. also לטוב לך ולעמך (C 27; in C 31–32: לטוב לך ולישראל). Curiously enough, this usage, which is very common in both BH and QH, as is indeed העם, is only rarely found in MH (which employs the word צִבּוּר, Bendavid, I, p. 357). It occurs in the Mishna approximately forty times, but is apparently restricted to more ancient sections, those which deal with the Temple and other subjects relating to the Temple period; cf. on ישראל in § 3.5.2.14. (On the strata of MH see § 3.7.1.3.) This is apparently also the case in the other Tannaitic texts. The subject, however, needs further study.

3.5.1.19   ואף על מטעת עצי המאכל :עץ מאכל (B 62)

MMT here uses the biblical expression (Lev 19:23) and not the mishnaic (Aramaicising) אילן מאכל (e.g., *m. Šebi.* 1:3). Indeed, אילן is not found in QH. In MH, עץ means only 'wood' not 'tree'; the biblical meaning can, however, be found in *t. ʿOr.* 1:5, and in the blessing formula בורא פרי העץ (Kutscher, *Words*, p. 73; *Studies*, p. תה.)

3.5.1.20   שראינו עמך ערמה ומדע תורה :עָרְמָה (C 27–28)

The word ערמה has here a positive meaning, 'wisdom', as is usual in BH and QH. In MH it is, with one doubtful exception, not attested, whether with this positive meaning or with the negative one of 'slyness, cunning'. For the vocalisation of ערמה in QH (עֶרְמָה or עָרְמָה), see § 3.1.1.2, and compare טמאה, טהרה.

3.5.1.20a   עַשְׁתֵּי עָשָׂר 'eleven' (A iii)

This number occurs fifteen times in QH. It is found in BH, but not in MH. For its etymology, see S. A. Kaufman, *The Akkadian Influence on Aramaic*, Chicago, 1974, p. 60.

3.5.1.21   עֵת: באחרית העת (C 30; cf. באחרית הימים C 14)

The word עת, though still attested in MH, does not mean 'time' there (as it does in BH, QH, and MMT), but denotes a short period, e.g.

העונה אחת מעשרים וארבעה משעה. העת אחת מעשרים וארבעה בעונה. והרגע אחת מעשרים וארבע בעת

An *ʿona* is the twenty-fourth part of an hour, an *ʿet* is the twenty-fourth part of an *ʿona*, and a *regaʿ* is the twenty-fourth part of an *ʿet*

(*t. Ber.* 1:1; cf. also Mekilta of R. Simʿon Bar-Yoḥai, ed. Melamed, p. 35). It is especially frequent in MH in the phrase מעת לעת.

Cf. in MMT also the conjunction מעת ש- (§ 3.5.2.27), and see the discussion of אחרית in § 3.5.1.1.

3.5.1.22 צְדָקָה '(act of) charity': see § 3.5.1.9.

3.5.1.22a צָרוּע: see § 5.3.1.2.

3.5.1.22b רֵאשִׁית 'first-fruits': see § 5.3.1.5.

3.5.1.23 רַע 'evil, wickedness': והרחיק ממך מחשבת רעה ועצת בליעל (C 29 MSᵉ), contrast MSᶠ: מחשבת רע

רע as an adjective is frequent in all phases of Hebrew; as a noun, however, as in MSᵈ, it is found in BH and QH, but not in MH. The usage in the variant reading in MSᵉ, with the adjective רעה used as a substantive, is, however, found also in MH. This may account for the Samaritan reading רעה in Gen 44:34 (= MT רע). Compare מחשבות רע (Pr 15:26), מחשבת רעה (Ezek 38:10), עצת רע (Ezek 11:2). Especially instructive is the phrase מחשבת רוע in 1QHᵃ 7:3 where רוע is parallel to רע (!), דמים and בליעל. For the use in substantives of the pattern *qall* (alongside *qull*), cf. other pairs of substantives: רַב and רוב in BH (cf. BDB, p. 913.1c), and קל (וחמר) and קול (וחמר) (MH), where no difference of meaning can be detected; cf. also *HDSS*, § 330.1a.

3.5.1.24 שוב 'return': [ולוא ישובו אחו[ר] לת[מיד] שישובו בישר[אל] (C 21–22); ושבתה אלו בכל לבבך (C 15)

Instead of using the verb שוב in the *qal* with the BH and QH sense of 'return', MH uses the verb חזר (not yet attested at Qumran); שוב is still used in MH, but only in the phrase עובר ושב (taken from BH) and in a few other special expressions. It is also used in the technical sense of 'to repent' (see Kutscher, *Words*, p. 76).

The usage in MMT is usually the biblical one. The expressions שב אחור and שב אל ה' are frequent in all periods of BH; in QH we find them four or five times in Kuhn's concordance and at least three times in the 4Q concordance. But it may be that in C 23 this verb had a special non-biblical, and also non-mishnaic, connotation. In QH שב אחור has the meaning of 'be cancelled'; the same may be true here, and שישובו may here have the opposite sense. The lack of context in MMT makes it impossible, however, to decide. (This meaning for שוב אחור was suggested by D. Flusser.)

3.5.1.25 שֶׁמֶשׁ: להערי[בו]ת השמש (B 15); עד בוא השמש (B 72)

MH generally uses the word חמה, with the biblical and Qumranic שמש appearing only in certain phrases or contexts (e.g., בא השמש, בין השמשות, סכי שמש, הערב שמש).

3.5.1.26 תּוֹעֵבָה: [שלו]א תביא תועבה א[ל ביתכה כי] התועבה שנואה היאה (C 6–7)

This word is very frequent in all BH and QH, but very rarely occurs in the Tannaitic literature, and then only when referring to biblical passages. Here too its occurrences and its context suggest that it could be explained by biblical influence. Note that the word שנואה is here the attributive of תועבה. This agrees with *Tg. Pseudo-Jonathan*'s rendition of this word, שניאה (contrast *Tg. Onqelos* מרחקא).

3.5.1.27 תּוֹרָה 'law, ordinance': מקצת מעשה התורה (C 27); ערמה ומדע תורה (C 28)

In MH this word generally refers specifically to 'the Torah', i.e. the Pentateuch as a whole (which is basically a code of law). This MH usage is, however, anticipated by passages in BH and QH referring to the individual law codes.

3.5.2 Post-Exilic Elements

3.5.2.1 ארץ ישראל: ואף על מטעת עצי המאכל הנטע בארץ ישראל (B 62–63)

The expression ארץ ישראל is rare in BH but very common in MH. In BH it is found more in the later books than in the earlier ones, and on the few occasions where it is found in the early books it does not denote a country as a complete geographical unit, but as either the area of Israelite settlement (Jos 11:22 [ארץ בני ישראל], 1 Sam 13:19), or the area of the kingdom of the ten tribes (2 Kgs 5:2, 6:23). It is an open question whether ארץ ישראל in the later writings (e.g., Ezek 40:3, 1 Chr 22:2, 2 Chr 2:16) refers to a geographical unit comprising the whole country. It is, however, clear that in MMT (as in 11QTᵃ 58:6) the term denotes the whole of the land of Israel as a geographical entity, or rather as an entity constituted by its purity and by the purity of its inhabitants (cf. also 4Q385 44 אדמת ישראל תאבד 5). Elsewhere in the DSS, in non-halakhic contexts, the term ארץ יהודה, or יהודה, is found. It appears that for halakhic purposes ארץ ישראל was preferred, while in other types of literature the historical name for the southern kingdom and the Persian province (Aramaic יהוד), יהודה (ארץ) = 'Judaea', continued to be used (cf. *Hebrew Encyclopaedia*, vol. 6, pp. 25–28, s.v. ארץ ישראל). Note that the *ṣade* in ארץ is in medial form. This is not typical of MSᶜ, which generally uses the final forms of מנצפ״ך (cf. מחוץ in B 66). Another exception to the rule is the *pe* in ואף על (B 62, 64; but ואף כתוב B 66). Is ארץ ישראל viewed as a combined word like ואף על?

3.5.2.2 בוא ל- 'Enter' followed by a place noun: לבוא למקדש (B 5); ואין להבי למחני הקודש כלבים (B 58)

In CBH the verb בוא 'enter' is generally attached to its adverb of place without any preposition. This is always the case when the adverb is a place name (e.g., לבוא מצרימה [Gen 12:11], ויבוא ירושלם [1 Kgs 3:15]). When the adverb is a place noun a preposition may be attached to it, but the usual preposition in this case is אל rather than ל- (ל- only occurs very rarely when a pronominal suffix is attached to the noun). In post-exilic Hebrew, however, בוא ל- 'enter' occurs more frequently. (For the usages in BH, see H. J. Austel, *Prepositional and Non-Prepositional Complements with Verbs of Motion in Biblical Hebrew*, Ph.D. Dissertation, University of California, Los Angeles, 1969, pp. 33, 44, 51–53, 78–98 [Austel unfortunately ignores the evidence of the *hipᶜil* conjugation]; for the use of בוא ל- in the Temple Scroll, see G. Brin, 'Philological Notes on the Temple Scroll', *Leshonenu* 43 [1979], pp. 24–25 [Brin's treatment is, however, inaccurate]). If one views the above cases of בוא ל- in MMT as a variant of בוא אל rather than of בוא without a preposition, the following references are relevant: Bendavid, I, pp. 369–370 and D. Talshir, 'A Reinvestigation of the Linguistic Relationship between Chronicles and Ezra-Nehemia', *VT* 38 [1988], pp. 179–180.)

It has been pointed out, on the other hand, that in MH the verb נכנס rather than בוא is used to denote 'entering' (Bendavid, I, p. 118; Schiffman, *Halakha*, p. 113, n. 195). בוא ל- is therefore untypical both of CBH and of MH.

3.5.2.2a בוא ל- 'have access to, be admitted'

When בוא ל- is not followed by a locative, it does not mean 'enter' (§ 3.5.2.2), but has other meanings. S. Lieberman (*JBL* 71 [1952], p. 202) has pointed out that בוא ליחד, and the like, mean 'to

apply for membership (of a sect)'. This is a technical usage found also in MH. In B 54 another expression occurs: באים לטהרת המקדש. This may well be a synonym of [י]גש לטהרת ה[קודש] (B 23). The latter is an equivalent of the BH phrase קרב אל הקדש and נגש אל הקדש. It has been suggested that נגש אל and קרב אל in BH mean 'have access to, be admitted' (J. Milgrom, 'The Cultic Use of קרב/נגש', *Proceedings of the Fifth World Congress of Jewish Studies*, vol. 1, Jerusalem, 1969, pp. 75–84). So also in QH and MH קרב ל- (as well as בוא ל-) means 'to admit' (Lieberman, ibid).

The semantic range of בוא ל- may well be identical with those of קרב אל and נגש אל, and the meanings 'to apply', 'to be admitted' and 'have access to' are very close to one other. We include this usage here believing that there is no real difference between בוא לטהרה and בוא ליחד. Otherwise the term would have been discussed in § 3.5.4.

3.5.2.2b [לבו]א עליהם

If the restoration is correct, and if women are referred to here, then the expression means 'to have sexual relations'. This expression is frequent in MH. In BH it occurs only twice (Gen 19:31; Deut 25:5), while בוא אל is much more common. In QH it occurs only once (see the concordance to the unpublished texts; see also S. Abramson, 'On a Peculiar Linguistic Feature in the Bible', *Sinai* 76 [1975], pp. 193–197).

3.5.2.3 בין in *hipᶜil*, in the sense of 'study, learn well', the object (a book or something written) being preceded by -ב: שתבין בספר מושה (C 10); הבן בכל אלה (C 28)

Hurvitz (*LBH*, p. 136) writes of this usage: 'Bacher had already noted that in the post-exilic passages Neh 8:8 ויקראו בספר בתורת האלהים . . . ויבינו במקרא and Dan 9:2 אני דניאל בינתי בספרים the verb בין approximates in meaning to the verb דרש. This approximation is associated with the later meaning of דרש (= 'study'). Just as דרש, so also בין, in both these later texts, is connected with books and the written word . . .' The lateness of this usage is also evident from a formal grammatical point of view; even if we ignore the meaning of the verb, the use of בין (whether in *qal* or *hipᶜil*) with the preposition -ב is only found in LBH, becoming even more common in QH.

Hurvitz (n. 181), following Rabin, notes the equivalence of Aramaic דרש ב- and of Hebrew הבין ב- in *b. Ḥag.* 13a; from the point of view of grammar and meaning, this usage should be seen as parallel to השכיל ב-, also frequent in QH.

3.5.2.4 בקש ש-: ובקש מלפנו שיתקן את עצתך (C 28–29)

The phrase בקש ש-, with בקש having its late meaning 'ask', not 'look for', and with אשר/ש- introducing an object clause, is found only once in BH, in the late passage Dan 1:8 (as בקש אשר); it has not yet been found in QH, which uses בקש + -ל + infinitive, although it appears in MH. Particularly instructive is the following example, which is also from other points of view similar to our text: על אחת כמה וכמה שלא יבקש מלפני הקב"ה שיתן לו אלא חנם (*Sipre Deut.*, Finkelstein's edition, p. 38–39). There are also other instances of object clauses preceded by -ש: אמר ש- (§ 3.5.3.2), חשב ש- (§ 3.5.4.3), הכיר ש- (§ 3.5.4.7).

3.5.2.5 בְּשֶׁל שֶ-: בשל שתשמח באחרית (B 16); בשל שא יהיה הטהר מזה על הטמה (B 12); בשל שלוא י[היו] העת (C 30) [cf. -ש בגלל (B 79), § 3.5.4.1]

This combination, meaning 'in order to' rather than 'inasmuch as', is found in Qoh 8:17 (אשר בשל) and in one of Bar-Kokhba's letters (*DJD* II, pp. 165–166; see Milik's note ad loc. and the parallels cited there). In Jonah it is used as a preposition rather than as a conjunction (באשר ל-, בשל; see BDB, p. 980 and the Aramaic parallels cited there). In standard MH it does not occur. N. H. Tur-Sinai was

of the opinion that MH's בשביל- is an expansion of בשל -ש (idem, apud Ben-Yehuda dictionary, vol. 14, p. 6841, col. ii, n. 2). Commentators on Qohelet compare it to the Aramaic בדיל ד-, which is the Aramaic Targum's equivalent of למען, and to its negative counterpart בדיל דלא (= לבלתי, פן). Note that the statement בשל שלוא י[היו] מסיא[י]ם את העם עוון (B 12–13) has a biblicising parallel in 1QS 5:14: בשל שלא) = פן; פן ישיאנו עוון אשמה). The Aramaic בדיל ד- already occurs in 11QtgJob 37:17 and in an Aramaic letter of Bar-Kokhba (Beyer, p. 352; see M. Sokoloff, *The Targum to Job from Qumran Cave XI*, Ramat-Gan, 1974, pp. 23, 145, and A. Tal, *The Language of the Targum of the Former Prophets*, Tel Aviv, 1975, p. 36).

It should be noticed that, on the one hand, של as a mark of the genitive (most current in MH) is not found either in the surviving text of MMT or in Jonah or Qohelet, while on the other hand, the word בשל (ש-), denoting cause or purpose, which occurs in various sources of the Second Temple period (and even in Tannaitic times), is not found in MH. These facts prove that the Hebrew sources differed as to the uses of (ב)של. They also imply that MH was not the spoken language of the author of MMT (cf. the uses of -ש, § 3.3.1.4).

3.5.2.6   זֶה הוּא: וזה הוא אחרית הימים (C 21)

The combination זה הוא is characteristic of MH. In CBH either הוא or זה is used.

There are, however, several occurrences of the combination in LBH (Qoh 1:17, 1 Chr 22:1). The parallel combination אלה הם occurs even in early biblical books (eight times in all; all the occurrences are in the priestly source; Mandelkern, p. 1285). In the DSS it occurs only in MMT and in 4Q186 8 ii 1. The question of the meaning of the combination and of each of its components needs further study (see Bendavid, II, pp. 741–745).

3.5.2.6a   זֹהר (*nip'al*) 'be careful': ואף על הסומים שאינם רואים להזהר מכול תערו[בת] (B 49–50); [כי לבני] הכוהנ[ים] ראו להזה'ר בדבר הזה (B 11–12)

In this last formula, the classical להשמר also occurs, taking the place of להזהר (B 26). Hurvitz (*P Source*, pp. 126–128) has demonstrated that the verb זהר is typical of post-classical compositions, and that the *nip'al* never appears in distinctly classical sources; in pre-exilic Hebrew, the regular equivalent of late BH נזהר is נשמר. In MSª there is a supralinear *yod* over the *reš*. The *hip'il* conjugation hardly fits here, and a plene spelling (לְהַזְהִיר) would be very surprising, though not impossible.

3.5.2.7   זֹונוּת (= זנות) 'illegal marriage': ועל הזונות הנעסה בתוך העם (B 75)

This form is also known from CD 8:5 (and perhaps 7:1), but also זנות is found in the parallel text of MS B and in other works from Qumran. In MH we find ואין לך זונות כזונות של ערביים (*Abot de Rabbi Nathan*, Version A 43a, MS New York); the ו after the ז was deleted in both words. The Samaritans' form in Num 14:33, זונתיכם (for MT's זנותיכם), is also relevant, but its pronunciation, *zunatikimma* (Ben-Ḥayyim, *SHG*, § 4.3.14), shows that it was taken to be the plural of *zuna* (= BH זונה); see also Milik, *Enoch*, p. 322, on the text of the *Midraš of Šemḥazai and Aza'el* (Version R, not Version S). On the meaning of this word, see § 5.7.17, and n. 83.

3.5.2.8   חוּץ לְ-, חוּץ מִן 'outside': חוץ ממ[חנה] (B 30); וחוצה למחנה (B 31)

The constructions חוץ ל- and חוץ מן are typical of late BH (cf. Neh 13:8); classical BH uses the construction מחוץ ל- (cf. מחוץ למחנה B 28). This explains why Deut 23:13, where MT has מחוץ למחנה, is rephrased in 11QTª 46:13 with חוץ מן העיר (on this identification of מחנה and עיר of Deut 23:13, see § 4 below), as it is also in the Peshitta of Deut 23:13 לבר מן משריתא; cf. also CD 11:5 חוץ מעירו and

CD 10:21 חוץ לעירו. MH also knows the construction חוץ מן, but in it the second, late construction, חוץ ל-, is more common (cf. Bendavid, I, p. 370; Qimron, *TSL*, A 17). On the use of חוצה with the same meaning as חוץ, see § 3.3.2.1.

3.5.2.9 חֲסָדִים in the phrase איש חסדים: זכור [את] דויד שהיא איש חסדים (C 25)

In BH and QH, a plural of חסד, referring to God, would need no justification. It refers also to human acts, however, in late biblical texts (Isa 55:3, Neh 13:14, 2 Chr 6:42, 32:32, 35:2), where it means 'deeds of kindness' (cf. BDB, and Kutscher, *Isaiah*, pp. 399–400); at Qumran we find a similar usage in the non-biblical phrase איש חסדים in 4Q375 2 ii 12 (of Moses) and in 4Q377 26 6 (probably of Moses). In MH the sense of the word חסדים is frequently narrowed to 'charity', especially in the phrase גמילות חסדים 'deeds of charity'; there is no trace of this further development in QH or in MMT.

3.5.2.10 טָהֵר (as a stative adjective): בשל שא יהיה הטהר מזה על הטמה (B 16)

The form הטהר, which occurs also in 11QTa 52:11 (though wrongly copied by the editor), might be merely a defective spelling for הטהור (cf. the parallel text in Num 19:19), though this would be contrary to the orthographic practice of our scribes. Perhaps we have here rather another pattern: טָהֵר; such a pattern is attested by some reliable manuscripts of Tannaitic literature (though, there, it is with the reflexive meaning 'one who purifies himself'), and perhaps also by Samaritan Hebrew (contra Ben-Ḥayyim, *SHG*, p. 194); cf. possibly also CD 10:10. Was this form vocalized after the pattern of its stative antonym טָמֵא?

3.5.2.11 טַהֲרָה

The word טהרה is regularly spelled 'defectively' in QH (more than forty times in the existing [published and unpublished] Qumran texts) and it is always so spelled in MMT. Only seldom does the plene spelling טוהרה occur in QH (two uncertain cases in 4Q manuscripts and לטו^הרה in 1QS at 6:22). We believe that QH's defective spelling represents the form טַהֲרָה as known in MH, whereas the plene spelling represents the form טָהֳרָה, as in BH (*HDSS*, § 100.2). For the meaning of the terms טהרה, טהרת המקדש and טהרת הקודש, see §§ 5.3.2.1, 5.3.2.5 and 5.3.3.6.

3.5.2.12 טִמְאָה

The word טמאה is always spelled defectively in Qumran manuscripts (some thirty times); this apparently reflects the form טִמְאָה as found in the Babylonian tradition of MH; BH's טָמְאָה would have been spelled טומאה, at least in some cases (*HDSS*, § 100, 2).

3.5.2.13 יוֹמִים (plural of יום): מיומ[י]ן (C 19 MSd; reading and context doubtful)

Such Aramaic plural forms of יום occur in QH (1QIsaa 1:1, 1QS 2:19, 3:5, 4Q175 [Testimonia] 4, and three more times in 4Q manuscripts). Such a form is also found in a Hebrew phrase in the *y. Berakot* 14:2. Cf. יומת (pronounced *yumat*) in the Samaritan Pentateuch, Deut 32:7 (= MT's יְמוֹת), as in Biblical Aramaic Ezra 4:15 (יוֹמָת).

3.5.2.14 יִשְׂרָאֵל 'the laity': משכתוב קודש ישראל (B 76)

The word ישראל has this meaning (cf. העם below 3.5.2.25) in this halakha, where it is opposed to בני אהרון and כוהנים. This usage, which is characteristic of the post-exilic social structure, can be found in later biblical books (BDB, p. 975, II, e), in QH (e.g., 1QS 8:5–6, 9:6) and in MH.

3.5.2.15 כְּשֶׁכָּתוּב: כשכתוב קודש ישראל (B 76 in MS^d; in MS^c משכתוב is found)

This term has an interesting history. It was current in post-exilic Hebrew in its biblicising form
כאשר כתוב (e.g., Dan 9:13, 1QS 8:14, 4Q177 often, CD, 4Q384 8 2, 4QpIsa^c [three times]; see J. A.
Fitzmyer, *Essays on the Semitic Background of the New Testament*, Montana, 1971, pp. 3–58, esp. 8–
9). In Tannaitic literature, surprisingly, it does not occur, but it does appear in the Amoraic
literature. The question of whether it is a loan translation of the Aramaic כדכתיב, and if so, from what
period, needs further study. (Cf. also משכתוב and שכתוב at § 3.5.4.6 below, and also § 5.3.2.6.)

3.5.2.16 לֵחָה 'moisture': כי לחת המוצקות והמקבל מהמה כהם לחה אחת (B 57–58)

This noun, in the feminine, also occurs in 11QT^a 49:12, in 4QTah^b (= 4Q277 1:5), in 4Q274 3 ii 5,
and, according to J. Baumgarten, in 4Q512 xii 4 (reading ליחות rather than the editor's לוחות; J. M.
Baumgarten, 'The Purification Rituals in *DJD 7*', in *Forty Years*, p. 207; cf. Qimron, *TSL*, B 15). In
BH, one finds only the masculine form of the noun, לֵח (Deut 34:7). In MH, לחה occurs frequently (on
its forms, see I. Bendavid, לֵחָה, *Leshonenu* 35 [1971], pp. 316–317).

3.5.2.17 לִפְנֵי referring to God: בעשותך הישר והטוב לפנו (C 31) (cf. 5.2.2c); ובקש מלפנו (cf. C 28)

In CBH, the preposition לפני is not used in such phrases. In the first phrase CBH would have בעיני, and
in the second either מן or מיד. The use of the word לפני in such expressions is characteristic of post-
exilic Hebrew and MH, cf. Esth 4:5, 8:5, Neh 2:5, 9:28, 2 Chr 31:30, 1QS 1:2, 5:20, etc. (Qimron,
TSL, A 22). Cf. the use of קדם in *Tg. Onqelos* to Deut 6:18 (= ועשית הישר והטוב בעיני ה' ותעביד דכשר
ודתקן קדם ה'). Note that לפני with בקש or שאל is not found elsewhere in QH.

The use of the word לפני (or קדם in Aramaic) when referring to God or to the king is
characteristic of the period and belongs to the courtly customs for speech to the king that were in
force during the Persian period. Objections can be raised to the alternative opinion that explains these
expressions as forms of anti-anthropomorphism (M. Klein, 'The Preposition קדם ("before") a Pseudo-
Anti-Anthropomorphism in the Targum', *JTS* 30 [1979], pp. 502–507; cf. Bendavid, I, pp. 373–374;
454–455; Brin, pp. 218–220).

3.5.2.18 מַדָּע: שראינו עמך ערמה ומדע תורה (C 27–28)

As noted in BDB, p. 396 I, this word appears late in BH (cf. also Qimron, *Gram.*, p. 294 # 23; Polzin,
p. 141). In sectarian compositions from Qumran it occurs four times, against the ubiquity of דעת
there; it should also be noted that the word מדע does not occur in Tannaitic literature. This apparent
Aramaic borrowing invaded the area of the original Hebrew infinitive דעת. The Aramaic nature of the
word can be recognized from its form, for the pattern מקטל in פ"י roots in Hebrew produces, for
example, מוצא or מושב, so that if the word were Hebrew we would find מודע; but in Aramaic, some
nominal and verbal forms from פ"י roots were formed on the analogy of פ"נ. M. Kister (personal
communication) mentions the parallel למדע תורתך found in the Saturday evening prayer.

3.5.2.19 מוּצֶקֶת (B 55–57)

This word would belong here (or in יצק after § 3.5.2.13) if we were to take into account only
morphological considerations; but for other reasons, especially semantic, we list and discuss it in
§ 3.5.4.4.

3.5.2.20 מַטָּעַת: מטע עצי המאכל (B 62)

The word מטע occurs ten times in QH: twice in 1QS, four times in 1QH^a and once each in 4Q418 81
13, 4Q423 2 7, 4QD^e and CD. In MH it is found in three passages in the *Tosepta: Šebiʿit* 1:1, 3;

Kilʾayim 3:3. BH uses instead the masculine synonym מטע, a form somewhat less frequent in QH (it appears four times in 1QHᵃ col. 8, and twice in *DJD* VII). It is not used in MH; cf. Qimron, *Gram.*, p. 297.

3.5.2.20a מן (= מקצת): see below, § 3.5.2.23

3.5.2.21 מעשה: on מעשי התורה see § 5.3.2.2

3.5.2.22 מצא with the sense 'to find out, to be aware (that something is so)': במצאך מקצת דברינו כן (C 30)

This usage is characteristic of the later books of the Bible: note ומצאת את לבבו נאמן לפניך in Neh 9:8; [. . .] ימצא כחש ואם לא ימצא נאמן [. . .] (4Q225 2 ii 8); and see נמצא אברהם נאמן ל[א]ל[ה]ים (4Q226 7:1); also 2 Chr 25:5, Dan 1:20, Qoh 7:26, Sir 44:20. Particularly instructive is the modification made by 1 Chr 20:2 to its earlier source, in 2 Sam 12:30:

| 1 Chr 20:2 | ויקח דויד את עטרת מלכם מעל ראשו וימצאה משקל ככר זהב |
| 2 Sam 12:30 | ויקח   את עטרת מלכם מעל ראשו   ומשקלה ככר זהב |

This construction is sometimes found in MH, both in the active (e.g., ובשחר עמד ומצאו מת *m. Tohar.* 5:7) and in the *nipʿal* passive (e.g., התורם קישות ונמצאת מרה *m. Ter.* 3:1); cf. also השתכח in Biblical Aramaic: תקלתא במאזניא והשתכחת חסיר (Dan 5:27). See also G. B. Ṣarfatti, 'The Use of the Syntagm נמצא עושה in Mishnaic Hebrew to Express Before-Future and After-Past Time', *Language Studies* 2–3, ed. M. Bar-Asher, Jerusalem, 1987, pp. 225–243 (English summary on p. XXI). Note that the sentence under discussion is an equivalent of a compound sentence such as במצאך שמקצת דברינו כן. The construction is discussed by Qimron in a forthcoming article.

3.5.2.23 מִקְצָת: invariably constructed, and very frequent in MMT (e.g. in B 1).

The word מקצת is derived from מן קצת, and it is in this form that it occurs in Aramaic, e.g., Dan 2:42 (cf. לקצת Dan 4:26), as also in some of the Hebrew deeds from the Bar-Kokhba period, where מן קצת means 'part of, some (of)' (*DJD* II, p. 226). The word מקצת first appears in LBH (especially with the meaning 'at the end of [a certain time]' and is used in MH. The Aramaic vocalisation of the word (cf. also מִנָת) betrays its origin; in early Hebrew, however, the preposition מ(ן) was perceived as an unseparated part of the word (cf. במקצת, למקצת).

MSᶠ has the reading מדברינו for מקצת דברינו. This use of מן alongside מקצת is to be found in other Hebrew and Aramaic sources, e.g. in the Aramaic of Dan (2:42): ואצבעת רגליא מנהון פרזל ומנהון חסף מן־הון מנהֵון מן־ קצת מלכותא תהוה תקיפה ומנה תהוה תבירה.

Note also the equivalent combinations ומקצת ראשי האבות (Neh 7:69) and ומראשי האבות (ibid. 70). Also Rabbinic Hebrew has both מקצת and מן, and the various sources differ in using the one or the other (Bendavid, I, p. 199). The partitive מן (synonymous with מקצת) occurs both in CBH and in LBH, but as pointed out in BDB, p. 580 II, it is typical of LBH and very rare in CBH. Note that in BH it refers to persons and not to objects. Cf. also H. Ewald, *Syntax of the Hebrew Language of the Old Testament*, Edinburgh, 1881, p. 41.

3.5.2.24 סֵפֶר מֹשֶׁה: (C 17, 21)

This phrase, an alternative name for 'the Torah', is also found in 2Q25 3. The editor, M. Baillet, draws attention to its lateness (*DJD* III, p. 90) and cites parallels from late biblical books (e.g., Neh 13:1) and from the Apocrypha; it is also found in Biblical Aramaic (Ezra 6:18). One can see its

prevalence in the later period from the modification made in the following parallel texts: בספר תורת משה (2 Kgs 14:6); בתורה בספר משה (2 Chr 25:4).

The phrase is not found in MH, but perhaps only out of theological concerns concerning divine authorship (cf. *Mekilta*, ed. Horowitz, p. 71); likewise תורת משה is found in LBH and QH, but only rarely in MH.

3.5.2.25 הָעָם 'the laity': (B 13, 75—cf. the use of ישראל in a similar sense, § 3.5.2.15)

The halakha in B 75–82 prohibits marriages between priests and women from lay families. Here the words ישראל and העם are opposed to כוהנים and בני אהרון. This restricted usage of העם is also found, though rarely, in CBH (e.g., Exod 19:24); only in post-exilic times, however, (e.g., Neh 10:34, 11QTa 35:11–14) does העם frequently have this technical meaning, which survives in MH.

3.5.2.26 עִמָּהֶם: בהיות טמאתם עמהם (B 67)

The form עמהם (instead of CBH's עמם) is typical of post-exilic Hebrew, and of QH (e.g., 1QM 1:2); in the unpublished texts from 4Q we have עמהם eight times against עמם five times. This is also the form which predominates in MH (cf. Gesenius, § 103, BDB s.v. עִם; Qimron, *Gram.*, p. 244 n. 61).

3.5.2.27 עֵת שֶׁ-: שמעת שיגלח וכבס [י]שב מחוץ [לאוהלו] (B 66–67)

In BH, עת אשר (as a conjunction = 'when') occurs only in the later books, e.g., ומעת אשר סר אמציהו (2 Chr 25:27; cf. Esth 5:13, Qoh 8:9). Also in QH we find עת אשר, e.g., in 4Q175 21, 4Q177 1 5, CD 10:15, 11QTa 33:2, 58:3 (E. Qimron, 'Notes on the Text of the Temple Scroll', *Tarbiz* 53 [1984], p. 141), and twice in *Jubilees* (but scarcely in מעת שׁ 4Q418 229 2). Even in MH (where עת itself has a specific sense, see § 3.5.1.21), we find, though very rarely, -עת שׁ as a conjunction, as, e.g., in *m. ʿOrla* 1:2. But -עת שׁ (or עת אשר) is typical of the Second Temple period, and not of any other. Note other temporal conjunctions formed with a noun + -שׁ or אשר or די, e.g.: -בזמן שׁ, -בשעה שׁ, בעדנא די (Dan 3:5, 15).

3.5.2.28 צִדְקִיָּה: (C 19)

In this word we find the suffix -יה, which is a by-form of the theophoric ending -יהו found in many pre-exilic proper names. The forms of this ending were discussed by Kutscher, who wrote:

As has been pointed out by N. H. Ṭur-Sinai, the plene forms (i.e. those with ו) are the rule for the First Temple period, whereas the defective forms (i.e., those lacking the final ו) are very rare in the literature of that period. This is true for the Neo-Babylonian inscriptions of Nippur and for the Elephantine Papyri (5th cent. BCE) as well as for Ezra and Nehemiah and the Jerusalem inscriptions (Kutscher, *Isaiah*, pp. 4–5).

The shortened forms predominate in 1QIsaa (as against the long forms in the MT). In the non-biblical material from 1–10Q we find, for instance, צדקיה (four times; never צדקיהו); ישעיה (five times; ישעיהו once), and ירמיה (seven times; ירמיהו twice). MH uses only the short forms.

3.5.2.29 קבל *piʿel* 'receive': כי לחת המוצקות והמקבל מהמה כהם לחה לחה אחת (B 57–58)

The *piʿel* קבל = 'to receive' is widely used in post-exilic Hebrew: it appears in LBH, QH, Ben-Sira and in both Tannaitic and Amoraic literature (and is also very common in Aramaic sources contemporary with them). In BH, however, קבל is clearly characteristic only of post-exilic writings. Note Deut 16:19 ולא תקח שחד, where *Tg. Onqelos* has ולא תקביל שוחדא; likewise we find in the *b. Ketub.* 105a, מקבלי שוחד (cf. A. Hurvitz, 'The Date of the Prose-Tale of Job Linguistically Reconsidered', *HTR* 67 [1974], pp. 20–23).

The verb קבל is employed here as a term for receiving a poured liquid in a container. Precisely this usage is frequent in MH (e.g., *m. Šabb.* 3:6), and can already be found in one late biblical passage, וישחטו הבקר ויקבלו הכהנים את הדם ויזרקו המזבחה 2 Chr 29:22 (although here no container is mentioned). The discussion by A. Hurvitz (*RB* 81 [1974], pp. 43–45), who assumes that in 2 Chr 29:22 דם + קבל is the equivalent of דם + לקח, is misleading; the former means 'to take the blood (from an animal) into a container' and the latter 'to take the blood (which is already in a container)' and, say, sprinkle it.

3.5.2.29a רָאוּי: כי לבני אהרן ראואי להיות [כי לבני] הכוהנ[י]ם ראוי להזהר בדבר הזה (B 11–12); . . . (B 16–
17); . . . [להש]מ[ר] ראוי הכו[הנ]ים [כי לבני] (B 25–26)

The word ראוי first occurs in LBH (Esth 2:9: הראויות לתת לה) where it has the sense 'destined'. (On this unusual meaning, see Lieberman, V, p. 952, n. 22.) In QH it is found in 11QTa 66:9: והיא רויה, and perhaps also in 1QM 17:9: רויי (J. Strugnell, 'Notes on 1QS 1, 17–18; 8, 3–4 and 1QM 17, 8–9', *CBQ* 29 [1967], p. 582). It occurs frequently in MH, sometimes (as in QH) with a legal sense, for instance *m. Giṭṭin* 10:5: האומר . . . עשו לה כנימוס עשו לה כראוי לא אמר כלום; compare the Aramaic כדחזי which is common in legal documents, and also appears as a translation of BH כמשפט (e.g., Lev 5:4).

The use of ראוי in MMT is, however, peculiar. It is followed by an infinitive, as it is in the biblical passage, and as it often is in MH. But while in these sources the word is inflected, e.g. במכות הראויות להשתלש (*m. Makkot* 3:11), in MMT it is not, and the logical subject is expressed by a prepositional phrase. Even if we were to take out the word ראוי and merely say לבני הכהנים להזהר, the infinitive would be imperatival and the meaning would be the same (see § 3.4.2.3).

Diachronically, this use of ראוי as an auxiliary verb should be compared to the similar use of certain other passive participles, for instance אסור and מותר. Such words occur in two equivalent constructions: אסור לך לעשות and אסורה את לעשות, both meaning 'you may not do'. It has been claimed that the former is earlier than the latter (Y. Breuer, 'On the Hebrew Dialect of the Amoraim in the Babylonian Talmud', *Language Studies*, II–III, ed. M. Bar-Asher, Jerusalem, 1987, pp. 132–134).

As regards ראוי, the former construction first appears in MH, e.g. ואם אינם ראוין לבוא ביש׳ (*m. Yebam.* 7:5), while the latter first occurs, according to Ben Yehuda's dictionary (vol. 13, p. 6302 II, bottom), in Medieval Hebrew. Its occurrence in MMT is therefore striking.

3.5.2.30 -שֶׁ or אֲשֶׁ

This word is very common in MMT, especially in introducing indirect speech. It is sometimes pleonastically repeated, as -ד is in Syriac (Nöldeke, § 369), before either subject or verb; B 55–56 is perhaps a case in point. In MMT, -שׁ has almost completely displaced אשר, and has even penetrated into the semantic realm of other conjunctions, for instance כי (cf. § 3.3.1.4). Its appearance at the beginning of a substantive relative clause is especially interesting, cf. שלוא ראה (B 53) = MH's frequent מי שׁ-. This use of -שׁ in introducing a substantive relative clause is also found in late biblical texts (Ps 137:8-9, Song 1:7, Qoh 6:10) and in CD 20:4.

Another peculiarity of -שׁ in MMT is its use before the passive participle in וע[ל ש]א כתוב (B 27) for ועל הכתוב, the regular BH and MH usage. Our construction is similar to הדבר אשר כתוב (CD 7:10, 19:7), and occurs in the Bar-Kokhba documents (שפתוח; *IEJ* 36 [1986], p. 206). It is also typical of certain traditions of MH. It may be compared with similar constructions of -שׁ or שהם followed by the participle, since the various sources of MH have variants such as הפתוח, שפתוח and שהוא פתוח; היושב, שיושב and שהוא יושב (cf. § 3.4.9; Kutscher, *Studies*, p. סג; Rosenthal, pp. 80–81; Bar-Asher, § 59; Nathan, pp. 315–316). It should be noted that in QH we sometimes find -ה instead of אשר before a verb in the perfect (for example הנשבע for אשר נשבע [*JJS* 39 (1988), p. 64]). Cf. also: Z. Ben-

Ḥayyim, 'Notes on Grammar and Lexicography', *Language Studies,* II–III, ed. M. Bar-Asher, Jerusalem, 1987, pp. 99–103; D. Talshir, 'A Reinvestigation of the Linguistic Relationship between Chronicles and Ezra-Nehemia', *VT* 38 (1988), p. 180.

In one passage in MMT, שלוא לזרוע שדו (B 78), שלוא does not introduce an indirect clause of prohibition but an independent clause denoting prohibition (see the discussion at § 3.4.2.1).

Note also the following passages where -ש is redundant: שאין (B 55), שאנחנו (B 73 MS[d]; = אנחנו in MS[c]). Cf. E. Qimron, 'The Particles אשר, ש and די Introducing a Main Clause in Hebrew and Aramaic', *Leshonenu* 46 (1982), pp. 27–38.

In QH, -ש is found only in certain manuscripts, among them 4QMiš C, 4QJub[e], 4Q385 (= Pseudo-Ezek.), 4QD[a] and 4Q448.

Scholars have noted that -ש is found mainly in post-exilic Hebrew (including MH), and that its few occurrences in earlier biblical texts apparently reflect the dialect of the north of the country (see Ben-Yehuda, vol. 14, p. 6779; A. Hurvitz, *LBH*, pp. 41, 172; E. Qimron, 'On Second Temple Period Hebrew in the Book of Psalms', *Bet Mikra* 73 [1978], pp. 140–141).

3.5.2.31   שלם   *qal* 'to be finished, completed', of a period of time: ושלמה השנה (A 20)

In BH, the *qal* שלם with the word ימים or the like as a subject, occurs in this sense only in Isa 60:20 (ושלמו ימי אבלך). In QH (including the unpublished texts), it is found in the *qal* (eight times), in the non-BH *nipʿal* (five times), and in the *hipʿil* (twice). Examples include 1QS 10:6, CD 4:8, 10, 10:10, 11QT[a] 45 7–8. It is frequently used in Aramaic where שלם is the translation of the Hebrew מלא (+ a time-span); so, for instance, *Tg. Onqelos* on Gen 29:21.

MH likewise uses שלם with words of time (e.g. עת) where BH would use מלא (Bendavid, I, p. 353); QH continues to use מלא side by side with שלם; see CD 10:1, 1QSa 1:10, 1QS 7:20, 22, 8:26 and two or three more examples in 4Q.

3.5.2.32   תַּעֲרֹבֶת   [להזהר] מכול תערובת ;(50–51 B) . . . להזהר מכול תערו[בת] ותערובת [א]שם אינם רואים:תערובת [ה]גבר (B 48)

The word first occurs with a similar sense in QH, in 11QT[a] 45:7 and 50:4 (Qimron, *TSL*, B 36). The biblical expression בני הַתַּעֲרֻבוֹת 'hostages' (2 Kgs 14:14) is less relevant here, for in BH the meaning of the word is 'pledge', not 'mixture'. The nominal pattern תִּקְטֹלֶת is characteristic of MH and of Aramaic (Qimron, *Gram.*, p. 109, n. 92). The plural of this word in reliable manuscripts of the Mishna is תַּעֲרוּבוֹת. This implies that the original form was *taqtūlt* rather than *taqtult*.

An examination of the use of the word in QH shows that it occurs in contexts of uncleanliness, or of sexual relations; see further § 5.3.2.4, and Qimron, *ʾal Yitʿarev*. See also: Yalon, *Scrolls*, pp. 94–95; and cf. μειγνυμι and μιξις (L-S, pp. 1092 and 1136).

3.5.2.33   תקן: (C 28, if the reading is correct)

See BDB, s.v., and Gesenius, § 91–92.

3.5.3   Usages Not Found before MH

3.5.3.1   אכל, in האכיל מהקדשים: אין להאכילם מהקו[ד]שים (B 71); see also להאכילם מכול תרומות הש] (4Q513 2 ii 3)

In the Bible one finds the expression אכל מן הקדשים in the *qal* (e.g., Lev 22:6, 7), but not with the verb in the *hipʿil*. In MH, on the other hand, expressions similar to ours are often found, the *hipʿil*

having the technical sense 'let eat', 'to accord the right to eat'; cf. הרי זה מאכילה בתרומה (*t. Yebam.* 8:3); שאין מאכילים טהרות לעם הארץ (*t. Dem.* 2:22).

In MH, as a general rule, after האכיל the permitted food is introduced by -ב (and so frequently also after the *qal*, e.g., אוכל בקדשים, *t. Nazir* 6:1); but with the *qal* we find also מן, e.g. in לאכל מן הפסחים (*m. Pesaḥ.* 10:6 and *t. Zebaḥ.* 5:12).

In sum, then, the expression in MMT is closer to MH than to BH, for in MMT, also, the use of the *hipʿil* is apparently technical, and its meaning is 'let X eat of'. This usage is found in ואין להגיעם בטהרת [הקו]דש (4Q513 2 ii 1), and perhaps in משיאים את העם עוון 'let the people bear punishment' (B 27); cf. also the commentary to B 58.

3.5.3.2 -אמר ש ... :שהם אומרים אנחנו המוצקות על ואף (B 55); ... אנחנו אומרים שכל עצם ... (B 73); cf. § 3.5.4.7 -הכיר ש and § 3.5.4.3 -חשב ש

Although a similar phrase for introducing indirect speech can already be found in LBH (in the form אמר אשר, Qoh 8:14; Neh 3:19), it is only in MH that we find -אומר ש in contexts of the determining of halakhic opinion, e.g. *m. Šeqal.* 4:1: אף אתה אומר שאינם באים אלא משל ציבור; cf. in the Midraš, מניין -אתה אומר ש (e.g., *Sipre Num.*, ed. Horowitz, pp. 130, 143).

In the Mishna the expression שאתם אומרים occurs, interestingly, in quotations from Sadducees (*Yad.* 4:6–7; it is here followed not by -ש and indirect speech, but by direct speech). Baumgarten (*Controversies*, p. 164) has already noted the polemical significance of this usage. One tradition of MH uses the form אָמְרוּ with the meaning 'they decided', in contradistinction with אָמְרוּ which means 'they said' and the like (see Y. Bentolila, *A French-Italian Tradition of Post-Biblical Hebrew,* Beer-Sheva, 1989, pp. 65–66, n. 290 [in Hebrew]). The phrase אני אומר is also used by Jesus in his polemics. Cf. also בית הלל אומרים and בית שמאי אומרים in the Mishna.

3.5.3.3 אַף

ואף occurs frequently in MMT when introducing a further statement: ואף על (B 13, 42, 52, 55 etc.); ואף כתוב (C 12); ואף הקללות (C 18); see also § 5.2.4.

The question is one of the relative frequency of אף and גם. אף is rare in BH, and even more so in QH (according to the 4Q and Kuhn concordances it occurs about seven times in QH, excluding its occurrences in the phrase ואף הואה). The word גם is usually found in its stead in both BH and QH (according to the same concordances, it occurs about eighty times in QH). In MH, on the other hand, as in MMT, only אף remains in use. Kutscher (*Words*, p. 75) was of the opinion that this MH preference for אף stemmed from the fact that it was, unlike גם, a word also found in Aramaic. It should be noted that the word is employed in MMT affirmatively. It opens a new statement, as does the word וכעת in official Aramaic letters, the word ועתה in Hebrew letters, and the word וגם in the other DSS. Similarly, in the phrase אף הואה (1QS 11:20 and elsewhere), the word אף is merely an affirmative. Cf. ... ואף אללי Mur 42:5. For similar use of אף in MH, see A. Weiss, משפט לשון המשנה, Vienna, 1867, p. 83; Epstein, p. 1007; Z. Ben-Ḥayyim, *The Literary and Oral Tradition of Hebrew and Aramaic Amongst the Samaritans*, III b, Jerusalem, 1967, p. 43 (in Hebrew). The Samaritans pronounce the word אפוא *afu* (= אף הוא; see Ben-Ḥayyim, *SHG*, p. 241 and the other sources cited there). It should be noted that the combinations ואף על and ואף הואה are usually written in one word (with medial *kap*).

3.5.3.4 וָלָד: שאיאכל את הולד (B 37); [א]ת האם ואת הולד (B 36); וָלָד

In both passages it is materially equally possible to read ילד; but the word ולד is more appropriate to the context, since the meaning seems to be 'embryo' or 'small baby' (which is what ולד means in MH),

while ילד more frequently means both 'a little child' and 'a big child'. The word ולד 'embryo' occurs in BH only in Gen 11:30 and (according to the *Ketib* of the *Madinḥaʾe*) in 2 Sam 6:23; the Samaritan version has ולד also in Exod 21: 22 (but reads ילד in Gen 11:30); for QH, cf. 11QTᵃ 50:10 and Qimron, *TSL*, B 8.

3.5.3.4a יָד 'handle': [אין לעשות מן עצמותמה] ומן ע[ו]ר[ות]מה ידות כ[לים] (B 21–22)

If the restoration [כ]לים is correct, ידות must mean 'handles'. The earliest attestation of יד (singular) with this meaning is 1QM 5:14. The plural form ידות, however, was not hitherto attested before the mishnaic period.

3.5.3.5 סוֹמֶה [ואף ע]ל הסומ[י]ם שאינם רואים (B 49–50)

This is the earliest attestation of this word, which was previously known to us only from MH and even later Hebrew. It does not occur elsewhere in QH. Morphologically, סומים here is a participle masculine plural from √סמי, a root found in MH. Despite the frequency of spellings such as סומא with an *ʾalep*, the verb in MH is conjugated only as a *lamed-yod* (cf. Haneman, p. 391); in MMT, too, the word is conjugated as *lamed-yod*.

3.5.3.6 עברה 'pregnant female': והדבר כתוב עברה (B 38)

The syntax here is awkward, but the halakha surely concerns pregnant animals (see § 5.7.8; note the form עברות cited there). The word עברה occurs in MH. In reliable manuscripts of the Mishna we find two forms: עֲבָרָה and עוּבָּרָה (cf. H. Yalon, *Introduction to the Vocalization of the Mishna*, Jerusalem, 1964, pp. 85–87; *Studies*, p. 108). The QH witnesses confirm Yalon's view that the form עֲבָרָה represents a Palestinian vernacular feature.

3.5.3.7 עַל גַּב :[ע]ל גב [ו]מהתערב בדברים האלה ומלבוא ע[ל]מהם ע[ל]ל גב (לגב or) אלה (C 8)

The context, though broken, apparently states that the sect broke away from the rest of the people because of the abominations that they would bring to the Temple. The phrase על גב, found only once in MMT (and not at all in BH or QH), is known to us from MH (see Lieberman's commentary on *Tosepta Beṣa*, p. 950). Its sense cannot be defined exactly, but it occurs in MH in contexts of the mixing of pure food. From a linguistic point of view we can say that, although the meaning of על גב is not clear, it had a pre-MH technical usage hitherto unattested. See also the commentary.

3.5.3.8 עשה :כי שלוא ראה ולוא שמע לוא ידע לעשות (B 53–54)

In this passage, עשה is used absolutely as a technical term meaning 'to maintain the precepts of the Torah'. For this meaning of עשה, cf. מעשי תורה (§ 5.3.2.2) and the literature cited there. It might be conjectured that the Sectarians interpreted the word עשה in this sense in Exod 18:20 ואת המעשה אשר יעשון (cf. LXX); cf. העושה מצוה אחת (*m. ʾAbot* 4:11). But whatever the source of this meaning, this sense of עשה was also in common use in QH (see § 5.3.2.2 and the literature cited there). The absolute use (without תורה, מצוה, or whatever as an object), unattested elsewhere in the DSS, occurs in *m. ʾAbot* 2:2.

3.5.3.9 פָּרַת הַחַטָּאת 'the red cow' (B 13)

The term פרת החטאת is found in MH, but not in BH or QH. In the Pentateuch the red cow is simply called חטאת, and this biblical usage seems to be reflected in MSᵇ's text of MMT before it was corrected: the word פרת was added later between the lines. Cf. § 5.3.3.2.

3.5.3.10 פרש מן [פרשנו מרוב הע]ם: (C 7)

The verb פרש, 'to separate oneself', is not found in BH, but is at home in MH, where it denotes, among other things, the act of leaving the community because of differences of opinion over halakha. In our broken text the usage seems the same as that of MH, cf. אל תפרוש מן הציבור (*m. ʾAbot* 2:4; in MH ציבור replaces עם, see § 3.5.1.18). Elsewhere in QH the expression סור מן is used instead of פרש מן to denote the sect's breaking away and dissent (e.g., סרו מדרך העם [CD 8:16; 19:29]; see § 4.1.4.2). On the use of נבדל in similar contexts, see D. Flusser, 'The Dead Sea Sect and Pre-Pauline Christianity', *Scripta Hierosolymitana* 4, Jerusalem, 1958, p. 231.

The terminology here differs from the standard sectarian use in QH. It may predate it, or it may be that our text here reflects the terminology of the sect's opponents.

3.5.4 New Words or Expressions

3.5.4.1 -בִּגְלַל שׁ בגלל שהמה קדושים: (B 79)

The word בגלל 'because' is rare in BH and MH, in both of which it is found only in the construct state or with suffixes. In QH, it is found only in a biblical quotation in 11QTᵃ 60:20 and a single occurrence in 4Q (cf. § 3.5.2.5). The combination בגלל שׁ- is not found in early sources, and would appear to be a loan translation of the Aramaic -בגלל ד or מן בגלל ד- (or, in Christian Palestinian Aramaic, -לגלל ד).

3.5.4.2 הַעֲרִיבוּת לכול אלה להערי[בו]ת השמש להיות טהורים: (B 15)

The word העריבות, a *hipʿil* verbal noun (see § 3.3.3.5), is not attested elsewhere in Hebrew; in the Amoraic literature the Aramaicizing equivalent הערבה is found. The phrase העריבות השמש is similar to MH's הערב שמש, but MH uses a different form for the verbal noun and the indefinite form of the noun שמש (cf. also העריב שמשו in MH [and apparently also אשר יעריב שׁ[משו] in 4QD], עריבת שמש in Karaite literature, במערב שמשא in a papyrus from Elephantine [Cowley 21:8], and במעלי שמשא [Dan 6:15]. Note that the noun שמש is not used freely in MH, a fact which indicates that this construct phrase does not belong to the standard MH language; cf. § 3.5.1.25). For a discussion of the connection between כבוא השמש, להעריבות השמש and הערב שמש, and the development of terms with verbal nouns from time expressions with infinitive, see Qimron, *Terms*, pp. 130–132. Note that the phrase in MMT is used adverbially.

For the use of the preposition -ל to denote a point of time in the future, cf. the regular MH use of למחר 'tomorrow', and of לעולם הבא or לעתיד לבוא in contrast to בעולם הזה (*m. ʾAbot* 4:1; see Segal, § 296). 11QTᵃ 49:20 has ויטהרו לערב instead of the ויטהר בערב of BH (Num 19:11).

3.5.4.3 חשב (שׁ-) 'to think (that), to decide': [ועל] האוכל [אנח]נו (B 29); ואנחנו חושבים שהמקדש ... (B 42) ואף חושבים אנחנו (B 37); .... חושבים שיאכל את הולד ...

The combination חשב שׁ- can also be found in MH, e.g. *m. Makš.* 4:7, 6:1. In both BH and MH, חשב usually means 'to plan'. Though there are (chiefly in BH) some additional senses, such as 'to reckon' and 'to account', the MMT meaning 'think (that), to decide' is not found either in BH or in MH (even though it is given in some dictionaries). For parallels to MMT's usage, see above on אמר שׁ- (§ 3.5.3.2) and הכיר שׁ- (§ 3.5.4.7).

3.5.4.4 יצק *hupʿal* participle: המוצקות (B 55–57)

The word occurs twice in LBH, in Zech 4:2 and 2 Chr 4:3, each time with a different meaning; in the former passage it means 'a pipe', and in the latter 'a casting'. Apart from MMT, the word is not found

in QH; it is also non existent in MH. The sense here would seem to be the same as that of MH's נצוק (*nipʿal* participle of צוק), 'an uninterrupted flow (of a liquid poured from vessel to vessel)'. For further details, see the halakhic discussion, § 5.7.13, the commentary, and Qimron, *Terms*, pp. 133–134.

3.5.4.5 כָּתוּב

A. משכתוב קודש ישראל :מִשכתוב (B 76; in MS^d we find the variant כשכתוב)

This expression is not known to us from any other Hebrew source and is apparently a mechanical translation from the Aramaic מדכתיב; see W. Bacher, *Die exegetische Terminologie der jüdischen Traditions-literatur*, Leipzig, 1905, p. 99, and cf. כשכתוב, § 3.5.2.15.

B. (C 20–21) ואנחנו מכירים שבאוו מקצת הברכות והקללות שכתוב בס[פר מו]שה :שכתוב

The word שכתוב cannot be understood as adjectival to the words הברכות והקללות: gender and number are incompatible and שכתוב (for the expected הכתובות, cf., e.g., 2 Chr 34:24) is, although possible, very unusual in such a construction (cf. § 3.4.5). It would seem then that שכתוב is another term, like כשכתוב and משכתוב referred to above, translated mechanically from the Aramaic, in this case from the phrase דכתיב meaning 'as is written'. On כתוב not followed by a biblical quotation, see § 5.3.2.6. The term שכתוב (= דכתיב) does not occur, as far as we can ascertain, in Tannaitic literature, but it is found in the later midrašim.

3.5.4.7 √נכר in -ש הכיר: ואנחנו מכירים שבאוו מקצת הברכות והקללות (C 20)

הכיר ש- means here 'to know, understand'; its use in this sense is uncommon, but it appears in Neh 6:12, and perhaps in classical BH (2 Sam 3:36). Note also 4Q18 13:2: הלוא תכיר והלוא תדע. We have not, however, found any other instance of the combination הכיר ש- or הכיר אשר (cf. § 3.5.3.2 -אמר ש, § 3.5.4.3 -חשב ש). Syntactically not far from this construction is the use of הכיר + infinitive (as in חשב לפעול, אמר לפעול) and Neh 13:24: ואינם מכירים לדבר יהודית); compare also the LBH constructions בקש לפעול (BDB s. vv).

MH has a construction with -הכיר ש, but somewhat different in meaning: אם מכרתו שהוא אוכל בתרומה (*t. Toh.* 5:8). Only in Aramaic do we find an exact parallel: -אכר ד is frequent in Christian Palestinian Aramaic with the same meaning as -הכיר ש in MMT.

3.5.4.8 נצל: on מצול see § 3.3.3.4

3.5.4.9 ערב: on העריבות see § 3.5.4.2

3.5.4.9a עשה זנות: ועל הזונות הנעסה (B 75)

The phrase עשה זנות is not known to us from any other Hebrew source, but it has an Aramaic parallel, למעבד זנו, in *Tg. Ruth* 3:10.

3.5.4.10 צוק (מוצקות): see יצק above

3.5.4.11 רבע *piʿel*, 'to mate, to breed': ועל בה[מתו הטהור]ה כתוב שלא לרבעה כלאים (B 76–77)

In BH the *qal* and *hipʿil* of רבע are used in this sense; here we have rather the (non-biblical) *piʿel*, with a causal meaning (as is further shown by the use in MS^d of the *hipʿil* [as in BH] as a variant of the *piʿel*). As far as we know, the *piʿel* is not attested in any other Hebrew source.

3.5.4.12 שָׁפֶכֶת: [וכרו]ת השפכת (B 39)

This passage relates to Deut 23:2, which reads וכרות שָׁפְכָה (in the Babylonian tradition also שׁפׄכֺה) 'a man whose member is cut off'. The form in MMT agrees with that of the Samaritan Pentateuch, שפכת, pronounced *ašfikot* (plural) in the Samaritan oral tradition; the Samaritan Targum ad loc., translating שפיכין, also took the form as a plural. However the spelling in most of the Samaritan Hebrew biblical manuscripts is defective. The form in MMT is apparently singular, most likely of the pattern קְטֶלֶת. Perhaps this was originally the case also in the Samaritan Pentateuch.

Is there any formal connection between the שָׁפֶכֶת* of MMT and the שָׁפְכָה of MT? Both may represent a feminine infinitive pattern of *qal*, שָׁפְכָה *šupuk* + *at*, while שָׁפֶכֶת represents *šipik* + *t* (cf. שׁפׄכֺה *šipik* + *at* in the Babylonian tradition). Such *qal* infinitive forms are interchangeable in the various tradition of Hebrew, e.g.: שְׁכְבָה, שְׁכְבָה and שְׁכֹבֶת (see I. Yeivin, *The Hebrew Language Tradition as Reflected in the Babylonian Vocalization*, Jerusalem, 1985 [in Hebrew], p. 943; Ben Ḥayyim, *SHG*, p. 206; and ש'כבת הזרע in Qumran [see the preliminary concordance]; see also Bauer and Leander, p. 469). It is less likely that שפכת represents שָׁפֶכֶת, but cf. the by-forms קָרֲחָה / קָרַחַת, שָׁרֶטֶת / *šurta* (in the Samaritan oral tradition), צָרֶבֶת / צָרְבָה (in the MH Babylonian tradition; Yeivin, ibid., p. 864).

3.5.4.13 √תוך (?) 'to cohere': שמקצת הכהנים ו[. . .] מתוככים ומטמאי[ם] את זרע [א]ין להתיכם (B 80–81); ולעשותם [עצם אחת] (B 44)

There is no verb from the root תוך in the Bible; a verb תוך is found in MH, but not with the meaning required here (see, for example, *m. Me'ila* 2:3 in reliable manuscripts and in Maimonides' commentary). The verb is also found in the Amoraic literature, where תוך means (*a*) 'to divide in the middle, to halve' and (*b*) 'to be between, to lie between'; cf. התויך = 'to place in the middle'.

Since all these usages are different from that of MMT, the exact meaning of תוך in MMT can be established only by its context. In both passages the subject matter is marital relations and impurity. We can even be more exact and assert that the verb תוך denotes the consequence of the marital relation. The phrase להתיכמה ולעשותם [עצם אחת] appears to be equivalent to Gen 2:23-24 ... ודבק באשתו והיו לבשר אחד (On the centrality of this verse for establishing the marriage laws in the DSS, see § 5.7.9, note. On Samaritan מכתב הדביקה based on this passage, see M. Gaster, *The Samaritans*, London, 1925, p. 72.)

How can the root תוך denote cohesion? We can perhaps use the root קרב as a parallel, since בתוך = בקרב. The root קרב has the sense 'adhere' (Ezek 37:7) and 'relate' (קרוב), and it may be that תוך has a similar range of meaning. Note that *Tg. Onqelos* renders עצמי ובשרי (Gen 29:14) with קריבי ובסרי.

3.6 The Nature of MMT's Language

We can now specify the nature of the language of MMT and determine its relation to the language of the other DSS. We can also define with greater accuracy the relationship between the language of MMT and MH.

3.6.1 The Grammar

Here are the conclusions to be drawn from each of the various phases of grammatical study (spelling, phonology, morphology and syntax).

3.6.1.1 Spelling

The spelling practices are identical with those of the other Qumran manuscripts. The few deviations to be found in one or other manuscript of MMT are minor and of a kind that can be found in other

Qumran texts. They include, for example, the defective spelling of the second person masculine singular pronominal suffix (ך- for כה-, cf. § 3.1.3), which exists in most manuscripts of MMT, and the spelling כי (rather than כיא), which also occurs in other scrolls from Qumran. The absence of vulgar spellings, such as the combination of historic and phonetic orthography in ראוש, would appear to be accidental and may be explained by the small quantity of text that has been preserved (§ 3.1.4.1); but we should note that cases of *ś* spelled with ס are more numerous in our manuscripts than in the other Qumran scrolls.

3.6.1.2 Phonology

The phonology, to the extent that it can be determined from our short and unvocalized text, is also very similar to that of the other Qumran scrolls. We have found only one feature previously undocumented in QH: ראואי (§ 3.2.2.4); this feature is, however, known from some traditions of BH and MH vocalisation, though only rarely betrayed by the spelling. We believe that it represents the usual Qumran pronunciation, though it is not elsewhere expressed by the spelling (cf. also באוו § 3.2.1).

3.6.1.3 Morphology

The morphology, too, is primarily Qumranic; it is quite similar to that of BH, and differs markedly from that of MH. MMT has a large number of QH features not found in MH. The consistent use of the relative -ש is what seems to distinguish MMT from the other Qumran scrolls (even though it is to be found, inconsistently, in some). This word is the conspicuous feature that gives MMT its prima facie MH appearance, but as we have seen, the usages of -ש in MMT and in MH are not identical.

3.6.1.4 Syntax

The syntax of MMT (including its use of tenses) is also mainly Qumranic; there are, on the one hand, many specific traits which distinguish it from MH syntax—for instance, the use of the infinitive as predicate (§ 3.4.2), the archaising and biblicising use of the conversive perfect (§ 3.4.11) and the temporal infinitive of the type בקטלו (§ 3.4.3); on the other hand, there are elements shared primarily with MH—the use of the participle and of היה + participle to express habitual action (§§ 3.4.1.4, 3.4.1.5). (For the other MH syntactical features, see §§ 3.4.4, 3.4.5, 3.4.6.) Generally speaking, MMT's syntax is closer to that of MH than is its morphology.

3.6.2 The Vocabulary

The grammar of MMT is thus primarily Qumranic. What, then, constitutes the special nature of the language of MMT? The relative pronoun -ש, and a number of syntactical constructions, are insufficient in themselves to give the text the markedly MH appearance that it has. What lends it this appearance is above all the vocabulary. An analysis shows that lexical material that is not found in CBH predominates in MMT, and that the overriding majority of these words belong to MH alone. This is so not only for the words listed in § 3.5.3, but also for the majority of the words dealt with in § 3.5.2. (For the words in § 3.5.4, see the next chapter.) An especially large number of MH words occur in the halakhic part of MMT (= B 1–82). The halakhic terms are of great importance, and most of those found in MMT belong exclusively to MH [(a) below] while only a few belong to BH [(b) below].

A.   (אנחנו) אומרים = 'we are of the opinion (concerning a halakha)'; מקבל = '(a vessel) receiving a poured liquid'; טהרה = 'ritually pure food' (so also QH); פרת החטאת = 'the red cow'; העריבות השמש =

'sunset'; להאכיל מן הקודשים = 'to permit (someone) to eat from the holy things', i.e., ritually pure food; מעשים = 'rules; precepts of action; halakhot'; ארץ ישראל = those parts of Palestine in which Jews reside and where the relevant halakha—of the tithes, etc.—is in force.

B.   צרוע = 'leper'; עץ מאכל = 'fruit tree'; מעשר הבקר והצון = 'tithe of the herd or flock'.
It is the MH vocabulary (particularly what is found in the halakhic part of the work) that gives MMT its MH appearance, even though its grammar (and especially its phonology and morphology) differs markedly from that of MH, and resembles that of QH.

Of special importance are those linguistic elements in MMT which have opposing usages in the other DSS: שֶׁ- (vs. אשר), בְּשֶׁל שֶׁ(לוא) (vs. [אשר לוא], למען [אשר לוא] or בעבור [אשר לוא] or פן), אַף (vs. גם), מלבוא (vs. מבוא etc.), אנחנו (vs. אנו), פרש מן (vs. סר מן), הכּיר שֶׁ- (vs. ידע כי), סוֹמֶה (vs. עור), מְקֶצֶת (vs. מן), נזהר (vs. נשמר), מְשֶׁכָּתוּב (vs. כאשר כתוב), להעריבות השמש (vs. כבוא השמש), מָצוּל (לערב, מצוּל (vs. נצל), שהם בָּאִים (vs. הבאים). In most of these cases the usages in the other DSS are those of BH, while those of MMT may well represent the vernacular. Note that some of these elements occur both in section B and in section C (cf. also §§ 3.4.1.5, 4.1.3.1 and 5.2.4).

3.6.3 Aramaic Elements

Not only MH elements but also Aramaic elements occur more frequently in MMT than in other Qumran manuscripts. However, because of the similarity between Hebrew and Aramaic, only in a relatively few cases is it possible to demonstrate clearly that a given word has been borrowed from Aramaic. The following items, which are not found in MH, may have been borrowed from, or influenced by, Aramaic: בְּשֶׁל שֶׁ 'so that' (§ 3.5.2.5); בִּגְלַל שֶׁ 'because' (§ 3.5.4.1); מַדָּע 'knowledge' (§ 3.5.2.18); מְשֶׁכָּתוּב, שֶׁכָּתוּב 'as is written' (§ 3.5.4.6); הכּיר שֶׁ- 'know, understand' (§ 3.5.4.7); and perhaps the predicative use of the infinitive (§ 3.4.2). Note, however, that some of these attestations in MMT are earlier than their Aramaic equivalents. There are other features which, although found in MH, may have been borrowed from Aramaic by both MH and QH. They are: מְקֶצֶת 'some' (Aramaic in vocalic pattern; § 3.5.2.23); רָאוּי 'obliged' (translated from חֲזֵי; § 3.5.3.10); מֵעֵת שֶׁ- (conjunction; § 3.5.2.27); שלם 'be fulfilled' (of a time-span; § 3.5.2.31); קבל 'receive' (§ 3.5.2.29); היה + participle (§ 3.4.1.4); וּמִלָּבוֹא (§ 3.3.3.2.1).

3.6.4 Elements Known from Samaritan Hebrew (or from Other Traditions)

A number of special elements, phonetic and morphological, that are found in MMT have parallels in other non-Tiberian traditions of Hebrew, and in particular in the Samaritan tradition. We have noted אתמה (§ 3.3.1.1.3); -המה (§ 3.3.1.2.1); the suffix יו > o (§ 3.2.2.1); ראוי (= ראוי; ראואי and ראו = § 3.2.2.3); the הקטילה pattern (§ 3.3.3.5); the form שְׁפֶכֶת (§ 3.5.3.12); and in the Babylonian tradition טְמָאָה (§ 3.1.1.2).

3.6.5 The Composition of the Language of MMT

From a linguistic point of view, the material in MMT can be divided into five categories:
(a)   Biblical elements (early and late)
(b)   Elements found first in MH
(c)   Elements borrowed from Aramaic
(d)   Elements known from non-Tiberian traditions of Hebrew
(e)   Elements attested only in the Qumranic tradition (there are also some elements which we may suppose to be Qumranic, although they are as yet only documented in MMT itself)

These are precisely the same elements that compose QH in general. In other words, the language of MMT has the same components as the other works composed at Qumran, although, as we have seen, includes more mishnaic and Aramaic elements (particularly in the lexicographical sphere).

There is no need to assume that MH itself had any influence on QH (or on LBH). The fact that many of the new features of QH differ from those of MH proves that they originated in a spoken dialect which differed from MH (especially with regard to grammar), while nonetheless sharing much in common with it (especially with regard to vocabulary). The features which resemble those of MH may well have come from this dialect rather than from MH itself. Some of these features may have come from Aramaic.

A number of explanations can be suggested for the high ratio of Aramaic and mishnaic elements:

(a)   MMT is a letter; its language is therefore closer to the vernacular than the language of a literary composition of another and higher genre would have been.

(b)   The letter is addressed to a person, probably a Pharisee, who understood and apparently spoke a kind of MH. Perhaps, then, words and terms were selected which would be understood by the addressee.

(c)   The subject matter led to the use of a specific and technical vocabulary and terminology.

No one of these factors by itself would suffice to explain all of the MH and Aramaic features. It seems, rather, that each of them has contributed certain elements to the character of MMT's language. Thus the preference for -ש might be explained by factor (a), while the use of the verbal phrase פרש מן העם (rather than the phrase סר מדרך העם, current in the literature of the Qumran sect) would be rather a consequence of factor (b); again the difference in vocabulary between the halakhic part and the homiletic part shows the effect of factor (c), the subject matter.[92]

It would thus appear that the language of MMT reflects, more than that of any other Qumran scroll, the Hebrew actually spoken in Qumran. This spoken language was distinct from the later MH, and it contained elements not known to us from other phases of the Hebrew language.

3.7 MMT's Language and its Relation to Other Types of Hebrew

This chapter does not aim at describing the whole history of Hebrew during the period when it was a living language (from the biblical times to the end of the Tannaitic period); it merely attempts to locate MMT's language among the other types of Hebrew. In so doing, it will also review several problems inherent in research on Hebrew during the period when it was a living language.

3.7.1 BH and MH

Early Hebrew, while it was a living language, displayed two major linguistic types, BH and MH, which differed from each other in grammar and vocabulary. Research into each of these types shows that neither was uniform; differences and variations are revealed in each, reflecting different times and locations. Stylistic differences are also to be found, but they will not be discussed here.

3.7.1.1 BH Dialects

Evidence for the existence of different Hebrew dialects is to be found in the Bible itself, particularly in the stories about the northern tribes of Israel and about the Kingdom of Israel (as distinct from that of Judah).[93] Some dialectical features occur in ancient inscriptions (for instance, the Samaria

---

[92] In the Damascus Covenant, the post-classical lexical elements found in the halakhic section are about twice as numerous as those found in the historical section. The two sections are equal in length.

[93] See, for example, Kutscher, *Words*, p. 34. There is further evidence not mentioned by Kutscher, e.g., the use of the relative -ש in northern texts and the use of pronouns for the second person feminine singular ending -*i*.

ostraca).[94] The later traditions of pronunciation—Samaritan, Tiberian, Babylonian and so on—also preserve older dialectical differences.[95] It has been suggested that MH was an off-shoot of one of the dialects spoken during the period of the First Temple; this would account for the existence of a few typically MH elements in the early books of the Bible.

3.7.1.2 Late BH

The language of biblical texts written during the post-exilic period (LBH)[96] differs markedly from CBH, and contains many new elements. Most of these elements have parallels in Aramaic or MH; most scholars have therefore assumed either that the language of the later books of the Bible is basically CBH influenced by those languages that were spoken by the Jews at the time (especially Aramaic), or that it is a mixture of CBH, MH and Aramaic.

3.7.1.3 The Uniformity of MH

Nor is MH itself uniform. It has been shown that several early 'biblical' elements survive into some early *mishnayot*.[97] Moreover, the Bar-Kokhba documents are written in a language that differs from that of Tannaitic works in some points, and some of these special features match those of BH.[98] As Kutscher has shown,[99] the 'biblical' words in the Bar-Kokhba letters were not an intentional imitation of BH, but rather living features of Bar-Kokhba's particular dialect. A few dialectical features also show up in the Copper Scroll,[100] a work to be located in the region of Judea, but whose ascription to the Dead Sea Sect is dubious.[101] Apparently the differences between the various MH pronunciation traditions reflect, among other things, differences between dialects. Elements differing from regular MH that would characterize only some dialects can furthermore be found in certain individual works of Tannaitic literature (such as *Sipre Zuta*, a work composed in Lydda). It is also possible that in Amoraic literature some traces of specific regional dialects have been preserved; not all deviations from Tannaitic Hebrew there can be said to reflect biblical or Aramaic influences on MH—they may

---

[94] Ibid.

[95] Kutscher, *Isaiah*, pp. 61–73; Ben-Ḥayyim, *SHG*, p. 253.

[96] On which see the works of Kutscher and Hurvitz.

[97] Epstein, p. 1129, e.g., למשכים, חבתי and החלו. The closeness to biblical language is particularly noticeable in the grammar and phraseology of *m. ʾAbot*; although a number of ancient linguistic traits found in *m. ʾAbot* could be explained as the result of scribal corrections (made under the influence of BH), this tractate certainly contains some archaic traits that were quite at home in the MH dialect peculiar to this early witness (see S. Sharvit, *Text and Language*, p. 7); M. Bar-Asher, 'The Historical Unity of Hebrew and Mishnaic Hebrew Research', *Language Studies*, I, pp. 95–99.

[98] In the Bar-Kokhba material published so far, we have found more than twenty-five linguistic elements (lexicographical and grammatical) that do not exist in Tannaitic literature. Most of them are known from BH, QH, Aramaic or Amoraic literature, but some are not known from any other source. In order not to prolong the discussion, we shall merely list these special features here, without comments and without reference to the sources (some of them have, of course, been discussed by Kutscher, *Studies*, pp. 54–70): כה (once in MH: *m. Soṭa* 9:6, in a speech attributed to God), חפץ 'want' (once in MH: *m. Ned.* 4:8, a votive formula), דאג, אזי 'care', מחוז 'port', מרק 'pay', זבנות, חרר, בסרון, באיה, מן רצונו, מן קצת, חנטין, תקומה 'here', הכה, של ה- (second person), המך (= תבואה), פניו (= פני), מקום (= מוקם), ת (= את), שיושב (= היושב), -ש (before the imperfect, denoting a command), גואין (= פניו), למרחשון בב (instead of במרחשון בX). We have not listed special word combinations, such as שידע יהי, בטוב אתן יושבים, כסף זוזין מאה וששים לך (with the Aramaic and LBH order). The above items illustrate the extent to which the language of the Bar-Kokhba documents differs from that of Tannaitic literature (MH¹).

[99] Kutscher, *Studies*, pp. 54–70.

[100] בבואר (x 5), של ה- (xii 4), המערבית (with article; iii 10), אמות שש (i 12), etc. Note that MH uses the word מבוי instead of BH מבוא. In the Copper Scroll, however, the BH form occurs (xi 16), and in the Bar-Kokhba documents another BH form occurs: מובא (Mur 30, l. 19; the editor reads מרבא; the reading מובא, suggested by Qimron, is supported by the Aramaic parallel מעלא which occurs in a similar deed [*Biblica* 38 (1957), p. 259]).

[101] There are, at any rate, no linguistic indications of such an affinity, cf. J. T. Milik, *DJD* III, pp. 275–278.

also reflect an authentic and distinct dialect of MH itself.[102] This may also be the case with regard to the Babylonian transmission of MH, which shows many isoglosses with the documents found in the Judean Desert.[103]

3.7.2 Methodological Considerations

In order to characterize the language of any given text from Qumran, we would have to analyze it as we have analyzed MMT, i.e., we would have to try to isolate those characteristics that are not common to all the phases of the history of Hebrew, and then identify the various components of the text's language. However, in view of the non-uniformity of both BH and MH (as described above), a number of methodological difficulties arise:

A.   It is not clear that features which cease to be in use in MH were not in use in the other dialects contemporary to MH. Thus, forms such as בקטלו (cf. below) or אנחנו in MMT may well have been features of the spoken language—not imitations of BH—for it is not clear why in this type of text a biblicising equivalent would be sought for such banal words or phrases. For the general vernacular nature of בקטלו and אנחנו we should note, in the case of the former, its attestation in contemporary Aramaic and in the Copper Scroll; in the case of אנחנו we note a similar word (אנחנא) in Aramaic.

B.   Those special features in QH that are not found in either BH or MH may well reflect contemporary spoken Hebrew (and not be the result of the influence of Aramaic or of an unsuccessful attempt to imitate BH); it is, however, just as likely that they are CBH features which are found uniquely in the Qumran tradition, not having being preserved in other traditions of CBH.

It should be recalled that, when we examine the language of any individual Qumran scroll or QH in general, we are comparing it a) to the Tiberian tradition of BH, and b) to a MH that has been recorded for us in a much later period. Notwithstanding these limitations, these two (Tiberian BH and MH) are the major sources available to us for comparative purposes, and the picture that has emerged from research reflects with sufficient reliability, we feel, the historical situation of the written language,[104] and so enables us to determine the location of various literary texts and their relationships to each other.

To give an example: it is certainly not by chance that the verb קבל is absent from biblical books written in the First Temple period, for there are contexts in those books in which קבל could have occurred but other words are used instead. From this we may conclude that this verb did not exist in the literary language of the kingdom of Judah, where CBH was written. But it would be going too far to deduce that this root first came into use in Hebrew during the exilic and post-exilic periods. It may just as well have existed in some Hebrew dialect at the time of the First Temple, although not in the literary CBH of Jerusalem; this after all was the case with the relative -ש, whose Hebrew antecedents are no less ancient and authentic than are those of אשר. In another place, E. Qimron has suggested that the information in the early sources does not reflect a single language as it developed and changed over time, but rather different types of Hebrew at different stages of development.[104a] All attempts to fit the surviving fragments of early Hebrew into a single historical sequence are misguided and

---

[102] e.g., קטלתוני (cf. E. Qimron, 'קטלתוני and Related Forms in Hebrew', *JQR* 78 [1987], pp. 49–55); נתפעל participle; תי- second person feminine. See also M. Sokoloff, 'The Hebrew of *Bereshit Rabba* According to MS Vat. Ebr. 30', *Leshonenu* 33 (1969), p. 41.

[103] Bar-Asher, pp. 205–218.

[104] Cf. A. Hurvitz, *LBH*, p. 43. It should be recalled that the written language is only an incomplete representation of any dialect of Hebrew, and that this is so especially in the field of vocabulary.

[104a] Qimron, 'Observations', in *Forty Years*, pp. 349–361.

misleading. However, since similar processes often occurred in different Hebrew dialects, the contrast between CBH and MH can help in dating the language of such other sources as the late biblical books and the Qumran scrolls. It is, however, doubtful whether MH had any influence on the grammar of QH or LBH.

3.7.3 The Hebrew of QH and MMT in the History of Hebrew

Broadly speaking, the language of the Qumran sectarian literature is similar (especially in phraseology and syntax) to the language of those biblical books that were written in the post-exilic period; it does have its own special traits, however, particularly in its morphology. Some of these traits are known from other traditions of Hebrew (mainly the Samaritan), while others are as yet unparalleled. (A description of QH's grammar, of its syntactical and lexicographical characteristics, and of how they differ from what is found in classical BH, is given in Qimron, *HDSS*.)

This literary language of the Qumran sect (QH) appears to have been different from the language spoken at Qumran. QH shows, even in the non-biblical manuscripts, the clear influence of BH, expressed in the use of biblical phraseology and of very short biblical allusions; there are also elements that appear to be mechanical retroversions in BH, or biblicising forms of MH words and phrases.[105] MMT's language appears to be closer to MH than to BH, since the specifically BH lexical elements in it (enumerated above, § 3.6.2) are few in number. Its grammar, however, is mainly the grammar of Qumran, one which differs extensively from that of MH. It can further be shown that even in those features which have parallels in MH the similarity is sometimes partial (cf. § 3.3.1.4).

Nevertheless, it could be claimed, on the basis of the similarity to MH, that the language of MMT reflects the Hebrew spoken at Qumran better than does the language of the other scrolls. Support for the approach suggested above can be found in the dialectical isoglosses shared by MMT (and QH) with the Bar-Kokhba documents, materials originating from the same geographical region, though considerably later. These isoglosses include גואים (§ 3.2.3), פניו (for פָּנוּי, pronounced *pano*, § 3.2.2.3), -בשל ש (§ 3.5.2.5) and the pronunciation of the gutturals (§ 3.2.1); cf. also אֵלֶּה (§ 3.3.1.3) which is not found in MH, but is common to BH, QH, MMT and the Bar-Kokhba material.

Further isoglosses are revealed when we compare the language of the Qumran scrolls as a whole (QH) with that of the Bar-Kokhba documents; features common to these materials which are not found also in MMT (e.g., the prosthetic א, the pronunciation of the sibilants, -ש denoting a command, etc.) are no doubt lacking in MMT only because it is so short.

3.7.4 Conclusions

To summarize: Ancient Hebrew was divided into dialects, so that any attempt to locate a given work merely on the basis of the Tiberian BH tradition, of MH, and of biblical Aramaic is not compatible with the linguistic reality. It is no wonder that many features are inconsistent with this approach,[106] though, at the same time, it can paint a generally satisfactory picture of the history of the written Hebrew language.

In dealing with Hebrew as a living language, we must recall that we are dealing with sporadic representations of the language, from different places and times, as transmitted to us in different traditions of pronunciation. This literary material does not represent a single language which developed over time, but rather different dialects that existed together and fought for hegemony in the literary language. In the First Temple period the dialect in Jerusalem prevailed. In Tannaitic times MH became the literary standard. It was in the post-exilic period that the struggle between the dialects

---

[105] Such as אשר instead of -ש; and see also Rabin, p. 148.
[106] Qimron, n. 104a above.

was fiercest, traces of which survived in contemporaneous texts and in later traditions of pronunciation.

The history of ancient Hebrew must therefore be the history of written Hebrew, a form of Hebrew which reflects the changes caused by struggles between the various dialects of Hebrew (and Aramaic) rather than a rectilinear historical development.

In light of these considerations, we can give a summary characterization of QH, of the Hebrew of MMT, and of their relationship to each other. QH in particular contains many new elements. Most of these elements have parallels in either MH or Aramaic (or both). Yet in QH there are many new elements which were not found in BH, and which do not appear in MH or in Aramaic. Some of these features survive in other traditions of Hebrew (especially in the Samaritan tradition), but not in the Tiberian tradition. The distribution of these shared features probably indicates that the features in question were at home in earlier classical Hebrew (though not attested in the MT) and still alive in the Hebrew dialect spoken at Qumran. It may likewise be assumed that not all of the characteristics which are common to BH and QH but absent from MH were taken from the Bible. It is a priori likely that some of them reflect the later Hebrew that was actually spoken.

The language of MMT most closely reflects the Hebrew spoken at Qumran. Its vocabulary resembles that of MH more than that of BH; its grammar resembles BH's more than MH's. Its dissimilarity to QH could perhaps be explained by postulating that MMT was one of the earliest works composed at Qumran, written before the sect developed or adopted a biblicising jargon;[107] but since we have no dated works from Qumran, great caution should be exercised in appealing to such considerations. Its similarity to MH results from the fact that both MMT and MH reflect spoken forms of Hebrew current in the Second Temple period.

---

[107] Cf. Rabin.

4. THE LITERARY CHARACTER OF MMT AND ITS HISTORICAL SETTING

4.1 Indications of Date

4.1.1 The Dating of the Manuscripts

THERE is much more agreement among scholars concerning the date of a manuscript of any individual work from Qumran than there is concerning the date of composition of the work itself. Paleography, archaeology, linguistics and radiocarbon dating all indicate that the non blical Qumran manuscripts come mainly from the two centuries after the Maccabean revolt.[1] The dating of MMT and of its manuscripts presents no exception to this pattern. As has been shown in the paleographical analysis of the individual manuscripts (above § 2.1), the oldest manuscript dates from about 75 BCE, and the youngest from about 50 CE. This gives us the latest possible date for the composition. However, since the work was copied over several generations, there likely existed even older manuscripts which have not survived: the oldest surviving manuscript is unlikely to have been the archetype.

4.1.2 Description of MMT

The fragments of these six manuscripts, when put into their relative order, attest a work of which at least some 130 lines are preserved. These come from at least three distinct sections, or literary divisions. The end of the work is preserved, but more sections could theoretically have stood before the first surviving part, for instance a title or a proem (which would have been appropriate as an introduction either to the first section or to the work as a whole). It is even theoretically possible that before the first preserved section there could have existed one or more other longer sections, although this is unlikely. In any case, what sort of texts these might have been cannot be determined with any certainty.

4.1.2.1 Section A: The Calendar and its Date

The first of the preserved sections of the text, section A in our composite text, is a calendar which is arranged in twelve or thirteen very narrow columns. These columns can be almost completely restored and reconstructed in MS[a] (this section does not survive in any other manuscript of MMT). The text lists, for each numbered month of a calendar, on what days of that month the Sabbaths and principal festivals fell. The calendar in this section belongs to the same school as that of the solar calendar frequently found at Qumran, as also in Jubilees and in other works and traditions listed by the late Annie Jaubert.[2] It appears to be in almost complete agreement with that form of the calendar showing a very full choice of festivals implied by the list of David's compositions in 11QPs[a] xxvii 2–11.

---

[1] See G. Bonani, M. Broshi, I. Carmi, S. Ivy, J. Strugnell, W. Wölfli, 'Radiocarbon Dating of the Dead Sea Scrolls', *Atiqot* 20 (1991), pp. 27–32.

[2] A. Jaubert, 'Le Calendrier des Jubilés et de la secte de Qumran: ses origines bibliques', *VT* 3 (1953), pp. 250–264.

MMT preserves only portions of such a list together with a concluding sum (364) of the days that make up the year. We can therefore ask whether the fragments, as far as they can be reconstructed, attested a complete sequence of festivals. We should note that there are no indications that there was any literary introduction to this calendar nor (significantly, in view of the character of the rest of the work) was there any polemic note in either the conclusion, or the body, of the list. It appears as uncontroversial in its intention as our 'thirty days hath September'.

4.1.3 Section B: The Halakhot

After section A, the calendar, comes section B, a passage consisting of a long sequence of polemically formulated legal statements. The relationship of this section, literary or ideological, either to the calendar, section A, or to the subsequent homiletic epilogue, section C, is not immediately clear—though the combination of a legal section (cf. section B) and a homiletico-paraenetic one (cf. section C) is, of course, also found in other works (for instance, in the Pauline Letters, which will be shown later to have some other formal analogies to MMT).

4.1.3.1 The Title of Section B (and of MMT as a whole)

The initial description of section B, ה[מעשים   מ[קצת ל שהם [ל] אלה מקצת דבריונ (B 1), closely resembles the end of C: ואף אנחנו כתבנו אליך מקצת מעשי התורה שחשבנו לטוב לך ולעמך ... בשל שתשמח באחרית העת במצאך מקצת מדברינו כן (C 26–30). This is a formal link between the legal and homiletic sections. Out of these phrases we have suggested a hypothetical (or, better, functional) title for the whole work: מקצת מעשי התורה or MMT. We do not imply that this was, in fact, the formal title of the whole work used by the author or the scribe, nor the title of any part or source of it. There is certainly no evidence that such a title covered the calendar.

Unfortunately, the special introduction to section B is partly damaged. It began with the phrase 'These are some of our rulings'. The group of statements will have been chosen or composed with controversial intent and would imply the exceptional importance of the topics dealt with in the controversy.

4.1.3.2 The Literary Forms of the Halakhot in Section B

Next we should consider the literary form of these legal pronouncements, and the conclusions that may be drawn from it for the understanding of the polemic and historical setting of MMT. Formally, we should note that these pronouncements are made by a group speaking in the first person plural: thus some sections are introduced חושבים / אנחנו אומרים ... ואף על 'and concerning x: we are of the opinion'. Usually the correct praxis prescribed by that group is contrasted with a divergent praxis of others, who are described in the third person plural, in phrases such as שהם עושים 'which they are accustomed to do', or an appeal may be made to what the addressees (in the second person plural) themselves know to be right, introduced by ואתם יודעים ש-.

4.1.3.3 The Identity of Author and Addressee in Section B

Now who, in this cast of persons, are 'we', 'you' and 'they'? An answer to this question is best postponed until we have looked at the evidence of section C, which presents a similar set of personal pronouns, analogously used. It will also be best to postpone untill then the historical localization of the halakhic positions and disputes which section B attests. We can already note, however, that the disputes are between the 'we' party and the 'they' party, while the 'we' party appeals to the 'you' party because they know what are the real implications of the Torah and what are the wrong practices. As will be shown, the halakha of the 'they' party conforms with that of the rabbis of the Mishna, and the

halakha (and the calendar) of the 'we' party conforms with that of the Dead Sea sect. (For details see chap. 5.) All of this will aid us in dating the work and in understanding its historical setting.

4.1.4.1 The Homiletic-Paraenetic Section C and its Dramatis Personae

The last part (section C) is of a different character, though the point of transition between section B and section C is not preserved. We have separated section B and section C according to content and to the absence of the characteristic formal markers of the legal pronouncements, but the two sections may fit more closely together, each being referred to as מקצת דברינו. Section C also is ascribed to the אנחנו 'we' group; the second plural addressees are sometimes divided into the singular 'thee' and the collective 'thy people (or Israel)': cf. section C, ll. 27, 31–32. The 'they' group is referred to as רוב העם from whom (and from whose practices) the 'we' group has separated. Clearly the dramatis personae of the first and second person groups are much the same as those in section B; the second person singular leader of the 'you' group is characterized in a far from hostile fashion: 'with you is wisdom and knowledge of Torah' (C 28) and 'as you do what is righteous and good in His eyes for your own welfare and for the welfare of Israel' (C 31–32). The contents relate to the eschaton, together with the coming to pass then of the various blessings and curses predicted in Scripture, and they insist on the importance of fearing the Torah and performing it—especially of performing it, presumably, according to the views of the 'we' party exemplified in section B. Note, however, the absence of 'conversion' and 'true path' language. Because of the fragmentary nature of the manuscripts and the uncertainty about the order of the text, the sequence of thought, the significance of the references to biblical historical figures and the linkage with section B are all far from clear.

4.1.4.2 Lexical Evidence for Dating Section C

Two minor elements in section C may provide pointers to its date:

A.   פרש The 'we' group says 'we have separated ourselves from the multitude of the people' (פרשנו מרוב העם) on halakhic grounds. The neutral, or even positive, use of the verb פרש to describe the creation of 'sects' [sic] and especially of MMT's sect is noteworthy. In rabbinic literature too, as S. Lieberman pointed out, פרושים originally did not designate just the 'Pharisees', but rather any separatist sect.[3] It is also uncertain whether it was originally negative, positive, or neutral in sense. פרש, when used of one's own group's separation, may point to a time earlier than the development of the standard Qumranic usage סור מדרך העם (e.g., in CD 8:16). We cannot discuss here the significance of this usage for the origins of the name of the Pharisees,[4] whoever first used it; we can note that the standard technical term used later by the Qumran sect to describe their own separation was the biblicising סור מדרך העם and not פרש מרוב העם. The sectarians called themselves סרי מדרך העם (CD 8:16),[5] which is a biblicising equivalent of פרושים. The simplest explanation for this change was that this once neutral term פרש later yielded at Qumran to the biblicising phrase סור מדרך העם as פרש became a specialized term referring to another specific sect's separation or at least describing a separation that was judged hostilely.

B.   דויד as Part of the Description of a Tripartite Canon

---

[3] Lieberman, pp. 53–54. D. Flusser, 'Some of the Precepts of the Torah from Qumran (4QMMT) and the Benediction against the Heretics', *Tarbiz* 61 (1992), pp. 357–366.

[4] On the meaning of this name, see A. I. Baumgarten, 'The Name of the Pharisees', *JBL* 102/3 (1983), pp. 411–428 (see the bibliography cited there).

[5] The Cairo Geniza manuscripts read סרו instead of סרי.

Can a date be extracted from the phrase [ובדוי]ד הנ[ביאים ו]בספר[י הנ]ביאים ובספר מושה בספר שתבין 'so that you may study (carefully) the book of Moses and the books of the Prophets and (the book of) David' (C 10)? Phrases of this kind occur in other passages that have, perhaps loosely, been called canon lists. Nevertheless, this does not give us a precise date for the evolution of a list of authoritative books or of a canon among one specific group. It is, however, worth noting that (*a*) a tripartite list is attested in about 135 BCE (in the three quotations from the prologue of the grandson of Ben-Sira),[6] (*b*) the title in MMT for the second section of the canon is הנביאים ספרי, and that this probably includes the historical books (the former prophets): at least in section C, MMT seems to treat Samuel-Kings as authoritative, and (*c*) the title of the third section, whatever it contained, is 'David'.

There are no other early lists in Hebrew which vary from the standard later Hebrew lists. Indeed, MMT's list may well be the earliest tripartite list, and so cannot be dated on the grounds of the typology of canon lists or of the detail in them. It is not clear whether 'David' refers just to the Psalter, or denotes a *Ketubim* collection, either one that was open-ended, or one that was closed.[7]

4.1.5 The Authority of MMT

Some material facts about the manuscripts of MMT may contribute additional arguments or details concerning the historical background of the work. Six manuscripts of the work were found in the principal library-cave at Qumran, and these were copied over a period of a century or more. In general, the presence at Qumran of such a number of manuscripts of a work indicates that it had substantial authority. The large number of manuscripts does not necessarily imply that MMT originated within the Qumran community. It could be a work of pre-Qumranic origin, but the large number of manuscripts present would imply that there was at Qumran a great and lasting interest in both the controversial and the legal positions of this document. If MMT was composed—or believed to have been composed—by the Teacher of Righteousness, this would explain the great authority assigned to it among the Qumran sectarians.

4.1.5.1 Language in General

It is difficult to draw any precise chronological or historical conclusions from the language of the document. It is hard to know at what precise point in time to insert the dialect of MMT. We may note isoglosses with Qumran Hebrew and post-exilic biblical Hebrew sufficient to place it in the last four centuries BCE, but these and similar phenomena lead only to a broad dating. It is equally hard to define the relationship between MMT and Qumran Hebrew texts, though its grammar is closely related to theirs. Since the spoken dialect found in MMT belongs to a line distinct from both post-exilic biblical Hebrew and Qumran Hebrew, and is not a direct antecedent of MH, typological dating is

---

[6] The formulas used in the prologue to Ben-Sira for his tripartite Scripture are:

του νομου και των προφητων και των αλλων των κατ αυτους ηκολουθηκοτων (1–2)

του νομου και των προφητων και των αλλων πατριων βιβλιων (8–10)

αυτος ο νομος και αι προφητειαι και τα λοιπα των βιβλιων (24–25):

To these we may compare the similar tripartite 'canon' formula in Luke 24:44, which ends in και ψαλμοις, the description in 2 Macc 2:13 of Nehemiah's policy of library collection (with no mention of the Torah), επισυνηγαγεν τα περι των Βασιλεων βιβλια και προφητων και τα του Δανιδ (και επιστολας Βασιλεων . . .), and Philo's list in *De Vita Contemplativa* (if it really is tripartite) (*a*) νομους (*b*) και λογια θεσπισθεντα δια προφητων (*c*) και υμνους και τα αλλα οις επιστημη και ευσεβεια συναυξονται και τελειουνται (§ 25). See H. M. Orlinsky, 'Some Terms in the Prologue to Ben Sira and the Hebrew Canon', *JBL* 110 (1991), pp. 483–490.

[7] One should note that another work in the immediately pre-Qumranic tradition, Jubilees, implies the twenty-two book canon, although it is unproductive to speculate whether this is identical with other twenty-two book lists. If so, what was being done about (*a*) Daniel, probably written several years later than Jubilees, and (*b*) Esther, not known in the Qumran library, and whose special festival of Purim is scarcely to be located in the Jubilees-Qumran calendar—and in honesty it should be noted that the authenticity of the Jubilees verse itself could be disputed.

again impossible. There are some lexical innovations, but all of them could have originated at any time during the Second Temple period. No Greek words occur. This need not imply anything, since Greek words are rarely to be found in other Hebrew compositions from Qumran, even the latest ones—the community was in many ways xenophobic. On the implication of the verb פרש, see above § 4.1.4.2a.

4.1.5.2 The Absence of Sectarian Terminology

The absence of some terms typical of, and frequent in, the standard works of the Qumran sect is also significant: e.g., the opponents are not called דורשי החלקות, בני השחת or the like, but הם. The usual Qumran self-descriptions, e.g., בני אור, בני צדק, are not used to denote the writer's group; instead we simply find אנחנו. This too goes hand in hand with other elements that suggest a dating prior to or very early in the organized existence of the Qumran movement (cf. also § 4.2.5).

4.2 Literary Purpose and Historical Background of MMT

What literary purpose and historical background can be postulated to explain such a composite or disparate work? The end of the work, and the collection of legal ordinances sent with it, seem designed to convince an individual and his people, the 'you' group, to adopt the practices of the senders of the work, rather than those of the 'they' group.

4.2.1 Literary Genre and Function of MMT: Epistle or Treatise?

In our preliminary presentations,[8] the literary genre of MMT as a whole was described as that of a letter. We should, however, have taken account of certain distinctions, familiar to students of ancient epistolography, between personal letters, epistles (which are less personal and more literary), public letters and treatises. In Hebrew we have too few examples of epistles and treatises to compare these genres formally with MMT, and the sub-distinction between single and plural authorship in each of these genres is probably unimportant from a formal point of view. The formal traits of the personal letter can be deduced from a quite large Hebrew corpus; most are distinct from those traits found in MMT, or are absent from MMT (perhaps because of its incomplete condition). MMT has few of the formal characteristics of the personal letter, and we should probably expect parallels rather in the epistle or in the treatise, though formal descriptions of these genres are hard to make. Formally speaking, the presence of an author and of addressees clearly places MMT in such literary genres. The contents of the section containing legal pronouncements are appropriately varied, as we expect of the body of many letters, and the homiletic tone of section C would, of course, not be inappropriate to the paraenetic-homiletic conclusions of many epistles, for instance the Pauline ones. More specifically, we have no evidence that the beginning of MMT, lost though it is, corresponded with the closely defined forms of the genres of the letter or of the epistle. The ending, however, does survive, and it has few of the formal features of letters or epistles. For example לטוב לך ולישראל (C 31–32) could be compared formally with אהוה שלום וכל בית ישראל, the closing greeting formula of one of the Bar-Kokhba letters (Mur 42:7). We may note further that MMT has no signature. It could be noted that the incipit of each halakha in section B, ואף על, corresponds to a frequent articulating feature, peri de ton, in the body of the Pauline epistles. One might object, however, that this is probably not a unique characteristic of letters, but rather is a way of indicating new sections of subject matter, a structure of

---

[8] E. Qimron and J. Strugnell, 'An Unpublished Halakhic Letter from Qumran', *Biblical Archaeology Today*, Proceedings of the International Congress on Biblical Archaeology, Jerusalem 1984, pp. 400–407; E. Qimron and J. Strugnell, 'An Unpublished Halakhic Letter from Qumran', *The Israel Museum Journal* 4 (1985), pp. 9–12.

lists; but note that in MMT and the Pauline letters, ואף על or peri de ton is followed by a statement of the law, which is introduced, e.g., by אנחנו אומרים.

The contents of MMT suggest that it should be classed with corporate or public letters sent from one group to another,[9] or even with treatises, rather than with the private letter. Unfortunately, while we have many examples of the last type, of the first and second we have only a few: a few group letters in post-mishnaic literature,[10] one or two in intertestamental literature[11] and others in the New Testament.[12] Treatises are represented at least by Hebrews (if not also by Luke and Acts). The distinction between the epistle and the treatise is hard to draw. Perhaps it rests on the greater importance laid on the subject matter of the treatise rather than on the addressee-dedicatee's reaction to that matter,[13] and on the presence or absence of precise introductory or concluding epistolary formulas.[14] It does not seem that a formal distinction should be made between private treatises addressed to an individual and public treatises addressed to several people, or to a group, as was done in the case of letters. Both types exist but they do not constitute a change in the formal nature of the treatise which will not vary according to the relatively unimportant circumstances of the real or pseudepigraphical address.

4.2.2 Identification of 'We' as Author of MMT and as a Party

In MMT the author is regularly referred to not by the first person singular but by the plural אנחנו, i.e., as a group. Although it is a truism that an individual, not a group, holds the pen, it is also quite possible that groups compose statements of community doctrine or law. There is no reason to postulate an auctorial 'we', with first person singular meaning, in this document. Such a usage is unattested in early Hebrew, although frequent in Greek literature and epistolography. These pronouncements of law are therefore to be taken as uttered in the name of the community which practised them. Of course, the writer will have been a significant member of the 'we' group, but it is not an unavoidable illation to make him necessarily the Teacher of Righteousness. In the history of Qumran studies, practically every nonbiblical work found there has been ascribed at some time or other to the Teacher of Righteousness. In the present case, however, we have real evidence that connects MMT to the Teacher of Righteousness (see § 4.2.7.1 below).

4.2.3 The Characterization of the 'We', 'You' and 'They' Groups

Our ability to identify which historical individuals and groups are intended will depend on our finding other historical details that fit MMT. If we assume that the work is to be explained as reflecting the history (or the prehistory) of the Qumran community, we must look for a time when the 'we' group, i.e., the writers, were in 'eirenic' discussion with the 'you' group—a group not so different from themselves as to be incapable of being won over to the writers' positions and practices, a group also referred to in the phrases לך ולעמך, לך ולישראל. The 'we' group recommended their own purity practices to the 'you' group, in contrast to the contrary practices of the 'they' group. It is not clear whether the singular 'thou', who is distinguished from עמך and ישראל, was a priest, a high priest, or just a leader—political, military, or other. A satisfactory identification can be provided in each case, but for the moment we will maintain the ambiguity. See also § 5.2.4d.

---

[9] Cf. D. Pardee et al., *Handbook of Ancient Hebrew Letters,* SBL Sources for Biblical Study 15 (1982).

[10] e.g., *t. Sanh.* 2:6 and parallels (*y. Sanh.* 18ᵈ, *y. Maʿaś. Š.* 56ᶜ, and *b. Sanh.* 11ᵃ⁻ᵇ).

[11] e.g., 2 Macc 1:1–2:18.

[12] e.g., the Pauline epistles, which form the largest Jewish corpus chronologically close to MMT.

[13] Though this is, of course, a very imprecise criterion.

[14] Though some candidates for being treatises also have these formulas at least partially, cf. the public festival letter in 2 Macc 1:10–2:18, or Hebrews.

4.2.4 The 'They' Group and the (Proto)-Pharisees

Apart from the attribution to them of certain halakhot, there is only scant evidence about the 'they' group. At one point we find the phrase פרשנו מרוב העם 'we have separated ourselves from the multitude of the people'. רוב העם can scarcely refer to the 'you' group (although they are referred to by the associated word עמך); it would be unlikely that the writers of MMT would have used פרשנו מרוב העם to refer to the group which they were trying to win over. Instead, the implication is that it refers to the 'they' group which either composed the רוב העם or of whom the רוב העם formed a part. The erroneous halakhic traditions of the 'they' group in section B were in all probability the same traditions that provoked the separation from the רוב העם in section C. The detailed discussion in our halakhic chapter will identify much of the halakha of the 'they' group with that of the Pharisees; it is interesting to note that we find a similar early association of the Pharisee group with the רוב העם attested also by Josephus, at a time which, we will shortly suggest, is about as early as MMT.[15]

4.2.4.1 Conclusion to the Form-Critical Discussion

The preceding form-critical discussion may help to bring us to a correct reading of the document as a polemic with an historical setting. By itself, however, it does not give us any date or historical setting for such a polemic. For this we will have to identify the participants in the polemic.

4.2.5 The Polemic in MMT

The existence of a polemic in MMT is, in itself, of great historical significance. Nowhere else in the Qumran literature is there any mention of such an effort to convince the leader of Israel of the validity of the sect's halakhic views and of the invalidity of those of its opponents. This contrasts with the prohibition of disputes with opponents found in the later *Serekh Ha-yaḥad*.[16] From MMT we learn that the sectarians did try to propagate their halakha elsewhere in Israel. This thus constitutes an important piece of evidence for the history of religions and the history of Israel.

There are other passages in the *pesharim* which perhaps also point to polemics between the Teacher of Righteousness and his opponents. Thus 1QpHab 5:8–12 refers to a polemic between the Teacher and the 'Liar', probably the leader of a rival sect (i.e., the Pharisees):

למה תביטו בוגדים ותחריש בבלע רשע צדיק ממנו פשרו על בית אבשלום ואנשי עצתם אשר
נדמו בתוכחת מורה הצדק ולוא עזרוהו על איש הכזב אשר מאס את התורה בתוך כול ע[צת]ם

'Why do you look on, O Liars, and keep silence when the wicked devours him who is more righteous than
himself'. Its interpretation concerns the House of Absalom and the members of their council who were silent
during the dispute with the Teacher of Righteousness and gave him no help against the Liar who flouted the
Law in the midst of their whole congregation.

In the light of MMT, we may conjecture that this dispute, too, concentrated on the correct performance of the Torah, which the Liar rejected. (Cf. the discussion on 4Q171, below § 4.2.7.1.)

Such polemics seem to have taken place only in the time of the Teacher of Righteousness, and to have ceased when the *yaḥad* was separated and firmly established. As mentioned above, 1QS 9:16–17 prohibits disputes with opponents. The interpretation of the Torah thus became an inner-community activity (ibid.). It is quite probable that the unsuccessful results of earlier polemics convinced the sect

---

[15] Josephus, *Ant.*, xviii 2, 4 (15).

[16] 1QS 9:16–17 ואשר לוא להוכיח ולהתרובב עם אנשי השחת 'He must not argue or quarrel with the men of perdition'. Schiffmann, *Sectarian*, p. 96, interprets this passage as referring to dispute in a court of law, but his interpretation hardly fits the continuation ולסתר את עצת התורה בתוך אנשי העול 'He shall conceal the Torah-counsel <from> the midst of the men of deceit'.

to abstain from them; such results may even have been the reason, or a reason, for the exile of the sectarians from Jerusalem and for the founding of the *yaḥad*.[17]

Finally, we should note that the tone of the polemic in MMT is moderate. The opponents are not called בני השחת or the like, but הם, and the addressee is treated with respect. It seems that at that time the sect still believed that at least the 'you' party, if not also the opponents, could be won over. The violent reaction of the Wicked Priest attested in the *pesharim* is therefore unexpected. It would be less so if we also supposed that the persecutions referred to a single event that took place on the Day of Atonement:[18] the Wicked Priest could have taken the adoption of a different calendar by the sect as undermining his authority and therefore would have attacked the Teacher of Righteousness on what, according to the sect's calendar, was the Day of Atonement, hoping thereby either to profane the observances of that day or to invalidate the sect's calendar as a whole.

4.2.6 Historical Identification of the Participants in the Polemic

4.2.6.1 Praxis of the 'We' Group and of the 'They' Group

As will be seen in detail in our chapter on halakhic questions, the praxis of the opponents (הם, in section B) is that attested in Tannaitic literature for the Pharisees and for the later rabbinic consensus, while that of the 'we' group is, as we might expect, that attested in the Dead Sea Scrolls, but also that attested in Tannaitic literature for the Sadducees, especially in their formal controversies with the Pharisees.

Other groups, such as the חסידים הראשונים, the טובלי שחרים, the מינים גליליים and the ביתסין, some of whom may occasionally have had legal and exegetical traditions in common with those of the Sadducees, and who also occasionally shared certain practices with the Qumran sect, cannot be compared with the Sadducees for the constancy of this agreement in law. (This is, of course, not to deny the reality of the shared ancestry of their traditions.) The relationship between 'Essene' and ביתסין is philologically hard to demonstrate, though in praxis the groups may have been close.

4.2.6.2 Sadducees and the Tripartite Presentation of the Jewish Parties

We seem to be drawn to the paradoxical conclusion that the authors of MMT were, according to the terminology of Tannaitic literature, Sadducees, although MMT itself seems to have been an ancestral document of the Qumran sect, i.e., by the nearly universal consensus of scholarship, of the Essenes. Can this paradox be alleviated? First, note that the word 'Sadducee' is ambiguous in early sources. In places it refers to the aristocratic and sometimes Hellenizing priestly group that existed in Jerusalem from the second century BCE to 70 CE, but in other contexts (which fit our document better) it refers to a conservative group of priests and their supporters, equally aristocratic of course, but no more Hellenizing than their contemporaries.[19]

It should be noted that Tannaitic literature does not seem aware of the commonplace tripartite division of the Jewish parties attested from Philo and Josephus onward in Hellenistic literature; it mentions occasionally a scattering of other sects, but regularly only Pharisees and Sadducees, never also the Essenes.[20] This position is strangely parallel to that of the writers of the New Testament, who also pass over the Essenes in silence. It is by no means obvious that the missing Essenes are to be identified with the mixed bag of 'others' mentioned in either the Gospels or the Tannaitic corpus.

---

[17] Cf. CD 6:20 ff.

[18] Cf. 1QpHab 11:2–8.

[19] Cf. Baumgarten, *Controversies*.

[20] But see Sussmann, pp. 40–44.

4.2.6.2.1 How Can the Qumranites be Identified with the Sadducees?

The evidence of MMT favors rather a straight identification of the proto-Qumranites with the Sadducees, combined with a recognition that in some Tannaitic sources the term 'Sadducees' is ambivalent, sometimes referring to the Hellenizing high priestly party, and at other times to their 'intégriste' rivals at Qumran and elsewhere. The Qumranites were certainly called, in biblical fashion, בני צדוק, and so presumably were the Hellenizing Sadducees—this was scarcely a name given by their rivals (as so often religious group-names are). It is peculiar that J. Le Moyne in his recent comprehensive treatment[21] did not propose dividing Sadducee traditions among more than one referent. This could have freed him from the necessity of trying to harmonize apparently different traditions ascribed to 'the Sadducee party' as if it were one. In the titles of political and religious parties it is not uncommon for the same etiquette to be used by two parties, although they are sometimes widely distinct in ideology (cf. the modern use of 'democratic', 'liberal', etc.).

As we try to harmonize the various data, MMT seems to be a document emanating from a priestly group related to the early Sadducees, and either identical with, or an ancestor of, the Qumran group; these groups were also in controversy with a rival group which we can probably define as the Pharisees or the proto-Pharisees, or at least adversaries who stood in a legal tradition related to that of the Pharisees and the later rabbinic establishment. Furthermore, the document is addressed to a third group, 'thou and thy people Israel'. We have little evidence to allow us to define this group historically, ideologically or sociologically. MMT represents an attempt to win over this third group to the praxis of MMT on several points, whether randomly selected or systematically structured, of purity legislation.

4.2.6.3 The Leader of the 'You' Group

In all these groups, MMT refers specifically to only one individual, the leader of the 'you' group. Can he perhaps be identified at some time in Qumran's history or prehistory?

4.2.6.4 MMT and the Question of the Wicked Priest's Usurpation of the High Priesthood

In discussions of the origins of the Qumran movement, and of the character of the schism it represents, it has often been maintained that the cause of the schism was a dispute about the Zadokite genealogy of the Priest-Teacher of Righteousness and of the Wicked Priest, and about the legitimacy of each one's claim to the Pontificate. MMT does not, however, discuss this aspect of priestly law at all, and unless the question of genealogical legitimacy has been falsely read by modern scholars into the history of Qumran origins—which is unlikely, since several of the texts are quite clear on the importance of this question—one must deduce that MMT reflects an early stage, before that genealogical question had become important, a stage when the leaders of the rival groups did not yet lay claim to being High Priest, or had not been recognized as such.

4.2.6.5 The Significance of the Expression 'You and Your People'

If we try to locate a three-party situation, such as MMT presents, in the history or prehistory of the Qumran sect, do not the references to the 'you' party with a leader and his עם point us to a political ruler of Israel?

That this singular addressee was the political leader of Israel is supported by the fact that MMT reminds him of David and the kings of Israel, and suggests that he should learn from their history. Would MMT have referred to one of the Hasmonean high priests—Jonathan, Simon, or Hyrcanus?

---

[21] J. Le Moyne, *Les Sadducéens*, Paris, 1972.

(On paleographic grounds we should look for an early rather than a late high priest.) Would the phrase and the situation have better fitted Alkimus, or even one of the priests from before the Maccabean revolt? Most, it is true, are unlikely candidates for potential converts, but in fact we know little about their legal views, and have only rough descriptions of the degree of 'Hellenism' of each. To place an antecedent of the sect in those days is not in itself unlikely, but to also find a fully formed Pharisee opposition group so early would be more difficult.

If the national leader addressed in section C, who is here clearly to be distinguished from the Pharisee 'they' group, was either Alkimus, Jonathan, Simon, or Hyrcanus (to confine ourselves to the most likely time-frame), we can legitimately be asked to explain the somewhat friendly attitude displayed in our letter to such a leader, compared with the unyielding hostility shown to the 'Wicked Priest' in the later Qumran pesher tradition, where he is depicted as being, or growing into, an arch-enemy. However, this difficulty is solved very simply by 1QpHab viii 8–10 16 which suggests that initially the 'Wicked Priest' and his group were well regarded by the Qumran group, and that only later did he aspire to power greater than was lawful for him and so receive the sect's condemnation. At that early stage, the then friendly national leader (who was later to become the Wicked Priest) and his group could have been expected to side with the 'we' group, i.e., the pre-Qumranic Sadducees, in their controversies with the 'they' group, their innovative proto-Pharisaic adversaries, on matters confined to purity and Temple-administration (matters of high importance also to the early Pharisees). The precise historical referent of certain phrases in 1QpHab, loc. cit., נקרא על שם האמת בתחלת עומדו and כאשר משל בישראל, is obscure, but in general one can say that 1QpHab's account of the national leader and later Wicked High Priest requires that he had an earlier term of office that was judged more positively at Qumran, while MMT shows a national leader, well regarded by the 'we' group, though perhaps inclining to the views of their Pharisee adversaries. No trace yet appears of any controversy about who might legitimately claim the high priesthood. The hypothetical identification of the leader of the 'you' group is surely not a certain one, but it must be seen how well it fits with known national high priestly leaders who have been plausibly identified by scholarship with the Wicked Priest,[22] i.e., Alkimus and the early Hasmoneans, Jonathan, Simon, and Hyrcanus. Of which of these chronologically plausible candidates is a change of belief and conduct attested such as would justify the changed judgement described in 1QpHab?

4.2.6.6 Alkimus

In Alkimus' career there seem to have been two periods, one during which he was well-received by the Scribes and Asidaeans, and one after he had executed sixty Asidaeans. We know almost nothing of the first period except that it was very brief. It was not his installation as high priest which alienated the Scribes and Asidaeans: the alienation was caused rather by his violence towards them. It is hard to know which party would have reacted hostilely to his destruction of the Soreg. His subsequent policy seems to have had few definable (and principled) religious characteristics, but rather was simply a conflict with Judas; there is no trace of Pharisee-Sadducee conflicts at that time. In some ways Alkimus fits the requirements of our text, but it is hard to see him as coexisting with a rival priest, the Teacher of Righteousness, as is attested in the later Qumran texts.

4.2.6.7 Jonathan Maccabaeus

In Jonathan's case, it is not clear whether his assumption of the high priesthood (which we would then identify hypothetically with 1QpHab's clause וכאשר משל בישראל) was also related to any adoption of

---

[22] I.e., excluding those who are too early (from Onias III ? to Menelaus) or too late (the Hasmoneans from Aristobulus onward).

Pharisaic positions in general; however, between the period 159–152 and 152–143 BCE, there is a clear change in the nature of his political power. MMT, which would have dated from the earlier period when Jonathan could be characterized by 1QpHab as 'faithful', is not yet aware of the problem in priestly succession that was to be posed in 152 by Alexander Balas' raising Jonathan to the high priesthood. The clear evidence for Jonathan's rule as general and for his subsequent high priesthood does not attest any general Sadducee-Pharisee struggle for the soul of Jonathan, but it should be noticed that it is during the account of Jonathan's time that Pharisees, Sadducees, and Essenes are first mentioned (Josephus, *Ant.*, xiii 171–173, although the passage does not constitute a precise dating).

4.2.6.8 Simon Maccabaeus

We can also notice two changes in the nature of Simon's political power: one in 142, after Jonathan's death, when he was promoted by the Seleucid power to be high priest, ethnarch and strategos, and another in 140, when the assembly of the Jews declared permanent the transfer of the high priesthood to his family. The promotion in 142 is unlikely to have been offensive except to those who would have already found it reprehensible that Jonathan, a priest of the same wrong family, should have accepted the high priesthood from Syrian sovereigns. On the other hand, it has been suggested that the shift of 140 BCE was different and more radical in nature from that of (152 and) 142 and far more reprehensible—though why a *de facto* Syrian transfer of the pontificate to the Maccabees would have seemed less wicked in Qumran eyes than a formal and *de jure* transfer to the same improper house has never yet been demonstrated from the texts, only hypothesized. The two periods of Simon's high priesthood, i.e., those beginning in 142 and in 140 BCE, are the only ones with religiously significant changes attestable. The sources also discuss the later war with the Syrians but, apart from the decree of 140, they say very little about the inner Jewish features of that religious shift or conflict to which MMT and 1QpHab would be referring, or about any 'Sadducee' or 'Pharisee' role therein.

4.2.6.9 John Hyrcanus

Hyrcanus can be more easily disposed of. An appropriate religious shift can be found (Josephus, *Ant.*, xiii 5–6 [288–296]), but it is impossible to relate this to what we know of the career of the Wicked Priest. Although no precise data is given, Hyrcanus' change of allegiance took place at the end of his rule, not in the earlier part of it (cf. the contrast of בתחלת עומדו with וכאשר משל בישראל)—in 124 he was still promoting the Maccabean and Pharisaic feast of Hanukka (2 Macc 1:19). Hyrcanus' turning from being a Pharisee-sympathizer to being a Sadducee was a further change in the wrong direction from what our documents require: admittedly questions of the high priesthood were involved, but these did not concern change from one high priestly family to another, but rather concern the question of the legitimacy of Hyrcanus' birth and, consequently, his fitness for the priesthood. It was on this question that Hyrcanus left the Pharisees for the Sadducees. In this context, 'Sadducees' may not mean 'Qumranian-Sadducees', but the Jerusalem sacerdotal aristocracy; in either case, this would be hard to reconcile with the situation presented in 1QpHab.

4.2.7.1 Dating MMT by Dating its Author

Can one define the date of MMT more exactly by studying what may be said of its author(s)? Though MMT is formally, and on internal grounds, a communal document, sent to the head of the 'you' group, the Leader of 'Israel', there is a later inner-Qumranian tradition in 4QpPsᵃ referring to a document of 'precepts and law' which the Teacher of Righteousness had sent to the Wicked Priest:

צופה רשע לצדיק ומבקש [להמיתו יהוה לוא יעזבנו בידו ולוא י]רשׁיעׄנוׄ
בהשפטו פשרו על [הכו]הֵן הרשע אשר צׄ[פה למור]ה הצד]ק ובקש] לֵהׄמׄיתו
[על דברי החו]קׄ והתורה אשר שלח אליו

'The wicked spies on the righteous and seeks to put him to death. But the Lord will not leave him (the righteous) in his (the wicked's) power, nor let him be declared guilty when he comes to be judged.' Its interpretation concerns the Wicked Priest who spied on the Teacher of Righteousness and tried to put him to death because of the precepts and the law which the latter had sent to the former.[23]

The phrase [דברי החו]קׄ והתורה could refer to MMT whose legal pronouncements are called דברים and מעשי התורה, and which is cast in the form of a letter or treatise having both sender (שלח) and addressee (אליו).[24] If 4QpPs[a] is referring to MMT, then the author of MMT is the Teacher of Righteousness, and the referee is the Wicked Priest. In this case we have to assume that MMT was written at the beginning of the period of office of the Wicked Priest when he was still considered legitimate by the sectarians.

4.2.7.2 The Date of the High Priesthood of the Teacher of Righteousness

Our knowledge of the Teacher's career would be increased if we could accept the hypothesis that he was in fact the accepted and legitimate high priest of Israel, reigning from the death of Alkimus until his own deposition at Jonathan's Syrian-sponsored accession to the pontificate, a period (160/159–152 BCE) whose memory was later blotted out by Hasmonean *damnatio memoriae*. Tolerance or good will between the two leaders would be hard to envisage after such a dethronement, but before it one can easily conceive of a period of good will between a conservative Zadokite high priest and the ideologically close Maccabean general and 'Judge', as I Maccabees presents him, who also can be traced back to the vicinity of the Asidean group. However, the hypothesis of the Teacher's high priesthood during the so-called 'intersacerdotium' is not an inescapable one. To satisfy the text of 1QpHab, one need only postulate that there was no hostility between the Teacher, whatever his priestly rank, and the Maccabees, in the period before one or the other Maccabee became High Priest and was denounced as 'Wicked Priest'. It is certainly possible that this change of attitude at Qumran was provoked by the Maccabean usurpation of the high priesthood, i.e., usurpation from candidates more legitimate in their view. MMT does not require a further hypothesis about the identity of the high priest or the leader of its own 'Zadokites' in 159–152 BCE, but such a hypothesis would certainly not be irreconcilable with MMT, and also not irreconcilable with the presence of several traits suggesting the primitiveness of MMT's theology vis-à-vis the standard sectarian theology of Qumran.

As we have said, it is not necessary to see in the Teacher of Righteousness the author of MMT; but he was certainly the leader of the movement out of which the Qumran movement was to emerge and of which MMT marks a pre-Qumranic stage. What we can know of him and his history must be reconcilable with what we know of his movement's history and prehistory, and each of these should illuminate the other, even if later traditions about these matters may contain legendary and inexact material.

In brief, while it is not necessary to assume that the Teacher of Righteousness was the author of MMT, it fits most of our evidence if we conclude that MMT was written in the Teacher's community

---

[23] J. M. Allegro, *Qumran Cave 4, I* (4Q158–4Q186), DJD V (Oxford, 1968), p. 45 (= 4Q171 3–10 iv 7–9). The text in the edition is inaccurate.

[24] Yadin *per contra*, *TS*, I, p. 396, believed that 4QpPs[a] may allude to the Temple Scroll. There is, however, nothing in the contents of the Temple Scroll that would support the possibility that it has been sent. The word שלח in 4QpPs[a] (or כתב as in MMT) refers to a letter rather than a big scroll written by God.

and reflects the earlier phases of its development, before it adopted its later and more developed forms shown in the writings composed at Qumran.

4.2.8 A Summary of MMT's Theologically Early Traits

To summarize these possibly earlier features: (*a*) MMT is a polemic work. Later, 1QS 9:16–17 forbids sectarians to dispute with בני השחת: Is MMT in conflict with this or does MMT in fact confirm this law's existence in that it sends its criticisms instead to a third party and not to the real adversary? (*b*) The use of פרש, neutrally or positively, is prior to the currency of the later sectarian phrase סור מדרך העם. It may also antedate the use of פרושים to refer to their opponents. (*c*) MMT is theologically less developed than the standard Qumran theology in its lack of dualistic language, typical community descriptions, apocalyptic ideas, and 'apocalyptic conscience'. (*d*) The choice of legal topics by MMT, and especially the non-choice of some topics as contrasted with the delectus of topics popular in the later Qumran literature, suggests, or at least is reconcilable with, an earlier date for MMT. MMT is concerned with the consequences of intermarriage for the purity of the priestly line, not with the legitimacy of the high priest himself. MMT implies that the 'we' group regularly administered the Jerusalem Temple. Qumran literature does not imply that, but rather the opposite, sometimes *e silentio* and sometimes most specifically.

4.2.9 Conclusion

To sum up, although each of the above pieces of evidence is, to some degree, hypothetical or inadequate, taken together, they tend to support the following picture. Our initial description of MMT, as a letter from the Teacher of Righteousness to the Wicked Priest, pleasantly startling though it was, is probably to be modified. Rather than a personal letter, it is probably a treatise on certain points of traditional Zadokite legal praxis. MMT is a group composition, originating in the Qumran group, or in one of its antecedents, probably between 159–152 BCE. At this early period in the evolution and history of the Qumran group, when their leader was probably the Teacher of Righteousness (the Zadokite priest who may well have been also the high priest of the time), the group sent an appeal to an individual leader and his people Israel, with an exhortation to follow their own lead in certain points of Zadokite praxis. This individual was in all probability the Maccabean political leader who was to be known to the Qumran community as the 'Wicked Priest' after his usurpation of the high priesthood. At the time of MMT's composition, however, relations between the two groups, the 'we' group and the 'you' group of MMT, seem relatively eirenic.

Perhaps we should see in MMT not an occasional treatise but a systematic exposition of the reasons why a group of Zadokites separated from another group (possibly also Zadokite in origin) who followed what would later be called Pharisaic law, and then from the 'majority of Israel' who also followed that group's teachings. In Tannaitic literature, the law of the opponents is called 'Pharisee', while that of MMT is, surprisingly, called 'Sadducee'; but we have suggested that this name was used both for the later Hellenizing Sadducees and for the early Zadokite Essenes.

Most of the topics of legal dispute are hard to date, as one would expect, but it is worth noting, as an indicator of a date before Jonathan's pontificate, that the question of which family might be high priest is passed by, while the questions of priestly marriages and priestly seed are on the agenda. More general, non-legal indicators of such an early date are the absence of the metaphysical dualist thought and organisational language normal among Qumran texts.

5. THE HALAKHA

5.1 The Halakha of the Qumran Sect and Scholarly Study of the Field

5.1.1 The Halakhic Writings

QUESTIONS of halakha (in the widest sense of the word) and of halakhic principles are treated in many sectarian writings from Qumran. But actual halakha, in the narrow sense of a religious law binding upon all Israelites, is to be found primarily in two works, the Damascus Covenant[1] and the Temple Scroll. The Damascus Covenant contains halakhot about the Sabbath, marital relations, purification rites, oaths and other matters. The Temple Scroll's halakhot cover many subjects, among them ritual purity (with or without any connection with the Temple), festivals, and sacrifices.

The following works also contain halakhot for all Israel, and not just regulations for the *yaḥad*:

1. 'Ordinances' (4Q159) in J. M. Allegro, *DJD* V, pp. 6–9.
2. 'Florilegium' (4Q174), ibid., pp. 53–57.
3. Some fragments of other manuscripts of 'Ordinances' (4Q513–514) in M. Baillet, *DJD* VII, pp. 287–298.
4. Some fragments from Cave IV(= 4Q251), which the editors called 4QHalakah. To date only one of these halakhic fragments has been published, frg. a5.[2]
5. 'Ritual of Purification' (4Q512) in M. Baillet, *DJD* VII, pp. 262–286. This work describes the purification procedures and the blessings which accompanied them. Another manuscript of this work (4Q423) is to be published by J. Strugnell.
6. Several manuscripts of a work called Tohorot (4Q275–284; unpublished).
7. A work containing halakhot and regulations which Milik calls SD (= 4Q265).
8. Some fragments of manuscripts with agriculture laws (4Q284a).
9. Legal matters may also be found in sapiential works, e.g. 4Q415 11 and 4Q418 167; 4Q421 12.

The subject matter of the Qumran calendar also belongs to the domain of halakha, although the literary genre 'calendar' is not itself halakhic; only a small amount of the extensive calendaric material found at Qumran has so far been published.[3]

In other works of the sect, such as the Manual of Discipline and the War Scroll, one finds rulings which relate to the sect and which reflect the views of its members on the study of the Torah and performance of the law. These rulings are also to be included within the general scope of halakha.[4] They do not, however, constitute halakha in the narrow sense of the term, since they are not binding

---

[1] Both in the fragments discovered in the Cairo Geniza and in those discovered at Qumran, only some of which have so far been published; see *RB* 73 (1966), p. 105; J. M. Baumgarten, 'The 4Q Zadokite Fragment on Skin Disease', *JJS* 41 (1990), pp. 153–165; *DJD* III, pp. 128, 181, and J. T. Milik, *Ten Years of Discovery in the Wilderness of Judaea*, London, 1959, pp. 38, 114 and 151–152. The fragments discovered at Qumran contain purity laws relevant to those of MMT.

[2] See Baumgarten, *Qumran Law*, pp. 131–142.

[3] See S. Talmon, 'The Calendar Reckoning of the Sect from the Judean Desert', *Scripta Hierosolymitana* 4 (1958), pp. 162–199; J. T. Milik (see n. 1), pp. 41 and 107–113; Yadin, *TS*, I, pp. 95–96 (who cites further literature); S. Talmon and I. Knohl, 'A Calendrical Scroll from Qumran Cave IV: Miš Ba (4Q321)', *Tarbiz* 60 (1991), pp. 505–521.

[4] Cf. Schiffman, *Halakha*, pp. 4–9.

on the whole people, but only on the *yaḥad*, a community which had taken upon itself extra obligations.[5] Nevertheless, they contain much important evidence about the legal system in force at Qumran and the way in which problems were decided, as well as the *yaḥad*'s attitude to matters of ritual purity and the like.[6] We can also learn about matters of this kind from other written sources, for instance the passages in Josephus and Philo concerning the customs of the Essenes (if these are to be identified with the Qumran sect).

5.1.2 The Study of the Qumran Halakha

Scholarly investigation of Qumran halakha (in the narrow sense of the word) has hitherto been mainly based on the Damascus Covenant, of which large fragments were discovered a century ago in the Cairo Geniza, and smaller fragments (most of which have not yet been published) at Qumran. The recently published Temple Scroll has greatly enriched our knowledge in this area, and its halakhot have been treated at length by Yadin. It is to be hoped that experts in the field will continue to clarify the Qumran halakha on the basis of the new material: it must be compared with rabbinic halakha, the Apocrypha, the Karaites' halakha[7] and the halakha of the Samaritans and the Falashas.

5.1.3. Bibliography on the Halakha at Qumran

To the best of our knowledge there is still no bibliography devoted exclusively to the halakha of the scrolls. Chapter XI in Jongeling's bibliography ('Qumran and Judaism; the Calendar') does not limit itself to halakhic topics, and is extremely incomplete.[8]

The following list contains studies on the Qumran sect's halakha in the strict sense of the word. Though it is not exhaustive, it will give an impression of the types of study being carried out in this field. (Studies on the halakha of *Jubilees* are not included here.)

Bibliography on the Halakha at Qumran

Altschuler, D., 'On the Classification of Judaic Laws in the Antiquities of Josephus and the Temple Scroll from Qumran'. *Association for Jewish Studies Review* 7–8 (1982–83), pp. 1–14.

Amusin, J. D., 'Spuren antiqumranischer Polemik in der talmudischen Tradition'. In *Qumran-Probleme*, ed. H. Bardtke, pp. 5–27. Berlin, 1963.

Baumgarten, J. M., 'On the Testimony of Women in 1QSa'. *JBL* 76 (1957), pp. 266–269.

——, 'The Dead Sea Scrolls: A Threat to Halakhah?'. *Tradition* 1 (1958–1959), pp. 209–221.

——, '1QSa 1:11—Age of Testimony or Responsibility?'. *JQR* 49 (1958–1959), pp. 157–160.

——, *Studies in Qumran Law*. Leiden, 1977.

---

[5] These rulings are in force only during the time of the dominion of wickedness (בקץ הרשע). The Damascus Document makes a distinction between everlasting laws (חוק עולם) and laws in force temporarily (בקץ הרשע); see, for instance, 15:5–7, and E. Qimron, 'Celibacy in the Dead Sea Scrolls and the Two Kinds of Sectarians', In *The Madrid Qumran Congress: Proceedings of the International Congress on the Dead Sea Scrolls, Madrid, 18–21 March 1991* (ed. J. T. Barrera and L. V. Montaner), Leiden 1992, I, pp. 293–294.

[6] Schiffman, *Halakha*, pp. 1–3.

[7] There are many halakhot from Qumran (attested in MMT and in other works) which correspond to the Karaite view and differ from that of the rabbis. This does not, however, necessarily support the suggestion of A. Geiger that the Karaites were the descendants of the 'Sadducees' (or of any other early sect). Such similarities may have resulted either from a similar interpretation of Scripture, or from the influence of earlier literature, such as Qumranic works (which the Karaites possessed) or the works of Philo (cf. B. Revel, *The Karaite Halakha*, Philadelphia, 1913).

[8] B. Jongeling, *A Classified Bibliography of the Finds in the Desert of Judah*, Leiden, 1971, pp. 105–110; cf. also J. A. Fitzmyer, S. J., *The Dead Sea Scrolls: Major Publications and Tools for Study*, Atlanta, 1990, pp. 180–186; and Fitzmyer's bibliography on CD in the Ktav reprint of S. Schechter, *Documents of Jewish Sectaries*, New York, 1970, pp. 25–34.

——, Review of *The Halakhah at Qumran*, by L. H. Schiffman. *Religious Studies Review* 6 (1977), p. 179.

——, Review of *Megillat ha-Miqdaš*. *JBL* 97 (1978), pp. 584–589.

——, 'The Pharisaic-Sadducean Controversies about Purity, and the Qumran Texts'. *JJS* 31 (1980), pp. 157–170.

——, 'Exclusions from the Temple: Proselytes and Agrippa I'. *JSS* 33 (1982), pp. 215–225.

——, 'Hanging and Treason in Qumran and Roman Law'. *Eretz Israel* 16 (1982), pp. 7*–16*.

——, 'Some Problems of the Jubilees Calendar in Current Research'. *VT* 32 (1982), pp. 485–488.

——, 'The "Sons of Dawn" in CDC 13:14–15 and the Ban on Commerce among the Essenes'. *IEJ* 33 (1983), pp. 81–85.

——, '4Q502, Marriage or Golden Age Ritual?'. *JSS* 34 (1983), pp. 125–135.

——, 'On the Non-ritual Use of *Maaser-Dekate*'. *JBL* 103 (1984), pp. 245–251.

——, Review of *Sectarian Law in the DSS* by L. H. Schiffman. *JQR* 75 (1984), pp. 434–435.

——, 'Halakhic Polemics in New Fragments from Qumran Cave 4'. In *Biblical Archaeology Today*, pp. 390–399. Jerusalem, 1984.

——, 'The First and Second Tithes in the Temple Scroll'. In *Biblical and Related Studies Presented to Samuel Iwri*, ed. A. Kort and S. Morschauer, pp. 5–15. Winona Lake, IN, 1985.

——, 'Halivni's Midrash, Mishnah, and Gemara' (a review). *JQR* 77 (1986), pp. 59–64.

——, 'The Sabbath Trumpets in 4Q493 Mᶜ'. *RQ* 12 (1987), pp. 555–559.

——, 'The Laws of ᶜOrla and First Fruits in the Light of Jubilees, the Qumran Writings, and Targum Ps. Jonathan'. *JJS* 38 (1987), pp. 195–202.

——, 'Qumran and the Halakha in the Aramaic Targumim'. *Proceedings of the Ninth World Congress of Jewish Studies, Bible Studies and Ancient Near East* (1988), pp. 45–60.

——, 'The Qumran-Essene Restraints on Marriage'. In *Archaeology and History*, pp. 13–24.

——, 'The 4Q Zadokite Fragments on Skin Disease'. *JJS* 41 (1990), pp. 153–165.

——, 'Recent Qumran Discoveries and Halakhah in the Hellenistic-Roman Period'. In *Jewish Civilization in the Hellenistic-Roman Period*. JSP Supp., vol. 10, pp. 147–158. Sheffield, 1991.

——, 'The Purification Rituals in *DJD* VII'. In *Forty Years*, pp. 199–209.

——, 'Disqualifications of Priests in 4Q Fragments of the Damascus Document, a Specimen of the Recovery of pre-Rabbinic Halakha'. In *The Madrid Qumran Congress: Proceedings of the International Congress on the Dead Sea Scrolls, Madrid, 18–21 March 1991* (ed. J. T. Barrera and L. V. Montaner), Leiden 1992, II, pp. 502–513.

Bietenhardt, H., 'Sabbatvorschriften von Qumran im Lichte des rabbinischen Rechts und der Evangelien'. In *Qumran-Probleme*, ed. H. Bardtke, pp. 54–74. Berlin, 1963.

Blidstein, G., '4Q Florilegium and Rabbinic Sources on Bastard and Proselyte'. *RQ* 8 (1972–1974), pp. 421–435.

Bokser, B. M., 'Approaching Sacred Space'. *HTR* 78 (1985), pp. 279–299.

Borgen, P., 'At the Age of Twenty, in 1QSa'. *RQ* 3 (1961–1962), pp. 267–277.

Bowman, J., 'Did the Qumran Sect Burn the Red Heifer?'. *RQ* 1 (1958–1959), pp. 73–84.

——, 'Contact Between Samaritan Sects and Qumran?'. *VT* 7 (1957), pp. 184–189.

——, *Samaritanische Probleme*. Stuttgart, 1967, pp. 77–96.

Broshi, M., 'Anti-Qumranic Polemic in the Talmud'. In *The Madrid Qumran Congress: Proceedings of the International Congress on the Dead Sea Scrolls, Madrid, 18–21 March 1991* (ed. J. T. Barrera and L. V. Montaner), Leiden, 1992, II, pp. 589–600.

Büchler, A., 'Schechter's Jewish Sectaries'. *JQR*, N. S. 3 (1912–1913), pp. 429–485.

Callaway, P. R., 'Extending Divine Revelation: Micro-Compositional Strategies in the Temple Scroll'. In *Temple Scroll Studies*, pp. 149–162.

Davies, P. R., 'Halakhah at Qumran'. In *A Tribute To Geza Vermes: Essays on Jewish and Christian Literature and History*, pp. 37–50. JSOT Supp., vol. 100. Sheffield, 1990.

Dion, P. E., 'Early Evidence for the Ritual Significance of the "Base of the Altar" around Deut 12:27 LXX'. *JBL* 106 (1987), pp. 487–490.

Eppstein, V., 'When and How the Sadducees Were Excommunicated'. *JBL* 85 (1966), pp. 213–224.

Erder, Y., 'The First Date in *Megilat Ta'anit* in Light of the Karaite Commentary on the Tabernacle Dedication'. *JQR* 82 (1992), pp. 263–283.

Falk, Z. W., 'בחוקי הגוים in Damascus Document IX 1'. *RQ* 6 (1967–1969), p. 569.

——, 'The Temple Scroll and the Codification of Jewish Law'. *Jewish Law Annual* 2 (1979), pp. 33–44.

Fitzmyer, J. A., S. J., 'The Matthean Divorce Texts and Some New Palestinian Evidence'. *Theological Studies* 37 (1976), pp. 197–226.

——, 'Divorce among First-Century Palestinian Jews'. *Eretz Israel* 14 (1978), pp. 103*–110*.

Flusser, D., 'The Last Supper and the Essenes'. *Immanuel* 2 (1973), pp. 23–27.

Gärtner, B., *The Temple and the Community in Qumran and in the New Testament*. Cambridge, 1965.

Ginzberg, L., *An Unknown Jewish Sect*. New York, 1976.

Golb, N., 'Literary and Doctrinal Aspects of the Damascus Covenant in the Light of the Karaite Literature'. *JQR* 47 (1956–1957), pp. 354–374.

——, 'The Dietary Laws of the Damascus Covenant in Relation to Those of the Karaites'. *JJS* 8 (1957), pp. 51–69.

Hoenig, S. B., 'On the Age of Mature Responsibility in 1QSa'. *JQR* 48 (1957–1958), pp. 371–375.

——, 'Halakhic Implications of the Dead Sea Scrolls'. *Tradition* 1 (1958–1959), pp. 64–76.

——, 'The Age of Twenty in the Rabbinic Tradition and 1QSa'. *JQR* 49 (1958–1959), pp. 209–214.

——, 'Qumran Rules of Impurities'. *RQ* 6 (1967–1969), pp. 559–567.

——, 'Sectarian Scrolls and Rabbinic Research'. *JQR* 59 (1968–1969), pp. 24–70.

——, 'An Interdict against Socializing on the Sabbath (Damascus Document 11:4)'. *JQR* 62 (1971), pp. 77–83.

Isaksson, A., *Marriage and Ministry in the New Temple*, Lund, 1965, pp. 45–47.

Jackson, B., 'Damascus Document IX 16–23 and Parallels'. *RQ* 9 (1977–1978), pp. 445–450.

Kimbrough, S. T., 'The Concept of Sabbath at Qumran'. *RQ* 5 (1964–1966), pp. 483–502.

Kister, M., 'Some Aspects of Qumranic Halakhah', In *The Madrid Qumran Congress: Proceedings of the International Congress on the Dead Sea Scrolls, Madrid, 18–21 March 1991* (ed. J. T. Barrera and L. V. Montaner), Leiden, 1992, II, pp. 571–588.

Knohl, I., 'Post-Biblical Sectarianism and the Priestly Schools of the Pentateuch: The Issue of Popular Participation in the Temple Cult on Festivals', In *The Madrid Qumran Congress: Proceedings of the International Congress on the Dead Sea Scrolls, Madrid, 18–21 March 1991* (ed. J. T. Barrera and L. V. Montaner), Leiden, 1992, II, pp. 601–609.

Kuhn, K. G., 'The Lord's Supper and the Communal Meal at Qumran'. In *The Scrolls and the New Testament*, ed. K. Stendahl, New York, 1957, pp. 65–93.

Lehmann, M. R., 'Talmudic Material Relating to the Dead Sea Scrolls'. *RQ* 1 (1958–1959), pp. 391–404.

——, 'Gen 2:24 as a Basis for Divorce in Halakha and New Testament'. *ZAW* 72 (1960), pp. 263–267.

——, 'Yom Kippur in Qumran'. *RQ* 3 (1962–1964), pp. 117–124.

——, 'The Temple Scroll as a Source of Sectarian Halakha'. *RQ* 9 (1978), pp. 579–587.

——, 'The Beautiful War Bride (יפת תאר) and Other Halakhot in the Temple Scroll'. In *Temple Scroll Studies*, pp. 265–271.

Leszynsky, R., *Die Sadduzäer*. Berlin, 1912, esp. pp. 142–67.

Levine, B., 'Damascus Document IX 17–22—A New Translation and Comment'. *RQ* 8 (1973), pp. 195–196.

——, 'The Temple Scroll—Aspects of its Historical Provenance and Literary Character'. *BASOR* 232 (1978), pp. 5–23.

Lieberman, S., 'Light on the Cave Scrolls from Rabbinic Sources'. *Proceedings of the American Academy for Jewish Research* 20 (1951), pp. 395–404 [= Lieberman, S., *Texts and Studies*. New York, 1974, pp. 190–199].

——, 'The Discipline in the So-called Dead Sea Manual of Discipline'. *JBL* 71 (1952), pp. 199–206 [= *Texts and Studies*, pp. 200–207].

Liver, J., 'The Sons of "Zadok, the Priests" in the Dead Sea Sect'. *RQ* 6 (1967), pp. 3–30.

Marmorstein, A., 'Eine unbekannte jüdische Sekte'. *Theologische Tijdschrift* 52 (1918), pp. 92–122.

Martinez, F. G., 'Les limites de la communauté: pureté et impureté à Qumran et dans le Nouveau Testament'. In *Text and Testimony, Essays on New Testament and Apocryphal Literature in Honour of A. F. J. Klijn*, edited by T. Baarda, A. Hilhorst, G. P. Luttikhuizen and A. S. van der Woude, Kampen, 1988, pp. 111–122.

——, 'Il problema della purità: la soluzione qumranica'. *RSB* 1 (1989), pp. 169–191.

Milgrom, J., '"Sabbath" and "Temple City" in the Temple Scroll'. *BASOR* 232 (1978), pp. 25–27.

——, 'Studies in the Temple Scroll'. *JBL* 97 (1978), pp. 501–523.

——, 'Further Studies in the Temple Scroll'. *JQR* 71 (1980), pp. 1–17, 89–106.

——, 'New Temple Festivals in the Temple Scroll'. In *The Temple in Antiquity: Ancient Records and Modern Perspectives*, ed. T. G. Masden, Provo, Brigham Young Univ. Press, 1981, pp. 125–133.

——, 'The Qumran Cult: Its Exegetical Principles'. In *Temple Scroll Studies*, pp. 165–180.

——, 'The Scriptural Foundations and the Deviations in the Laws of Purity of the Temple Scroll'. In *Archaeology and History*, pp. 83–99.

——, 'Deviations from Scripture in the Purity Laws of the *Temple Scroll*'. In *Jewish Civilization in the Hellenistic-Roman Period*, JSP Supp., vol. 10. Sheffield, 1991, pp. 159–167.

——, 'First Day Ablution in Qumran', In *The Madrid Qumran Congress: Proceedings of the International Congress on the Dead Sea Scrolls, Madrid, 18–21 March 1991* (ed. J. T. Barrera and L. V. Montaner), Leiden, 1992, II, pp. 561–570.

Murphy-O'Connor, J., 'A Literary Analysis of Damascus Document VI2–VIII3'. *RB* 67 (1970), pp. 210–232.

——, and Y. Yadin., 'L'attitude Essénienne envers la Polygamie et le Divorce'. *RB* 69 (1972), pp. 98–100.

Neusner, J., 'The Fellowship (חבורה) in the Second Jewish Commonwealth'. *HTR* 53 (1960), pp. 125–142.

——, '"By the Testimony of Two Witnesses" in the Damascus Document IX 17–22 and in Pharisaic-Rabbinic Law'. *RQ* 8 (1973), pp. 197–217.

——, 'Damascus Document IX 17–22 and Irrelevant Parallels'. *RQ* 9 (1978), pp. 441–444.

Newton, M., *The Concept of Purity at Qumran and in the Letters of Paul*. Cambridge, 1985.

Noack, B., 'The Day of Pentecost in Jubilees, Qumran and Acts'. *ASTL* 1 (1962), pp. 73–95.

Qimron, E., 'Davies' the Damascus Covenant' (a review). *JQR* 77 (1986), pp. 84–87.

——, 'The Holiness of the Holy Land in the Light of a New Document from Qumran'. In *Pillars of Smoke and Fire—The Holy Land in History and Thought*, ed. M. Sharon, Johannesburg, 1988, pp. 9–13.

——, "'שבועת הבנים'" in the Damascus Covenant 15 1–2'. *JQR* 81 (1990), pp. 115–118.

——, 'Celibacy in the Dead Sea Scrolls and the Two Kinds of Sectarians'. In *The Madrid Qumran Congress: Proceedings of the International Congress on the Dead Sea Scrolls, Madrid, 18–21, March 1991* (ed. J. T. Barrera and L. V. Montaner), Leiden, 1992, I, pp. 287–294.

——, and J. Strugnell., 'An Unpublished Halakhic Letter from Qumran'. In *Biblical Archaeology Today*, Jerusalem, 1984, pp. 400–407.

——, 'An Unpublished Halakhic Letter from Qumran'. *The Israel Museum Journal* 4 (1985), pp. 9–12.

Rabin, C., *Qumran Studies*. Oxford, 1957, pp. 82–94.

Rabinovitch, N. L., 'Damascus Document IX 17–22 and Rabbinic Parallels'. *RQ* 9 (1977–1978), pp. 113–116.

Reeves, J. C., 'What Does Noah Offer in 1QApGen X, 15?'. *RQ* 12 (1986), pp. 413–419.

Robinson, A., 'A Note on Damascus Document IX 7'. *RQ* 9 (1977–1978), pp. 237–240.

Rosenthal, J., 'The Sabbath Laws of the Qumranites or the Damascus Covenanters'. *Biblical Research* 6 (1951), pp. 10–17.

Rosso-Ubigli, L., 'Il documento di Damasco e la Halakah Settaria'. *RQ* 9 (1978), pp. 357–399.

Rubinstein, A., 'Urban Halakhah and Camp Rules in the Cairo Fragments, Damascus Covenant'. *Sefarad* 12 (1952), pp. 283–296.

Scheiber, A., 'Ihr soll kein Bein dran zerbrechen'. *VT* 13 (1963), pp. 95–97.

Schiffman, L. H., *The Halakhah at Qumran*. Leiden, 1975.

——, 'The Qumran Laws of Testimony'. *RQ* 8 (1975), pp. 603–642, and 9 (1977), pp. 261–262.

——, 'The Temple Scroll in Literary and Philological Perspective'. In *Approaches to Ancient Judaism*, 2, ed. W. S. Green, Brown Judaic Studies, vol. 9. Chico, 1980, pp. 143–155.

——, 'Jewish Sectarianism in Second Temple Times'. In *Great Schisms in Jewish History*, ed. Jospe, S. Wagner, New York, 1981, pp. 1–46.

——, *Sectarian Law in the Dead Sea Scrolls: Courts, Testimony and the Penal Code*. Brown Judaic Studies, vol. 33. Chico, 1983.

——, 'Legislation Concerning Relations with non-Jews in the Zadokite Fragments and in the Tannaitic Literature'. *RQ* 11 (1983), pp. 379–389.

——, 'Purity and Perfection: Exclusion from the Council of the Community in *Serekh Ha-Edah*'. In *Biblical Archaeology Today*, Jerusalem, 1984, pp. 373–389.

——, 'Exclusion from the Sanctuary and the City of the Sanctuary in the Temple Scroll'. *Hebrew Annual Review* 9 (1985), pp. 301–320.

——, 'The Sacrificial System of the Temple Scroll and the Book of Jubilees'. In *Society of Biblical Literature 1985 Seminar Papers*, ed. K. H. Richards, Atlanta, 1985, pp. 217–233.

——, 'Reproof as a Requisite for Punishment in the Law of the Dead Sea Scrolls'. In *Jewish Law Association Studies*, ed. B. S. Jackson, Atlanta, 1986, pp. 60–74.

——, 'The King, his Guard and the Royal Council in the Temple Scroll'. *Proceedings of the American Academy for Jewish Research*, 54 (1987), pp. 237–259.

——, 'The Laws of War in the Temple Scroll'. *RQ* 49–52 (1988), pp. 299–311.

——, 'The Law of the Temple Scroll and its Provenance'. *Folia Orientalia* 25 (1988), pp. 85–98.

——, 'Architecture and Laws: The Temple and its Courtyards in the Temple Scroll'. In *From Ancient Israel to Modern Judaism: Intellect in Quest of Understanding*, Brown Judaic Studies, vol. 159. Atlanta, 1989, pp. 267–284.

——, *The Eschatological Community of the Dead Sea Scrolls: A Study of the Rule of the Congregation*. SBL Monograph Series, vol. 38. Atlanta, 1989.

——, '*Shelamim* Sacrifices in the Temple Scroll'. *Eretz-Israel* 22 (1989), pp. 176*–183*.

——, 'The Temple Scroll and the System of Jewish Law of the Second Temple Period'. In *Temple Scroll Studies*, pp. 239–255.

——, '*Miqṣat Maʿaseh Ha-Torah* and the Temple Scroll'. *RQ* 14 (1990), pp. 435–458.

——, 'The Prohibition of the Skins of Animals in the Temple Scroll and *Miqṣat Maʿaseh Ha-Torah*'. *Proceedings of the Tenth World Congress of Jewish Studies. Division A: The Bible and its World* (1990), pp. 191–198.

——, 'The Law of Vows and Oaths (Num 30, 3-16) in the Zadokite Documents and the Temple Scroll'. *RQ* 15 (1991), pp. 199–213.

——, 'Qumran and Rabbinic Halakhah'. In *Jewish Civilization in the Hellenistic-Roman Period*, pp. 138–146. JSP Supp., vol. 10. Sheffield, 1991.

——, 'Laws Pertaining to Women in the Temple Scroll'. In *Forty Years*, pp. 210–228.

——, 'The Furnishings of the Temple According to the Temple Scroll'. In *The Madrid Qumran Congress: Proceedings of the International Congress on the Dead Sea Scrolls, Madrid, 18–21 March 1991* (ed. J. T. Barrera and L. V. Montaner), Leiden, 1992, II, pp. 621–634.

Schubert, K., 'Ehescheidung im Judentum zur Zeit Jesu'. *Theologische Quartalschrift* 151 (1971), p. 23 ff.

Schwartz, D. R., 'Laws and Truth: On Qumran-Sadducean and Rabbinic Views of Law'. In *Forty Years*, pp. 229–240.

Siegel, J. P., 'The Employment of Palaeo-Hebrew Characters for the Divine Names at Qumran in the Light of Tannaitic Sources'. *HUCA* 42 (1971), pp. 159–172.

Slomovic, E., 'Toward an Understanding of the Exegesis in the Dead Sea Scrolls'. *RQ* 6 (1969), pp. 3–15.

Strugnell, J., and E. Qimron: see under Qimron.

Sweeney, M. A., 'Sefirah at Qumran: Aspects of the Counting Formulas for the First-Fruits Festivals in the Temple Scroll'. *BASOR* 251 (1983), pp. 61–66.

Urbach, E. E., 'Yigael Yadin's Contribution to Judaic Studies'. *Eretz-Israel* 20 (1989), pp. xviii–xxiv.

VanderKam, J. C., 'The Temple Scroll and the Book of Jubilees'. In *Temple Scroll Studies*, pp. 211–236.

Vermes, G., *Annual of Leeds University Oriental Society* 6 (1969), p. 65.

——, 'Sectarian Matrimonial Halakhah in the Damascus Rule'. *JSS* 25 (1974), pp. 197–202.

Vivian, A., 'I sacrifici prescriti nel *Rotolo del Tempio*'. *Rotolo del Tempio*, pp. 251–292.

Wacholder, B. Z., *The Dawn of Qumran*. Cincinnati, 1983.

——, 'Rules of Testimony in the Qumranic Jurisprudence: CD 9 and 11Q Torah 64'. *JSS* 40 (1989), pp. 163–174.

Wieder, N., *The Judean Scrolls and Karaism*. London, 1962.

Yadin, Y., 'A Midrash on 2 Sam VII . . .'. *IEJ* 9 (1959), pp. 95–98.

——, 'A Note on 4Q159 (Ordinances)'. *IEJ* 18 (1968), pp. 250–252.

——, 'Pesher Nahum (4QpNahum) Reconsidered'. *IEJ* 21 (1971), pp. 1–12.

——, and J. Murphy-O'Connor: see under Murphy-O'Connor.

Zahavy, T., 'The Sabbath Code of Damascus Document X 14 – XI 18; Form-Analytical and Redaction-Critical Observations'. *RQ* 10 (1981), pp. 589–591.

אורבך, א', 'הדרשה כיסוד ההלכה'. תרביץ כז (תשי"ז-תש"ח), עמ' 175-176.

באומגרטן, י', 'הלוח של ספר היובלים והמקרא'. תרביץ לב (תשכ"ג), עמ' 317-328.

בר, מ', 'הכתות ומחצית השקל'. תרביץ לא (תשכ"ב), עמ' 298-299.

בר-אילן, מ', 'האם מסכתות תמיד ומידות הן תעודות פולמוסיות?'. סידרא, ה (תשמ"ט), עמ' 27-40.

גולדברג, א', 'המדרש הקדום והמדרש המאוחר'. תרביץ נ (תשמ"א), עמ' 94-106.

הר, מ"ד, 'מי היו הבייתוסים?'. דברי הקונגרס העולמי השביעי למדעי היהדות, כרך ג' (תשמ"א), עמ' 20-21.

——, 'הרצף שבשלשלת מסירתה של התורה'. ציון (1980), עמ' 43-56.

זוסמן, י', 'חקר תולדות ההלכה ומגילות מדבר יהודה: הרהורים תלמודיים ראשונים לאור מגילת מקצת
        מעשי התורה'. תרביץ נט (תש"ן), עמ' 11-76. (נוסח מקוצר הופיע בספר 'מגילות מדבר יהודה: ארבעים
        שנות מחקר', בעריכת מ' ברושי ואחרים, עמ' 99-127, ירושלים, תשנ"ב.

חגי, ש', 'הטהרה והטומאה אצל כתות מדבר יהודה'. מחניים סב (תשכ"ב), עמ' 80-83.

טלמון, ש', 'חשבון הלוח של כת מדבר יהודה'. בתוך עיונים במגילות מדבר יהודה, בעריכת י' ליוור, עמ' 24-39,
        ירושלים, תשי"ז.

ידין, י', 'מגילת מלחמת בני אור בבני חושך', ירושלים, תשי"ז, עמ' 60-81 (חובת הגיוס), עמ' 181-190 (ממנהגי
        העדה).

——, 'תפילין של ראש מקומראן', ירושלים, תשכ"ט (= ארץ ישראל ט).

——, 'מגילת המקדש', א, ירושלים, תשל"ז, עמ' 74-136, 215, 294-215.

ליהמן, מ"ר, 'מגילת המקדש כמקור להלכה כתתית', בית מקרא כה (תשל"ט - תש"ם), עמ' 302-308.

——, 'אשת יפת תואר והלכות אחרות במגילת המקדש', בית מקרא לג (תשמ"ח), עמ' 313-316.

——, 'מסות ומסעות', ירושלים, תשמ"ב.

ליוור, י', 'מחצית השקל במגילות מדבר יהודה', תרביץ כא (תשכ"א), עמ' 18-22.

לייבל, ד', 'שבת של כת מדבר יהודה', תרביץ כט (תש"כ), עמ' 296.

לשם, ח', 'מגילת ברית דמשק', מחניים ס"ב (תשכ"ב), עמ' 74-79.

סגל, מ"צ, 'ספר ברית דמשק', השילוח כו (1912), עמ' 390-406, 483-506.

סופר, ע', 'מפני תרעומתן של מינים', סיני צט (תרא-תרב [תשמ"ו]), עמ' לח-מז.

פלוסר, ד', 'מחצית השקל באונגליון ואצל כת מדבר יהודה', תרביץ לא (תשכ"ב), עמ' 150-156.

——, 'הסעודה האחרונה והאיסיים', יהדות ומקורות הנצרות, תל אביב, תשל"ט, עמ' 115-119.

——, מקצת מעשי התורה וברכת המינים, תרביץ סא (תשנ"ב), עמ' 333-374.

פלק, ז', 'מגילת המקדש והמשנה הראשונה', סיני פג (תשל"ח), עמ' ל-מא.

קימרון, א', 'אל יתערב איש מרצונו בשבת (ברית דמשק יא 4)', דברי הקונגרס העולמי התשיעי למדעי היהדות,
        חטיבה ד, כרך ראשון - העברית ולשונות היהודיים, ירושלים, תשמ"ו, עמ' 9-15.

——, 'על שגגות וזדונות במגילות מדבר יהודה: עיון במונחים המשמשים לציונם', דברי הקונגרס העולמי העשירי
        למדעי היהדות, חטיבה א, המקרא ועולמו, ירושלים, תש"ן, עמ' 103-110.

——, 'מונחי ההלכה במגילות מדבר יהודה וחשיבותם לחקר תולדות ההלכה', מגילות מדבר יהודה: ארבעים שנות
        מחקר (בעריכת מ' ברושי ואחרים), ירושלים, תשנ"ב, עמ' 128-138.

קיסטר, מ', 'עוללות מספרות קומראן', תרביץ נז (תשמ"ח), עמ' 315-325.

רוזנטל, י', 'השתלשלות ההלכה בספר ברית דמשק', ספר היובל לכבוד הרב שמעון פדרבוש (בעריכת י"ל
        מימון), ירושלים, תש"כ, עמ' 293-303.

שוורץ, ד', 'מקוללי אלהים ואנשים (מגילת המקדש סד 12)', לשוננו מז (תשמ"ג), עמ' 18-24.

שרביט, ב', 'השבת של כת מדבר יהודה', בית מקרא כא (תשל"ו), עמ' 507-516.

שיפמן, י', 'הלכה, הליכה ומשיחיות בכת מדבר יהודה', ירושלים, תשנ"ג.

——, 'טומאה וטהרה לפי כת מדבר יהודה', בית מקרא כו (תשמ"א), עמ' 18-27.

5.2   The Character and Formulation of the Halakha of MMT

5.2.1   The Halakhic Topics Treated in MMT

MMT differs in its character from all halakhic texts hitherto published. It is not a collection of halakhot (or ordinances) arranged systematically according to subject, but rather a work which lists some (מקצת) special halakhot in which the sect differs from its opponents. It appears that the halakhot listed in this text occupied a central place in the halakhic controversies that took place between the sect and its opponents. According to what is now preserved of the manuscripts, these halakhot seem to belong to several areas: (a) the cultic calendar;[9] (b) ritual purity (especially in connection with the Temple) and the sacrificial cult; and (c) laws on marital status (in connection with the priests and the Temple).[10]

It need hardly be said how important all these halakhic topics are for communal religious life. On the importance of the calendar one need only read the article by S. Talmon,[11] who remarks that there is no barrier to communal religious living as tangible as a difference in the calendar; this constitutes an unmistakable mark of withdrawal from the larger community. As for the laws concerning ritual purity and the Temple cult, halakhot in these areas—because of their abundance—are to be assigned a central place among the earliest halakha.[12] In early Judaism, contaminating the Temple was considered the most severe sin.[13] We may especially note that most of the disputes with the 'Sadducees' recorded in our early sources involve matters of ritual purity. The last area dealt with, that of marital status, is of course a central area of halakha, and any dispute on this matter would create barriers to a communal religious life.[14]

In fact, MMT deals primarily with the three topics that stood at the center of the controversy between the Jewish religious parties of the Second Temple period. All are issues with regard to which a lack of consensus would make it impossible to coexist within a single religious community. Disagreement on these issues is what created the sects. MMT gathers together the main points of halakha on which its authors differed from the community at large, and from it we learn what were the matters that they themselves considered to be of central importance.

5.2.2   Other Sources for Early Halakha Comparable to MMT

Halakhot from the Second Temple period can be found both in contemporaneous sources (such as the Apocrypha and the writings of Josephus and Philo) and in later sources (such as rabbinic literature and that of the Samaritans and the Karaites).[15] The rabbinic sources explicitly ascribe halakhic views

---

[9] This material constitutes a formally distinct section of the work which comes before the section devoted to halakhot. See § 4.1.2.1.

[10] Only one marital halakha is preserved and it is in B 75–82 (cf. B 39–49 and § 5.7.9). Halakhot involving this area of law are found in other writings of the sect, and it seems strange at first that we do not find mention in this text of such key issues as the prohibition of bigamy which was accepted by the sect. One should, however, recall that the section that follows B 82 is missing, and it is possible that the missing section (whose extent is difficult to estimate) contained further laws relating to marital status. This hypothesis finds further support in frg. 8 of the papyrus MSe, in which the words תערובת 'sexual intercourse' (see below § 5.3.2.4) and האשה 'the woman' are found. The proper place of this fragment would seem to be in the gap at the end of section B.

[11] Cited in n. 3, pp. 163–166. Note that all the separatist sects emphasized differences in the calendar. Even in the time of the Geonim, calendric questions played a central role in the controversy between Palestine and Babylon.

[12] J. Neusner, *The Idea of Purity in Ancient Israel*, Leiden, 1973.

[13] Sussmann, p. 26, n. 66.

[14] Cf. *m. Yebam.* 1, 4 and Ginzberg, pp. 127–128. Note that this topic is one of the 'three nets of Belial' mentioned in CD 4:15.

[15] Schiffman, *Halakha*, pp. 9–19.

to the Sadducees and to the other sectarians. Two or three of the halakhot found in our work (those touching ritual purity) are specifically mentioned in early rabbinic literature as positions held by the Sadducees in their controversies with the Pharisees: those on streams of liquids (*m. Yad.* 4:6–8) and on the red cow (*m. Para* 3:7), and perhaps those on the purity of hides and bones (cf. § 5.7.6).

With regard to other halakhot in MMT, those about which no explicit evidence of controversy with any sect is to be found in rabbinic literature, we may still deduce that such controversy existed, either from the formulation of the rabbinic halakhot, or from comparison of rabbinic halakhot with the corresponding halakhot found in the law of the DSS.[16]

5.2.3 Some Principles of MMT's Halakha and their Consequences

A.   In all of the halakhot we may discern the sect's pronounced tendency toward strictness. Several scholars have written about the halakhic principles of the sect;[17] it is not our intention to deal exhaustively with this subject, but merely to point out the contribution made to the subject by MMT.

First of all, one should note that MMT is a written halakhic text from the Second Temple period. As has been pointed out,[18] the Pharisees at that time maintained the principle of not writing down halakhot, believing that the Torah was the only written law, and that it had been transmitted from Sinai together with an oral law; henceforth no prophet would have the authority to introduce any halakhic innovation.

Other sects did not believe in the oral law; they maintained that obligatory laws should be written down, and that the Pentateuch was not the only source for halakha (they believed in esoteric apocalyptic writings which supplemented the Mosaic Law).[19] MMT, however (unlike the Sadducean Book of Decrees), does allude to the biblical source of most of its halakhot (cf. §§ 5.2.4g and 5.3.2.6).

B.   In the Epilogue we find a number of passages which apparently deal with the principles underlying halakha, principles with which we are also familiar from other sectarian writings. We shall deal with some of them briefly.

[כתב]נֹו אליכה שתבין בספר מושֹׁה [ו]בֹספרֹי הנֹבֹיאים ובדויֹׁ[ד]

We have written to you so that you may study carefully[20] the book of Moses and the books of the Prophets and the writings of David[21] . . . (C 10)

The term הבין בספר refers to an exact study of Scripture, according to exegetical methods similar to the midrash of the rabbis. The members of the sect believed that all the particulars of the commandments had been written down in the Bible, which contained both 'clear laws' (נגלות) and 'hidden laws' (נסתרות). The latter, in their view, could be discovered by thorough, careful and intensive searching in the Scripture.[22]

---

[16] Ibid., pp. 22–76; Yadin, *TS*, I, pp. 400–401.

[17] Epstein, pp. 692–706; Baumgarten, *Qumran Law*, pp. 13–35; Halivni, pp. 38–43.

[18] Baumgarten, *Qumran Law*, p. 34; Ginzberg, p. 106. Does the sentence והדבר כתוב עברה (B 38) refer to such a book? See also 11QTᵃ 56:3–4 and Yadin, ad loc.

[19] For a discussion of this problem, see Halivni, pp. 38–43.

[20] On the phrase הבין בספר, see § 3.5.2.3.

[21] On the use of דויד to refer to the third part of the biblical canon, see the commentary, ad loc.

[22] The terms נסתרות and נגלות also mean unintentional and intentional sins (see E. Qimron, על שגגות וזדונות, *Proceedings of the Tenth World Congress for Jewish Studies, Division A, The Bible and its World*, Jerusalem, 1990, pp. 108–109). For the view that all the particular commandments can be found in the Bible, cf. the words of ʾAnan חפישו באורייתא שפיר; cf. Mahler, p. 134, and N. Wieder, *The Judean Scrolls and Karaism*, London, 1962, pp. 53–89. Wieder compares the halakhic principles of the sect with those of the Karaites; both are opposed to the concept of an oral

If in fact this passage refers to the study of the law, it also implies that one may (through careful study) derive halakha from biblical books other than the Pentateuch (ספר משה). This contrasts with the view of the Talmud that legal principles may not be derived from the Prophets.[23]

C.   It seems that the sectarians strove to observe the commandments in accordance with the literal sense of Scripture, and condemned any tendency to adapt the commandments to the needs of the time. This attitude is perhaps alluded to by the biblical formula לעשות הטוב והישר לפניו 'to do what is good and righteous before Him', which is quoted in C 31, the conclusion of the work; this formula, in the sect's opinion, referred to the perfect performance of the biblical commandments according to the will of God.[24] This may be deduced especially from the opening of the Manual of Discipline, where the formula is mentioned as one of the principles of the sect's doctrine:

לעשות הטוב והישר לפניו כאשר צוה ביד מושה וביד כול עבדיו הנביאים

To do what is good and righteous in His eyes, as He has commanded it through Moses and through all His servants the prophets (1QS 1:2–4)[25].

This formula is equivalent to the expression לעשות רצון אל; both reflect the attitude of the sectarians towards the biblical law, which is 'the will of God.' Thus the sectarians are called עושי רצונו (cf. עושי התורה); the opponents of the sect, by contrast, are depicted as doing their own will, e.g. CD 3:2–3, 11–12; עשה (בחר ב)רצון רוחו CD 2:20–21; בעשותם את רצונם ולא שמרו את מצות עשיהם[26] עשה הישר בעיניו CD 3:6; or הלך בשרירות לבו. They are further condemned for their lenient attitude toward the laws of the Torah: כי בחרו בקלות (4Q171 1–2 i 19).[27]

D.   This attitude of the sect can also be seen in the halakhot themselves, with the rigid and consistent interpretations given in them to terms from the Torah, as compared to the more fluid and more innovative rabbinic interpretations of these same terms.

---

law, believing that the details of all laws are contained in the Torah (some of them are 'hidden', but can be revealed through careful study). This view differs from that of the Sadducees, who did not insist on a biblical source for all their halakhot. (See J. M. Baumgarten, 'Halivni's Midrash, Mishna, and Gemara', *JQR* 77 [1986], pp. 62–64.)

[23] For further discussion of the attitudes of the rabbis and the Karaites towards this question, see Mahler, p. 134, n. 33; Ginzberg, p. 137, n. 119; Urbach, 'Halakha and Prophecy', *Tarbiz* 18 (1947), pp. 12–19; A. Leshem, *Sabbath and Festivals of Israel*, 1, Tel-Aviv, 1969, pp. 30–32; Schiffman, *Halakha*, p. 26. It should be noted that MMT deals with the observance of commandments, not with the manner in which they are deduced; it makes only passing reference to such fundamental questions.

[24] Cf. also the phrases דורשי רצונו 1QS 5:9 (contrast לעשות את רצון אל 1QS 9:13 etc., עושי רצונו 4Q173 1 ii 5, בעשותם את רצונם CD 2:12, where the suffix refers to the people's will, not to God's). Wernberg-Møller, p. 13, writes: 'The sole aim of the Torah study was the detection of the will of God, and the members set themselves the goal of living accordingly (1:3; 8:5)'; cf. also *m. 'Abot* 2:4, 5:20. On the linguistic relationship between עשה + רצונו and עשה + הטוב בעיני, see A. Hurvitz, 'The History of a Legal Formula: *kol ʾašer-ḥapeṣ ʿaśah* (Psalms 115:3, 135:6)', *VT* 32 (1982), p. 264. The rabbis understood the formula לעשות הטוב והישר as referring to any pietistic and stringent approach to the performance of the commandments (especially those governing relations between man and man); the rabbis themselves did not consider such an approach to be obligatory, but rather as connected to the rule לפנים משורת הדין 'beyond the strict letter of the law'; see B. de Vries, 'Halakha' in *Encyclopaedia Hebraica*, 14, p. 508. Note that the rabbis deduced this principle also from the expression ואת המעשה אשר יעשון, Exod 18:20. On the word מעשה in MMT and its technical meaning, see § 5.3.2.2 below.

[25] Note that the Hagiographa are not mentioned here, since 1QS here refers to the words of God through His messengers, and not to the Scriptures themselves.

[26] There may have been a special stress on the suffix, which refers to the opponents rather than to God. A similar view of the contrast between the commandment of God and the commandment of the sages is found in the New Testament (see M. Kister, 'Plucking of Grain on the Sabbath and the Jewish-Christian Debate', *Jerusalem Studies in Jewish Thought*, 3 [1983–4], pp. 364–366).

[27] Cf. CD 1:14–20. See also M. Kister, 'Notes on the Dead Sea Scrolls', *Tarbiz* 57 (1988), pp. 315–316.

Thus, for example, MMT identifies the מחנה 'camp' mentioned in the Torah, with Jerusalem; in contrast the rabbis distinguished between three types of camp, and so sometimes interpreted מחנה as referring to Jerusalem (מחנה ישראל), sometimes as referring to the Temple Mount (מחנה לויה), and sometimes as referring to the Temple (מחנה שכינה; see § 5.4).

The word אהל in the laws of the Torah is interpreted in the DSS as a 'house' or 'any dwelling place'. Thus MMT takes the word אהל in the verse וישב מחוץ לאהלו in Lev 14:8 as בית 'house': אדם הצ[רועים באים ע]ם טהרת הקודש לבית (B 68; see § 5.7.15f). Similarly the word אהל in Num 19:14 כי ימות באהל was interpreted in 11QTᵃ 49:5 as בית 'house'.[28]

A tendency toward stringency is evident also in the use of the word טהור. For the sectarians, איש טהור in connection with the red cow rites (and elsewhere) meant one who had undergone the entire process of purification which was held not to be completed until the sun had set.[29] The rabbis maintain that one who has immersed himself in a *miqve* can also be defined איש טהור even before sunset (see § 5.7.5d).

E.   In all these examples there is a clearly discernable tendency towards literalness, stringency and uniformity of interpretation. Similar principles of literalness and stringency can be found also among some early rabbinic sages; compare the approach of the school of Shammai, generally more 'severe' than that of Hillel. This did not however prevent the two schools from having a communal religious life. The sect, on the other hand, was not willing to compromise either on the calendar or on halakhic issues, and for this reason its members separated themselves from the rest of the Jewish people. It would appear that this fact is stated explicitly in the Epilogue:

[פٔרٔ]שנו מרוב הע[ם] ומכול טמאתם ו[מהתערב בדברים האלה ומלבוא ע[מהם] לגב אלה

[. . .] We have separated ourselves from the multitude of the people and from all their impurities and from intermingling in these practices and from participating with them in these (practices) (C 7–8).

Here we have the earliest evidence for the use of the term פרש[30] as designating withdrawal from the general community. We also find here the words על גב (or לגב), which are used in rabbinic literature in contexts referring to participation in purity.[31] A similar rabbinic passage (*m. Yebam.* 1:4, summarising the disputes between the school of Hillel and the school of Shammai) also contains the term על גב (but obviously not the term פרש):

אף על פי שאילו פוסלין ואלו מכשירין לא נימנעו בית שמי מלישא נשים מבית הלל ולא בית הלל מבית שמי, כל הטהרות והטמאות שהיו אלו מטהרין ואלו מטמאין לא נימנעו עושין טהרות אלו על גב אלו

Though these declared ineligible what the others declared eligible, the [men of the] school of Shammai, nevertheless, did not refrain from marrying women from [the families of] the school of Hillel, nor the [men of the] school of Hillel [from marrying women] from [the families of] the school of Shammai. [Similarly in respect of] all [questions of ritual] purity and impurity, where these declared clean what the others declared unclean, neither of them abstained from preparing pure food with each other.

---

[28] Yadin, *TS*, II, pp. 212–213.
[29] Baumgarten, *Qumran Law*, p. 160.
[30] On the importance of the word פרש for the identification of the Pharisees, and the understanding of the name פרושים, see § 4.1.4.2.
[31] Cf. Lieberman, V, pp. 950–951.

5.2.4 The Formulation of the Halakhot

A.   The halakhot are formulated in a form and style that is in accordance with their polemical purposes. They are worded in a rather stereotyped manner. Many of them open with (*a*) the particle phrase ועל or ואף על 'and concerning',[32] followed by (*b*) a noun or several nouns or a noun phrase indicating the subject of the halakha. After this,[33] there may follow a statement reflecting either (*c*) the view of the sect, or (*d*) the (wrong) practice of its opponents.[34] In both cases the plural participle is used, preceded by a personal pronoun in the third or in the first person, e.g.:[35]

a	b	c
ואף על	המוצקות	אנחנו אומרים שהם שאין בהם טהרה

a	b	d
[ועל]	[העמוני] והמואבי . . .	שהם באים בקהל

B.   Other halakhot are formulated in a concise apodictic form, consisting of an infinitive form (e.g. ואין להבֿי למחני הקֿודש כלבים 'one may not let any dog enter the holy camp'[36] [B 58]), or (less frequently) a nominal sentence (e.g. ומעשר הבקר והצון לכוהנים הוא 'and the tithe of the cattle and the flock belongs to the priests' [B 63–64]), an imperfect form, or (once) a 'modal' participle. All of these halakhot present the view of the sect, whether in the affirmative or in the negative. In this type, the halakha sometimes opens with the subject, which may be introduced by ו(אף) על, but the infinitive (or the nominal clause) replaces the participle.

C.   Typical of the halakhot is the justificatory clause, which opens with words such as כי or ש-, בשל, as in: כי ירושלים היאֿ מחנה הקדש 'For Jerusalem is the holy camp . . .' (B 59–62); בשל שא יהיה הטהר 'So that the pure should sprinkle upon the impure' (B 16). These justificatory clauses

---

[32] In the preserved text of MMT, ועל occurs four times and ואף על occurs six times (in the restored text ועל seems to be somewhat more frequent). Evidently (ו)על is what marks the beginning of a new halakha, occurring either with ואף or without it. ואף alone has a more general nature; it rather marks a new statement (like וכעת in official Aramaic letters—cf. 3). Thus we find ואף על המוצקות (B 55) denoting the new subject, and then ואף המוצקות (B 56) denoting another statement on this same subject; ואף על הצרועים (B 64) and then ואף כתוב (B 66). It is only in one passage that ועל does not mark a new halakha: ועל בהמתו הטהורה . . . (B 76–77). In the two halakhot which have no heading neither על nor אף is used but rather ו 'and' (see table). This use of על in halakhic headings is also found in CD: על הטהר במים 'concerning the one who purifies himself in water' (12:10); על השבת לשמרה כמשפטה 'concerning the Shabbat to be kept properly' (12:14); על השבועה 'concerning oaths' (9:8); cf. Ruth 4:7. Sometimes it designates halakhic terms: על ההון 'civil cases' (CD 9:22), ואף על[ ] על הנפש 'concerning capital law' (4Q159 2–4:5). Note that ואף (always with a *waw*) is frequent also in C. In B 49 ואף על[introduces the reference to the blind and in B 52 it introduces the reference to the deaf. Although ואף על occurs twice, the subject of the blind and the deaf forms a single halakha. This may be inferred from the concluding statement in B 53–54: כי שלוא ראה ולוא שמע . . .. It is even possible that the halakha concerning the blind and the deaf is dependent on the preceding one (see § 5.7.10).

[33] Syntactically, in the sentence ואף על x אנחנו אומרים, the phrase אנחנו אומרים should not be taken as the subject and the predicate of ואף על x, the latter phrase being simply the heading. Note that in l. 13, אנחנו אומרים is missing after the heading ועל טהרת פרת החטאת. On the other hand, in a construction ואף על x שהם עושים, the phrase שהם עושים is apparently a part of the heading.

[34] Note that in the homiletic part of the Damascus Document general violations of the law by the opponents are formulated with the past tense; the specific violation, however, is formulated with the participle. Thus 4:5: הם נתפשים וגם מטמאים הם את המקדש אשר אין הם מבדיל כתורה ושוכבים את, and 5:6–8: בשתים בזנות לקחת שתי נשים בחייהם הרואה את דם זובה ולוקחים איש את בת אחיהו ואת בת אחותו.

[35] The participle construction with the personal pronoun may also occur later on, after the incipit of the halakha, e.g. והמה באים לטהרת המקדש (B 54).

[36] In this particular case there is no heading.

clearly serve the work's polemical purposes.[37] In a few cases the justificatory clauses refer not only to the adjacent halakha but to several preceding halakhot (B 26–27; 38; 53–54).

D.   Other typical elements are the use of the expression ‏ואתם יודעים ש‎- (B 68, 80; cf. C 14, 15) and ‏כי לבני אהרן/הכוהנים ראוי להזהר‎ (B 12, 16, 26). The former refers to the addressees, the leader of Israel and his ministers (see § 4.2.3). The latter refers to the priests who were responsible for the purity of the Temple, or to their chief, the addressee (see the commentary).

E.   Finally, it may be observed that, in spite of the generally stereotyped formulation, there are some variations. Some halakhot are very short, and only describe either the (wrong) practice of the opponents or the (correct) view of the sect (though sometimes both the opponents' practice and the sect's view are stated). Some halakhot develop a more complex structure as the polemic is expanded by justificatory clauses and even the occasional citation of scriptural proof-texts. Nevertheless there is extensive use of a fixed pattern.

F.   In most of the halakhot there are allusions to the biblical passages on which the particular halakha is based. Some words from each biblical parallel occur in the halakha of MMT (sometimes in a grammatical form different from that of the source). This helps us to understand the topic of some halakhot even where the text is damaged and to restore the text with considerable confidence. In fact, MMT actually consists of certain precepts of the Pentateuch as understood by the sectarians. The parallel passages are as follows (the details are to be found in the discussion of the individual halakhot):

B 6–8	//	Lev 6:21
B 9–11	//	Lev 7:15
B 13–16	//	Num 19
B 21–24	//	Lev 11:24-25, 27-28, 39-40, etc.
B 28–34	//	Lev 17:2
B 36–38	//	Lev 22:28
B 39–40	//	Deut 23:2-4 and Gen 2:24
B 61–62	//	Num 15:30-39 (?)
B 62–63	//	Lev 19:23-25
B 64–67	//	Lev 13:46; 14:8
B 69–70	//	Lev 4:13-14; 5:1-4; Num 15:27-31
B 72–74	//	Num 19:16-18
B 75–82	//	Lev 21:7, 13-16

---

[37] The construction with causal clauses containing ‏את/הם‎ followed by a participle is very common in formulations of the polemic between the Sadducees and the Pharisees in *m. Yad.* 4:6–8, cf. ‏הרי הם אומרים‎. For a discussion of the Jewish predilection for justificatory law, see Halivni, pp. 9–17.

Subject	Headline				The Halakha (or Practice)					Additional Statements		
	ואף על	ועל	x	אנחנו אומרים ש-	pt. (± הם)	inf. (± אין)	impf.	nom. statement	אתם יודעים ש-	כי לא ראוי	Scripture or reasoning
Wheat of Gentiles	-	[+]	+	-	+	+[+]	-	-	-	-	-
Sin Offering	-	[+]	+	-	++[++]	-	-	-	-	-	-
Sacrifice of Gentiles	-	+	+	[+]	+	-	-	-	-	-	+
Cereal Offering	[+]	-	+	-	++	-	-	-	-	+	+
Red Cow	+	-	+	-	-	+	-	-	-	+	+
Hides	+	+[+++]	++	-	[+]	+	+	-	-	?	-
Slaughtering	-	[+]	+	+	[+++]	-	-	+++	-	-	+
Pregnant Animals	-	[++]	+[+]	+	-	[+]	+	-	[+]	-	+
Entering the *Qahal*	-	[+]	+	+	+++	+++	-	-	[+]	+	-
Blind and Deaf	[+]+	-	++	+	+	-	-	-	-	-	+
Liquid Streams	+	-	+	+	-	-	-	+	-	-	?
Dogs	-	-	-	-	-	+	-	+++	-	-	++
Fruits of the 4th Year	+	-	+	-	-	-	-	+	-	-	-
Cattle Tithe	-	-	+	-	-	-	-	+	-	-	-
Lepers	+	+	+	+	+	+	++	-	+	-	++
Human Bones	-	+	+	+	-	-	-	+	-	-	-
Illegal Marriage	-	+	+	-	++	+	-	-	+	+	+++

5.3   The Halakhic Terminology of MMT

In the area of halakhic terminology and its history, MMT makes an important contribution. The work is filled with expressions typical of juridical literature. Some are expressions which are already common in the Bible, others are expressions familiar to us from other writings of the Qumran sect, and still others were known to us hitherto only from rabbinic literature. These in the last group constitute the most significant contribution of MMT. We shall here list the relevant expressions according to the above classification.

5.3.1   Biblical Juridical Expressions Still Used at Qumran but for which Rabbinic Literature Uses Other Expressions:

5.3.1.1   עץ מאכל (B 62)

Contrast אילן מאכל in rabbinic literature (see § 3.5.1.19).

5.3.1.2   צרוע (B 64)

In rabbinic literature only מצורע is found. In the Bible, as well as in the Temple Scroll, both צרוע and מצורע are found.

5.3.1.3   מעשר הבקר והצאן (B 63–64)

Thus we find in the Bible מעשר בקר וצאן (Lev 27:32), whereas in rabbinic literature we find מעשר בהמה.[38]

5.3.1.4   בוא השמש (B 72)

This is the biblical phrase, as opposed to הערב שמש in rabbinic literature, and להערי[בו]ת השמש (B 15). בא השמש occurs in *m. Menaḥot* 10:3, however, which records an early anti-Sadducean practice; cf. בוא השמש in 11QTᵃ 50:4 and § 3.5.1.25.

5.3.1.5   ראשית 'first fruit' (B 63)

In rabbinic literature the words בכורים and תרומה are preferred.

5.3.2   Specifically Qumranic Juridical Expressions

Expressions which are confined to the Qumran sect merit a more detailed discussion.

5.3.2.1   טהרת המקדש (B 54)

This expression designates the pure food which was brought to the Temple and kept in ritual purity. It differs in sense from טהרה (see § 5.3.3.6). The former refers to the sacred food eaten in the Temple, whereas the latter refers to ritually pure food eaten elsewhere.[39] This term is typical of QH, while its equivalent קדשים (or קודש) is used in BH, in QH and in MH (see B 71). Eating of טהרת המקדש (or קודשים) requires the highest degree of purity.[40] See also § 3.5.2.11.

---

[38] On the possibility of supplementing מעשר לבהמתמה (i.e. the rabbinic phrase) in 11QTᵃ 60:2, see § 5.7.14.

[39] The contrast between the two terms is evident in 11QTᵃ 47:10–18, where טהרתמה in l. 10 refers to the pure food of Israel, and טהרת המקדש in l. 17 refers to the sacrifices.

[40] See n. 166.

5.3.2.2 מעשים

In MMT laws are not called halakhot, מצוות and the like, but rather מעשים (B 2) and מעשי התורה (C 27). The singular מעשה, referring to law in general, is apparently found in the Bible: 'And thou shalt teach them the statutes and the laws, and shalt show them the way wherein they must walk, and the law (המעשה) that they must perform' (Exod 18:20).[41] It is only from the Second Temple period and onwards, however, that we find widespread use of the plural מעשים as a term specially designating the laws or commandments of the Bible.[42] The term מעשים in this sense is also found in some other Qumranic works (4Q174, 1–2 i 7, 1QS 6:18 [מעשיו בתורה]).[43] The Dead Sea sectarians did not employ the term halakhot, which was used by their opponents.

5.3.2.3 דבר = 'cases', 'custom', 'commandment'

In MMT, (דבר(ים refers to commandments; thus אלה מקצת דברינו (B 1), להזה'ר בדבר הזה (B 12), etc.[44] In 1QS 11:14 and elsewhere the commandments are designated דברי אל, cf. similarly עוברי דברו (1QS 5:14), ואלה המשפטים אשר ישפטו בם במדרש יחד על פי הדברים (1QS 8:22).[45] In 1QS 1:24 דבר מתורת מושה the word דברים may mean 'specifics of the commandments'.[46] Note that the Septuagint renders והדבר הקטן (Exod 18:22) as βραχεα των κριμα των 'the minor juridical cases'. (For the possible influence of Exod 18 on the development of the terminology at Qumran, cf. on מעשה above. Does מהדרך [C 12] also refer to the commandments, as in Exodus 18? In MH we find, for example, שמונה עשר דבר [t. Šabb. 1:16].)

5.3.2.4 ערב referring to impurity

תערובת in QH sometimes refers to impurity, and specifically to impurity due to sexual relations. Thus the phrase תערובת הגבר[47] is used in MMT in contexts referring to forbidden sexual relations (B 48). Similar meanings of ערב are found in two other places in the Qumran Scrolls:

---

[41] The rabbis interpreted המעשה here to refer to civil law (b. B. Meṣ. 30b). The Septuagint renders המעשה as τα εργα = המעשים. See also Ibn Ezra ad loc.

[42] S. Lieberman, 'ספר המעשים—the Book of Decisions', Tarbiz 2 (1931), pp. 377–379. עושי התורה is used to signify both 'those who perform commandments of the Torah' and 'those who study the Torah'; cf. S. Abramson, 'מלשון חכמים', Leshonenu 19 (1954), pp. 61–66. In MMT we find לעשות alone in the sense 'to act according to the law' (B 54). A detailed discussion of מעשה in the teachings of Jesus and the rabbis is to be found in D. Flusser, Die rabbinischen Gleichnisse und der Gleichnisserzähler Jesus, Frankfurt-am-Main, 1981, pp. 101 ff. For further discussion, see M. A. Friedman, 'Marriage Laws Based on Maʿasim Livne Ereṣ Yisrael', Tarbiz 50 (1981), p. 211, n. 10.

[43] See Baumgarten, Qumran Law, pp. 82–83, and Licht, Srakhim, p. 135. The terms מעשים and מעשים בתורה are equivalent. They interchange in the manuscript of Serekh Hayaḥad. Thus in col. 5, l. 27, 1QS has ומעשיו while 4QSᵈ has ומעשיו בתורה; in l. 24, 1QS has ומעשיהם while 4QSᵈ has ומעשיהם בתורה. Compare also B 2 to C 27 and 1QS 5:21 to 5:23.

[44] דבר in the sense 'commandment' is found in the Bible (see BDB, p. 183, col. i, meaning no. IV, 2), as in עשרת הדברים 'the ten commandments'. It is more widespread in the later books of the Bible than in the earlier ones, cf. דבר המלך (translated מלת מלכא in Aramaic).

[45] With regard to דברים = 'Wörte des Gesetzes', see D. Flusser (n. 42 above), pp. 99–101.

[46] על פי הדברים is interpreted by Licht as meaning 'according to each specific case'. He cites parallels from 1QS. Wernberg-Møller translates 'according to the cases' and writes: 'for דבר as a judicial expression (also in 6:1) cf. Ex XVIII 16, 22 . . .' See also Flusser, ibid. (n. 42), pp. 98–115; Schiffman, Sectarian, p. 73 and elsewhere; M. Weinfeld, The Organizational Pattern and the Penal Code of the Qumran Sect, Göttingen, 1986, p. 17, n. 49. Note that in 11QPsᵃ 119:43 למשפטך substitutes לדבריכה of the MT.

[47] The word גבר in this phrase is an extra-specification; cf. תשמיש and תשמיש המיטה with the meaning 'intercourse' in MH. The word גבר appears to be a subjective genitive, as is זכר in למשכבי זכר 1QSa 1:10; contrast BH where זכר in למשכב זכר is an objective genitive. Cf. also the phrase מן כל טומאת כל גבר in the Aramaic Testament of Levi (Beyer, p. 117).

A.   In the Temple Scroll ‏[ת]ערובת המת‏ (50:2; cf. 45:4–7) apparently means 'corpse-defilement', 'contact with a corpse, transmitting impurity'.

B.   In the Damascus Covenant we find a halakha which has presented difficulties: ‏אל יתערב איש‏ ‏מרצונו בשבת‏ (11:5). Of all the interpretations that have been suggested for this passage, the only one which we consider plausible is that which sees it as a prohibition against defiling oneself on the Sabbath, especially by intentional sexual contact.[48]

5.3.2.5   ‏חוק ומשפט וטהרה‏

One should note the terminology used for the various classes of laws in MMT B 52–53: ‏ואף על החרשים‏ ‏שלוא שמעו חוק ומשפט וטהרה ולוא שמעו משפטי ישראל‏ 'And concerning the deaf who have not heard the laws and the judgements and the purity regulations, that is to say, have not heard the ordinances of Israel'. Interestingly, a similar division of the laws into three classes is found in 1QS 6:21–23: ‏ואם יצא‏ ‏לו הגורל לקרבו ליחד יכתובהו בסרך תכונו בתוך אחיו לתורה ולמשפט ולטוהרה ולערב את הונו ויה' עצתו ליחד‏ ‏ומשפטו‏. If there was indeed at Qumran a real distinction between three classes of laws, a comparison of these two sources demonstrates that the term ‏חוק‏ in MMT B 39–40 parallels ‏תורה‏ in 1QS 6:22 (= the rulings of the Torah); ‏משפט‏ (= civil law)[49] is found in both sources, as is ‏טהרה‏ (= purity regulations, cf. B 13). Note how in both sources, at the end of each passage, ‏משפט‏ has also a more general meaning. The use of ‏טהרה‏ to denote a special class of laws suits the centrality of this realm in early halakha.[50] In the light of these distinctions it would be worthwhile to check to what extent the Qumran writers took care to distinguish precisely between the use of each of these terms.

5.3.2.6   ‏כתוב‏

This word is known in MH as a technical term introducing scriptural citations.[51] In MMT it never introduces biblical verses.[52] It sometimes precedes a description or paraphrase of a biblical verse, as in:

‏ועל בה[מתו הטהור]ה כתוב שלוא לרבעה כלאים‏

'And concerning his (i.e. Israel's) pure animal it is written that one must not let it mate with another species' (B 76–77);

‏[ו]אף כתוב שמעת שיגלח וכבס [י]שב מחוץ [לאוהלו שבעת י]מי‏ם

'And it is written that after he (i.e. the leper) shaves and washes he should dwell outside his tent seven days' (B 66–67);

‏וע[ל העושה ביד רמה כת]וב שהואה בוזה ומגדף‏

'And concerning him who purposely transgresses the precepts it is written that he despises God and blasphemes Him' (B 70).

---

[48] H. Leshem, 'The Damascus Scroll', *Maḥanaim* 62 (1962), pp. 75 and 77–78; Qimron, *ʾal Yitʿarev*; Yalon, *Scrolls*, pp. 94–95.

[49] For ‏על הנפש‏ 'criminal law', and ‏על ההון‏ 'civil law', see *HDSS*, pp. 107 and 111.

[50] Cf. *m. Ḥag.* 1:8 and J. N. Epstein, ‏מבוא לנוסח המשנה‏, Jerusalem and Tel-Aviv, 1957, p. 47. Cf. also B. Cohen, 'The Classification of the Law in the Mishneh Torah', *JQR* 25 (1934–1935), pp. 522–524.

[51] On the formulas used at Qumran to introduce scriptural citations as compared with those found in other sources, see J. A. Fitzmyer, 'The use of Explicit Old Testament Quotations in Qumran Literature and in the New Testament', *NTS* 7 (1960), pp. 297–333; Halivni, pp. 14–15.

[52] There is only one place where ‏כתוב‏ could even possibly be introducing a biblical verse: ‏משכתוב קודש ישראל‏ (B 76). In that passage ‏כתוב‏ could conceivably be introducing Jer 2:4, though even here the context makes it doubtful whether the expression ‏קודש ישראל‏ really refers to that verse.

At B 38 it does not refer to any specific verse at all: והדבר כתוב עברה 'And the ruling refers (to) a pregnant animal'.

It would therefore seem that כתוב is not intended to introduce a verbatim quotation from Scripture, but rather to introduce the statement which was derived from such a verse. This use of the word כתוב is distinctive of MMT, but כתוב (or אמר) followed by a paraphrase is also found in the Damascus Covenant.[53]

The connection between the use of this term at Qumran and the question of the writing down of halakhic works other than the Torah needs further study: note especially the last passage quoted above (B 38) and cf. § 5.2.3a; cf. also §§ 3.5.2.15 and 3.5.4.6.

5.3.3 Juridical Expressions Hitherto Known Only from Rabbinic Literature

Particular significance should be attached to those expressions which were hitherto known to us only from rabbinic literature. MMT contains a substantial number of such terms, a fact which reveals much about the development and sources of halakha.[54] The following are the most important individual terms:

5.3.3.1 העריבות שמש 'sunset' (B 15)

= הערב שמש in MH; contrast בוא השמש in BH (cf. §§ 3.5.1.25 and 3.5.4.2).

5.3.3.2 חטאת in the following expressions:

A. פרת החטאת = the red cow (B 13). פרת החטאת is the phrase which replaces BH's החטאת or פרה (see *m. Para* 2:1; 4:1). MS[b] originally contained the BH term, and the word פרת was added between the lines (cf. § 3.5.3.9).

B. מי החטאת (B 14–15; see the commentary). מי חטאת (without the definite article) is the normal expression in rabbinic literature, as against מי נדה of BH and QH. מי חטאת is in fact found once in the Bible (Num 8:7; cf. Zech 13:1), but in Num 19 we find only the more widespread term מי נדה. Cf. also the QH phrases מי דוכי (1QS 3:9) and מי טהר[ה] (11QT[a] 50:2), and Qimron, *Terms*, pp. 134–135.

5.3.3.3 ארץ ישראל (B 63)

Regarding the possibility that in MMT this is not a geo-political expression, but rather a geo-halakhic one (as it is in the Reḥob inscription l. 13),[55] see § 3.5.2.1.

5.3.3.4 על גב when used in contexts of participation in ritual purity (C 8)

Although this preposition appears here in the homiletic C, it is clearly at home also in halakhic usage and of the utmost importance for the laws of ritual purity (see § 3.5.3.7). It is hard to suggest a precise translation.

5.3.3.5 מוצקות 'an uninterrupted flow of liquid' (B 55, 56, 57)

This is the equivalent of נצוק in MH (see § 3.5.4.4).

---

[53] See Ginzberg, pp. 192–200. J. M. Baumgarten, 'A "Scriptural" Citation in 4Q Fragment of the Damascus Document', *JJS* 43 (1992), pp. 95–98.

[54] See Qimron, *Terms*.

[55] See Y. Sussmann, 'The Boundaries of Eretz-Israel', *Tarbiz* 45 (1976), p. 247.

5.3.3.6 טהרת הקודש (B 65, 68)

Cf. also טהרת]הקו[דש 4Q513 2 ii 1—an obscure text. This term occurs only once in BH, in 2 Chr 30:19, where it is used in connection with the Passover that was celebrated at the Jerusalem Temple in the reign of Hezekiah (cf. 1 Chr 23:28). It is also found in MH, where it designates a high degree of ritual purity, namely that required for eating the sacred food; but eaters of Ḥullin could also observe such a high degree of ritual purity (cf. *m. Ḥag.* 2:7 and *m. Ṭohar.* 2:7). The term טהרה (also טהרת הרבים and טהרת ישראל) is more frequent in QH, and mostly refers to the pure food of the *yaḥad*, members of which observed their טהרה at higher degrees, namely that of טהרת הקודש.[56] See §§ 3.5.2.11 and 5.3.2.1.

Note also the following terms and idioms:

5.3.3.7 האכיל מהקודשים

Meaning 'let someone eat of sacred food' (see § 3.5.3.1).

5.3.3.8 אומרים 'decide on halakha' (B 50, etc)

The term has a distinct polemical nuance (see § 3.5.3.2).

5.3.3.9 קבל 'to receive (liquid in a container)' (B 57)

This MH usage does in fact appear once in the Bible, in Chronicles (see § 3.5.2.29).

5.3.3.10 ראוי 'liable, obligated' (see § 3.5.2.29a).

5.3.3.11 מחנה הקודש (B 58, 60)

Refers to 'the camp' mentioned in the Torah, which is here identified as Jerusalem (see below n. 63); in BH and MH the simple מחנה is sufficient, and the phrase is not known to us from any Hebrew source other than MMT.

5.4 The Scope of the Laws of Purity

5.4.1 In General

One of the central questions in the rules of ritual purity involves the different degrees of sanctity of various places with regard to purity and defilement. According to G. Alon's[57] analysis, there existed among the Jews in antiquity two positions on the matter:

A.   The minimalist position, which restricted the application of the laws of purity to the Temple and the priesthood.

B.   The maximalist position, which applied the laws of defilement and purity to all places and to the whole of the Jewish people.

---

[56] On the possibility that there was a distinction between degrees of ritual purity at Qumran, see Yadin, *TS*, II, p. 214, and compare also the expression טהרת אנשי הקודש in 1QS 5:13, 8:17; cf. also n. 63 below. The term טהרת הקודש appears on ostraca from Masada (see Yadin and Naveh, pp. 34, 36).

[57] Alon, pp. 176–198. For a critique of his thesis, see Ḥ. Albeck, 'טומאת הגוף והידים וטומאת אוכלים', תורה שבעל פה, 6 (1964), pp. 24–32.

The first view predominated among the rabbis, while the second view predominated among the Essenes; nevertheless, echoes of the second view can be detected in rabbinic writings,[58] especially where early Pharisaic views are recorded.

The Temple Scroll has presented us with new material relating to this question. Yadin[59] accepted Alon's view, and explained the evidence in the Temple Scroll accordingly. In his opinion, the Temple Scroll accepted the maximalist approach, 'extending the laws of the 'camp' to the Temple, the 'city of the Temple', and the cities'. Jerusalem is the 'city of the Temple', and those regulations of purity which the Bible applies to the Temple apply to the whole of Jerusalem.[60] B. Levine disagrees with this approach, arguing that in the Temple Scroll Jerusalem is no more holy than other cities, and that the 'city of the Temple' there does not denote Jerusalem but rather the Temple complex.[61]

As can be seen from the above-mentioned studies, the problems with which the halakha had to deal arose from the fact that the biblical verses dealing with questions of purity refer mainly to the purity of the Tabernacle and of the camp. How was one to equate these concepts with the topographical realities of the Second Temple period? The developed rabbinic halakha adopted the minimalist approach, in that it did not confine itself to a single equivalent for the biblical 'camp', but declared that there were three camps in the Torah: the camp of God, the camp of the Levites and the camp of the Israelites. Similarly there were three sections in Jerusalem: the Temple (the camp of God), the Temple Mount (the camp of the Levites), and the rest of Jerusalem (the camp of the Israelites).[62] The rabbis restricted the operation of most of the purity laws to the Temple itself, the camp of God.

5.4.2 The View of MMT

A.   The sanctity of various places is discussed in two passages in MMT: in a halakha dealing with the entry of dogs into Jerusalem (B 58–62), and in a halakha concerning slaughtering in the camp (B 27–33, related to Lev 17). The first passage contains a brief discussion of the sanctity of Jerusalem in a justificatory clause while the second has a long discussion dealing with Jerusalem, with the Temple and with the concept of 'outside the camp'. Unfortunately, the second text is only partially preserved. The passages are:

1.   כי ירושלים היאה מחנה הקדש והיא המקום שבחר בו מכל שבטי ישראל כי ירושלים היא
ראש מחנות ישראל

For Jerusalem is the camp of holiness[63] and is the place which He has chosen from among all the places of the tribes of Israel. For Jerusalem is the chief of the camps of Israel (B 59–62).

---

[58] In Alon's opinion, the Sadducees accepted the first position, while the Karaites had a variety of different approaches to this matter.

[59] Yadin, *TS*, I, pp. 277 ff.

[60] Bickermann, pp. 103–104 states that before its widening in the Hasmonean era, Jerusalem was no more than a sort of a precinct of the Temple. It was for this Jerusalem, which was afraid of impurity, that the edict of Antiochus III was made.

[61] B. Levine, 'The Temple Scroll—Aspects in its Historical Provenance and Literary Character', *BASOR* 232 (1978), pp. 13–17; but J. Milgrom, *Studies* 1, pp. 26–27, accepts Yadin's view on the meaning of 'city of the Temple'. See Baumgarten, Review. Cf. also: Ginzberg, pp. 73–74; L. H. Schiffman, 'Architecture and Law: The Temple and Its Courtyards in the *Temple Scroll*', in *From Ancient Israel to Modern Judaism: Intellect in Quest of Understanding*, Brown Judaic Studies 159, Atlanta, 1989, pp. 267–284; Sussmann, p. 34 and n. 108.

[62] See *t. Kelim B. Qam.* 1:12 (Zuckermandel, p. 570), and *Sipre* on Numbers § 2 (Horovitz, p. 4).

[63] The expression מחנה הקודש is not known from other sources. It was probably formed by analogy with the expressions עיר הקודש and הר הקודש in Second Isaiah. On the use of the word קודש in relation to Jerusalem, in connection with Second Isaiah, see Yadin, *TS*, I, p. 281 (and Haran's article cited there). Dr. P. Segal has suggested (personal communication) that the word הקודש in the expression under discussion refers to God. This can be supported from the variant expression מחני קד[וש] ישראל (4QTah[a] 1 i 6, if our restoration is correct).

Thus 'Jerusalem' = 'the place which He has chosen' = 'the camp of holiness'[64], while the other cities are called merely 'the camps of Israel'.[65] Consequently, all regulations governing the sanctity of 'the camp' apply to the whole of Jerusalem, which is called at Qumran ראש מחנות ישראל, מחנה הקודש and עיר המקדש.

2.   ואנ̇ח̇נו חושבים שהמקדש [משכן אוהל מועד הוא וי]רושלי̇[ם] מחנה היא וחוצה למחנה

[הוא חוצה לירושלים ו]הוא מח̇נ̇ה ער̇[י]ה̇ם . . . [כי ירושלים] ה̇יא המקום אשר [בחר בו] מ̇כול

ש̇ב̇[טי ישראל]

And we are of the opinion that the sanctuary is the 'tent of meeting', and that Jerusalem is the 'camp', and that 'outside the camp' is outside Jerusalem, that is the encampment of their settlement . . . For Jerusalem is the place which He has chosen from among all the places of the tribes of Israel (B 29–33).

Here, too, Jerusalem is identified with the 'camp' and the 'place which He has chosen'.[66] There was also an identification of המקדש (with the 'tent of meeting'?), and another of מחוץ למחנה, 'outside the camp', though these two are now lost. The word עריהם, if the reading is correct, may refer to the settlements of the Land of Israel (= גבולין in MH).

B.   The contrast between this view and the rabbinic view about the identification of the camp apparently caused a controversy over the identification of 'outside the camp'. The rabbis sometimes interpreted 'outside the camp' as meaning 'outside the Temple',[67] and followed certain practices inside Jerusalem which, according to the sectarians, should be followed only outside Jerusalem. Thus the words וחוצה למחנה [הוא חוצה לירושלים] may represent another polemical statement (if our restoration is correct). This would account for the apparently reversed order of the subject and predicate in this nominal sentence; the subject of the controversy is the term 'outside the camp' which was therefore put at the beginning of the sentence.

C.   In both passages in MMT, Jerusalem is identified with both 'the camp' and 'the place which He has chosen . . .' Why does MMT need to mention the latter identification? Certainly one would not expect to find here a polemic against the Samaritans. One should rather assume that the identification of the 'chosen place' was another part of the controversy between the sectarians and their opponents with regard to the scope of the purity laws and perhaps other issues. The statement in MMT that Jerusalem is the place which He has chosen may well refer to the view of the opponents that the 'chosen place' is the Temple and not all of Jerusalem.[68]

D.   In the light of these identifications, it appears that Yadin was correct in claiming that in the Temple Scroll Jerusalem is more sacred than the other settlements: in MMT it is deemed 'the camp' (and Deut 23:15 commands 'thy camp shall be holy'). Nevertheless, it would appear that the sanctuary

---

[64] The identification of 'the Camp' with Jerusalem is also found in Karaite works; cf. Yadin, *TS*, I, p. 279, n. 6.

[65] On the significance of the contrast between 'the camp of holiness' and 'the camp(s)' for the distinction between the *yaḥad* and the rest of the sect, and for the celibacy in the *yaḥad*, see E. Qimron, 'Davies' The Damascus Covenant', *JQR* 77 (1986), pp. 86–87.

[66] In the Bible, the word בחר frequently refers to Jerusalem. In 2 Chr 7:16 (cf. also verse 12) it refers to the Temple (cf. the parallel text in 1 Kgs 9:3 where the verb בחר is not found). It seems that what is really meant in the Bible is the Temple rather than all Jerusalem (see S. R. Driver, *Deuteronomy*, ICC, New York, 1916, p. 140). We believe that such was the view of the rabbis. We were unable to find an explicit discussion of this question, but the phrase בית הבחירה, which is an epithet of the Temple, may well have been modelled on the biblical phrase המקום אשר יבחר. There is also a distinction between the Temple and the cities (including Jerusalem: see *m. Roš Haš.* 4:1 and *Sipre* on Deut 12:5).

[67] Ibid.

[68] Ibid.

was a separate area—and one more sacred than Jerusalem—as may be surmised from the fact that it is mentioned before Jerusalem (B 24).[69] Such a separation is also attested in 11QT^a 46:9–11, where a wide rampart (fosse; חיל) is to be made in order to separate the holy (Temple) from the rest of the city.[70]

Other settlements are here called מחנות; similarly, in the Qumran Scrolls they are called ערים, מושבות, מושב המחנות and מחנות.[71] Consequently, their sanctity is of a lesser degree. It seems to us that MMT distinguished at least four degrees of holiness with regard to places:[72] the Temple, Jerusalem, other settlements, and areas outside settlements (see below, in the discussion of the leper § 5.7.15).

As regards the degree of purity to be kept by priests and laymen, MMT states that Israelites are 'holy', but the priests are 'most holy' (B 79; see § 5.7.17; on the term טהרת הקודש see § 5.3.3.6). Nevertheless, from other DSS one may learn that not all the members of the sect maintained the same degree of ritual purity (see § 5.3.3.6 and n. 65).

E.   The scope of the purity laws is obviously wider in the DSS than in rabbinic literature. But it is premature to postulate a general principle of 'expanding the areas of holiness'. The application of the laws of the purity of 'the camp' to Jerusalem may have followed simply from the identification of the 'camp' with Jerusalem. In any case, it is doubtful whether a general principle of broadening the applicability of laws would be consistent with the sect's halakhic system.[73] It seems rather that in this matter the sect tried to conduct itself according to the laws of the Torah as they were translated into the reality of the Second Temple period.

F.   The topic of the scope of the purity laws involves the laws concerning exclusion; according to the Torah, not only impurity, but also certain classes of people, must be kept away from holy places. We distinguish two kinds of exclusion: (1) exclusion or isolation of impure people; (2) preventing of certain classes from entering holy places. The latter is generally connected with the biblical term בוא בקהל , which is interpreted in the DSS as referring not only to marriage but also to entering the

---

[69] One may reach the same conclusion from analysing some of the halakhot of MMT that deal with the purity of the sanctuary, e.g. § 5.7.11 and § 5.7.12. There is no mention of the Temple Mount as a separate entity either in MMT or in the Temple Scroll. Halivni (p. 24) has claimed that in early passages of the Mishna the Temple Mount, הר הבית, means the Temple proper, and that only after its refurbishing and enlargement by Herod did the Temple Mount become a distinct sacred place (but see J. M. Baumgarten, 'Halivni's Midrash, Mishna, and Gemara', *JQR* 77 [1986], p. 60).

[70] ועשיתה חיל סביב למקדש . . . אשר יבדיל בין מקדש הקודש לעיר 'You shall make a fosse around the sanctuary . . . that will separate the most sacred area from the city'. Milgrom has pointed out that the phrase מקדש הקודש is 'significant for the system of holiness gradations adopted by the scroll: the distinction between the Temple and the Temple-city is that between the most sacred and sacred. There is practically no difference between them in regard to impurity prohibitions: both Temple and Temple-city are off limits to the impure. But there is a world of difference in regard to the positive qualifications for entering either sphere: all who are pure may enter the Temple-city, but not necessarily the Temple' (Milgrom, *Studies* 2, p. 96). For the distinction between טהרה 'pure food' and טהרת המקדש 'sacred food', see § 5.3.3.6, and for the distinction between קודש (= Israel) and קודש קודשים (= the priests [or the priestly angels]) in the DSS, see § 5.7.17d.

[71] The word מחנה in the singular can designate either Jerusalem (as in our passage), or another city (as in CD 13:4, 5, 7, 13).

[72] As against the ten degrees attested in rabbinic sources (*m. Kelim* 1:6–9). These degrees of holiness with regard to places can be traced also in the Temple Scroll. As Milgrom has noted (*Biblical Archaeologist* 41 [1978], p. 114), the laws of purity in the Temple Scroll are arranged in the following sequence: 'Temple, Temple city, other cities and the land'. But the Temple Scroll distinguishes further degrees of holiness in the Temple proper. Thus when describing the Temple courts (from the inner to the outer, cols. 35 ff), it specifies those who are not allowed to enter each of these courts.

[73] It is worth mentioning that Alon himself, p. 175, admits that even in the Torah the purity laws sometimes apply not just to priests and Temple, but to all Israel, and not just in the Temple. See also Ḥ. Albeck (n. 57 above). A new approach to this subject has recently been suggested by J. Milgrom, 'The Scriptural Foundations and the Deviations in the Laws of Purity of the Temple Scroll', in *Archaeology and History*, pp. 83–99.

Temple (see § 5.7.9) and communal gatherings. The subject has recently been treated by Schiffman.[74] In order to understand its implication for the question of the degrees of purity at Qumran, however, a more extensive study is needed. I give here a list of the relevant passages in the DSS and a table based on the evidence in these passages (the numbers in the table refer to the passages).

I. The Passages:

1 = B 39–54; 2 = B 64–72; 3= 11QT^a 39:5–11, 40:6; 4 = 11QT^a 45:7–18; 5 = 11QT^a 46:16–18; 6 = 11QT^a 48:14–49:4; 7 = 11QT^a 49:16–50:16; 8 = CD 12:3–6; 9 = CD 15:13–17 (according to the Geniza MS^a and 4QD^a); 10 = 1QSa 1:25–2:11; 11 = 1QM 7:3–6; 12 = 4Q174 1–2 i 3–4.

II. The Table:

Kind of Exclusion Classes	Entering the Temple	Entering Jerusalem	Entering Other Cities	Intermingling with Israelites	Marrying Israelites	Communal Gatherings
Ammonite, *mamzer*, etc.	- (1) (12)	+	+	+	- (1)	?
Ger (to 4th generation)	- (3) (12)	+	+	+	- (Torah)	- (?)
Ben Nekhar	- (12)	+	+	+	- (?)	-
Deformed person	-	? (4)	+	+	+	- (9) (10) (11)
Mindless	- (1)	? (4)	+	+	+	- (8) (9)
Senile						- (10)
Woman and child	- (3)	+	+	+		- (9) (10) (11)
Leper	- (4) (5)	- (4) (5)	- (6)	-	-	- (10) (11)
Zav and *zava*	- (4) (5)	- (4) (5)	+	- (6)	-	-
Nidda and *yoledet*	- (Torah)	?	+	- (6)		-
Corpse contaminated	- (4)	-(4)	+	- (7) ?		-
Semen contaminated	- (4) (5)	- (4) (5)	+	+		- (11)
Purified person on the seventh day	- (2)	+ (4)	+	+		?

NOTES TO THE TABLE:

1.   Reading the table from top to bottom one sees that while all these classes are to be kept away from the Temple and apparently also from communal gatherings, only impure people are to be kept away from Jerusalem. There is also a difference between the Temple and Jerusalem in the case of the purified person on the seventh day.

2.   Marriage with an Israelite is forbidden also for priests (see § 5.7.17).

3.   On the senile, see the discussion by Schiffman (n. 74 above) and idem, *The Eschatological Community of the Dead Sea Scrolls*, Atlanta 1989, p. 49.

4.   The blind and the deaf have two reasons for being excluded by the sectarians: they are deformed and they are considered mindless (see § 5.7.10). MMT and CD 15:16 refer explicitly to the blind who cannot see, i.e. who are mindless.

---

[74] L. H. Schiffman, 'Exclusion from the Sanctuary and the City of the Sanctuary in the Temple Scroll', *Hebrew Annual Review* 9 (1985), pp. 301–320.

5.   It has been suggested that the sentence וקדשום שלושת ימים (1QSa 1:25) means 'They shall keep them away from women for three days' (see Nachmanides on Exod 19:10 and E. Qimron in the article mentioned in n. 75 below, pp. 311–312).

6.   On the captive woman, see Yadin, I, pp. 364–367, and Milgrom, *Studies*, 2, pp. 104–105.

5.5 The Halakhot in the Order of their Appearance in the Text

The following halakhot or halakhic topics are mentioned in the extant fragments of MMT:

1.   Gentile wheat should not be brought into the Temple (B 3–5). Very little of this halakha has survived and even the key words דגן הגוים are doubtful.

2.   A halakha about the cooking of offerings (B 5–8). Also this halakha is quite fragmentary and we have not managed to reconstruct a coherent law from its scanty remains.

3.   A halakha about sacrifices from gentiles (B 8–9). The text is very fragmentary but the subject of the halakha is quite clear.

4.   The cereal offerings should not be left overnight (B 9–13).

5.   The purity of those preparing the red cow (B 13–17).

6.   Several halakhot concerning the purity of hides (B 18–24).

7.   The place of slaughtering and offering sacrifices. The text is damaged and is composed of fragments from various manuscripts (B 27–35).

8.   'The mother and the child.' This deals with the slaughter of pregnant animals (B 36–38).

9.   Forbidden sexual unions. There were apparently a number of halakhot here, but the text is very fragmentary (B 39–49).

10.   The banning of the blind and deaf from the 'purity of the Temple' (B 49–54).

11.   The purity of the 'liquid streams': this concerns liquids poured from a pure vessel into an impure one (B 55–58).

12.   Dogs should not enter Jerusalem (B 58–62).

13.   The fruit of the fourth year is to be given to the priests (B 62–63).

14.   The cattle-tithe is to be given to the priests (B 63–64).

15.   Several regulations about the impurity of the leper during the period of his purification, and about his isolation until final purification (B 64–72).

16.   The impurity of human bones (B 72–74).

17.   Marriages between priests and Israelites are apparently forbidden (B 75–82).

We have enumerated here seventeen halakhic subjects dealt with in MMT. On some of the subjects (e.g., lepers) several halakhot are given. The work will have included, of course, a number of further halakhot in those parts where the text is defective (e.g. in B 2–3), in the few missing lines following B 24, 34, and after the end of the preserved parts of B.

5.6 The Arrangement of the Halakhot in MMT

Though it is difficult to discern any strict method in the arrangement of the halakhot, it is possible to see how certain halakhot that have something in common are grouped together. It appears that association of words and ideas plays a central role in the arrangement of the halakhot (cf. § 5.5 no. 6).

Here then are the groups into which the halakhot fall, according to the listing in § 5.5 of the individual topics:

(*a*)   Nos. 1–5 deal with sacrificial offerings; they conclude with a halakha on the laws of the red cow (which is a sin-offering).

(*b*)   Nos. 6–8 deal with sacrificial animals.

(c)   Nos. 9–10 deal with those banned from the Temple.

(d)   Nos. 11–12 are purity laws.

(e)   Nos. 13–14 deal with gifts to be made to priests.

(f)   Nos. 15–16 are further purity laws (cf. d).

(g)   No. 17 deals with incest; the missing text after it may have contained other incest halakhot.

5.7   The Particular Halakhot

We shall deal with each of the halakhot in the order of its appearance in the text.

5.7.1   On Gentile Grains of Wheat

[ועל תרומת ד]גֹֿן ה[ג]וים שהם ...] ומֹגיעֹ[י]ֹם בה אֹ[ת   ]ֹהם ומט[מאים אותה ואין לאכול]
מדגֹן [הג]וֹֿֿים [ואין] לבוֹא למקֹ̇ׄש

And concerning the sowed gifts of the new wheat grains of the gentiles that they . . . and let their . . . touch it
and defile it, and no one should eat any of the new wheat grains of the gentiles, nor shall the grains be brought
into the sanctuary (B 3–5).

The text is damaged and its exact content is unknown: the heading is almost entirely lost, but can be
restored from the traces and confirmed by its re-occurrence in l. 5 (מדגן [הג]וים). The word דגן in
legal texts from Qumran means 'the new grains of which the best part should be given to the Temple'.
In one passage it is explicitly identified with דמע 'the first and best grains'.[75] The restoration תרומת
(or alternatively מתנת) adds nothing to דגן. The word ומגיעים apparently relates to contact with
something impure, but it is not clear whether it refers to the gentiles or to the opponents. The logical
subject of לבוא is either the grains (if one reads לבוא) or 'anyone' (if one reads לביא = להביא). From
the text that has been preserved it is clear that grains of gentiles should not be brought to the Temple.

We do not know of any rabbinic halakha that discusses explicitly the purity of heave offerings of
gentiles' grains. Sources such as *m. Terumot* 3:9 and *t. Terumot* 4:12 seem to be irrelevant. The only
source that may have some relevance is *t. Makširim* 3:3–4.[75a]

If our restoration (ואין לאכול) is correct, then other sources that deal with eating the bread of
gentiles may also be relevant: see Dan 1:8, Tob 1:10–11, and Jdt 10:5.[76] Note also that the Falasha do
not eat the bread and flour of gentiles, though they do eat the unground wheat of gentiles.[77]

In sum, even though only part of the text has been preserved, it is obvious that the purity of the
grain of the gentiles was a controversial subject in the Second Temple period. The sectarians forbade
the acceptance of heave offerings given by gentiles, as they did sacrifices offered by gentiles (see
§ 5.7.3).

---

[75] *DJD* III, p. 300; see E. Qimron, 'Biblical Philology and the Dead Sea Scrolls', *Tarbiz* 58 (1989), pp. 304–307
and 310 n. 77.

[75a] See E. Urbach, *The Halakha: Its Sources and Its Development*, Israel, 1986, pp. 14–15.

[76] Cf. H. Mantel, 'The Ancient Halakha', *Dine Yisrael* 5 (1974), p. 187.

[77] Aescoly believes that the prohibition on eating such bread and flour arises either from fear of impurity caused by
the liquids that may have touched the flour or the bread, or because of the impurity of the gentile mill stones. See A. Z.
Aescoly, ספר הפלשים, Jerusalem, 1943, pp. 50–51 (see the references there).

5.7.2 The Cooking of the Purification Offering

A.   [ועל] זֹב[ח] החטאת] שהם מבֹשלֹים [אות]ה בכֹלֹי [נחושת ומ . . . ים] בה] את] בשר זבחיהֹם

             וֹמֹ[. .].יֹם בעֹזֹרֹ[ה ומ . . ים] אֹותֹ[ה] במרק זבחֹם

> And concerning the sacrifice of the purification offering that they cook in a copper vessel and that they . . . in it the flesh of their sacrifices and that they . . . in the Temple court and that they . . . it with the broth of their sacrifices (B 5–8).

This passage apparently alludes to Lev 6:21: וכלי חרש אשר תבשל בו [החטאת] ישבר. ואם בכלי נחשת בשלה ומרק ושטף במים. The dependence of our text on this biblical source is evident from the use of the words בשל, כלי and מרק which occur (albeit in different grammatical forms) in both texts.[78] If the reading [עזר]ה is correct, it should be compared to חצר אהל מועד of Lev 6:19.

B.   Lev 6:17–22 states that the purification offering is most holy and may be eaten by priests in the enclosure of the tent of meeting. If it was boiled in an earthen vessel, then that vessel should be broken; if in a copper vessel, then the vessel should be polished and rinsed with water. The rabbinic explanation for this treatment of the vessel is that its purpose is to avoid the problem of נותר 'forbidden sacrificial remnants.' The rabbis did, however, permit the copper vessels in which the purification offering was cooked to be used repeatedly without being scraped.[79]

C.   It is possible that MMT is protesting against the violation of the law of נותר or against the cooking of other sacrifices in the vessels of the purification offerings. There were several participle forms in this halakha, and more than one accusation may have been made here. Since these participles have not been preserved, we cannot tell what the accusations were. Furthermore, the pronominal suffixes are ambiguous and various reconstructions are possible (see below).

D.   If the reading [בעזר]ה is correct, then it may be assumed that one of the accusations is related to the Temple court, but we cannot offer even a plausible guess as to what it may have been.[80] The word עזרה is not attested with the meaning 'court' in the literature of this period; the Temple Scroll still uses the older term חצר.

E.   It is also possible to restore

           [ועל] זֹב[חי העם] שהם מבֹשלֹים [אות]ם בכֹלֹי [הכוהנים ומ . . ים] בה]ם את] בשר זבחיהֹם . . .

in which case the passage could be compared to 11QTᵃ 35:10–15. We prefer, however, the other restoration, which is based on the similarity in phraseology to Lev 6:19.

5.7.3 Sacrifices Offered by Gentiles

           ועל זבֹח הגוים [אנחנו חושבים שהם] זובֹח[ים] אל ה[ֹ] [ ] שֹא היֹא [כ]מֹי שזֹנֹת אליו

> And concerning the sacrifice of the gentiles: we are of the opinion that they sacrifice to the . . . that it is like (a woman) who whored with him (B 8–9).

---

[78] ומֹרַק in the biblical passage is a verb which means 'to polish', while מרק here must be a noun meaning 'broth'. If MMT really refers to Lev 6:21, its author may have associated the verb and noun as Kimḥi did (וכן נקרא למים שנתבשל בהם הבשר מָרָק לפי שיש בו מריקת הבשר, *Book of Roots* s.v. מרק). The rabbis maintained that the verb מרק in Lev 6:21 means 'to wash in boiling water' (*m. Zebaḥ.* 11:7; and *b. Zebaḥ.* 97ᵃ).

[79] See the sources in *Torah Shlema*, 26, p. 206 ff.

[80] 11QTᵃ 35:10–15 and 37:8–38:10 specifies separate places for each sacrifice (cf. also 17:12; see Milgrom, *Studies* 1, pp. 506–509).

The text is, again, poorly preserved, and the scant remains tell us little about what is being said about sacrifices offered by gentiles. Even the subject matter of this halakha cannot be established with certainty, since the word זבח is materially uncertain, though it fits the context and seems to be the only plausible reading.[81] This is also the case with the reading כמי שזנת,[82] according to which sacrifices offered by gentiles are apparently referred to as whoring after idols.[83] The preserved text suggests that this halakha consisted of no more than a short statement of the wrong practice of the opponents, and that it contained no contrasting law.

Fortunately we possess some interesting parallels on this subject. They enable us to follow the ancient discussion of this topic, and to surmise what may have been the content of the halakha in MMT.

If, in fact, the passage in MMT forbids the acceptance of offerings from gentiles, then it contrasts with the developed rabbinic halakha, which did not. During the Second Temple period this question was a matter of controversy (as Josephus reports, *J. W.*, 2:17:2). Echoes of this dispute are found in rabbinic literature and in Karaite works. It appears that those who forbade the acceptance of gentile offerings based themselves on Lev 1:2 'If one of you (מכם) shall offer . . .' (where 'of you' implies 'not of the gentiles'). The whole subject has recently been thoroughly dealt with by I. Knohl.[84] It appears that the refusal to accept sacrifices from gentiles, attested in Karaite writings, in *Pirqe Rabbi Eliezer* and in other rabbinic sources, originated in sectarian views from the Second Temple period.[85]

In view of the information in the above sources, it is quite likely that our text did, in fact, include here a halakha forbidding offerings from gentiles (cf. § 5.7.1).

5.7.4 Leaving Overnight the Cereal Offerings of the Sacrifices

[ואף על מנחת] זבח השל[מים] שמניחים אותה מיום ליום וֹאֹף [כתוב] שהמנׄ[חה

נא]כׄלׄת עלׄ הׄחלבים והבשר ביוםׄ זׄ[וֹב]חׄם]

And concerning the cereal offering of the sacrifices for well-being which they (the opponents) leave over from one day to the following one (i.e. leave after sunset), and it is written (in the Torah) that the cereal offering is to be eaten after the suet and the flesh (are sacrificed), namely on the day that they are sacrificed before sunset (B 9–11).

It is not easy to establish the subject of this halakha, since the beginning of its heading is missing. Our restoration of the heading is based on the fact that the word מנחה is the subject in the second statement. Since this word is determinate here (שהמנחה), it must have been mentioned before (in the heading).

If this was the case, our halakha would parallel the sectarian practice concerning the cereal offering found in 11QTᵃ 20:12–13:

ביום ההוא תאכל [ולוא תבו]אׄ עׄל[וֹ]יה] השמש

It (the cereal offering) should be eaten on the same day before sunset.[86]

---

[81] The traces fit זפת better than זבח.

[82] Materially, כמו שזפת is also possible. For other possible readings, see § 1.2.3.2.1.

[83] In Exod 34:15-16, eating of the sacrifices of gentiles and whoring after their idols are mentioned.

[84] I. Knohl, 'The Acceptance of Sacrifices from Gentiles', *Tarbiz* 48 (1979), pp. 341–347. See also Sussmann, p. 33, n. 97.

[85] See, however, Y. Gilat, 'A Comment to "The Acceptance of Sacrifices from Gentiles"', *Tarbiz* 49 (1980), pp. 422–423.

[86] Note also that in ll. 3–9 the sacrifice for well-being and their fats are mentioned, as is the case in MMT.

As Yadin noted,[87] this statement is opposed to the rabbinic halakha that ordained that the cereal offerings should be eaten not only in daytime but also at night: מנחות . . . ונאכלות ליום וללילה עד חצות 'Cereal offering . . . shall be eaten during the day and the night up to midnight' (*m. Zebaḥ.* 6:1; cf. *Sipra*, Finkelstein's facsimile edition, pp. 148–149). This accords with the general rule that in sacrificial matters night follows day.[88]

How did this controversy arise? Since the biblical source does not specify the time at which the cereal offerings are to be eaten, it was deduced from Lev 7:15 (cf. Lev 22:29), a passage whose phraseology is very similar to our passage in MMT. The law in Leviticus states:

ובשר זבח תודת שלמיו ביום קרבנו יאכל לא יניח ממנו עד בקר

> And the flesh of his thanksgiving sacrifice of well-being shall be eaten on the day when it is offered; none of it shall be left over until morning.

As we have seen, the rabbis interpreted the word יום as including also part of the following night, according to their general rule that in sacrificial matters night follows day, and in accordance with the second statement in this biblical source (לא יניח ממנו עד בקר). What was the view of the sect as reflected in MMT? The word יום in both the biblical source and in the expression ביום זוב[חם] is taken to mean on the same day (i.e. before sunset). This is evident from the accusation at the beginning of the halakha שמניחים אותה מיום ליום. When one leaves something after sunset one leaves it from one day to the next (the beginning of the day occurring in the evening). The phrase מיום ליום occurs elsewhere in the DSS, and has been correctly interpreted.[89]

This interpretation of the biblical source would hardly conform with the second statement in this biblical law (לא יניח ממנו עד בקר). How would the sect explain the apparent contradiction between the two statements in this law?

To answer this question, one should note that a similar contradiction occurs in the biblical law about the hired worker, a law that uses similar phraseology: while Deut 24:14 states שכרו ביומו תתן ולא תבוא עליו השמש, Lev 19:13 states לא תלין פעלת שכיר אתך עד בקר. The sentence ולא תבוא עליו השמש in Deuteronomy makes it clear that יום here means 'until sunset'. The rabbis therefore maintained that these two laws speak of two different kinds of hired workers, a day worker and a night worker. The sect apparently noticed the similarity between the law of the hired worker and that of the leaving over of the sacrifice, since the Temple Scroll transfers the modifying sentence ולא תבוא עליו השמש of Deut 24:14 to the law of the leaving over of the sacrifices (see above). Our suggested explanation therefore includes both these laws.

We believe that the sect interpreted the word יניח in Lev 7:5 as equivalent to תלין in Deut 24:14 (cf. Exod 23:18). The sect interpreted the law as being that the cereal-offering should be eaten before sunset so that nothing would be left over for the next morning.[90] Similarly, in the case of the hired

---

[87] *TS*, I, p. 89.

[88] *B. Ḥul.* 83ᵃ and Baumgarten, *Qumran Law*, p. 126; for the time at which sacrifices should be eaten, see *Encyclopedia Talmudica* (English), II, pp. 233–235.

[89] CD 7:3, 9:6—Wernberg-Møller, p. 100; Schiffman, *Sectarian*, p. 91. This is, in fact, also the meaning of this phrase in BH: see Rashi on Num 30:15. The influence of this biblical passage on our halakha is evident also from the similarity between the construction ביום שומעו there and ביום זוב[חם] here. Note that in *m. Ned.* 8:1 the phrase מיום ליום has a different meaning.

[90] The phrase עד בקר would be the equivalent of לבקר in Deut 16:4. The statement שהמנחה נאכלת על החלבים והבשר is unclear, since one is permitted to eat the cereal offering but not the fats of the sacrifice. The word נאכלת refers, therefore, only to the cereal offering, and על החלבים והבשר means 'as long as the fats and the meat are allowed to be sacrificed', namely, until sunset. Accordingly, the words ביום זוב[חם] should be taken as an apposition to על החלבים והבשר. It is less likely that נאכלת means 'should be consumed' in contrast with the meaning of this verb in Lev 7:15-16. For the expression על החלבים, cf. Lev 8:26 and 11QTᵃ 22:7.

worker, one should give him his wages before sunset and not leave them overnight in order to give them to him the next morning.

Our interpretation is also valid if we restore l. 9 as זבח השלמים [תודת]. In this case, however, the use of the word שהמנחה (determinate) in the second statement presents some difficulties, and the halakha would not be parallel to that of the Temple Scroll.

Finally, we should examine the possibility of restoring our passage as זבח השלמים [נדבת], and explaining it as referring to the sacrifice of well-being offered as a freewill sacrifice, which is mentioned in Lev 7:16-17. Opinions in fact differed as to the time of this sacrifice.[91] But the text from MMT could hardly be interpreted as dealing with this controversy, since the expressions מיום ליום and ביום זובחה would be appropriate only for a sacrifice that is to be eaten on a single day.

5.7.5 The Red Cow

A.   In Num 19:1-10, God commands Moses and Aaron to prepare the ashes of a burnt red cow which are to serve as a 'water of lustration', i.e. water which purifies from corpse uncleanness. Three people participated in the preparation of the ashes, one of them being Eleazar the Priest.

Our halakha centers on those who take part in the preparation of the ashes and the sprinkling of the purifying waters. The halakha declares that after their immersion they must wait until sunset before performing their tasks:

ואף על טהרת פרת החטאת השוחט אותה והסורף אותה והאוסף את אפרה והמזה את [מי]
החטאת לכול אלה להערי[בו]ת השמש להיות טהורים בשל שא יהיה הטהר מזה על הטמה כי
לבני אהרן ראוי להיות מן]

> And concerning the purity regulations of the cow of the purification offering (i.e. the red cow): he who slaughters it and he who burns it and he who gathers its ashes and he who sprinkles the water of purification—it is at sunset that all these become pure (after their immersion) so that (in accordance with the Scripture) the pure man may sprinkle upon the impure one. For the sons of Aaron should [. . .] (B 13–17).

B.   The purity of those who participate in the red cow ritual was a subject of much controversy during the Second Temple period. Thus we read in *m. Para* 3:7 that the rabbis intentionally defiled the priest who was to burn the cow, and then immersed him; immediately thereafter he had to perform his task without waiting for sunset. This was aimed at showing the invalidity of the view of the Sadducees, who maintained that the cow was to be prepared by those on whom the sun had set after their immersion:

ומטמין היו את הכהן השורף את הפרה מפני הצדוקים שלא יהו אומ': במעורבי שמש היתה נעשת

> They [the Sages] defiled [deliberately] the priest who was to burn the cow, on account of the Sadducees, so that they would not [be able to] say: only by those on whom the sun had set (after their immersion) was it [= the cow] prepared.[92]

---

[91] See *Sipra*, Finkelstein's facsimile edition, p. 160; *Kether Torah* commentary on this verse; Revel, p. 26, and Baumgarten, *Qumran Law*, p. 126.

[92] Cf. *t. Para* 3:7–8, and S. Lieberman's remarks in *Tosefet Rishonim*, pp. 218–219; S. H. Kuk, *ʿIyunim U-Meḥqarim*, I, pp. 49–55. The Karaites criticized the rabbis on this subject. Thus Elijah of Nikomedea in *Gan Eden*, p. 126, III states:

תמיה אני מבעלי הקבלה איך אמרו שהשורף והאוסף טבול יום והכתוב הורה שהיא צריכה טהרה כמו שבאר והניח
אותה אל מחוץ למחנה אל מקום טהור ולא עוד אלא שאמר ואסף איש טהור. ואיך יתכן שיהיה טבול יום והכתוב
קרא לטבול יום טמא שנאמר ורחץ במים וטמא עד הערב . . . והם אומרים כשהיו רוצים לשרוף פרה היו מטמאים
שמשיה בשרץ והיו טובלים ואחרי כן עושים את הפרה וכל זה מצד קנאה כדי לעמוד כנגד מי שהיה עומד לנגדם.

C. The controversy mentioned in the above-mentioned sources centers only on the purity of those engaged in the preparation of the cow (Num 19:1-10).[93] MMT, however, mentions also the man who sprinkles the water of purification. The sprinkling of the water of purification, mentioned in verses 18–19, is in fact a separate ritual, so that one may wonder why MMT combines the two topics. Since the controversy centers on the preparation of the cow, it is also unclear why the sectarians sought support for their view in Num 19:19 והזה הטהור על הטמא rather than in Num 19:9 ואסף איש טהור. As far as we know, no controversy with the Sadducees over the sprinkling of the water is recorded. Surprisingly, the rabbis too use verse 19 (on sprinkling) as support for their view that a *ṭebul yom* is qualified to officiate at the ceremony of the preparation of the red cow (see *b. Yoma* 43ᵇ).[94]

D. The contrast with the rabbinic view relates to a much broader problem: is the *ṭebul yom* (in rabbinic terminology) considered clean or unclean? This topic has been treated recently by Y. Yadin[95] and J. M. Baumgarten.[96] Baumgarten writes:[97] 'Although levitical law repeatedly insists on sundown as a necessary sequel to immersion, the Pharisees maintained that this was requisite only for the consumption of sacrifices or teruma . . . the Pharisees could point to passages such as Lev 14:8, 15:13 and 16:28 which refer to immersion without mentioning sundown'.

The need to wait until sunset that is expressed in MMT is also mentioned in a number of halakhot in the Temple Scroll.[98] It appears again in another passage from MMT: in the rulings concerning the purification of the leper, MMT declares that the leper must wait until sunset on the eighth day of his purification before he may eat of the sacred food. This is contrary to the view of the rabbis, who did not require the leper to wait until sunset. The author of the *Tosfot Yom Tov* commentary on the Mishna, R. Yom Tov Lipmann Heller, has already suggested that such would have to have been the view of the Sadducees, in accordance with their position on the question of the red cow (see below § 5.7.17).

A detailed description of the ritual of the red cow occurs in another work from Qumran (4QTahᵇ; 43.316). This work deals, among other things, with the sprinkling of the water of purification, and says that the sprinkling should be done only by a pure priest. It rules ועלול אל יז על הטמא. The word עלול is not easy to interpret; perhaps it is from the Aramaic root חלל 'immerse'; cf. the MH term טבול (יום).

This text apparently rules that the water of purification should be sprinkled on a person who was contaminated by a human corpse on the eighth day of the purification process. But this interpretation depends almost entirely on the restoration of the text.

I am astonished at the bearers of the tradition, at how they have claimed that those who burn [the cow] and gather [its ashes] are *ṭebul yom* (i.e., have been immersed, but have not then waited until sunset); whereas Scripture instructs that purity is demanded, as is explained 'and (he) shall deposit them outside the camp in a clean place'. It is stated, moreover, 'and a man who is clean shall gather up'. And how is it conceivable that he could be a *ṭebul yom* when Scripture refers to a *ṭebul yom* as unclean for it is written 'and he shall wash himself in water and be unclean till sunset'? . . . And they say that when they wanted to burn the cow they used to defile those involved in the preparations by means of a creeping thing, and they immersed and then they would prepare the cow, all this being a consequence of their intense desire to contradict their opponents.

[93] Actually, the Mishna mentions only the priest who was to burn the cow (see Sussmann, p. 28, n. 74).

[94] Cf. the discussion in *Sipre* on Numbers (Horowitz ed., pp. 157–158). The difficulty of this source in *Yoma* has been discussed by Yom Tov Lipman Heller in his commentary on *m. Para* 3:7. See also *Encyclopedia Talmudica* (English), II, pp. 604–613 (especially p. 613).

[95] Yadin, *TS*, I, pp. 329–334.

[96] *Controversies*, pp. 157–161.

[97] Ibid., p. 158.

[98] Yadin, *TS*, I, pp. 340–341.

E.   One of the sources relevant to this controversy was the passage in Deut 23:12 concerning nocturnal impurity: והיה לפנות ערב ירחץ במים וכבא השמש יבא אל תוך המחנה. B. Revel has demonstrated[99] that, contrary to the rabbinic view, the Karaites interpreted the phrase לפנות ערב as designating the time immediately preceding sunset. They deduced from this passage that immersion—permitting contact with purity—should only be performed immediately before sunset, thus in effect eliminating the status of *ṭebul yom*. In all likelihood, this was also the regular custom among priests, as noted by Ḥ. Albeck.[100]

In the light of this practice, it comes as no surprise that the passage in Deut 23:12 was construed differently in both the Samaritan Pentateuch and the Temple Scroll. The Samaritan Pentateuch reads: לא יבא אל תוך המחנה כי אם רחץ בשרו במים ובא השמש ואחרי כן יבוא אל המחנה, and 11QT[a] 45:9–10 reads: וביום השלישי יכבס בגדיו ורחץ ובא השמש. אחר יבוא אל המקדש. The same construction is found in 11QT[a] 51:5: וכבס בגדיו ורחץ במים ובאה השמש. אחר יטהר. The use of the consecutive perfect (ובאה השמש) in these three passages indicates that sunset immediately followed washing and immersion. If it did not, a construction such as וכבס בגדיו ורחץ במים וכבוא השמש יבוא אל המקדש would have been used. This construction with וכבס ... ורחץ ... ובא השמש followed by אחר is also found elsewhere in MT (for example, Lev 14:18; 22:6-7).

F.   According to *Tg. Pseudo-Jonathan*, the entire ritual of the red cow is to be performed by priests. Geiger assumed that this would have been the view of the Sadducees.[101] The passage in MMT can hardly support Geiger's assumption.[102] The passage from 4QTah[b] (above, d), however, stipulates that the water of purification should be sprinkled by איש כוהן טהור (cf. גבר כהין דכי in *Tg. Ps.-J.*).

G.   In summary, the sectarians insisted on the need to wait until sunset in a number of laws of the Torah where the word טהר appeared. The rabbis, on the other hand, held that it was necessary to wait until sunset only where Scripture explicitly said so. This was one of the main issues of controversy among the Jews of the Second Temple period.

5.7.6   The Purity of Hides

A.   In B 18–20, mention is made of hides in relation to the Temple:

[על] עורות הבק̇[ר ... מן עורות]יהם כלי̇[ם ... להביא]ם למקד̇[ש]

And concerning the hides of the cattle [. . .] vessels from their hides . . . to bring them to the Temple.

The text is so fragmentary that we can do no more than guess what it may have said. Possibly there stood at this point a halakha concerning the hides of clean animals similar to the halakha in the Temple Scroll (51:1–6). The Temple Scroll declares that hides of animals that were slaughtered outside the sanctuary are not to be brought into the city of the Temple. It further establishes the principle that the degree of purity of the hide of an animal is equal to the degree of purity of its flesh. Since only the

---

[99] Revel, p. 35. On the question of the ablution on the first day for removing the first uncleanness, see Milgrom, *Studies* 1, pp. 512–518; Baumgarten, *Controversies*, pp. 159–160.

[100] See Ḥ. Albeck's commentary on *m. Berakot* 1:1, and his additions at p. 325. See also J. M. Baumgarten, 'Qumran and the Halakha in the Aramaic Targumim', *Proceedings of the Ninth World Congress of Jewish Studies, Bible Studies and Ancient Near East*, Jerusalem, 1988, pp. 53–55; Sussmann, p. 35, n. 112.

[101] See Bar-Ilan, pp. 129–146.

[102] Priests are mentioned in the sequel כי לבני אהרן ראוי להיות מ[ן B 16–17; this passage apparently discusses the responsibility of the priest for the purity of the Temple cult, however, rather than implying that the red cow ritual should be performed by priests. It is similar to the sequels in ll. 12–13 and 25–27.

flesh of an animal that was slaughtered on the Temple altar may be eaten in Jerusalem, only hides of an animal that had been slaughtered on the altar of the Temple can be used in Jerusalem.[103]

B.   B 21–22 may well have contained a halakha about hides and bones of unclean animals. Because the text is so badly preserved we can only say with certainty that the controversy here was about the purity of some kind of hides and bones.[104] The fact that in the following passage (ll. 22–23) the purity of the hides and bones of a clean animal is discussed, however, leads us to assume that there was a polemic here concerning the purity of some other kind of hides and bones, no doubt those of unclean animals. Note that also in the biblical source, Lev 11, defilement from the carcass of unclean animals is discussed before defilement from clean animals.

Accordingly, we restore the text as follows:

ואף על עורֹ[ות ועצמות הבהמה הטמאה אין לעשות מן עצמותמה] ומן עֹ[ו]רֹ[ות]מה ידות כֹ[לים]

And concerning the hides and bones of unclean animals: it is forbidden to make handles of vessels from their bones and hides (B 21–22).

The biblical law in Lev 11 states that the carcass of an unclean animal transmits defilement. The rabbis, however, ruled that the defilement is associated only with the flesh, not with the hides and bones.[105] One is therefore allowed to make vessels from the hides and bones of unclean animals.

What was the stand of the sectarians on this point? According to 11QT^a 51:4–5, there is no difference, with regard to defilement, between the hides or bones of a carcass and its flesh. This subject has been dealt with by Yadin[106] and Baumgarten.[107] They both mention the edict of Antiochus III, which forbade bringing hides of unclean animals into Jerusalem.[108] Baumgarten further maintains,[109] following Geiger,[110] that such was the view of the Sadducees as reported in *m. Yad.* 4:6:

הרי הם אומרים: עצמות חמור טהורין ועצמות יוחנן כהן גדול טמאין

Behold, they (the Sadducees!) say: the bones of an ass are clean, but the bones of Johanan the High Priest are unclean (after his death).

C.   B 22–23 discusses the purity of the hides of the carcass of a clean animal:

[ואף על עֹ]וֹר נבלת [הבהמה] הטהורה הנושא אֹ[ו]ֹת(ה) נבלתֹה [לוא י]ֹגֹש לטהרת הֹ[קודש]

And concerning the hides of the carcass of a clean animal: he who carries such a carcass shall not have access to the sacred food.

In this passage the subject matter is clear; it is carrying—not touching—with which the text is concerned. The restoration הֹ[קודש] is to be preferred to הֹ[מקדש] since the Temple is discussed in ll. 18–20 (only the hides of an animal which has been slaughtered in the Temple can be used there).

---

[103] See Yadin, *TS*, I, pp. 308–311, and the parallels and the references there; see also the discussion (below b and c) on the hide from the carcass of an unclean animal and the hide from the carcass of a pure animal. The Samaritans wrote their Torah Scrolls on the hides of sacrificial animals (Geiger, *Studies*, p. 74).

[104] The word עצמות has not been preserved here. We restored it on the assumption that handles (ידות l. 21) may have been made of bones. The combination ידות כלים occurs in MH in the context of purity (e.g. *m. Miqw.* 1:10).

[105] *M. Ḥul.* 9:1–2, and elsewhere.

[106] Yadin, *TS*, I, p. 338–341.

[107] *Controversies*, pp. 161–163.

[108] Bickerman, pp. 86–104; Milgrom, *Studies* 2, p. 98.

[109] Ibid.

[110] *Studies* 2, pp. 70–82; see the criticism of L. Ginsberg there on pp. 388–389. See also S. Lieberman, *Greek and Hellenism in Jewish Palestine*, Jerusalem, 1962 (Hebrew), pp. 229–230. For the view of the Karaites, see Revel, p. 42.

What do we know about this subject from other sources? Lev 11:39 states that whoever touches or eats or carries the carcass of a clean animal will be impure until evening. As we have seen (in b, above), the rabbis rule that the defilement is associated only with the flesh, not with the hide and bones. We further observed that the sect did not distinguish between the purity of the flesh of a clean animal and the purity of its hide and bones.

It is clear, then, that the sectarians' view regarding the defilement produced by the hides and bones of an animal differed from that of the rabbis. It is, however, unclear why the sectarians distinguished between the hides of carcasses of clean animals and those of unclean animals.

The subject of the impurity of the various kinds of hides is a very complicated one, as one may learn from the works cited in our discussion. We have only briefly surveyed some of the sources: further study is needed.

In order to understand the exact attitude of the sect to this subject and the contribution made by MMT, we should treat together all the evidence found in the DSS. In MMT there were at least three different halakhot concerning hides. Combining the evidence of MMT and that of the Temple Scroll, we can see that the sect probably distinguished several degrees of purity in hides:

(a)   Hides of a sacrificed animal; such hides are always pure
(b)   Hides of an animal that was slaughtered for secular consumption; such hides are pure outside Jerusalem, but inside Jerusalem they are impure
(c)   Hides of the carcass of an unclean animal; such hides are always impure
(d)   Hides of the carcass of a clean animal; such hides were regarded as clean for ordinary purposes (in the cities), but those who carry them may not have access to the purity[111]

If this analysis is correct, then the principle כבשרמה תהיה טהרתמה ('their [i.e. the hides'] purity shall be like [that of] their flesh') found in the Temple Scroll is not applicable to all kinds of hides. For a similar attitude with respect to the impurity of human bones, see § 5.7.16.

5.7.7   Where Animals Should be Slaughtered

Ll. 27–35 apparently contained halakhot concerning where animals should be slaughtered. Unfortunately, the text of these lines is damaged in all the manuscripts, and it is only by combining a number of tiny fragments from three different manuscripts that we have been able to produce a partial reconstruction. The subject matter is presented in the heading:

[וע]ל שא כתוב [איש כי ישחט במחנה או ישחט] מחוץ למחנה שוֹר וכשב ועז

And concerning that it is written: if a person slaughters inside the camp, or slaughters outside the camp, cattle or sheep or goat (B 27–28).

This seems to be no more than a paraphrase of Lev 17:2 et seq.[112] Elaboration on this source and on Deut 12:29ff. is found in the Temple Scroll. This scroll forbade the secular slaughter of animals in Jerusalem and its environs, and demanded that in Jerusalem, and within a three-day radius of Jerusalem, all slaughter be performed within the sanctuary and on the altar (52:13–16). Hence the statement [אי]נם שוחטים במקדש ('they are not slaughtering in the sanctuary', B 35) may also refer to the practice of the opponents regarding secular slaughtering. Our fragmentary text does not

---

[111] e.g., for making a Torah Scroll (contrast the rabbinic view, b. Šabb. 108ᵃ) or for special meals. As far as we can tell from the evidence adduced by Geiger (ibid.), the Samaritans did not forbid the use of hides from the carcass of a clean animal for ordinary purposes. They only avoided such hides on Sabbath or during Passover, and did not use them for making a Torah scroll. On the attitude of the Karaites, see Geiger (ibid.). For a similar attitude in rabbinic literature, see Alon, p. 156 and Bar-Ilan, p. 223.

[112] We are obliged to Dr. P. Segal for his suggestion to restore או ישחט instead of our restoration והם שוחטים.

contribute anything new on the subject of slaughtering; the reader is referred to the discussion of the relevant passage in Yadin's edition of the Temple Scroll, pp. 241–242, where references are given to a variety of sources, among them Karaite works. For the identifications in ll. 28–33, see § 5.4.2.

The adverbial expression בצ]פון המחנה] apparently refers to slaughtering; cf. Lev 1:11: ושחט אתו על ירך המזבח צפנה. The rabbis ruled that some kinds of sacrifices must be slaughtered in the northern part of the court, and others slaughtered elsewhere.[113]

5.7.8 The Slaughter of Pregnant Animals

A.   Ll. 36–38 contained two halakhot concerning the slaughtering of a female animal and its unborn offspring on the same day:

[ועל העברות א]נ̇ח̇נו חו]שבים שאין לזבוח א]ת̇ האם ואת הולד ביום אחד [. . .] ועל̊ האוכל̊
[אנח]נו חושבים שאיאכל את הולד [שבמעי אמו לאחר שחיטתו ואתם יודעים שהו]א̇ כן
והדבר כתוב עברה

And concerning pregnant animals, we are of the opinion that the mother and its fetus may not be sacrificed on the same day . . . And concerning the eating of the fetus, we are of the opinion that only provided that it has been ritually slaughtered may the fetus found in its dead mother's womb be eaten. And you know that it is so, namely that this ruling refers to pregnant animals.

The text dealing with this halakha is damaged; in MS[c] only the ends of the lines have survived. Fortunately there is a small fragment from MS[d] which enables us to reconstruct most of the text, though both the combination and the reconstruction are tentative. The outlines of the controversy can in any case be discerned even without a reconstruction.

The words האם ואת הולד ביום אחד [את] echo Lev 22:28 ושור או שה אותו ואת בנו לא תשחטו ביום אחד. It appears that MMT applied this biblical law to pregnant animals. This can be inferred from the word עברה 'pregnant'.[114] Two statements can be distinguished: (1) it is forbidden to slaughter pregnant animals and (2) a fetus found alive within a (dead) pregnant animal must be ritually slaughtered before it may be consumed. Both rules oppose the rabbinic halakha in which the fetus is viewed as part of the mother and not as an independent entity.

The subject is also discussed in the Temple Scroll:

ולוא תזבח לי שור ושה ועז והמה מלאות כי תועבה המה לי ושור ושה אותו ואת
בנו לוא תזבח ביום אחד ולוא תכה אם על בנים

And you shall not sacrifice to Me a cow or a sheep or a goat when they are pregnant, for they are an abomination to Me. And you shall not slaughter a cow or a sheep, it and its young, both on the same day, so as not to kill the mother with its young (52:5–7).

B.   These laws should be viewed in the framework of the general juridical problem of whether the embryo is a living creature or merely a part of its mother. The Dead Sea sect, Philo, and the Karaites all maintained that it is a living creature, while the rabbis maintained that it is a part of its mother.[115]

---

[113] *M. Zebaḥ.* 5:1. If in fact צפון המחנה refers to slaughtering, MMT implies that at the time of its composition the Temple Mount was the northern border of Jerusalem (Dr. P. Segal in personal communication).

[114] The reading עֲבֵרָה 'transgression', is less probable; the word is not attested either in QH or in BH.

[115] Several rabbis, however, maintained that the embryo was not a part of its mother (see A. Aptowitzer, 'The State of the Embryo in Jewish Law of Punishment', *Sinai* 6 [1942], pp. 9–32). For a discussion of the slaughtering of pregnant animals and of the status of the embryo, see Albeck's commentary on the Mishna, order *Qodashim*, p. 377, and the literature cited there; see also Geiger, *Urschrift*, pp. 343–346; Alon, pp. 279–280 and, most recently, Yadin, *TS*, I, pp. 312–314, 336–338; M. Weinfeld, 'Killing an Embryo: The View of Israel's Tradition in Comparison with Others', *Zion* 42

C.   The question arises, concerning the first part of this passage, whether it deals with sacred or non-sacred slaughter. The Temple Scroll deals only with sacrificial offerings, since it states 'you shall not slaughter to Me'.[116] In MMT, the sanctuary is mentioned in l. 35, at the conclusion of a section prohibiting the slaughter of clean animals outside the sanctuary (cf. § 5.7.7). The juxtaposition of these matters with the halakha under discussion implies that sacrificial animals are dealt with here. The second part of the halakha, however, includes the verb אכל, which refers to non-sacred slaughter.

It is possible that during the Second Temple period there was a controversy over the question of whether the law of 'it and its young' applied only to sacrificial animals or to non-sacred slaughter as well. According to Philo, it applied also to non-sacred slaughter, but Josephus mentions it only in connection with the slaughter of sacrifices. In rabbinic sources the law of 'it and its young' is discussed with regard to both sacred and non-sacred animals.[117]

5.7.9   Those Forbidden to Enter the Congregation

A.   [ועל העמו]ני והמואבי [ו]המזר ופ[צוע הדכה וכרו]ת השפכת שהם באים בקהל
[. . . ונשים] לוקחים [להיו]תם עצם אחת [ובאים למקדש . . .] טמאות. ואף חושבים אנחנו
[שאין . . . ואין לבו]א עליהם [. . . וא]ין להתיכם ולעשותם [עצם אחת . . . ואין להבי]אם
[למקדש . . . ואתם יודעים שמק]צת העם [. . .] מתוכ]כים [כי לכול בני ישראל ראוי להזהר] מכול
תערובת [ה]גבר ולהיות יראים מהמקדש.

And concerning the Ammonite and the Moabite and the *mamzer* and him whose testicles have been crushed and him whose male member has been cut off, who nevertheless enter the congregation of Israel . . . and take wives to become one (flesh and) bone and enter the sanctuary . . . impurities. And we are of the opinion that one must not . . . and one must not cohabit with them (i.e. the women), and one must not let them be united with an Israelite and make them (i.e. the man and the woman) one (flesh and) bone, and one must not let them enter the sanctuary . . . And you know that some of the people . . . and become united. For all the sons of Israel should beware of any forbidden unions and be full of reverence for the sanctuary (B 39–49).

B.   MMT's lengthy discussion on this subject is poorly preserved, and as a result our conclusions are based largely on conjecture. Let us first outline those sources which help us to reconstruct what is being said in MMT. The Torah speaks of the classes of persons listed here, and says that they shall not enter the congregation of the Lord (Deut 23:2-4). The expression 'enter the congregation of the Lord' has been explained in two different ways. In Lam 1:10 it is understood as referring to entry into the sanctuary,[118] while the rabbis explained it as referring to marriage with Jewish women. The rabbis interpreted the masculine form of the words 'Ammonite', etc. (in the biblical verse), as excluding

---

(1978), pp. 129–142 and particularly p. 142 (Hebrew); Milgrom, *Studies* 1, p. 522. See also the references cited in P. Segal's article in שנתון המשפט העברי 13 (1987), p. 217, n. 12, and Sussmann, p. 35, n. 110.

[116] And perhaps the use of תזבח rather than תשחט as in Lev 22:28 is intended to emphasize this matter; contrast Brin, p. 205.

[117] See Albeck's commentary on the Mishna, order Qodashim, p. 377. In 4Q269 [= D^e] we find the phrase בהמה [וחיה עבר]ה, which proves that the law applied also to non-sacred animals, חיה being an edible non-sacred animal. Contrast *Sipra* (Finkelstein's facsimile edition, p. 439): שור-לא חיה. A different question arises from the Temple Scroll: whether 'it and its young' applies only to female animals or also to males (in MMT pregnant animals are spoken of, thus excluding males). Yadin (*TS*, I, p. 49) cites many sources to support the former view. In our opinion it can indeed be shown that the Temple Scroll held that the law applied to the mother alone. As Brin points out, the conclusion of the section, the phrase 'so that you will not strike the mother with her offspring' does not constitute a separate law, and this, we believe, proves that 'it' is the mother. Note the similarity between אם על בנים in the Temple Scroll and את האם ואת הולד in MMT.

[118] Baumgarten, *Qumran Law*, p. 77, interpreted Neh 13 as testifying to this effect. But see Z. Falk, 'Those Excluded from the Congregation', *Beth Mikra* 62 (1975), pp. 342–351.

Ammonite or Moabite women from this prohibition.[119] In this they differed from the Karaites, who also prohibited marriages with Ammonite women and the like, and found it understandably difficult to explain the case of Ruth the Moabitess. The same attitude is found in the *Tg.* Ruth 2:10–13 (which is apparently of a sectarian origin).

This question is further addressed in 4Q174 (Florilegium) 1–2 i 3–4:

הואה הבית אשר לוא יבוא שמה [איש אשר בבשרו מום] עולם ועֹמוני ומואבי וממזר ובן נכר
וגר עד עולם

That is the House unto which shall not enter [a man with] an incurable [defect in his flesh] and an Ammonite and a Moabite and a *mamzer* and a foreigner and a proselyte until eternity.

Baumgarten[120] has analysed this text, comparing it to other relevant sources; he shows that the sectarians interpreted those biblical sources which forbade entry into the congregation as prohibiting entry into the sanctuary.

C.   What do we find in MMT? It appears that the halakha consists of four sections.

The first begins with the opening formula ועל x. It is followed by a plural participle with the third personal plural pronoun הם (B 39–42). This section is to be interpreted as stating that those forbidden to enter the congregation do, in fact, enter it. They marry Israelite women[121] and cause impurity.

The second section opens with the words ואף חושבים אנחנו followed by negated infinitives denoting prohibitions (B 42–46). This section surely gives the sectarians' halakhic views. These views are that no one should have intercourse with women from these groups, and that one should not let men of these groups marry Israelite women[122] or let them enter the sanctuary.

The third section presumably opened with the words ואתם יודעים שמק[צת העם followed by plural participle(s) (B 46–47). This section denounces the practice of those who do not accept the sectarians' views.

The fourth section, opening with [כי לבני ישראל], consists of infinitives denoting commands or prohibitions. It seems to be a concluding statement to the effect that Israelites should refrain from sexual relations with the above-mentioned groups, and that they should be full of reverence for the sanctuary. On the similarity in construction to B 63–71, see § 5.7.17b.

The mention of the sanctuary here clearly refers to the prohibition against the entry of these classes of people into the sanctuary, though the expression בא בקהל seems to have a more general meaning (see Baumgarten, ibid.). It seems to us that, according to the sect, the prohibition against entering the congregation included at least two different items:

1.   a prohibition against marrying members of certain groups

[119] Cf. E. E. Urbach, *The Sages: Their Concepts and Beliefs*, Jerusalem, 1979, pp. 376–377.

[120] *Qumran Law*, pp. 75–87; cf. also M. Kister, 'Notes on the Book of Ben-Sira', *Leshonenu* 47 (1983), pp. 131–132; see also his additions in *Leshonenu* 53 (1989), p. 43. (We do not agree with Baumgarten's opinion that בן נכר here does not mean 'gentile'.)

[121] The word לוקחים apparently means 'marry wives' (see § 3.5.2.15a). This agrees with the immediate continuation [תם עצם אחת [להיו], which alludes to the creation of Eve in Gen 2:21-24 (see the next note). The order of the words in לוקחים נשים rather than [נשים] לוקחים is, however, somewhat irregular in Hebrew.

[122] The expressions להתיכמה and מתוככים seem to have the same meaning as the verb דבק in Gen 2:21-24; the phrase [תם עצם אחת [להיו] and its causative equivalent [עצם אחת/בשר אחד] would parallel ודבק באשתו להתיכמה ולעשותמה in Genesis (see § 3.5.4.13). The passage in Gen 2:24 may have been a central source for the sectarians' conceptions of marriage (and divorce). It is also referred to in a sapiential work (4Q416, to be published by J. Strugnell), where we find: [לך and מאמה הפרידה ואליכה, את אביֹה [וֹ]אֹת אמֹה followed by בהתחברכה יחד התהלך עם עזר בשרכה לבֹשר אחד. The verb חבר is here synonymous with the verbs תוך in MMT and דבק in the biblical source.

2.   a prohibition against members of these groups entering the sanctuary[123]

The dispute between the sect and its opponents apparently concerned only the question of entering the
sanctuary and marrying women from these groups. The rabbis maintained that the biblical law means
only that these groups should not marry Israelite women.[124] Philo and the Karaites interpreted the
biblical law to mean that the *mamzer* is not to intermingle with the community of Israel, and not as
referring to marriage.[125]

5.7.10   The Blind and the Deaf

A.   [ואף ע]ל הסומ[י]ם שאינם רואים להזהר מכול תערו[בת] ותערובת [א]שם אינם רואים
              ואף על החרשים שלוא שמעו חוק ומשפט וטהרה ולא שמעו משפטי ישראל כי שלוא ראה
              ולוא שמע לוא ידע לעשות והמה באים לטהרת המקדש

> Also concerning the blind who cannot see so as to beware of all mixture, and cannot see the mixture that incurs
> reparation-offering; and concerning the deaf who have not heard the laws and the judgements and the purity
> regulations, and have not heard the ordinances of Israel. They, i.e. both the blind and the deaf, should revere
> the sanctuary. Since he who has not seen or heard does not know how to obey the law: nevertheless they have
> access to the sacred food (B 49–54).

The structure of this passage is problematic. The passage contains two 'sentences' which open with the
phrase ואף על. Neither of them has a predicate. In the first, one might take the infinitive להזהר as a
predicate ('should beware'), but then the two sentences would not have parallel structures. It is better
therefore to interpret them as defective sentences whose predicates should be supplied from the
preceding sentence להיות יראים מהמקדש. Alternatively, one could take these two sentences as rubrics
(§ 5.2.4).

The first of the two sentences deals with the blind and the second with the deaf, but the conclusion
of the passage (the explanation) applies equally to the blind and the deaf. This proves that MMT treats
these two classes alike;[126] the reason for treating them alike is not that the members of these classes all
have defects, but rather that none of them are able to act in accordance with the laws of purity.

B.   There is no exact parallel to our ruling in the DSS, but a similar halakha is found in the Temple
Scroll 45:12–14:

              כול איש עור לוא יבואו לה כול ימיהמה ולוא יטמאו את העיר אשר אני שוכן בתוכה

> 'No blind men shall enter into it all their days lest they defile the city in which I dwell'.

Yadin[127] connected this passage with other texts from Qumran which lay down that persons with
defects are forbidden to enter Jerusalem (the city of the Temple) or the camp, lest they profane what
is holy. In his opinion, the source of this prohibition is Lev 21:17, where priests with defects are
forbidden to sacrifice burnt offerings. He suggests that the Temple Scroll expanded the prohibition to
include all of Israel, and broadened the area to which the law was applicable to include all of
Jerusalem.[128] The word עור in the Temple Scroll refers, in his opinion, not only to the blind, but also

---

[123] On the obligation to revere the sanctuary, see *Talmudic Encyclopedia* (Hebrew), 17, pp. 495 ff. On the distinction
between the sanctuary and Jerusalem, see § 5.4.2d.

[124] See *m. Yad.* 4:4. It appears that the words א[לבו]א עליהם and לוקחים in MMT refer to the practice of the opponents
of the sect of marrying Ammonite and Moabite women. This supports Urbach's assumption (n. 119 above) that this
rabbinic halakha is ancient.

[125] See Revel, pp. 66–67.

[126] Note however that before the word ואף in l. 47 there is (in MS[a], but not in MS[c]) three-quarters of a line blank.

[127] Yadin, *TS*, I, p. 224; II, p. 136.

[128] We suggest rather that the sectarians based their ruling on Deut 18:13 תמים תהיה עם ה' אלהיך which they
understood to mean 'you shall be without blemish when you are near God'. The phrase תמימי רוח ובשר (1QM 7:5) may

to people with other types of defects. Yadin's interpretation should be reconsidered, however, in the light of our halakha. Perhaps the halakha in the Temple Scroll, like the one in MMT, merely rules that a blind person is forbidden to enter Jerusalem lest he approach the holy things and profane them through 'mixture'.[129] If so it would follow that there is no need to resort to the forced explanation that the blind here stand for other people with defects of various sorts.

One should not, however, overlook the differences between the Temple Scroll and MMT: (1) The Temple Scroll mentions only the blind, whereas MMT deals with both the blind and the deaf; (2) The Temple Scroll speaks of Jerusalem (= the Temple city), whereas MMT deals with the Temple.

C.   What was the attitude of the rabbis on this subject?

The rabbis did not treat the blind and the deaf as forming a single category. A deaf person was treated as mindless (in the same category as an imbecile or a minor).[130] The blind were not seen as mindless, but merely as incapable of carrying out certain practices.

As regards the deaf, the Mishna in *Terumot* 1:1 states that a deaf man may not set aside *Teruma*, and that if he does his act is not valid. The Tosepta in *Terumot* 1:1 adds that the deaf may have access to the pure food eaten in Jerusalem.[131] The practice of the opponents in MMT conforms, then, with that of the rabbis. The rabbinic source, however, does not mention either the blind[132] or the Temple.

We were unable to find any particular biblical passage on which this ruling is based. Nevertheless, the justificatory clause—which implies that one should be capable of seeing and hearing in order to behave in accordance with the precepts of the law—may have been drawn from one or more of several biblical passages, for instance Deut 5: 24 (ושמענו ועשינו) and Deut 4: 9 (פן תשכח את הדברים אשר ראו עיניך).

5.7.11   Streams (מוצקות)

A.   In B 55–58 there is a discussion on the מוצקות:

ואף על המוצקות אנחנו אומרים שהם שאין בהם טהרה ואף המוצקות אינם מבדילות בין הטמא לטהור כי לחת המוצקות והמקבל מהמה כהם לחה אחת

And concerning (unbroken) streams of a liquid (poured from a clean vessel into an unclean vessel): we are of the opinion that they are not pure,[133] and that these streams do not act as a separative between impure and pure liquids, for the liquid of the streams and that of the vessel which receives them are alike, being a single liquid.

well allude to this biblical passage as understood by the sectarians, since it follows a list of deformed persons and is followed by the sentence כי מלאכי קודש עם צבאותם יחד. Note the use of the preposition עם in both the biblical source and in this passage.

[129] Similarly, MMT casts doubt on Bar-Ilan's view (p. 189) that the blind are discussed in *m. Ḥul.* 1:1 because of their defect.

[130] *B. Ḥag.* 2b and *Talmudic Encyclopedia*, s.v. חרש.

[131] See Sussmann, p. 34 and n. 106.

[132] The contrast with the rabbinic view is related to a much broader problem: to what extent are the blind and the deaf capable of carrying out the laws of the Torah? According to *m. Ḥul.* 1:1, a blind person is permitted to slaughter. This is in contrast with the view of the Karaites (also found in Eldad Ha-Dani, ed. Müller, p. 78). We may assume that the view of the Dead Sea sect was similar to that of the Karaites, since according to MMT (in contrast to the rabbinic conception mentioned above), the blind as well as the deaf are incapable of carrying out the laws of the Torah. With regard to the deaf, the contrast with the rabbinic view seems to be minor, since even the rabbis consider the deaf to be mindless and incapable of carrying out the laws of the Torah. This rabbinic view, however, applies only to those who are mute as well as deaf. If the law in MMT applies also to the deaf who are not mute, then the contrast with the rabbinic view is greater than appears at first glance.

[133] Literally 'have no purity in them'.

Since the word ואף is repeated in this passage, we must distinguish two separate rulings concerning streams.

1.   Streams poured into an unclean vessel are unclean.

2.   These streams are to be considered as connecting a pure liquid and an impure liquid (so that if the receptacle contains an impure liquid, then the liquid in the upper vessel is also rendered unclean).

B.   Both these rulings have their parallels in rabbinic sources.

The first ruling occurs in *m. Yad.* 4:7 as a subject of controversy between the Sadducees and the Pharisees. The view of the author of MMT is identical with that of the Sadducees as represented in the Mishna:

אומרים צדוקין: קובלים אנו עליכם פרושים שאתם מטהרין את הנצוק

'The Sadducees say: We protest against you, O Pharisees, for you pronounce clean the unbroken stream (of liquid poured from a clean vessel to an unclean one)'.

The second ruling occurs in *m. Tohar.* 8:9:

הנצוק והקטפרס ומשקה טופח אינן חיבור לא לטומאה ולא לטהרה

An uninterrupted flow (of a liquid poured from vessel to vessel), a current on sloping ground and the dripping of moisture are not considered a connective (of the two liquids) either for communicating uncleanness or for producing cleanness.

The identification of מוצקות in MMT with MH נצוק was already suggested by Yadin.[134] According to this suggestion we would take the word מוצקות as the *hop'al* participle of יצק. Cf. the form מוצקות in Zechariah 4:2 (though with a different meaning)[135] and cf. § 3.5.4.4.

Once again we have a halakha which was the subject of controversy between the Sadducees and the Pharisees.[136] The fact that the controversy is mentioned both in MMT and in the Mishna shows how important it was. It probably involved the purity of the pools (מקואות) and the purity of the water channels of the Temple.[137]

5.7.12 The Ban on Bringing Dogs into Jerusalem

A.   ואין להבי למחנה הקודש כלבים שהם אוכלים מקצת [עצ]מות המק[ו]דש ו]הבשר עליהם
כי ירושלים היאה מחנה הקדש והיא המקום שבחר בו מכול שבטי ישראל כי ירושלים
היא ראש מחנות ישראל

And one must not let dogs enter the holy camp, since they may eat some of the bones of the sanctuary while the flesh of the sacrifices is still on them. For Jerusalem is the camp of holiness and is the holy place which He has chosen from among all the places of the tribes of Israel. For Jerusalem is the capital of the camps (i.e. settlements) of Israel (B 58–62).

This halakha is well preserved and clearly formulated. Its concern is with the purity of Jerusalem.[138] It rules that dogs are not to be brought into Jerusalem, since they may defile the sacred food. The

---

[134] Yadin, *TS*, II, p. 213. The subject, however, is foreign to the Temple Scroll. See also Baumgarten, *Controversies*, pp. 163–164.

[135] It is less plausible to take מוצקות as 'pipes' and explain the passage accordingly; cf. however *m. Kelim* 2:3.

[136] From *m. Makš.* 5:9 we learn that the School of Shamai was more stringent than the School of Hillel with regard to streams.

[137] See *t. Miqw.* 4:6, and J. Patrich in *Cathedra* 17 (1981), pp. 11–23, and also ibid., pp. 223–224.

[138] The author, as he states later, uses the term מחנה הקודש as an epithet for Jerusalem. On the phrase עצמות המקדש, see below.

passage contains an apodictic prohibition (ואין להבי) followed by two causal clauses (שהם אוכלים[139] and כי ירושלים; see § 5.2.4).

From the first of these causal clauses it seems that dogs (rather than other animals) are involved not because they are impure, but because it is their habit to dig up bones; thus they may eat the flesh that remains on the bones of the sacrificial animals.[140] The second causal clause is apparently not an organic part of the halakha (see § 5.4), but it may imply that the polemic between the sectarians and their opponents was on the question of whether dogs should be excluded only from the Temple proper or from the whole of Jerusalem.[141]

In any case, the opponents of the sect did keep dogs in Jerusalem, and the sect considered this to be a severe transgression. We have not been able to find an exact parallel to such a halakha, nor can we find any biblical source from which it might have been deduced. There are, however, a number of sources which shed some light on our passage.

B. The Edict of Antiochus III (recorded by Josephus) forbade bringing the flesh or the hide of unclean animals into Jerusalem, and forbade the rearing of such animals in Jerusalem. As Bickerman has shown,[142] the aim of this edict was to prevent the defilement of Jerusalem. The edict does not concern the eating of the flesh of the sacrifices, however, but the impurity of carcasses.[143]

In *m. B. Qam.* 7:7 there is an ancient prohibition against raising chickens in Jerusalem, lest they defile the holy things: אין מגדלים תרנגלים בירושלם מפני הקדשים 'No one may raise chickens in Jerusalem because of the sacrifices'.

Dogs are mentioned in connection with sacred food in some other sources,[144] e.g. in the New Testament: 'Do not give dogs the sacred food; do not cast your pearls before swine' (Matt 7:6). The dog is here conceived of as an unclean animal that should be kept away from the sacred food, and is coupled with pigs.[145] It is possible that this coupling of dogs and pigs originated in a halakha like ours that regards the dog as an unclean creature which ought to be kept away from the sacred food.

The above sources tell us about the precautions taken by Jews in Jerusalem to avoid the defilement of the Temple by unclean animals, whether dead or alive.

There are still some unsolved questions: Why does MMT mention only dogs? Did they allow other animals to be brought into Jerusalem (contrast the Edict of Antiochus III, or the mention of the chicken in the rabbinic sources)? Note 11QT[a] 46:1–2, where עוף טמא is mentioned in connection with

---

[139] From the formal linguistic point of view, this phrase may also be taken as a relative one; causal clauses in MMT begin with כי rather than -ש (see § 3.3.1.4).

[140] Jars have been found at Qumran containing animal bones. Some scholars maintain that they are bones from sacrifices, others that they are from the common meal at Qumran, but all agree that the bones were preserved in the jars because of considerations of purity. It may be that the bones of the sacrifices were buried temporarily in Jerusalem so that the flesh might be consumed, and that these bones were then collected and preserved. If so, then a danger existed that during the temporary burial dogs or other animals might dig up the bones and eat the flesh that remained on them (cf. Baumgarten, *Qumran Law*, pp. 59–61).

[141] We are obliged to Dr. P. Segal for this suggestion.

[142] Pp. 88–104; cf. also Yadin, *TS*, I, p. 240.

[143] Bickerman, ibid.

[144] But not in rabbinic sources. In the sources discussed by Sussmann (p. 34), neither sacred food nor Jerusalem is mentioned.

[145] A similar juxtaposition of pigs and dogs is found in the LXX to 1 Kgs 22:38, 'And the swine and the dogs licked the blood'. (Our thanks to M. Weinfeld for these references.) See also Isa 66:3-4; *t. Yebam.* 3, and Lieberman's commentary; *t. B. Qam.* 8:17; *b. B. Qam.* 80[a], 83[a]. We note that the Hittites regarded the entry of a dog and pigs into the temple, and their coming in contact with the sacrifices, as an act which is not in accordance with the will of the gods. See *Encyclopaedia Biblica*, s.v. כלב and חזיר; Bickerman ibid.; J. C. Moyer, 'Hittite and Israelite Cultic Practices: A Selected Comparison', in *Scripture in Context, II*, Winona Lake, IN, 1982, pp. 29–33.

the Temple. Were dogs mentioned here only because they dig up bones, or also because of the impurity ascribed to them (as the above mentioned sources teach us)?

5.7.13 The Fruits of the Fourth Year

A.   ואף על מטעת עצי המאכל הנטע בּאֹרץ ישראל כראשית הוֹא לכוהנים

And concerning (the fruits of) trees with edible fruit planted in the Land of Israel: the fruit produced by such trees in their fourth year is to be dealt with like first fruit belonging to the priests (B 62–63).

According to the wording of the text, it seems that this apodictic halakha is based on Lev 19:23-25:

וכי תבואו אל הארץ ונטעתם כל עץ מאכל וערלתם ערלתו את פריו. שלש שנים יהיה לכם ערלים
לא יאכל ובשנה הרביעית יהיה כל פריו קדש הלולים לה׳ ובשנה החמישת תאכלו את פריו להוסיף
לכם תבואתו. אני ה׳ אלהיכם.

When you enter the land and plant any tree for food, you shall regard its fruit as forbidden. Three years it shall be forbidden for you, not to be eaten. In the fourth year all its fruit shall be set aside for jubilation before the Lord, and only in the fifth year may you use its fruit that its yield to you may be increased. I the Lord am your God.

(Note the similarity in wording between the two passages: הארץ in Leviticus and ארץ ישראל in MMT;[146] ונטעתם in Leviticus and מטעת in MMT; עץ מאכל in Leviticus and עצי המאכל in MMT; לה׳ in Leviticus and לכוהנים in MMT.)

The halakha in MMT seems to say that the fruits of the tree or of the vineyard in its fourth year[147] belong to the priests, just as the first fruits belong to the priests. This ruling is presumably based on the phrase קדש הלולים לה׳.

B.   What do we know from other sources about this subject? The rabbinic halakha rules that during the fourth year after their planting, the fruits of a tree or vine are to be treated like second tithe, i.e. they or their money value are to be brought to Jerusalem to be consumed there. This is how Josephus reports the rule in *Antiquities of the Jews*. In *Tg. Pseudo-Jonathan*, however, it is laid down that the fruits belong to the priests. This is also the position of the Samaritans and the Karaites. The Book of Jubilees also states: ' . . . so that they might offer up in the juice the first of the wine and the oil as first fruit upon the altar of the Lord who will accept it. And that which is left the servants of the house of the Lord will eat before the altar which receives (it)' (7:36).[148] From the comparison with ראשית in MMT, we may infer that the fruit in the fourth year is an offering given to God and eaten

---

[146] The phrase בארץ ישראל in MMT may simply be an allusion to הארץ in Lev, but it may also imply that this precept is in force only in the land of Israel. This is in contrast with the view of some of the rabbis that it is in force also outside the land. With regard to ʿorla, all the rabbis agree that it is in force also outside the land (see *Encyclopedia Talmudica*, III, 41–41).

[147] Even though neither the fruit nor the fourth year are mentioned here. It is also possible to interpret the passage as dealing with the fruit tithe; Lev 27:30 states that such a tithe is to be given to the priests, and in both Lev 27:30-32 and MMT B 62–64 the law about the fruits of the tree is followed by the law about the cattle tithe. It is, however, preferable to interpret it as dealing with what is 'holy for giving praise', both because of the wording and because there is no mention of a tithe. There seems to be no connection between the halakha here and in Neh 10:36-38.

[148] For references and discussion on these sources, see Geiger, *Urschrift*, pp. 116–118; Albeck's commentary to *Zeraʿim*, pp. 243–244; Revel, pp. 17–18; Zunz, הדרשות בישראל, p. 421 n. 35; E. Itzchaki, *Sidra* 1 (1985), p. 50; Sussmann, p. 33, n. 96; and M. Kister, 'Some Aspects of Qumranic Halakhah', *The Madrid Qumran Congress: Proceedings of the International Congress on the Dead Sea Scrolls, Madrid, 18–21 March 1991* (ed. J. T. Barrera and L. V. Montaner), Leiden 1992, II, pp. 576–588.

by the priests in the inner court.[149] It should be brought to the Temple at a fixed time, and may not be redeemed by its owner (contrast the rulings of *Tg. Pseudo Jonathan*, the Samaritans and the Karaites).[150]

The fruits of the fourth year ('holy for giving praise') also appear among the priestly gifts itemized in the Temple Scroll at the beginning of col. 60 (see the following paragraph on the cattle-tithe).[151] Similarly in 4QD[e] 2 ii 6 the word מטעת occurs among the priestly gifts.

It seems, then, that during the Second Temple period it was widely held that the fruits of the fourth year belong to the priests, although this view was not unanimous. Some held, however, that they do not belong to the priests. Echoes of the ancient dispute on this issue can be found in rabbinic literature.[152]

Both the fruits of the fourth year and the cattle-tithe (to be mentioned below) are designated 'holy . . . unto the Lord'. The halakhic dispute centers on the interpretation of this expression.[153]

5.7.14   Cattle-Tithe

ומעשר הבקר והצון לכוהנים הוא

And (likewise) the tithe of the herd and of the flock should be given to the priests (B 63–64).

The tithe of the cattle and of the flock ('tithe of the herd', מעשר בהמה, in rabbinic terminology) is mentioned in Lev 27:32 and 2 Chr 31:6, and perhaps in 4QD[e] 2 ii 7–8. According to the literal sense of the verse in Leviticus, this tithe is sacred to the Lord, and belongs to the Temple or to the priest:[154]

וכל מעשר בקר וצאן כל אשר יעבר תחת השבט העשירי יהיה קדש לה׳

And all the tithe of the cattle or the flock, whatsoever passes under the rod, the tenth shall be holy unto the Lord.

The rabbinic halakha rules, concerning the tithe of the herd, that the blood is to be sprinkled and the fat offered upon the altar, while the flesh belongs to the owner and is to be consumed in Jerusalem (like the second tithe). The priests have no part in it.[155]

In contrast, some texts from the Apocrypha, Philo, the Karaites and other sources say that this tithe is sacred to the priests and is to be given to them like the firstborn.[156] The cattle tithe is apparently listed among the priestly gifts in the Temple Scroll, at the beginning of col. 60:

---

[149] See Deut 18:12-13. 11QT[a] 38:1–7 specifies the places in the inner court where the first fruits and, apparently, also the fruits of the fourth year are to be eaten (see E. Qimron, 'New Readings in the Temple Scroll', *IEJ* 37 [1987], p. 33).

[150] J. M. Baumgarten, 'The Laws of ʿOrlah and First Fruits in the Light of Jubilees, the Qumran Writings, and Targum Ps. Jonathan', *JJS* 38 (1987), pp. 195–202.

[151] See Yadin, *TS*, I, pp. 162–163.

[152] See Geiger and Yadin, *TS*.

[153] Cf. Lev 23:20; 27:21; Num 5:8; 18:8-20.

[154] Y. Kaufman, תולדות האמונה הישראלית, I, p. 148; Haran in *Encyclopaedia Biblica*, s.v. מעשר, col. 206. According to Kaufman (ibid.), this tithe was not an obligatory annual gift, but was given as the result of a vow or as a voluntary offering; but cf. J. Milgrom, *Cult and Conscience: The Asham and the Priestly Doctrine of Repentance*, Leiden, 1976, pp. 55–58; Alon, p. 294.

[155] See *m. Zebaḥ.* 5:8, and Albeck's introduction to his commentary on *m. Zebaḥ.* (order *Qodašin*, p. 7). The rabbis explained that the priests had no part in it because it was not mentioned among the priestly gifts. See Rashi's commentary on the verse in Leviticus.

[156] See *Jub.* 32:15, Tob. 1:6, and the parallels from Philo and the Karaites cited by Revel, pp. 79–80.

וכול תנופותמה וכול בכורות̇ן̇י̇]המה ה̇זכרים וכול̇ מע̇ן̇ש̇̇]ר̇] לבהמתמה וכול קודשיהמה אשר
יקדישו לי עם כול קוד̇]ש̇[הלוליהמה . . .

And all their wave-offerings and all their firstborn males[157] and all the tithe of their cattle tithes[158] and all their
holy offerings which they sanctify to me, and all their holy fruit offerings of praise . . .

Our halakha, then, represents the prevailing view in the Second Temple period, and is based on the
literal interpretation at that time of the expression 'holy unto the Lord'.[159]

5.7.15   The Impurity of Lepers

A.   The halakhot about lepers in early rabbinic sources are very detailed since the problems
involved were particularly complex. The main difficulty lay in identifying the various types of
'leprosy' and in defining the degrees of purity and impurity proper to each type. Most of the halakhot
about lepers in rabbinic sources contain details about the symptoms of leprosy, about isolating the
leper, and about how to decide when to declare the leper pure or impure. Such details were also
discussed in Qumran halakha, as can be inferred from a fragment of CD found in Cave 4.[160]

MMT, however, is not concerned with such details. It concentrates instead on the problems of
keeping lepers away from the Temple and away from things that are ritually pure. What interests
MMT is therefore the degree of impurity that lepers have during the various stages of their
purification. In order to understand the text in MMT we must first turn to its biblical sources and to
rabbinic practice.

B.   The Bible (Lev 14:1–32) distinguishes three stages in the purification of a healed leper; the
directions for the treatment of each stage end with the word וטהר 'and he becomes pure':
1.   When the healed leper enters the camp, after shaving himself and immersing himself for the
first time, it is written: ורחץ במים וטהר 'and he should wash with water, and become pure'. During this
stage, which lasts for seven days, he is not allowed to enter his tent (14:8).
2.   On the seventh day, after shaving and immersing himself for a second time, it is written: ורחץ
את בשרו במים וטהר 'then he should wash his flesh with water, and become pure' (14:9).
3.   On the eighth day, when he brings his offerings, it is written: וכפר עליו הכהן וטהר 'and the priest
will atone for him, and he will become pure' (14:20).

C.   The rabbis' definition of the degree of purity at each of these three stages is given in *m. Neg.*
14:2–3[161] (see also 14:8–9). According to the rabbis, it is only while the leper is kept outside the camp
that he is highly impure and conveys defilement even by entering a house (*m. Neg.* 13:7 ff.). The first
stage of the purification process begins immediately after he shaves for the first time and is permitted
to enter the city. The severe impurity of leprosy now ceases, and the leper is only slightly impure:

---

[157] On the reading בכורותיהמה, see E. Qimron, 'Studies on the Text of the Temple Scroll', *Leshonenu* 42 (1978), p.
145.

[158] On this restoration, see J. Milgrom, *Studies* 1, pp. 519–520 and E. Qimron, 'Notes on the Text of the Temple
Scroll', *Tarbiz* 53 (1983), p. 141 (Qimron was unaware of Milgrom's suggestion).

[159] This expression is also found in Lev 27:30, which was consistently taken by the rabbis to apply to the second
tithe; cf. J. M. Baumgarten, 'The First and Second Tithes in the Temple Scroll', *Biblical and Related Studies Presented to
Samuel Iwri*, ed. A. Kort and S. Morschauer, Winona Lake, IN, 1985, pp. 5–15.

[160] J. T. Milik, *RB* (1966), p. 105. Other laws about lepers occur in fragments of the Damascus Document from
Cave 4 (see Baumgarten's article cited in n. 1) and in 4QTah[a] (unpublished).

[161] The Mishna (ibid.) states that there are three degrees of purity of the leper, but commentators on the Mishna are
divided on the question of whether these degrees are parallel to the three stages mentioned in the Bible, or parallel to the
three stages in the purification of the leper (i.e. טבול יום אוכל במעשר, הביא כפרתו and העריב שמשו אוכל בתרומה,
אוכל בקודשים).

טהר מלטמא בביאה והרי הוא מטמא כשרץ

And thus he became so clean that he no longer conveyed impurity by entering (a house), yet he still conveyed impurity like a creeping thing.[162]

During the second stage, starting with immersion on the seventh day, the leper is considered as a *ṭebul yom* ('one that had immersed himself on the self-same day', i.e. ritually pure), and may therefore eat of the second tithe:

טהר מלטמא כשרץ והרי הוא טבול יום

He became so clean that he no longer conveyed uncleanness like a creeping thing, but was become (like) one that had immersed himself the self-same day (ibid.).

In order to achieve even higher degrees of purity he must wait until after sunset (on the seventh day), and then bring his offerings on the eighth day:

העריב שמשו אוכל בתרומה הביא כפרתו אוכל בקדשים

After he had awaited sunset (on the seventh day) he could eat of the heave-offerings; and after he had brought his offerings of atonement (on the eighth day) he could eat of the hallowed things (ibid.).[163]

D.   The sectarian views, as presented by MMT, are at several points much more strict than those of the rabbis. MMT considered lepers as carrying the impurity of leprosy (טמאת נגע) until the very last stage of purification, which (in its view) came at sunset on the eighth day (see below):

[ואף בהיות לה[מ]ה ט[מ]אות נ[גע] אין להאכילם מהקו[ד]שים עד בוא השמש ביום השמיני

Moreover, since they (still) have the impurity of leprosy one should not let them (the lepers) eat from the sacred food until sunset on the eighth day (B 71–72).

E.   Before discussing the evidence in MMT, we present a passage from the Temple Scroll which illuminates MMT and is illuminated by it. 11QTᵃ 45:17–18 discusses the leper who enters Jerusalem and the Temple during his purification process. The text is fragmentary and ambiguous, but may be restored in the light of MMT as follows (the underlined text is that of the 11Q fragments: see Yadin, II, p. 189):

---

[162] The Mishna (ibid.) adds (in agreement with Lev 14:8 . . . וישב מחוץ לאהלו 'and he shall sit outside his tent . . .'): מנודה מביתו שבעת ימים ואסור בתשמיש המטה 'he was banished from his own house for seven days and he was not allowed to have sexual relations (with his wife)'. The rabbis took the word אהלו in the biblical verse as a metonym for 'wife' (אין אהלו אלא אשתו), and deduced that the leper is banned from having sexual relations with his wife (see *Sipra Meṣora*, ed. Weiss 71ᵇ [ed. Finkelstein, p. 293] and *b. Mo'ed Qat.* 15ᵇ). Some commentators (see Hagaon R. Eliyahu of Wilna on Mishna, *Sipra* and *b. Mo'ed Qatan*, ibid.) have maintained that the leper was also to be kept out of his house; not, however, because he had any additional degree of impurity, but because of the scriptural decree that he must be treated as a מנודה (cf. *Tiperet Yisrael* on the Mishna, ibid.).

[163] Thus after sunset on the seventh day he is almost completely pure; but before eating from the sacred food he must still bring certain offerings (כפרתו) and (according to the rabbis' decree) must, on the eighth day, undergo another immersion (see *m. Ḥag.* 3:3, and *b. Yebam.* 74ᵇ).

וכול צרוע ומנוגע לוא יבואו לה עד אשר יטהרו. וכאשר יטהר והקריב את [חטאתו יקרב אל
הטהרה בתוך עיר המקדש. ר]ק לוא יבוא אל המקדש [ולוא יואכל מן הקודשים. ובבוא השמש
ביום השמיני מן הקודשים יו[אכל ואל המקדש יבוא].

None afflicted with leprosy shall enter it (i.e. Jerusalem) until they are purified (on the seventh day). And when
he is purified and brings his purgation-offering he may have access to the purity within the Temple city. But he
shall not enter the sanctuary, nor eat of the sacrifices. And when the sun sets on the eighth day he may eat of the
sacrifices and enter the sanctuary.

This passage refers to Jerusalem, while MMT refers to other cities.[164] Milgrom has pointed out[165]
that 'whereas 11QT^a presumably will follow the Torah in allowing the healed leper to enter the
camp/city after the first day ablutions, it does not permit him to enter the Temple-city until the second
set of ablutions, on the seventh day'. In other cities, however, the lepers were quarantined until they
had reached that stage (see n. 170). Both sources agree that a healed leper may not eat of the sacred
food (nor enter the Temple) until sunset on the eighth day. He may, however, eat pure food at an
earlier stage, perhaps on the seventh day or perhaps (if our reconstruction of the text in the Temple
Scroll is correct) only after bringing his offering on the eighth day.[166]

F.   Let us now see what can be deduced from the damaged text of MMT (B 64–72) about the
various degrees of purity of the leper.

ואף על הצרועים א̇נ̇ח̇נו א[ומרים שלוא י]בואו עם טהרת הקודש כי בדד י[י]ה̇יו [מחוץ לבית]

(B 64–66).

The sense of this passage depends on our restoration of the last two words. Following Lev 13:46,
בדד ישב מחוץ למחנה מושבו, one could restore [מחוץ למחנה], and suggest that MMT contained no more
than a quotation. But if this was indeed the case, then why does the text use the polemic expression
אנחנו אומרים, instead of saying, for instance, . . . ועל הצרועים כתוב? It is possible that MMT interpreted
the biblical phrase מחנה מושבו as 'dwelling places' rather than 'the camp of his dwelling' (i.e. any city
in which the leper may live; cf. the uses of the word מושב in CD 12:22, 13:20).[167] If this is so, then
MMT is not merely quoting the biblical source, but is criticizing the opponents of the sect who did not
exclude lepers from every city. As is well known, the rabbis excluded lepers from those cities which

---

[164] For the restoration, cf. Lev 12:14: בכל קדש לא תגע ואל המקדש לא תבא. Note that 11QT^a 49:2–4 apparently
discussed the need to isolate the healed leper in the cities.

[165] *Studies* 1, p. 514.

[166] In any case, a distinction is made here between pure food (טהרה) and sacred food (קודשים; cf. § 5.3.2). 11QT^a
63:14–15 also makes such a distinction and requires a longer period of purification before allowing access to sacred food.
According to Milgrom (*Studies* 2, pp. 104–105), this passage also presents the scheme of seven and eight days of
purification. Here follows the text with Milgrom's translation: ולוא תגע לכה בטהרה עד שבע שנים וזבח שלמים לוא
תואכל עד יעבורו שבע שנים 'she [the captive woman] shall not touch your pure food seven years, and she may not eat of
the well-being offering until seven (full) years have elapsed'. Milgrom's translation can be improved: עד שבע שנים is
equivalent to עד השנה השביעית 'until the (beginning of) the seventh year' (see G. Haneman, 'On the Meaning of the
Phrase בן כך וכך שנים', *Studies in Hebrew and Semitic Languages Dedicated to the Memory of Professor E. Y. Kutscher*,
Ramat-Gan, 1980, pp. 103–109); יעבורו means 'are completed' (see H. Yalon, עבר שמשמעותו מלא, *Bulletin of Hebrew
Language Studies*, ed. H. Yalon, Jerusalem, 1963, pp. 42–44). Cf. 1QSa 1:8–10:

ובֹ[ן] עשרים שנ[ה] . . . ולוא י[קרב] א[ל] אשה . . . כיאם לפי מולואת לו עש[רי]ם̇ שנה.

And in his twentieth year . . . and he shall not [approach] a woman unless he has completed (his) twentieth year.

[167] This practice could also have been deduced from Num 5:3, where the form מחניהם may have been interpreted by
the sect as a plural denoting the cities of Israel. But in this biblical passage the word מחנה occurs twice in the singular, and
the sect interpreted it as referring to Jerusalem rather than to other cities. This is why the Temple Scroll (46:16–18; 48:14–
17) excluded corpses and those suffering from gonorrhea only from Jerusalem, and not from other cities (see Milgrom,
Studies 1, p. 516, contra Yadin).

had been walled since the days of Joshua, but not from other cities of lesser holiness.[168] This solution seems forced and hardly fits the continuation, which concerns the isolation of the healed leper.

The best solution is to restore [מחוץ לבית]. The passage is then no more than the heading to the polemic mentioned in the two lines that follow. The whole passage (ll. 64–68) states that lepers during the first stage of their purification (i.e. after their first shaving) are to be isolated inside cities, since they transmit defilement if they enter houses.[169] Here MMT is probably criticizing the practice of opponents who allow healed lepers to enter a house where sacred food (טהרת הקדש) is to be found.[170]

G. In ll. 68–70 there is a statement of a polemical nature beginning with the words ואתם יודעים. Only about half the text has been preserved. We have nevertheless been able to discover the biblical verses on which the passage is based, and thus to reconstruct it. We believe that נעלה ממנו should be compared to ונעלם ממנו in Lev 4:13-14, 5:1-4, and that the words בוזה ומגדף should be compared to גדף and בזה in Num 15:27-31 (we are indebted to Menachem Kister for this last suggestion). Thus the text should be restored as follows:

ואתם יודעים [שעל השוגג שלוא יעשה את המצוה] ונעלה ממנו להביא (ח) חטאת[171] וע[ל
העושה ביד רמה כת]וֹב שהוא בוזה ומגדף.

Here MMT draws the attention of the addressees to the fact that the opponents of the sect, in allowing the lepers to touch pure food before completing the last stage of their purification, are intentionally transgressing. In such a way they are despising God.

H. B 71–72 deals with the last stage of the purification process:

[ואף בהיות לה]מֹ[ה ט]מֹאוֹת נ[גע] אין להאכילם מהקו[ד]שים עד בוא השמש ביום השמיני

Moreover, while they (still) have the impurity of leprosy, one should not let them eat of the sacred food until sunset on the eighth day.

The Bible in Lev 14 mentions neither waiting for sunset on the eighth day nor immersion. The rabbis maintain that if the leper has made his purification offering, then he may eat of the hallowed things on the eighth day, without waiting for sunset (*m. Neg.* 14:3); but they rule that the leper must immerse himself if he is to be fit to eat of the hallowed things.[172] The ruling in MMT is in accordance with the ever more stringent approach characteristic of the sect in matters of ritual purity; they require that a sunset intervene even in cases where the Bible does not explicitly demand it. It is possible that they found support for this interpretation in the occurrence of the word וטהר 'and he shall be clean' (Lev 14:21) that occurs at the end of the description of the sacrifices to be performed by the leper on the eighth day. Menachem Kister has suggested that the sect deduced its view from Lev 22:4-8, where the

---

[168] *M. Kelim*, 1:7, and see the commentators. In contrast, according to 11QT[a] 48:14–15, lepers were banished from all cities.

[169] The LXX renders אהל in Lev 14:8 as οικου, i.e. בית (as it does in Num 19:14).

[170] According to 11QT[a] 46:16–18, all types of impure persons should be excluded from Jerusalem. This rule did not apply to other cities: 11QT[a] 48:14–17 implies that only lepers should be excluded from them; other impure persons need only be isolated in the city (see Milgrom, *Studies* 1, p. 516, contra Yadin). A striking parallel which confirms this interpretation and our restoration (מחוץ לבית) occurs in 4QTah[a] (= 4Q274)1 i 1–2: בדד לכול הטמאים ישב ורחוק מן הטהרה שתים עשרה אמה בדברו אליוֹ ומערב צפון לכול בית מושב ישב רחוק כמדה הזות. This text rules that healed lepers are to be isolated in the northwest part of each city; they may not mingle with other kinds of impure persons, nor may they have access to the pure food.

[171] It is unlikely that the word חטאת refers to the sin-offering of the leper, mentioned also in the Temple Scroll (Yadin, *TS*, II, pp. 194–195).

[172] *M. Ḥag.* 3:3.

Bible mentions both the purification of the leper and the eating of hallowed things after purification and sunset; but the reference there is to the eating of hallowed things by anyone who touches an impure person, and not by a leper (see the opinion of Yom Tov Lipman Heller, below).[173]

We noted above (§ 5.7.5) that Yom Tov Lipman Heller, in his commentary on *m. Para* 3:7, already postulated that the 'Sadducees', in conformity with their position on the purity of the red cow, ruled that a leper only became pure after sunset on the eighth day.

> ... ותמיהני שהרי נמצא בכתוב ג״כ שנקרא טהור כשלא העריב שמשו במצורע ורחץ את בשרו
> במים וטהר ... ואולי שבכולם מצריכים [הצדוקים] הערב שמש ולמדין מובא השמש וטהר

And this is surprising, since there are also verses in Scripture where a leper is termed clean even before sunset: 'he shall wash his flesh in water and then he shall be clean . . .' It is possible that the Sadducees ruled that waiting until after sunset is necessary in all cases, deriving this ruling from (the words) 'and the sun shall set and he shall be clean'.

In cases of severe impurity, the sect apparently demanded a purification period of seven (full) days before eating sacred food (see n. 166). Waiting until sunset on the eighth day ensures that seven days have been completed.

5.7.16 Human Bones

A.   ועל̇ [טמאת נפש] האדם אנחנו אומרים שכול עצם ש[היא חסרה] ושלמה כמשפט המת או
החלל הוֹא

And concerning the impurity of a dead person we are of the opinion that any quantity of human bone, whether it has flesh on it or not, should be treated according to the law of the corpse of someone who has died of natural causes or that of someone who has been killed (B 72–74).

The interpretation of this halakha depends on the restoration of the lacunae. According to the surviving wording of the passage it seems to refer to Num 19:16-18:

> וכל אשר יגע על פני השדה בחלל̇ חרב או במת או בעצם אדם או בקבר יטמא שבעת ימים ...

And whosoever in the open field touches one that is slain with the sword, or one that dies of himself, or a bone of a person, or a grave, shall be unclean seven days . . .

This passage occurs in the Temple Scroll with some variations:

> וכול איש אשר יגע על פני השדה בעצם אדם מת ובחלל̇ חרב או במת או בדם אדם מת או
> בקבר וטהר כחוק המשפט הזה

And whosoever in the open field touches the bone of a dead person or one that is slain with the sword or one that dies of himself or the blood of a dead person or a grave should be purified according to this ritual (11QTᵃ 50:4–6).

Yadin[174] notes that the added word 'dead' is directed against the rabbinic position, which regards the phrase 'or a bone of a person' as meaning a limb from a living person.

B.   What is the point being made in this passage? If we wish to maintain that the passage rules that bones from a living person do not defile, then we should read: שכול עצם ש[ל אדם מת] ושלמה ... 'that

---

[173] Cf. J. Milgrom, 'The Scriptural Foundations and the Deviations in the Laws of Purity of the Temple Scroll', *Archaeology and History*, p. 94.

[174] Yadin, *TS*, I, p. 258; cf. Baumgarten, *Controversies*, pp. 161–163.

every bone of a dead person and whole . . .' With this reading the halakha would depart from that of the rabbis in the direction of leniency,[175] which would be exceptional in MMT; it is not clear why the fact that the rabbis saw fit to add a prohibition should trouble the sect. Nor is it clear how the words שכול and ושלמה here connect to this subject. Moreover, the phrase נפש (ה)אדם can mean 'a corpse' (cf. Num 19:11, 13), so that the restored word מת would be superfluous.

Another possibility is to restore שכול עצם ש[היא שבורה] ושלמה, the word שבורה being in contrast to שלמה. This restoration could be supported by a polemic text of the Karaite Kirkisani: 'Then they claim that a person who touches a dead man's bone does not become unclean if it was broken; because of the expression או בעצם אדם "or a bone of a man" (Num 19:16). Woe unto him who said this. Do you see that he did not know that a piece of bone is bone, even if it be a splinter, just as the smallest piece of flesh is flesh?' (*Kitab al-anwar*, p. 20:9–11; we are indebted to R. Steiner for this reference). As far as we know, the view that Kirkisani attributes to the rabbis is not in fact theirs. We should therefore reject the above-mentioned restoration.

Consequently, the restoration ש[היא חסרה] seems best. According to this reading, the passage relates to the following point: according to the rabbinic halakha, a bone from a dead person transmits impurity, but only by contact and by being carried, not by overshadowing. It can defile by overshadowing only when there is a certain quantity of it and it has its 'proper flesh'. If it has no flesh on it, it does not transmit impurity at all (see *m. Ohal.* 2:1–3; but note the view of R. Neḥunia in *m. ʿEd.* 6:2–3).[176]

MMT (according to our reading) stipulates that any amount of bone, however small, no matter whether it has flesh on it or not, transmits impurity like a corpse or a slain person.

We conjecture that the sect deduced from Num 19:16-18 that a bone bears the same impurity as does the whole corpse. According to the sect's interpretation of this source, there would be no distinction between bones, the corpse and the slain. For a similar attitude toward the bones and the hide of a dead animal, see § 5.7.6.

5.7.17 The Ban on Marriage between Priests and Israelites

A.   The last halakha to have been preserved opens with the words ועל הזונות הנעסה בתוך העם 'And concerning the *znut*[177] that is performed among the people[178] . . .' (B 75). It apparently deals with the marriage between priests and Israelites, which is here called זנות 'illegal marriage' or 'marriage to outsiders'.[178a] The halakha goes on to say that Israel is holy and that just as it is forbidden to combine diverse kinds (כלאים) or mixed threads (שעטנז), so also is it forbidden to combine Israelites who are

---

[175] Baumgarten, *Controversies*, p. 161, n. 17.

[176] Note the expression חסר העצם in this source. See also *Sipre* on Numbers, sections 128–129 (Horowitz, pp. 165–166). For other rabbinic sources, see Sussmann, p. 32, n. 90.

[177] The word זנות in the Dead Sea Scrolls (see below) refers to all kinds of illegal marital acts, including (as here) forbidden marriages that fall under a ban analogous to that on 'diverse kinds'. See the discussion of *porneia* in J. A. Fitzmyer, 'The Matthean Divorce Texts and Some New Palestinian Evidence', *Theological Studies* 37 (1976), pp. 197–226, and note the similar use of the term נאוף in Karaite literature (N. Wieder, *The Judean Scrolls and Karaism*, London, 1962, p. 131, n. 2).

[178] I.e., Israel in the broader sense of the word, and not only the lay Israelites (though later the term 'the people' is used in the latter sense).

[178a] Our interpretation of the passage is mainly based on the restoration שמקצת הכהנים ו[העם מתערבים] at the end of l. 80. J. M. Baumgarten (personal communication) assumes that MMT refers to marriages of both priests and laymen with aliens. If this were the case, one would have to restore, e.g., מתערבים בגוים (rather than מתערבים) at the end of l. 80, while there is not enough space for such a restoration. On the other hand it is possible that more than one type of illegal marriage was included under the heading ועל הזונות הנעשה בתוך העם, namely that other types were mentioned in the lacuna after l. 82. In any case, the expression בתוך העם in the heading seems to refer to the people of Israel, and not to gentiles.

'holy' with priests who are 'most holy'[179] (קודש קודשים). At the end, it states (as far as we can tell from the damaged text) that some of the priests were at that time marrying Israelites, thereby contaminating their holy seed with women who are outsiders.

B.   The syntactic structure of this halakha is almost the same as that of the halakha about those forbidden to enter the congregation (§ 5.7.7); here, too, we find an alternating use of participles (denoting the actual practice) and infinitives (denoting the correct ordinance). Content (both halakhot deal with forbidden marriage) and phraseology (ערב, מתוככים, אתם יודעים שמקצת העם etc.) are also similar. This halakha, like the other, consists of four sections:

The first section begins with the opening formula (ועל הזונות) and with a participle (הנעסה) denoting the practice that is condemned (B 70–71). The second section consists of a sequence of sentences of the pattern (כתוב) x על + ואף + negated infinitive, comparing intermarriage with *kil'ayim* and *sha'atnez*. At the end of this section comes the argument (ש ... בגלל) (B 76–79). The third section opens with the words ואתם יודעים שמקצת הכהנים ו]העם, followed by participles describing the actual practice of the people (B 80–82). The last section, of which only כ]י remains, may have contained a concluding apodictic statement of the kind we find in B 43–44 and B 48–49.

C.   From where was this halakha derived? At first glance, it seems to have no basis in the Torah. But the wording of MMT ll. B 80–82 (טמא + זרע + בתוך העם) is reminiscent of Lev 21:15 (ולא יחלל זרעו בעמיו). Both passages refer to priests. The biblical passage (Lev 21:13-14) deals specifically with the high priest and states that he must take for his wife only a virgin from his own family (מעמיו), not a widow, a divorcee, a 'profaned' woman or a harlot. The traditional interpretation of the word מעמיו is 'from his own people', i.e. from the people of Israel. This interpretation is supported by the parallel law in Ezek 44:22 which has בתולה מזרע ישראל (instead of בתולה מעמיו).[180] But the use in Leviticus of the plural noun, 'his peoples', scarcely fits this interpretation. Consequently, מעמיו was understood by several early sources as 'from his own family', i.e., paternal kin (or tribe),[181] and the Samaritans even read מֵעַמּוֹ, interpreting it as 'from his household'.[182]

---

[179] At first sight, it might seem reasonable to suppose that this lengthy section (B 70–77) contained several distinct halakhot, including some on diverse kinds and on mixed threads. But what is here stated concerning *kil'ayim* and *sha'atnez* adds nothing to the laws of the Torah on these topics, and does not fit the heading זנות; moreover, the text proceeds to state 'because they are holy . . .', and it is clear that this assertion refers back to the people of Israel, who were mentioned some lines earlier, in the heading of the halakha on *znut*. It is clear that the laws on diverse kinds and mixed threads were mentioned here only as examples or by way of comparison: just as it is forbidden to mix these things, so also is it forbidden to mix Israelites (who are holy) and priests (who are 'holy of holy', i.e. 'most holy'). Such a comparison is found in the Damascus Covenant, in 4QD^f 1 i 9–10 (and 4QD^d [underlined]):

וגם אל יתנהֹ לאשר לוא הוכן לה כי [הוא כלאים ש]ור וחמור ולבוש צמר ופֹשתים יחדיו

And he (the father) may not marry her to someone who is not proper for her, because this is (like) mating an ox with an ass or wearing clothes made of (both) wool and flax.

Forbidden marriages are also compared with *kil'ayim* and *sha'atnez* in rabbinic and Karaite sources.

[180] D. Hoffmann, ספר ויקרא, 2, p. 69: Y. Kaufman, תולדות האמונה הישראלית, I, Jerusalem and Tel-Aviv, 1961, p. 63.

[181] For the sources (e.g., the LXX, Philo and Josephus) and the various opinions as to the meaning, see Geiger, *Studies*, pp. 131–136, with L. Ginzberg's objections, ibid., pp. 404–407. In addition to most of the studies mentioned in our discussion here, note the commentaries on Lev ad loc., and Revel p. 77, together with the references quoted by him. Cf. also Rashbam on Lev 21:4.

[182] See Geiger, ibid.; Z. Ben-Ḥayyim, *SHG*, p. 68. According to Benjamin of Tudela, Samaritan priests used to marry only the daughters of priests; see Geiger, ibid. and R. Kirchheim, כרמי שומרון, Frankfurt, 1852 (repr. Jerusalem, 1970), p. 19.

Even if the sectarians understood מעמיו as meaning 'from his own tribe (or family)',[183] it would still not be clear how our halakha on all priestly marriages could have been derived from Lev 21:14, which apparently dealt exclusively with the high priest. One might suggest that the sectarians extended this law from the high priest to other priests, either by claiming that every priest may become the high priest,[184] or by claiming that the sons of Zadok are descendents of the high priest, and should therefore follow the biblical laws directed to him.[185] (Note that the sect probably did not consider the high priest of its time to be legitimate.) These explanations are, however, somewhat speculative. It is more likely that the sectarians deduced this halakha from their understanding of the root זנה. It is possible that זונה in Leviticus was understood as a 'a female outsider'.[186] In both Lev 21:14 and 21:7, the word זונה can hardly mean 'harlot',[187] and it may well have been interpreted by the sect as a 'female outsider'. As Albeck has pointed out, this interpretation is especially plausible in Lev 21:14.[188]

D.   There is another biblical source which may have been taken as a basis for this ruling: 1 Chr 23:13, ויבדל אהרן להקדישו קדש קדשים הוא ובניו עד עולם. The sect may well have understood this verse as saying 'Aaron was set apart to be hallowed, he and his sons for ever as most holy'. They may have deduced from it that priests should be separated from the Israelites. Thus we read in 1QS 9:5–6:

בעת ההיאה יבדילו אנשי היחד בית קודש לאהרון להיחד קודש קודשים ובית יחד לישראל
ההולכים בתמים דרך ...

At that time the men of the community shall separate themselves as a house of holiness (consisting) of Aaron to participate (with the community) as most holy, and a house of community (consisting) of Israelites who walk in integrity ...

In 1QS 8:5ff, we find oppositional phrases similar to those of MMT:

בית קודש לישראל וסוד קודש קודשים לאהרון ...

A house of holiness[189] (consisting) of Israelites and a most holy congregation (consisting) of Aaron ...

The dependence of 1QS on 1 Chr 23:13 has already been noted by commentators on 1QS.[190] Now we are able to understand better the meaning and the implications of the term קודש קודשים (or קדושי קדושים), which refers in the DSS[191] to priests (or to angels).

---

[183] According to this interpretation, מעמיו 'from his tribe' is contrasted here with זונה 'a woman from another tribe', just as בתולה is with אלמנה וגרושה (see below).

[184] Cf. *m. Yebam.* 5:4 and *Keter Torah* on Lev 21:14:
יש מפרשים 'יקח אשה' שנכנס לכהונה גדולה אבל קודם לכך הדבר עובר ויש משיבים שהכהונה הגדולה משתלשלת
והראוי להיות כהן גדול יש לו להזהר ... ואמר לכהן הדיוט 'קדוש הוא לאלהיו' ונאמר לכהן גדול 'ולא יחלל זרעו בעמיו'.
אומרים בעלי הקבלה 'איש מזרעך' כולל בין כהן גדול בין כהן הדיוט.

[185] Geiger, *Studies*, p. 135.

[186] Cf. נפקת ברא in Aramaic, יוצאת חוץ in MH, and בראה, the *Samaritan Targum*'s equivalent for זונה. The Targumic *Tosepta* to Judg 11:1, as quoted in the commentary of Qimhi, ad loc., says that a woman who married a man from another tribe was called פונדקיתא (= זונה).

[187] See *b. Yebam.* 61ᵇ.

[188] The word זונה is used in this verse in opposition to מעמיו 'from his tribe', just as אלמנה וגרושה is used there in opposition to בתולה.

[189] בית קודש here is an equivalent of בית יחד in 1QS 9:6; note also: אנשי הקודש and אנשי היחד; עצת הקודש and עצת היחד.

[190] Wernberg-Møller, p. 125; Licht, p. 172.

[191] Cf. D. Flusser, 'The Dead Sea Sect and Pre-Pauline Christianity', *Scripta Hierosolymitana* 4, Jerusalem, 1958, p. 231.

E.   Are there rulings similar to ours in other sources? The most striking parallel occurs in the *Testament of Levi*, where Isaac addresses Levi:[192]

לקדמין היזדהר לך ברי מן כל פחז וטמאה ומן כל זנו(ת). ואנת אנת(ת)א מן משפחתי סב לך
ולא תחל זרעך עם זניאן ארי זרע קדיש אנת וקדיש זרעך

First of all, be on guard, my son, against all fornication and (sexual) impurity, and against all *znut*. And you, take to yourself a wife from my family, and do not defile[193] your seed with female outsiders, because you are holy seed and your seed is holy (34:14–21; Beyer, p. 117).

Here, as in MMT, one finds the word זנו(ת) (with the same special meaning), the expression 'defile seed with outsiders' (זניאן = זונות), and the combination זרע + קדש. Yet the passage from the *Testament of Levi* (unlike that of MMT) is a clear example of a ruling in favour of endogamy.

In rabbinic literature we find no exact parallel to our halakha. Yet some passages treat unfavourably marriages between priests and Israelite women:[194]

קנס קנסו חכמים בהן כדי שיהא אדם מדבק בשבטו ובמשפחתו

The rabbis have punished them so that everyone should marry with his own tribe and kinship (*Y. Ketub.* 1:5 and *Qidd.* 4:4 [= 66b]).[195]

11QT^a 57:15–19 rules that the king must marry a woman 'from the house of his father, from his own family'. This ruling is in opposition to the rabbinic position, as has been pointed out by Yadin.[196] Yadin recognized the similarity between the wording in the Temple Scroll, in the instructions of Abraham in Gen 24:37, and in the story of the daughters of Zelopeḥad (Num 36:6-8); he himself, however, maintained that the sect applied the law relating to the marriage of the high priest to the king. We prefer to make a distinction between those sources that deal with the older custom (one with explicit biblical precedent) of marrying within one's own family, and the laws of the high priest (see below). The law about the king's marriage in the Temple Scroll seems to belong to the first category.

F.   There is evidence that in the Second Temple period priests would marry only women from priestly families.[197] Several scholars, however, treated together the question of marriages between priests and Israelites and the custom, frequent in the Second Temple period, of marrying women from the same tribe (or family).[198] They adduce many attestations of this custom from early sources.[199] Ginzburg states explicitly that the laws concerning marriages between priests and Israelites were not

---

[192] Cf. J. M. Baumgarten, 'Halakhic Polemics in New Fragments from Qumrân Cave 4', *Biblical Archaeology Today*, *Proceedings of the International Congress on Biblical Archaeology*, Jerusalem, 1984, pp. 392–395.

[193] M. Kister has directed our attention to a similar interpretation of חלל in *Sipra Qod.* 7 (Finkelstein's facsimile edition, p. 406): ‎אל תחלל את בתך יכול לא יתננה ללוי ולא יתננה לישראל?‎ . . . .

[194] Cf. A. Büchler, הכוהנים ועבודתם, Jerusalem, 1966, pp. 67–68. Büchler states that intermarriage among priestly families was the custom during the Second Temple period. Cf. also D. Flusser in the newspaper הארץ, August 23, 1985, pp. 16–17.

[195] L. Ginzberg, ad loc., added that Origen in his commentary on the Pentateuch (Num 27:11) mentions this view as having been transmitted by his Jewish teachers.

[196] ‎ובורר לו נשים מכל מקום שירצה כהנות לויות וישראליות‎ (*t. Sanh.* 4:2; cf. Yadin, *TS*, I, pp. 354–355).

[197] Geiger, ibid., p. 134.

[198] e.g., Y. Grintz, פרקים בתולדות בית שני, Jerusalem, 1969, pp. 54–55 (see the references there); Ḥ. Albeck, ‎תורה שבעל פה‎', הנישואים בימים קדומים‎ 3 (1961), pp. 9–16; Yadin, *TS*, I, pp. 353–355; Revel, p. 77 (and the references there); P. Segal, 'The "Divine Death Penalty" in Hatra Inscriptions and the Mishna', *JJS* 40 (1989), p. 51, n. 27.

[199] To those adduced by others (e.g. Tob. 1:9, 4:12) we add *Tg. Ruth* 3:10.

based on the special holiness of the high priest, but on the custom of marriage within the family.[200] MMT proves, however, that at an early date the ban on marriage between priests and Israelites was based on the special holiness of the priests. This sheds new light on the whole problem. The various sources, both those that mention marriages between priests and Israelites and those involving the custom of marrying women from the same tribe or family, need further study in the light of MMT.

5.8 MMT and the History of Early Halakha

5.8.1 The Tripartite Division in Judaism

As is well known, the Jews in the Second Temple period were divided over questions of halakha. Josephus tells us that there were three groups among the Jews. This is confirmed by *pNah*, where the names אפרים, יהודה and מנשה refer to the Dead Sea sect, the Pharisees and the Sadducees respectively.[201] Further groups, such as בית פלג and בית אבשלום, are mentioned in the DSS, but they should be classified as sub-groups of the עם הארץ, referred to there as פתאי אפרים and פתאי יהודה.

There are also three groups in MMT: the group of the author, referred to by the first person plural in the phrase 'we decide' (henceforth the 'we' group); the group of the addressee, referred to by the second person singular in the phrase 'you know' (henceforth the 'you' group); and the group referred to by the third person plural in the phrase 'they are doing' (henceforth the 'they' group; see §§ 4.2.2–4.2.4).[201a]

5.8.2 Identification of the Groups in MMT

The 'we' group is clearly the Dead Sea sect. This is evident not only from the fact that the manuscripts of MMT were found at Qumran (and not elsewhere), but also from the agreement that exists between the halakhic views of the author and those found in the other DSS (see §§ 5.4, 5.7.4, 5.7.6, 5.7.8, 5.7.9, 5.7.13, 5.7.14, 5.7.15, 5.7.16). The sectarian calendar in MMT also points to the same conclusion.

The identity of the 'you' group may be established from the Epilogue, in which the addressee is referred to as a leader of Israel. It appears that he was one of the Hasmonean kings. The pPs 37 indicates that the addressee may have been the famous Wicked Priest. We read there that the Wicked Priest tried to kill the Teacher of Righteousness because of a halakhic text which the latter had sent him. It appears that this text was MMT (see § 4.2.7.1).

The 'they' group is the Pharisees. This is evident from the similarity between the halakha of the opponents of the sect and rabbinic halakha: the 'they' group must have been the predecessors of the rabbis, namely the Pharisees.

5.8.3 The Reasons for the Schism

From MMT we learn the reasons for the schism; up to now we have had no explicit evidence on this subject. Josephus[202] gives the impression that the sects were primarily divided over theological questions, for instance those relating to the resurrection of the dead or the role of Divine Providence. He was concerned to produce an explanation that would make sense to his Greek (and Roman) readers. But the fact that only matters of practice are mentioned in MMT confirms the view that it

---

[200] Ibid., p. 405.

[201] D. Flusser, 'Pharisees, Sadducees and Essenes in Pesher Naḥum', G. *Alon Memorial Volume*, Jerusalem, 1970, pp. 133–168 (Hebrew).

[201a] Note the somewhat different use of the personal pronouns in 1QH^a 2:28–29 and elsewhere in this scroll.

[202] *Ant.* XIII 171–173; XVIII 2–17.

was not dogma, but law that was apt to produce lasting schisms in Judaism.[203] It can be seen once again how important the laws of purity were to all parties of that period.

5.8.4   Controversial Halakhot

MMT contains the largest surviving corpus of early controversial halakhot, though such halakhot also appear in other sources, both sectarian and rabbinic. It has already been noted that two[204] of the halakhic views which the Mishna explicitly ascribes to the Sadducees occur in MMT.[205] There are also cases where a custom explicitly ascribed to other sectarians in rabbinic sources resembles a law known from the DSS or from the evidence on the customs of the Essenes in Greek sources,[206] and other cases where the rabbinic sources refer implicitly to sectarian practices known from MMT or other DSS.[207] Similarly, there are, in the DSS, implicit references to the halakha of the Pharisees.

5.8.5   The Sectarians in Rabbinic Sources

The rabbis refer to their opponents by a number of names, among them צדוקים and בית סין. There are many difficulties in correlating the sects referred to by these names with the sects described by Josephus and other Greek authors. Furthermore, the various Hebrew sources sometimes contradict each other. It is, at any rate, clear that while the halakhic polemic in MMT and in the other DSS sources is directed only against the Pharisees, the rabbinic sources are concerned with a number of different sects.

The cornerstone of all research in this area must be the fact that the halakhic views ascribed to the Sadducees and other sectarians in the rabbinic texts often agree with those of the Dead Sea sect. In such cases, it seems that the rabbis are either referring to the Dead Sea sect itself, or to other sects that shared its extreme halakhic views. In other instances, however, the rabbis refer to the views of other sects.

Any attempt to identify the sectarians mentioned in the rabbinic literature must take the following considerations into account:

A.   A given sectarian practice mentioned by the rabbis may not be confined to a single heretical group. This is obviously the case as regards the law concerning the red cow: according to the Hebrew sources it was the custom both of the Sadducean priests in the Temple and of the Dead Sea sect to wait until sunset before performing the ritual of preparing the ashes or using the water of purification.

B.   The rabbis and their predecessors knew of the practices of a number of heretical groups, including the Dead Sea sect. But they were not concerned precisely to identify each group; they were interested only in halakhic practices. This explains the existence of inconsistencies in the rabbinic texts.

---

[203] Ginzberg, p. 105; Revel, p. 3 (citing Geiger). Revel adds: 'This is particularly true of the Karaites who differ in nothing but religious practices from the rest of Israel'.

[204] Or maybe three; see § 5.7.6b.

[205] Baumgarten, *Controversies*.

[206] Lieberman, *Texts and Studies*, pp. 190–199; Baumgarten, *Controversies*; Baumgarten, *Polemics*; A. Sofer 'מפני 'תרעומתן של מינים, *Sinai* 99 (1986), pp. 38–47; Y. Erder, 'The First Date in *Megilat Taʾanit* in Light of the Karaite Commentary on the Tabernacle Dedication', *JQR* 82 (1992), pp. 263–283.

[207] Ibid.

5.8.6 Early Rabbinic Halakha

MMT's contribution to our knowledge of the history and character of the halakha of the various groups in this period is of the highest importance. The conformity of the halakha of the 'they' group with rabbinic halakha proves that the 'they' group was the predecessor of the rabbis, hence probably of the Pharisees.[208] It further shows that the rabbinic halakha concerning those topics discussed by MMT was established at a very early date, thereby disproving Geiger's theory that the Pharisaic halakha represents a 'new halakha'. The Pharisaic halakha, in fact, contains both old and new rulings; on some occasions its roots are very old,[209] dating back to the time of the Teacher of Righteousness. Unfortunately, we have no evidence concerning the halakha of the period between Ezra and the Teacher of Righteousness, but it stands to reason that the stabilization of rabbinic halakha as regards the topics discussed in MMT took place at the time of the Teacher of Righteousness, and that the polemics with the sectarians contributed much to rabbinic halakha. Only a few traces of the old polemics have so far been found, but now that scholars are aware of the significance of these polemics for the establishment of early rabbinic halakha, it may be that more will be uncovered.

ELISHA QIMRON

---

[208] The same picture emerges from other DSS. In all cases where we find an explicit reference to the practices of the opponents, these practices conform with those of the rabbis. Thus, in CD, the opponents of the sect are accused of permitting polygamy (4:20–5:5) and marriage between uncle and niece (5:7–8); the accusation of having intercourse with menstruants (5:7) is not specified. In 4Q513 3–4, the opponents are accused of harvesting the ʿOmer on Sabbath (see Baumgarten, *Controversies*).

[209] This is confirmed by other considerations, among them being: (*a*) The tradition concerning the oral transmission of halakhot is very old (Baumgarten, *Studies*, pp. 13–35); (*b*) Many halakhic terms which were hitherto considered characteristic of rabbinic literature actually occur already in the DSS (see Qimron, *Terms*).

APPENDIX 1

THE HISTORY OF THE HALAKHA AND THE DEAD SEA SCROLLS
PRELIMINARY TALMUDIC OBSERVATIONS ON
MIQṢAT MAʿAŚE HA-TORAH (4QMMT)[1]

THE study of the halakha in the writings of the Dead Sea sect preceded the discovery of the scrolls themselves by some forty years, beginning with the discovery and publication of a few worn-out folios of an ancient sectarian work from the Cairo Geniza approximately eighty years ago. The noted scholar Solomon Schechter, who salvaged the remains of the Geniza for future generations, discovered ten folios from a hitherto unknown work. He immediately grasped the significance of these fragments, which he identified with extraordinary acumen and intuition as the remnants of a sectarian document from the Second Temple period, and published under the title 'Fragments of a Zadokite Work',[2] a work later to be known as the Damascus Covenant. The entire second part of this document deals with matters of a halakhic nature, which were discussed at length by Schechter, and shortly thereafter by most other members of the scholarly community. Thus, paradoxically enough, while investigation of the halakha of the Dead Sea sect preceded the discovery of the scrolls by some forty years, halakhic inquiry has been the most neglected area in DSS research during the past forty years, ever since the sensational discovery of the sect's prolific writings in their original form.

A proper appreciation of this situation calls for a brief survey of the history of scholarly research on the ancient, pre-mishnaic halakha, taking us back another eighty years, to the first half of the nineteenth century.

[1]

One of the prime goals set for itself by the *Wissenschaft des Judentums* in its initial stages was the study of the history and development of the halakha—the attempt to reveal the process of the evolution and development of the halakha, and bridge the wide gap in Jewish history between Bible and Mishna. One stands awed by the remarkable phenomenon of a fully developed halakhic system, governing all aspects of life and crystallised to its most minute details, which emerges fully formed in the classical halakhic literature of the Tannaim. How did all this evolve? What were the stages of its development? What changes did the halakha undergo from biblical times up to its final consolidation in Tannaitic literature? The great pioneers of the *Wissenschaft des Judentums* sought to fill this huge void, which extends over most of the Second Temple period, some proceeding forward from the Bible (e.g., A. Geiger), while others turned backward from rabbinic literature (e.g., Z. Frankel).

---

[1] Originally read at a symposium on 'Forty Years of Qumran Research', held at the Hebrew University of Jerusalem in June 1987. The text is reproduced here in translation, with selected footnotes; extensive documentation appears in the Hebrew version (*Tarbiz* 59 [1989–1990], pp. 11–76). I wish to thank Dr. L. Moscovitz for preparing this English version, and Dr. B. M. Lerner for his meticulous reading of the translation.

[2] *Documents of Jewish Sectaries*, I, Cambridge, 1910 (henceforth: Schechter).

From the forties to the sixties of the previous century, many bold steps were taken in this direction, which were considered the cornerstones for an understanding of Pharisaic-rabbinic Judaism at the time. In Geiger's words, in one of his last studies on this subject: 'Such research into the early halakha is extremely profound and most important; no other inquiry into the history of the Jewish religion and its sages can compare with it'.[3] The problems facing these scholars were immense, foremost among them being the nature of the sources: the material then available was either tangential (the Apocrypha and Pseudepigrapha, Philo, Josephus, the New Testament, the ancient biblical versions, etc.)—works which were not primarily concerned with the halakha, and whose provenience and ideological stance are not clear to us; or relatively late sources (i.e., rabbinic literature), whose traditions and historical information are unverified, and which present a one-sided position. These scholars offered interesting proposals, keen suggestions and bold hypotheses, but they often indulged in far-fetched conjecture. Nor was their research free of contemporary *Tendenzen*, and there was no lack of explicit declarations along these lines. Geiger, the great opponent of contemporary Orthodox halakha, conscripted his research into the history of the ancient halakha, with all his brilliance and learning, toward furthering his ideological goals.

Indeed, these two problems—the lack of reliable sources, for which brilliant yet unfounded conjectures substituted, and the extremely radical approaches characteristic of earlier scholarship—led to decline and regression among both Orthodox and progressive scholars. Despite the remarkable accomplishments of these pioneers, their efforts were not fortunate enough to be continued by worthy successors. Thus, Frankel and his students directed their inquiries to other areas of research, less sensitive but more well-grounded: the historical and philological study of rabbinic literature. Not the history of the halakha, but the discovery of earlier strata of halakhic literature; no longer the early halakha, but rather the early Mishna—the remnants of ancient *mishnayot* in the Mishna of the later Tannaim—became the subject of inquiry. These goals, though perhaps more modest, stood on much more solid ground. This approach dominated scholarship almost up to the present generation. In the words of J. N. Epstein, in his introduction to mishnaic source-criticism:[4] 'Here we stand on firm and solid ground'—'here', of course, referring to the study of the literary sources of the Mishna. Similarly, Epstein declared at the beginning of his introduction to Tannaitic literature: 'This introduction deals with the Mishna as a literary work (!) and with the history of its sources'.[5] In his quest for information about collections of ancient halakhot stemming from the period before the destruction of the temple, Epstein found himself compelled to rely, *inter alia*, on traditions cited by fourth-century Church Fathers (Epiphanius and Jerome), who mentioned the *deuterosis* of the Hasmoneans and of Hillel and Shammai. Just one generation ago, who would have even imagined that remnants of a halakhic work from that very period—the era of the Hasmoneans and the *zugot*—would ever reach us in their original form?

Schechter's previously-mentioned discoveries from the Cairo Geniza aroused great hopes and renewed interest in the history of the halakha in the beginning of this century. As indicated above, Schechter identified several folios from the myriad tattered Geniza fragments as the remains of a sectarian work from the Second Temple period. As far back as 1902, he hinted, with considerable hesitation, that a great find—on the order of his discovery of the Hebrew original of fragments of Ben Sira—had once again fallen his way.[6] Schechter toiled over the analysis and publication of these fragments while he was still in Cambridge. However, the work appeared only in 1910, years after

---

[3] A. Geiger, '*Ha-Halakah Ha-Qedumah*', *Ozar Neḥmad* 3 (1860), p. 127.

[4] J. N. Epstein, '*Mevoʾot Le-Sifrut Ha-Tannaʾim*', Jerusalem and Tel-Aviv, 1957, p. 459.

[5] Ibid., p. 13.

[6] See A. S. Oko, *S. Schechter—A Bibliography*, Cambridge, 1938, p. 61; *Letters of S. Z. Schechter to S. A. Poznanski*, ed. A. Yaʿari, Jerusalem, 1944; Hebrew; (henceforth: *Letters to Poznanski*), p. 14.

Schechter had left for the United States, where he was occupied primarily with academic and public affairs. Schechter held great hopes for these fragments, and in a letter to Poznanski (September 1910), he claimed that they were 'the most momentous discovery restored to us by the Geniza'.[7] Indeed, these fragments, which were later to become known as the Damascus Covenant, occupied Schechter for many years.

Schechter's introduction to the fragments was extremely brief (approximately twenty pages), yet today, eighty years later, it is amazing to note how accurately he perceived the significance of this material, at a time when only these few fragments were available, in a late (eleventh-twelfth century) and corrupt copy, when no one ever dreamed of finding original literary discoveries from the Second Temple period. Indeed, Schechter's bold breakthrough was met by considerable misgivings. It is well worth returning to these few pages in order to realise how contemporary scholars, armed with dozens of original works from the sect, continue to hash out endless studies which merely repeat the same fundamental points already grasped by Schechter—viz., that these fragments comprise a sectarian work composed in Second Temple times and stemming from an anti-Pharisaic group, which resembled the circle of the author of the book of *Jubilees*, on the one hand, and the Sadducees, on the other. Moreover, Schechter maintained that the remnants of anti-sectarian polemic found in rabbinic literature were directed against the halakhic views and philosophical outlook of this sect. Schechter also assumed that fragments of these works reached the early Karaites, whose halakhot reveal considerable similarity to those of the sect. In a brief note, Schechter also alluded to the importance of the few fragments at his disposal for research on the history of the halakha in general: 'It need hardly be pointed out that there are both in the Hagada and in the Halakha of our Sect features which strikingly recall the famous hypothesis of Geiger regarding the Sadducees and the Old Halakha'.[8] Similarly, in another letter to Poznanski: 'I alluded to this find in a very brief note, because I intend, God willing, to devote a special study to the early halakha, a subject which has not yet been clarified',[9] although this special study unfortunately never materialised.

The publication of Schechter's work immediately aroused a great sensation, and the following six years (1910–1916) witnessed the appearance of numerous studies which dealt with the fragments from different perspectives. Some of these studies were authored by scholars of halakha and rabbinic literature (e.g., L. Ginzberg, W. Bacher, L. Blau, A. Büchler, H. P. Chajes, A. Marmorstein), and others by biblical scholars and students of the Apocrypha, Pseudepigrapha, and early Christianity (e.g., E. Meyer, W. Bousset, H. Gressmann, R. Eisler, G. F. Moore). However, with the intensification of hostilities during World War I and Schechter's demise (in 1915), interest in the fragments gradually died out. And since Charles included the 'Fragments' in his great edition of the Apocrypha and Pseudepigrapha, the work has been discussed primarily in this context.

Subsequently, most prominent scholars of halakhic literature refrained from discussing the work for its own sake, and it failed to generate renewed interest in the study of the history of the halakha in general. This is not surprising, since many leading scholars questioned the very assumption that these were fragments of an ancient work from Second Temple times, while others challenged Schechter's identification of the fragments (e.g., Büchler, who considered them a Karaitic work, or Ginzberg, who identified them, of all things, as a Pharisaic document!). Since these scholars possessed only a fragmentary and late copy, undoubtedly marred by scribal errors (and perhaps by later additions as well), students of rabbinic literature seem to have abandoned the investigation of the work for its own sake. From here on, to the extent that such scholars engaged in any research on the history of the

---

[7] *Letters to Poznanski*, p. 48.

[8] Schechter, p. xxi, n. 35.

[9] *Letters to Poznanski*, p. 48.

early halakha, they dealt with the Damascus Covenant only in passing—e.g., Albeck, in his important study of the halakha in *Jubilees*.[10]

In any event, Schechter's great expectations were already frustrated during his lifetime, and he felt that only new discoveries could rectify the situation. As a result of the criticism leveled at him from different directions, Schechter wrote: 'I have no intention of arguing now until the matter becomes clearer. In general I must say that [scholars] . . . have been arguing about the matter as if "the opposite must be correct" . . . in any case, Heaven forbid that I grow angry at those who take issue with me. Let us hope that new folios will be discovered, even if they disprove my conjectures, so that the truth may be established conclusively'.[11] Schechter was referring, of course, to the discovery of additional fragments from *the* Geniza, for who would have ever imagined that not only would additional individual folios (and not just other late copies) be discovered, but numerous, diverse works in original copies from the Second Temple period, including the Damascus Covenant itself! Indeed, these new discoveries enable us to 'conclusively establish the truth'; and I dare say that not only do they fail to 'disprove' Schechter's 'conjectures', but they actually confirm his suggestions in general terms.

The great surprise came forty years ago, with the sensational discovery of the Dead Sea scrolls. Indeed, very soon after the discovery of the scrolls in the Judean Desert, the close connexion between the new documents and the folios which Schechter had found in the Geniza became clear. E. L. Sukenik described his initial attempts to identify the scrolls as follows:[12] 'I showed the new scrolls to two of my colleagues in the Hebrew University'. One of these was apparently Ḥ. Albeck (who wrote in his introduction to the Mishna: 'After Prof. Sukenik had purchased some of the scrolls . . . he asked me whether I noticed any similarity between them and other ancient works [viz., to verify that the scrolls were not forgeries], and I immediately answered in the affirmative: "The Damascus Covenant!"')[13] Indeed, as far back as his first publication,[14] Prof. Sukenik prepared a short list of parallel terms and phrases in the newly-discovered scrolls and the Damascus Covenant. The connexions between these documents became increasingly clear, and were already summarised by H. H. Rowley in 1952, in his study of the Damascus Covenant.[15] At about the same time, the existence of the first fragments of the Damascus Covenant among the Dead Sea scrolls became known. As far back as 1957, J. Milik[16] alluded to fragments of different copies of the Damascus Covenant, which paralleled and supplemented Schechter's fragments, as well as some entirely new fragments, some of which contained new and important halakhic material. Scholars gradually became aware of other halakhic fragments among the sect's writings, including fragments possibly deriving from the Damascus Covenant (and perhaps other works). However, none of these discoveries led to a renewed awakening of research into the history of the early halakha. To be sure, immediately after the publication of the first scrolls, the illustrious talmudic scholar S. Lieberman published two important articles demonstrating how the scrolls and rabbinic literature complement and illuminate each other,[17] but these initial steps (and others) were not followed by serious endeavours, especially insofar as research on the history of the halakha was concerned.

---

[10] Ḥ. Albeck, *Das Buch der Jubiläen und die Halacha*, Berlin, 1930.

[11] *Letters to Poznanski* , p. 50.

[12] E. L. Sukenik, *Ha-Megillot Ha-Genuzot, Seqirah Sheniyyah*, Jerusalem, 1950, p. 14.

[13] Ḥ. Albeck, *Mavo La-Mishnah*, p. 15, n. 44.

[14] E. L. Sukenik, *Megillot Genuzot—Seqirah Rishonah*, Jerusalem, 1948, p. 21.

[15] H. Rowley, *The Zadokite Fragments and the Dead Sea Scrolls*, Oxford, 1952.

[16] J. Milik, *Ten Years of Discovery in the Wilderness of Judea*, trans. J. Strugnell, London, 1959, p. 151.

[17] S. Lieberman, 'Light on the Cave Scrolls from Rabbinic Sources', *PAAJR* 20 (1951), pp. 395 ff; 'The Discipline in the So-Called Dead Sea Manual of Discipline', *JBL* 71 (1951), pp. 199 ff.

At the same time (the early 1950s), F. Baer published his essay on 'The Historical Foundations of the Halakhah',[18] which called for a renewed examination of the foundations and development of the halakha during the Second Temple period. This article, and a series of additional studies by Baer which followed in its wake,[19] appeared shortly after the sensational discovery of the Dead Sea scrolls; these studies were not written directly in connection with the scrolls, although they were not totally divorced from them either (just as they could not be divorced from the dramatic events of those days; in Baer's own words, we must seek to understand 'the approach of those ancient pietists who established the foundations of talmudic and rabbinic Judaism, Christianity, and European culture, and ultimately all of our history in the Diaspora, on the basis of which we could have renewed our [national] existence even now, if only we were worthy of it . . .'[20]). However, Baer arrived at greatly exaggerated conclusions in these studies, in line with his general historical approach and his deep faith in the unity of Jewish history from the time of the 'ancient pietists' of the Second Temple period up to the days of the medieval German pietists, and he attributed the historical and halakhic realia of the scrolls to other periods and groups, as is well known.[21] In any event, it should be noted that these inspired studies failed to encourage additional research into the history of the halakha in direct connection with the documents of the Judean Desert.

However, it was primarily the manner in which the halakhic material was published and the way it was handled which discouraged scholars. Rumors of different finds and hopes for additional discoveries caused scholars to delay any serious study of the sect's halakha *per se* until publication of the finds, and these were late in coming. A considerable number of the fragments of the halakhic works have not been published at all, and a critical edition of the most important halakhic work—the Damascus Covenant—based on the fragments of the Dead Sea scrolls remains a desideratum. Aside from various rumors, some encouraging and others discouraging, it was not at all clear what material was available and what could be expected. Nevertheless, two lengthy works of prime importance—the Manual of Discipline and the Temple Scroll—are exceptions to the rule. Indeed, the scholarly community is greatly indebted to the editors of these works, who dealt, *inter alia*, with the halakhic aspects of this material—first and foremost, Y. Yadin and J. Licht. Even though these scholars did not specialise in the field of halakha, they nevertheless devoted serious efforts to the clarification of the halakha in the documents which they edited, and made significant contributions to an understanding of the halakha in both scrolls. However, the halakha of these works is unique, and this point must be taken into consideration in any discussion of the subject: this halakha is either particularistic, viz., an internal halakha, regulating life within the community (in the Manual of Discipline), or a quasi-utopian halakha (in the Temple Scroll). It is quite clear that these works also include numerous details relating to halakhot of a general nature, as well as fundamental halakhic principles, which accurately reflect the sect's halakhic milieu. Nevertheless, these treatises cannot be considered halakhic tracts in the usual, broad sense of the term.

As for the remnants of other halakhic works (and we are dealing only with fragments here)— works dealing neither with the Bible, biblical interpretation, or the unique milieu of the sect, works which are strictly halakhic in nature—works of this sort have not yet been published, with the exception of scant fragments. The reasons for this situation are numerous—first and foremost, because the extant material is generally highly fragmentary, so that any discussion of it, not to mention its reconstruction and publication, are highly problematic. Secondly, most of the scholars

---

[18] *Zion* 17 (1951), pp. 1 ff (Hebrew).

[19] See H. Beinart, 'The Writings of Prof. I. F. Baer (A Bibliographical List)', *Zion* 44 (1979), p. 333 (Hebrew).

[20] Baer, see above, n. 18.

[21] See E. E. Urbach, '*Yemei Ha-Bayit Ha-Sheni Utequfat Ha-Mishnah Be-ʿEinei Yizhaq Baer*', *Proceedings of the Israel Academy of Sciences and Humanities*, 6 (1984), pp. 59–82.

who were assigned these fragments for study and publication were far-removed from the field of halakhic inquiry. But aside from these objective considerations, I believe that this material caused a certain confusion, perhaps even disappointment, to scholars. Initially, there were great expectations that the writings of the sect would reveal its members to be the precursors of a spiritualistic, evolving, antinomian religion stressing vision and spirit, not the meticulous observance of religious commandments. Gradually, though, it became clear that the members of the sect meticulously observed the Torah's precepts, minor and major, and fought zealously for the supremacy of the halakha in all its minute details, according to their own interpretation. Examination of the specific contentions of the sect's members against their opponents reveals that the members of the sect held that their adversaries 'violated the law' (CD 1:20) and 'did not observe the precepts of God' (CD 2:18), 'doing as they wished and not observing the commandments of their Creator' (CD 2:20–21). And observance of these precepts meant observance according to the understanding of the sect, following the interpretation of the Teacher of Righteousness. Only *they* fulfilled the commandments 'according to its [correct] interpretation' and 'according to the precepts of the members of the new covenant' (CD 6:18–19), whereas the others 'overstepped the bounds set by the ancients' (CD 1:16). This is the essence of the dispute between 'all who overstepped the bounds of the Law' (CD 2, 20:25) and 'all who observe these laws, coming and going according to the Torah, and listening to the voice of the Teacher' (ibid. 27), who demand that their fellows 'act according to the [correct] interpretation of the law' and 'according to the precepts of the members of the new covenant' (CD 6:14, 19), 'acting zealously for the law' (1QS 9:23).

Indeed, it is no coincidence that the halakhic compositions—the Manual of Discipline, the Damascus Covenant, and the new scroll, which I shall discuss at some length below—are the most frequently encountered of the sect's extant writings, and fragments of numerous copies of these works have been unearthed. From what has been published (or alluded to) to date, it is clear that fragments of approximately *twelve* different copies of the Damascus Covenant are extant, among them numerous halakhic fragments. It is also clear that the entire structure of the work—particularly the second section, viz., the halakhic material—is in need of revision and rearrangement. In any event, in light of this situation, it is not at all surprising that scholars have avoided re-examining and re-analysing the specific halakhot of the sect before the publication of this material in its entirety.

The most vivid impression arising from a study of all these works, as well as the additional, presently unpublished halakhic material (which I have had the opportunity to glimpse at briefly)— material so fragmentary that it is doubtful whether it will be possible to extract anything of value from it—is their remarkable resemblance to the halakhic world of the talmudic rabbis: we find similarities of language, terminology, halakhic particulars, and the entire conceptual scheme. Some of the parallel terms were already noted by Schechter,[22] who was followed by others, but as Lieberman wrote in connection with the Damascus Covenant: 'This document abounds in good Hebrew words and expressions which occur in Rabbinic literature in greater number than all editors of it were aware of'.[23] This similarity is even more pronounced in the new material, and it is especially prominent in the new scroll (MMT), which contains concepts, terms, and expressions that are surprisingly, and at times astonishingly close to the world of the Tannaim. The publication of MMT was originally entrusted to the devoted care of J. Strugnell and E. Qimron, who requested me several years ago to examine the numerous halakhic rulings in this scroll; in the course of doing so, I had occasion to consider the halakha of the sect in general, and the position of these rulings within the framework of the rabbinic world.

---

[22] Schechter, p. xi and *passim*.
[23] S. Lieberman, *Greek in Jewish Palestine*, New York, 1941, p. 135 n. 151.

[2]

The scroll itself is not particularly long—the original work apparently contained some 150 lines, of which approximately 120 have been reconstructed (for the sake of comparison, the Temple Scroll contains over one thousand lines). This composition reached us in highly fragmentary form, and has been skillfully reconstructed by professors J. Strugnell and E. Qimron from countless minute bits and pieces belonging to six different copies of the work, some on parchment and others on papyrus. It may thus be assumed that the main part of the work is now in our hands. The entire opening section is missing, and there are quite a few lacunae later on, but the work itself—its aim, significance and the remnants of most of its paragraphs are quite clear. This scroll will undoubtedly stand in the centre of all future discussion of the halakha and identity of the sect and the history of the halakha in general. When Prof. Strugnell requested me several years ago (1982) to advise him regarding the halakhic matters in the scroll, I was astonished by its similarity to and affinity with rabbinic literature—I must admit that I initially entertained certain doubts as to whether this work was later than the halakhic literature of the Tannaim—but the reasons for this similarity soon became clear to me. Many years have passed, and bits and pieces of information, as well as unfounded theories—some in my name and others not—have been circulating, and I would therefore like to present an accurate summary of the evidence and the matters under discussion as I understand them.

This is a polemical document about halakhic matters. The author appeals to his opponents and attempts to persuade them to accept his views regarding specific halakhot. The work is written as a personal epistle—apparently, from one of the leaders of the sect to a leader of the opposing group[24]—and is couched in relatively mild language. The introduction to the work is missing—and thus it is unclear who is addressing whom, why, and on what occasion—but from the conclusion it is clear that the author still hopes to persuade his audience. He appeals to them 'for your own benefit and for the benefit of your people', and once again: 'It shall be accounted to you as righteousness when you do the upright and good before Him—for your benefit and for the benefit of Israel' (C 27–32), because 'we recognise that some of the blessings and curses written in the book of Moses have befallen us', and 'this is the end of days when [the people of] Israel shall repent' (C 20–21). Therefore, 'we have written to you . . . for we thought that it was for your benefit and for the benefit of your people, as we have seen your cleverness and knowledge of the Law; understand all this, and request of Him that He refine your wisdom and keep your evil thought and wicked counsel asunder from you, that you may rejoice at the end of time' (C 26–30).

From the extant material, it would appear that the work originally included an introduction and a personal appeal (which have not survived); these were followed by a calendar enumerating the Sabbaths and festivals of the year in the correct order (parts of the upper half are extant); next there follow paragraphs of halakhot (approximately twenty in number) disputed by the sect and its opponents; and finally, a conclusion and blessings (selections from which have been cited above).

The following introduction appears at the beginning of the halakhic paragraphs, after the calendar: 'These are some of our words regarding the Law of God—some words regarding the deeds (ma'aśim; sing. ma'aśeh) which we think . . .'; and similarly at the end of the work, in the sections quoted previously: 'We too have written to you some of the deeds (ma'aśei) of the Law which we thought were for your benefit and for the benefit of your people'. From the expressions 'some words

---

[24] Judging from the contents of the epistle, it would appear that the addressee was either an important functionary (the High Priest or the 'Wicked Priest'?) who officiated in the temple according to the 'lenient' halakha, or a person who supported such practices (the King, a religious leader, or the 'Preacher of Falsehood'?).

regarding the deeds' and 'some of the deeds of the Torah', we may infer that the letter discusses specific halakhot whose details were disputed by the sect and its opponents. It is possible that the term *maʿaseh* is already used here in the sense of 'performance of a religious precept', 'halakha'—a usage reminiscent of the later Palestinian expressions *maʿaseh* and *sefer ha-maʿasim* in the sense of 'halakhic ruling', 'halakhic work' (and as demonstrated by S. Lieberman,[25] the term *maʿaseh* in Palestinian literature refers to a halakhic ruling or halakha in general). In any event, the editors have decided to call our scroll *Miqṣat Maʿaśe Ha-Torah*.

This new scroll, which is entirely devoted to halakha, and contains paragraph after paragraph of specific halakhot, is unique, and differs in many respects from all other halakhic works of the sect discovered to date. I would like to single out the following three areas in particular:

(1)   Halakhic Polemic

MMT presents detailed paragraphs of halakhot disputed by the sect and its opponents. By contrast, it is not clear whether the halakha in the other works of the sect (as well as in the Apocrypha and elsewhere) was unique to the sect or was unanimously accepted: whenever such halakha deviates from the norm found in rabbinic literature, it is usually not clear whether these rulings merely reflect a particular stage in the development of the halakha—what Geiger termed 'the ancient halakha'—or a sectarian halakha, viz., not a different stage, but a different approach to the halakha.

(2)   Areas of the Halakha

The halakha of MMT does not govern the communal life of the sect. This halakha is not unique to the members of the sect, as in the Manual of Discipline, nor is this a comprehensive utopian and exegetical halakha dealing with all of the Torah's laws, as in the Temple Scroll. Rather, this is a halakha which applies to the entire Jewish people, a practical halakha disputed by the different groups, dealing with practical ramifications of specific halakhot in various areas of communal life: the calendar and festivals, ritual purity, the sanctuary and sacrifices, the priesthood and the priestly gifts.[26]

(3)   Similarity to the Halakhic Milieu of the Talmudic Rabbis

Due to the general nature of these halakhot and the polemic against the halakha of the sect's opponents, there are both numerous points of similarity to as well as divergence from Tannaitic rulings. This similarity manifests itself in the following areas: formulation—the rulings in MMT are formulated in paragraph after paragraph of specific halakhot, one after the other, as in the Mishna; terminology—a developed halakhic terminology, hitherto known only from rabbinic literature, already appears here, fully crystallised and formulated in fixed phraseology; and, above all, in content—specific halakhot known to be the subject of polemics in rabbinic literature against dissident sects are presented here in detail, but from the viewpoint of the rabbis' opponents.

The scroll contains approximately twenty paragraphs of halakhot, some brief and others longer. The polemic is apparent from the beginning of the work, as well as from its conclusion, and occasionally from the wording of the paragraphs themselves, in which the opposing views of the different sides are stressed, e.g.: 'And concerning . . . we say . . .'; 'and concerning . . . we think . . .'; 'and you know that . . .' Occasionally explanations are provided as well: 'Because . . .', 'for the reason that . . .', 'on account of the fact that . . .'; or 'it is written', 'and the matter is written'. However, the

---

[25] S. Lieberman, '*Sefer Ha-Maʿasim—Sefer Ha-Pesaqim*', *Tarbiz* 2 (1931), p. 377.

[26] It is noteworthy that MMT contains no halakhot pertaining to the Sabbath and the festivals, the laws of incest, or laws relating to monetary matters. See nn. 66–67 in the Hebrew version.

positions of both sides are not always clear, not only because the scroll does not present them explicitly, but also because the text is damaged and extremely fragmentary. Occasionally we can only conjecture or guess how the lacunae are to be restored, based on comparison with other paragraphs of the scroll, other works of the sect (the Damascus Covenant, Manual of Discipline, and Temple Scroll), and particularly rabbinic literature. However, it should always be kept in mind that such conclusions are based on an extremely fragmentary text, restoration of whose lacunae remains conjectural.

The basis for the arrangement of the halakhot and their juxtaposition to one another is not always clear. Most of these halakhot belong to the realm of ritual purity, the temple, and the priesthood; prohibited marriages and incestuous relations were apparently included here only insofar as they are related to the laws of the priesthood and the temple.[27]

As stated previously, the phraseology and terminology of the scroll are highly reminiscent of those found in rabbinic literature, and I shall cite but a few of these terms—*parat ḥaṭṭaʾt, haʿarev shemesh, muzzaqot/nizzoq, yedot kelim, ṭaharat ha-qodesh, taʿarovet* (in a different sense from the usage attested in rabbinic literature), *ʾeretz yisraʾel* (in the halakhic sense), *raʾuy* and others.

The common denominator of all of these halakhic rulings is that they are invariably stringent. The author inveighs against his opponents, protesting that they permit what is forbidden and declare ritually clean what is impure. Occasionally he reproves his readers and admonishes them: '[For it is fitting that the sons of] the priests be careful regarding this matter, that they will not bring iniquity upon the people' (B 12–13; also B 26–27); 'for . . . it is fitting that the children of Israel be mindful . . . and fear the temple' (B 48–49). This stringency is extremely prominent, as the members of the sect are invariably consistent in their stringent rulings: what is forbidden is always forbidden, and what it unclean is absolutely unclean. This characteristic of sectarian halakha was already noted by Geiger[28] and others, and most recently (and emphatically) by Lieberman.[29]

One wonders who are the two opposing parties who polemicised against each other in *Miqṣat Maʿaśe Ha-Torah* and what camps they represent. What sort of halakhot do they observe? And what is the relationship between these halakhot and those of the rabbis (i.e., the Pharisaic-rabbinic halakha)?

On the one hand, the halakhic tradition of the new scroll, like its idiomatic expressions and terminology, is generally identical with that found in the other writings of the Dead Sea sect (to the extent that comparative material is extant); taken all together, these constitute a single literary and halakhic corpus. On the other hand (as was already noted on occasion by some scholars), this halakha is clearly contrary to the halakha accepted in rabbinic literature. In all sections of the document where the view of the sect can be determined conclusively, the halakha which the sect challenges is Pharisaic. Moreover, in those cases where the talmudic rabbis explicitly contrast their views with an opposing, sectarian view, the sectarian halakha accords with the halakha of the scroll, whose author wages battle against rabbinic halakha.

I shall now cite several prominent examples explicitly recorded in rabbinic literature—all told, there are not that many—beginning with the most well-known of them, *m. Para* 3:7: 'The priest burning the [red] heifer was rendered ritually unclean because of the Sadducees, so they would not say that [the purification ceremony] was performed by [ritually clean] people for whom the sun had [already] set [*meʿorevei shemesh*]'.[30] This was not merely a theoretical discussion; the rabbis report actual clashes between the Pharisaic sages and certain high priests, who insisted that the ceremony be

---

[27] See above, n. 26.

[28] *Ha-Miqra We-Targumaw*, Jerusalem, 1949, p. 88 and *passim*.

[29] S. Lieberman, see above, n. 17, where rulings in the Damascus Covenant are ascribed to 'ultra-pious extremists'.

[30] According to the Pharisaic-rabbinic halakha, an unclean person was permitted to perform the purification ceremony immediately after immersion, without waiting for sunset. See also *m. Para* 5:4.

performed by priests who were fully clean, having waited until the sunset after immersion. Thus, the rabbinic sources relate that Rabban Yoḥanan ben Zakkai intentionally defiled a high priest and compelled him to immerse just before performing the purification ceremony that same day. Similarly, Ishmael ben Phiabi initially performed the purification ritual with priests who had immersed and waited until after sunset, but after the rabbis intervened, he repeated this ritual with other priests immediately after they immersed.[31]

MMT states explicitly: 'And also with regard to the purification of the heifer [brought as] a sin-offering [*parat ḥaṭṭaʔt*], the one who slaughters it and the one who burns it and the one who collects its ashes and the one who sprinkles the water of purification—it is by sunset that all these become clean, and the pure shall sprinkle on the impure. For so it is fitting for the sons of Aaron . . .' (B 13–17). Clearly, the halakha of the scroll is identical to that which the talmudic rabbis attributed to the Sadducees.

And another example, taken from the famous Mishna in *m. Yad.* 4:6 ff., which reports several disputes between the Sadducees and the Pharisees, all phrased in a manner reminiscent of MMT: 'The Sadducees say: "We complain against you, Pharisees, *for you say* . . ."' And in *m. Yad.* 7, ibid.: 'The Sadducees say: "We complain against you, Pharisees, for you declare unbroken columns of liquid [*nizzoq*] incapable of transmitting ritual impurity"' (viz., liquid poured from one container into another, thereby joining ritually unclean liquid in the lower container to ritually clean liquid in the upper container).

MMT states explicitly: 'And even with regard to unbroken columns of liquid [*muṣṣaqot*] we say that they have no purity. And even unbroken columns of liquid do not separate between the pure and the impure, for the moisture of the columns of the liquid and that which receives from them is all one moisture' (B 55–58).

[Note that the word 'even' (*ʔap*) appears twice in the halakha in MMT, and this wording may indicate that the text should be divided into two sub-sections. Aside from the passage from *m. Yad.* cited previously (and *m. Makš.* 5:9), the term *niṣṣoq* also appears in *m. Tohar.* 8:9: 'An unbroken column of liquid . . . is not [deemed] a connective, either with regard to impurity or purity'. With regard to impurity, as stated above in *m. Yad.*, an unbroken column of liquid does not render liquid in the upper container impure; with regard to purity, it cannot join two separate ritual baths (*miqwaʔot*), neither of which contains the requisite minimum quantity of water (forty *seʔah*), into a single, halakhically valid *miqweh*. Even so, the Mishna states explicitly that if the lower *miqweh* contains the required amount of water, then the upper *miqweh* is also halakhically valid, even if it does not contain the required amount of water, since it is connected to the lower one by the unbroken column of liquid, as stated in *m. Miqw.* 6:8: 'The upper *miqweh* can be rendered fit [by adding valid water] from the lower one [to the upper one].'

MMT rules strictly about both of these laws: (*a*) Unbroken columns of liquid 'have no purity'—viz., the water in the upper *miqweh* is not rendered fit for ritual immersion by virtue of the unbroken column connecting this water with the lower *miqweh*. (*b*) An unbroken column of liquid joins the impure liquid in the lower container to the upper one, rendering the contents of the upper container impure. However, the matter still requires further investigation.]

Attention may further be drawn to the famous dispute between the Sadducees and the Pharisees about the celebration of Pentecost 'on the day after the Sabbath'. Although this law is not explicitly discussed in the halakhic sections of MMT, it is alluded to in the scroll's calendar: 'On the fifteenth thereof is the festival of Weeks'—in the third month, as in *Jubilees*, in accordance with all the other writings of the sect. Some scholars, among them the noted talmudic scholar, Ḥ. Albeck, in his study of

---

[31] *T. Para* 3:6, 8 (Zuck., p. 632) and parallels.

Jubilees,[32] have already noted that 'the day after the Sabbath' (*mimoḥorat ha-shabbat*, Lev 23:15) refers to the Sabbath after Passover, not the Sabbath during the intermediate days of the festival.[33] In any event, 'the day after the Sabbath' does not refer to the day after the festival, as interpreted by the rabbis, but rather means 'Sunday', the first day of the week (= 'after the Sabbath'). Here too, the scroll follows the Boethusian (Sadducean?) view.

It is possible that still another dispute between the Pharisees and the Sadducees alluded to in rabbinic literature is mentioned explicitly in MMT. In the series of disputes between the Sadducees and Rabban Yohanan ben Zakkai in *m. Yad.* 4, mention is made of the purity of a 'donkey's bones' (M. 6). This ruling is fully consistent with the view of the rabbis, who distinguished between the flesh and bones of the carcasses of forbidden reptiles and other animals (clean or unclean): 'The flesh of animal corpses and forbidden reptiles [is unclean], which is not the case with their bones' (*m. ʿEd.* 6:3; see also *m. Ṭohar.* 1:4 and elsewhere). Likewise, in the *Sipra*, the rabbis repeatedly emphasised the interpretation of the relevant biblical expressions: 'Their corpses—and not their bones';[34] 'flesh'—and not bones'.[35] However, it is not clear from *m. Yad.* (see above) what the Sadducees' position was regarding this halakha, and the traditional commentaries differ on this issue.[36] Basing himself on the wording of the Mishna ('they [= the Pharisees] say'), Geiger[37] inferred that the Sadducees disagreed, ruling that even the bones are unclean. Yadin also noted, and rightly so, that according to the Temple Scroll, the Dead Sea sect disagreed with the rabbinic view, as stated there explicitly: 'Whoever carries their bones and carcasses, skin, flesh and nails *must wash his clothing'*.[38] In fact, it would appear that the lacuna in MMT B 21–23, too, should be restored as follows: 'Even the skins and the bones of unclean animals . . . and even the skins of the carcasses of clean animals . . .' (unfortunately, the text is extremely fragmentary here, although in any case this ruling is explicitly mentioned in the Temple Scroll).

The viewpoint of the sect is evident not only in the instances cited above, where the rabbinic sources state explicitly that the Sadducees and Pharisees disagreed, but also in the case of other halakhot. Careful examination of rabbinic literature reveals that MMT reflects sectarian halakha, and contains rulings which previous scholars have conjectured to be of sectarian origin. For example:

'A fetus is considered a limb of his mother (ʿubbar yerekh ʾimmo)'—In his commentary on the Temple Scroll,[39] Yadin correctly explained that a fetus in its mother's womb is impure because it is not considered a 'limb' of its mother. However, he failed to note that Geiger had already suggested more than a century ago that this issue was the subject of a sectarian dispute,[40] and once again, this conjecture is apparently confirmed by MMT (although here, too, the text is damaged; see lines 36–38).

Produce of the fourth year—Produce of the fourth year is holy to God and the priests, as in *Jubilees* (following the interpretation of Albeck[41] and others). This ruling appears explicitly in MMT:

---

[32] See above, n. 10, p. 16.

[33] See p. 30, and n. 81a, of the Hebrew version.

[34] *Shemini* 10:2 (55b); ibid., 10:5–10 (58d), and elsewhere, in *Torat Kohanim*, ed. Weiss, Vilna, 1862.

[35] Ibid., *Zav* 12:15 (36a).

[36] See n. 86 in the Hebrew version.

[37] *'ʿAl Devar "Eizeh Mahaloqet bein Ha-Zeduqim We-ha-Nilwim ʿAleihem U-Vein Ha-Perushim'*, *He-Ḥaluz* 6 (1862), p. 18.

[38] Y. Yadin, *Megillat Ha-Miqdash* II, Jerusalem, 1977, p. 51, l. 4 (henceforth: MHM).

[39] MHM I, p. 50, l. 10 (II, p. 157). See also MHM I, p. 306.

[40] Geiger, *Ozar Neḥmad* 3 (1860), p. 12 ff; *Ha-Miqra We-Targumaw*, p. 343 and *passim*.

[41] See above, n. 10, pp. 30-33.

'Even trees planted for food in the Land of Israel shall be like the first[-offering] for the priests, and the tithe of cattle and sheep is for the priest' (B 62–64).[42]

As stated above, the scroll's text is extremely fragmentary at times, to the point where it is impossible to extract anything of value from the fragments, but even in such cases it is possible that the remaining words and letters allude to sectarian practices, e.g., the prohibition of gentile sacrifices (B 8–9),[43] and possibly a prohibition against marrying Ammonite and Moabite women (line 35), as opposed to the rabbinic view: "An Ammonite" [Deut 23:4]—but not an Ammonite woman; "and a Moabite"—but not a Moabite woman' (m. Yebam. 8:3; y. Yebam. 9c).

There are other halakhot, too, regarding which MMT rules stringently, while the rabbis were apparently lenient (although these laws are not explicitly discussed in rabbinic literature). For example (line 53): 'Dogs shall not be brought to the holy camp, for they [might] eat some of the bones of the temple'—and this refers to all of Jerusalem, as stated below (line 55): 'Jerusalem is the holy camp'. However, according to the rabbis, this is not forbidden; the talmudic sages only mention a prohibition against raising chickens in Jerusalem because of the sacrifices (m. B. Qam. 7:7 and parallels), but they were apparently lenient about raising dogs, and indeed they explicitly mention 'the high priest's dog', albeit sarcastically and ironically (t. Kelim B. Qam. 1:6). However, there may be another allusion to this ruling in the strange conversation between R. Eliezer—the noted exponent of Shammaitic teaching[44]—in t. Yebam. 3 (and parallels), where R. Eliezer replied to all the questions posed to him by asking: 'Is it permitted to raise chickens? Is it permitted to raise pigs? Is it permitted to raise dogs?' Indeed, Rabbi Eliezer said: 'One who raises dogs is like one who raises pigs' (t. B. Qam. 8:17), and elsewhere (t. B. Bat. 1:9): 'One who raises bees is like one who raises dogs'— although the matter requires further investigation.

Similarly, we find a prohibition forbidding blind and deaf people from coming in contact with ritual purity in the Temple—a prohibition apparently appearing in the Temple Scroll as well (p. 45, lines 12–14), although MMT provides the reason for this prohibition: Whoever 'does not see and does not hear does not know how to observe' purity. Here too, this halakha is opposed to the view of the rabbis; t. Ter. 1:1 states explicitly of the sons of Yohanan ben Gudgada,[45] who were deaf-mutes, that 'all ritually pure food in Jerusalem was prepared relying on them [ʿal gabban] . . . for ritually pure food does not require intention'.

As stated above, all the halakhic rulings in MMT are stringent—I shall not go into further detail on this point—and this stringency is systematic and fully consistent, applying to all details and aspects of any given halakha. Thus, for example, the 'camp' mentioned in the Bible refers to the entire city of Jerusalem, and hence all strictures governing the biblical 'camp' apply to it, as stated explicitly in MMT (cf. Yadin's remarks,[46] following G. Alon): 'For Jerusalem is the holy camp'.

The expression 'holy to the Lord' always refers to the Temple and the priests; therefore, produce of the fourth year and first-born animals are given to the priests (in contrast to the rabbinic view).

A fetus is not considered a limb of its mother, so the fetus must be slaughtered;[47] the prohibition against slaughtering such an animal together with its mother (Lev 22:28) applies here; a fetus in its mother's womb confers ritual impurity.

---

[42] See J. M. Baumgarten, 'The Laws of ʿOrlah and First Fruits in the Light of Jubilees, the Qumran Writings and Targum Ps.-Jonathan', JJS 38 (1987), pp. 195–202.

[43] See n. 97 of the Hebrew version.

[44] Note that the rulings of Beit Shammai bear a certain similarity to those of our sect (cf. below).

[45] According to m. Ḥag. 2:7, this rabbi 'ate food prepared according to the purity laws applying to sacred food all his life'.

[46] MHM, I, p. 215 ff.

[47] If its mother had been slaughtered while it was still in the mother's womb; see m. Ḥul. 4:5 and parallels.

'Pure' means absolutely pure, so a person who was ritually unclean renders objects which he touches impure until after sunset of the day he immersed. The same applies to the preparation of the red heifer (see above) and the purification of lepers on the eighth day.[48]

[3]

I shall not continue by discussing specific halakhot mentioned in the scroll; instead, I shall concentrate on the general significance of the scroll and its broad implications. MMT is not an incidental list of halakhot, but a collection of specific rulings on issues wherein the members of the sect considered themselves separate and distinct from the rest of the Jewish community. The importance of this document lies in the fact that it reflects the sect's own conception of its uniqueness, of what distinguished it from the rest of the Jewish community; and what distinguished it and served as the backbone of its sectarian polemic was not religious doctrines, theology, or national or political issues, but halakha. To be sure, there were undoubtedly differences regarding these areas as well, but the main issue of concern to the scroll's author, on account of which he appeals to his opponents 'for your benefit and the benefit of your people . . . that you may rejoice in the end of time', is the *halakha*—viz., specific halakhot which, in his opinion, are improperly observed by his opponents, who are too lenient.

At first sight, the sect does not seem to differ in this respect from the Pharisaic sages, as the members of the sect bear no small resemblance to other extreme, halakhically stringent groups within the Pharisaic fold itself, e.g., Beit Shammai. But even though Beit Hillel's views were eventually accepted as authoritative, Beit Shammai was never excluded from the Jewish community or from the circle of the talmudic rabbis, the Pharisaic scholars. What then renders our stringent group a sect? It seems that the answer to this question was provided by both the sages of the Mishna and by the sect's own members. The Mishna (*m. Yebam.* 1:4, following the reading of manuscripts Kaufmann, Parma, and Lowe) states: 'Even though [Beit Shammai] disqualify and [Beit Hillel] declare permissible, Beit Shammai did not refrain from marrying the women of Beit Hillel, nor Beit Hillel those of Beit Shammai'. And in the Tosepta (*t. Yebam.* 1:11): 'Even though [Beit Shammai] prohibit and [Beit Hillel] permit, they did not refrain from preparing ritually clean food *relying on one another*'.[49] By contrast, the author of our scroll states explicitly (and I shall have occasion to refer to this below) that the sect was unwilling to accept the majority view and abandon its strictures. Indeed, it was against this background that they seceded from the rest of the people, as the author states: '[And we avoided] joining with them and coming [together] wi[th them] and *relying on them* [*ʿal gav ʾelleh*]' (C 8)—note the identical phraseology and terminology: 'preparing ritually pure food *relying on them* [*ʿal gav ʾellu*]'—and as Lieberman noted elsewhere,[50] 'the expression *gav* occurs in this unique sense in the Mishna and Tosepta'.

Who then is the author of the scroll, and whom does he represent? I shall not suggest far-flung conjectures or attempt to solve all the problems—it is possible, perhaps, that the author was the 'Teacher of Righteousness' himself, or some other leader of the sect. However, the more important question is: whom does he represent, viz., how are we to identify the sect? As is well known, endless studies have been written about this question. Since the discovery of fragments of the Damascus Covenant in the Geniza, every conceivable possibility has been suggested: Sadducees, according to

---

[48] In contradistinction to *m. Neg.* 14:3 (see nn. 111–112 in the Hebrew version).

[49] The conceptual basis of these rulings is, of course, problematic; see n. 119 in the Hebrew version.

[50] *Tosepta Ki-Fshuṭa, Bezah,* vol. 5, New York, 1962, p. 950.

Schechter; Pharisees, according to Ginzberg[51] and others; Essenes according to others, Christians or Judaeo-Christians, Karaites, and others.

These hypotheses have been restated and rediscussed with increased vigor since the discovery of the Dead Sea scrolls, and every conceivable—and inconceivable—sect, sub-sect and combination of sects has been suggested to identify the Dead Sea sect. There is no doubt in my eyes that the new scroll, *Miqṣat Maʿaśe Ha-Torah*, will stand in the center of all such discussion, and that halakhic considerations will prove decisive in resolving this issue. Indeed, in the last section of our document, the author speaks explicitly of the reason for the group's secession as a sect—viz., the halakha—and it is in this sectarian connection that the term *parush* ('separatist') appears for the first time in ancient literature. Immediately after the list of halakhot we read: '[And you know that] *we separated* from the majority of the people, and we refrained [?] from joining them regarding these matters and coming together with them [and] relying upon them' etc. (C 7–8). It is thus quite evident that the members of the sect considered themselves 'separatists' (*porshim*). Even so, this should certainly not be taken as support for the view of those scholars (Ginzberg, Rabin and others) who identified the sect with the Pharisees, for we have already seen that all of the sect's halakhot are clearly anti-Pharisaic. This is merely another expression of the separatist ideology of the sect, which seceded from the Jewish community, and 'separated from the settlement of the wicked [p]eople to go to the desert' (1QS viii 13)—an attitude already noted by scholars on the basis of similar expressions, such as *bdl*, *swr*, etc. Much has been written about the etymology and usage of this ambiguous expression—*perushim*—a derogatory term (*poresh*) when used by one's opponents, or an expression of praise (*parush*) when used by the sect's own members. Apparently, the sources used this term in both senses. One example should suffice to illustrate this point: an ancient *baraita* cited in the Babylonian Talmud (*Pesaḥ.* 70b)[52] relates of a sage in the time of the temple (apparently a contemporary of Shemaʿyah and Avtalyon) as follows: 'It was taught: Yehudah ben Dortai *separated* (*parash*), he and his son Dortai, and he went and settled in the South. He said: If Elijah comes and asks Israel, Why did you not bring the festival offering on the Sabbath, what will they say to him?' Here we have a description of an individual who disagreed with the sages regarding sacrificial procedures, who 'separated' from the Jewish community and settled in the South (the Judean desert?). And in the course of analysing this 'separatist's' view, Rav Yosef (read: Ashi) is quoted as retorting: 'Are we to stand up and explicate the motives of *separatists* [*perushim*]?'—i.e., is it necessary to analyse the exegesis of such separatists, who 'separated themselves from the Sages' (following Rashi)? Here is a figure seemingly reminiscent of the separatist sects who settled in the wilderness (as they themselves state: 'we *separated* from the majority of the people'!), and indeed, R. Yehiel Heilperin comments: 'He was apparently a Sadducee'![53]

Indeed, there is no doubt in my mind that decisive conclusions regarding the identity of the Dead Sea sect can only be drawn from the well-defined and unequivocal discipline of the halakha. As noted above, it is quite clear that the halakha represented by our scroll is unquestionably Sadducean, i.e., it accords with the halakha explicitly described by the rabbinic sources as Sadducean. On the other hand, it is becoming increasingly clear—and apparently justifiably so—that the Dead Sea sect is to be identified with the Essenes. How then can these two conclusions be reconciled—Sadducees according to the halakhic definition of the rabbis, yet a sect identical in all other respects with what is known about the Essenes?

---

[51] To be more exact: 'Hyper-Pharisees'.

[52] According to the *editio princeps*, Venice (1520?); see R. N. N. Rabbinovicz, *Diqduqei Soferim, Pesaḥim*, Munich, 1874, p. 210.

[53] *Seder Ha-Dorot* 2, Warsaw, 1870, 83c. Needless to say, I do not wish to imply that Yehudah ben Dortai was a member of the Dead Sea sect (or of any other identifiable sect); I merely wish to note that here we have an example of a zealous separatist who seceded from the community because of an halakhic disagreement.

I believe that the various (interchangeable) epithets used to denote the different sects in rabbinic literature, as well as the usage of these terms in other sources, require further investigation. As is well known, the fundamental question concerning the use of these epithets in rabbinic literature is the total absence of the appellation 'Essenes'.[54] Instead, the sources speak of Boethusians (*baytusim*), or *beit sin* (following the reading of the reliable manuscripts of the Mishna, Tosepta, and Yerushalmi), sects whose identity is uncertain and which are not mentioned at all in the other sources (Josephus, etc.). Nevertheless, all sources assume the tripartite division of these sects, and the same apparently applies to the members of the Dead Sea sect itself, who employed the typological designations Judah, Ephraim, and Manasseh.[55] This problem has been discussed since the beginning of serious historical inquiry into rabbinic literature, beginning with R. Azariah de Rossi in the Renaissance, and continuing with the pioneers of the *Wissenschaft des Judentums*—Geiger, Frankel, and others. Aside from the problem of the various appellations and the sects which they designate, there is another question, no less important (which, however, has not been explicitly discussed to date): was the Essenes' halakha similar to that of the Pharisees, the Sadducees, or different from both? Various hypotheses have been suggested regarding these issues, beginning with R. Azariah de Rossi's suggestion that the Essenes are identical with the *baytusim* (Boethusians) / *beit sin* mentioned by the rabbis (along with the Sadducees), and followed by the identification of the Essenes as Pharisees (*hasidim*, *haverim*, people who ate ordinary food following the purity laws governing sacred food; so already Frankel,[56] and most recently Baer[57] and others), who opposed the Sadducees and Boethusians.

But, the generally accepted views regarding the essential characteristics of the Sadducees and Pharisees are also in need of revision, and most recently E. E. Urbach has criticized 'the conjectures and theories suggested by scholars regarding the nature of the two parties'.[58] Indeed, it is not just the conjectures of previous scholars, but first and foremost the sources themselves which are in need of re-examination. The prevalent conception of Sadducees in rabbinic literature as heretics and freethinkers, together with Josephus' description of the Sadducees as high priests and aristocrats, engendered the widespread conception of an aristocratic, almost secular sect. An extreme caricature along these lines was indeed drawn by such conservative scholars as Yizhak Isaac Halevi,[59] and is widely encountered among such eminent talmudic scholars as H. Albeck, who wrote: 'This group of nobles, raised and educated in hellenistic culture, claimed outwardly, for purposes of argumentation, that they opposed only [the oral] tradition. But inwardly most of them had contempt not only for the Oral Law, but also for the written law'.[60]

[I should note in passing that the numerous textual variants between the terms *minim*, *meshummadim*, 'Sadducees' and other appellations for heretics in the printed editions of the Babylonian Talmud contributed, wittingly or unwittingly, to this conception, although I cannot go into additional detail here. Nevertheless, it is noteworthy that in most cases where the term 'Sadducees' appears in the printed editions of Babylonian Talmud, completely different readings are found in the manuscripts, and as R. N. N. Rabbinowicz noted in connection with the first occurrence of this term

---

[54] See the detailed discussion of the talmudic sources in the notes to the Hebrew version, pp. 41 ff.

[55] See D. Flusser, '*Perushim Zeduqqim We-ʾIsiyim Be-Fesher Nahum*', *Essays in Jewish History and Philology in Memory of Gedalyahu Alon*, Tel-Aviv, 1970, pp. 133–168.

[56] 'Die Essäer nach talmudischen Quellen', *MGWJ* 2 (1853), pp. 30 ff; 61 ff.

[57] *Yisraʾel Ba-ʿAmmim*, Jerusalem, 1955, p. 43.

[58] *Ha-Halakhah, Meqoroteha We-Toldoteha*, Givatayim, 1984, p. 77.

[59] *Dorot Ha-Rishonim*, I/3, Frankfurt, 1906, pp. 359, 362, 416, and *passim*.

[60] '*Le-Mahaloqet Ha-Perushim We-Ha-Zeduqqim Be-ʿInyenei Ha-Miqdash We-Qodoshaw*', *Sinai* 52 (1963), p. 1.

in the Talmud [*Ber.* 7a], 'it is absolutely impossible to rely upon the printed texts in such matters'.[61] According to the printed editions, Adam was a Sadducee [*b. Sanh.* 38b], as are people who defiantly eat non-kosher meat [*b. Hor.* 11a]. Similarly, the Talmud's statement that certain types of heretics 'descend to Gehenna and are judged there for generations on end' [*b. Roš Haš.* 17a] refers to Sadducees and Boethusians, according to Rashi in the printed editions.]

The above-mentioned conception of the Sadducees is also highly prevalent among non-Jewish scholars, who portrayed the Sadducees as the heirs, in effect, of the hellenists who preceded the Hasmonean revolt, and even as collaborators with the Roman government.[62]

This conception also gave rise to the frequently encountered axiom that any literary document or sect which demands the scrupulous observance of religious practices must be Pharisaic—so, e.g., the book of Judith, and *Jubilees*, according to many scholars;[63] so, too, the Damascus Covenant according to Ginzberg, Albeck, and, most recently, Rabin.[64] Similarly, Rappaport,[65] Frankel, and in modern times Baer[66] and others, maintained that the spiritualistic Essenes, devoted to a life of contemplation and religious observance, were actually Pharisees. This 'Pharisaic' conception of the Essenes as a sect of *ḥaverim*, who prepared ordinary food according to the purity laws and separated completely from mundane matters, actually gained increased popularity with the discovery of the Dead Sea scrolls.

However, as Geiger[67] already pointed out, the Sadducees should be seen as the representatives of a social class and political party with religious and halakhic principles and traditions of their own—traditions which are seemingly conservative, stringent, and uncompromising. But to cite Urbach once again:[68] 'Aristocrats and plebians, conservatives and modernizers, were to be found in both parties'. I believe that the inconsistencies in the description of the Sadducees in the various sources, talmudic and extra-talmudic, merely reflect different sides of the same coin. The priestly nobility were apparently not the only adherents of Sadducean halakha. The Sadducean halakha mentioned in rabbinic literature was followed not only by the Sadducean aristocrats of the other sources, but also by popular classes and fanatical religious sects, who even fought on its behalf. These sects waged a dual battle: a religious-*political* struggle (ethical and social) against the priestly Sadducean aristocracy, on the one hand, and a religious-*halakhic* struggle against the opponents of the strict Sadducean tradition (i.e., the Pharisees), on the other. Only from the perspective of the Pharisees were all the opponents of Pharisaic tradition who followed similar halakhic practices included in the same category—those who deny the authoritative Pharisaic interpretation of the Torah's commandments. All of these were termed 'Sadducees', regardless of whether they were 'Sadducees' by virtue of their social and political status, or only because of their halakhic tradition.

---

[61] *Diqduqei Soferim, Berakhoth*, Munich, 1867, p. 24. Note that most of the variants stem from censorship of the printed editions; see n. 153 in the Hebrew version.

[62] See, e.g., E. Schürer, G. Vermes, F. Millar and M. Goodman, *The History of the Jewish People in the Age of Jesus Christ*, Edinburgh, 1973–87, I.212; II.412 (henceforth: Schürer).

[63] Schürer III/1, pp. 219, 313–314 and n. 14. See J. M. Grintz, *Sefer Yehudit*, Jerusalem, 1957, p. 47.

[64] *Qumran Studies*, Oxford, 1957, pp. 82–94.

[65] *Toledot R. Elʿazar Ha-Qallir, Bikkurei Ha-ʿIttim*, 10 (1829), n. 20 (end), pp. 118–119.

[66] See above, n. 57.

[67] See above (n. 28), p. 69 ff, 88, and *passim*.

[68] See above, n. 58.

The talmudic rabbis knew about Sadducees and Boethusians,[69] but different terms are used in different sources;[70] the expression encountered most frequently in halakhic contexts is 'Sadducee', which gradually acquired a derogatory and contemptuous connotation. Indeed, in practice, the Pharisees clashed over the observance of the temple laws with the descendants of the Sadducean high priests in Jerusalem, and not with the separatist sects who had left the city and settled in the desert. Certainly, in retrospect, the rabbis did not distinguish between the different groups, and in halakhic discussions they generally mention only two fundamental approaches, 'ours' and 'theirs'—the Pharisaic and Sadducean views. Even though the rabbis were fully aware of the situation which obtained during the period before the destruction of the temple, and they knew that 'Israel went into exile only after they had become twenty-four classes of heretics' (y. Sanh. 10:29c), they also knew about 'Boethusians' who went up to Maʿaleh ʾAdummim, apparently from Jericho to Jerusalem (t. Roš Haš. 1:15). In their disputes with sects from the Second Temple period, the talmudic sages mention not only Sadducees and Boethusians, but also 'morning immersers' (t. Yad., end) and 'Galilean heretics' (m. Yad. 4:8, according to the manuscripts). But when they mention clashes with the high priests in the temple or discuss conflicting halakhic views, they generally speak only of 'Sadducees', an inclusive term apparently referring both to Sadducees and Boethusians.

In the Mishna (according to the manuscripts and *editio princeps*) the expression generally used is Sadducees—*beit sin* (Boethusians) appears only once (m. Menah. 10:3), apparently for a special reason.[71] In other Tannaitic sources, the two expressions appear along side of each other, and are used interchangeably in the parallel texts.[72] However, the prevalent, inclusive expression used for halakhically deviant sects is 'Sadducees', just as the even more inclusive expression *minim* is used to denote both 'Sadducees' and 'Boethusians'.[73]

A brief summary should suffice here: those scholars who maintained that the *beit sin* (Boethusians) mentioned in rabbinic literature are Essenes were apparently correct.[74] Lieberman, too, was apparently of this opinion (although he merely alluded to it in subdued fashion, as was his wont in such cases): 'Since we have proven the existence of *beit sin* (in two words), it is quite possible that the expression *beitsin*, which occurs frequently in the manuscripts, is a combination of *beit sin* . . .'; 'the view of the author of *Me ʾor ʿEinayim* [and others] that *beit sin* means 'House of the Essenes' is worthy of study and consideration'.[75] However, the view accepted by most DSS scholars—and justifiably so— that the members of the Judean Desert sect were Essenes, continues to gain additional support: the Essenes were apparently the 'Boethusians', as suggested by Grintz[76] and others, but, as is now evident from *Miqsat Maʿaśe Ha-Torah*, the halakhic position of the sect was Sadducean (as defined by rabbinic literature). This is not at all surprising, if indeed we assume that the halakha of the Boethusians—viz.,

[69] The Mishna mentions the Boethusians only once (in connection with the calendar; see below, n. 71), while the Tosepta invariably refers to 'Boethusians', even where the Mishna or parallel sources speak of Sadducees (this dichotomy also finds expression in the citations of Tannaitic sources in Amoraic material). Thus, the interchanges between 'Sadducees' and 'Boethusians' in the parallel sources apparently stem, at least in part, from different branches of Tannaitic literary tradition. For extensive documentation of this point, see nn. 166, 171 in the Hebrew version .

[70] See the detailed discussion of this point in the Hebrew version, pp. 48 ff (and notes).

[71] See the detailed discussion in the Hebrew version, nn. 81a, 166.

[72] See nn. 166, 167, and 171 in the Hebrew version.

[73] *Minim* often denotes people who espouse heretical beliefs of all sorts, whereas 'Sadducees' refers to the adherents of sectarian halakha. Note, too, that virtually all disputes in classical rabbinic literature between the Pharisees and Sadducees/Boethusians deal with halakhic matters, not with religious doctrines; cf. nn. 175–176 in the Hebrew version.

[74] For the etymology of Essenes/*beit sin*, see n. 177 in the Hebrew version.

[75] *Tosepta Ki-Fshuṭa, Sukkah*, vol. 4, New York, 1962, p. 870.

[76] 'Anshei Ha-Yahad—ʾIsiyim-Beit (ʾA)sin,' *Sinai* 32 (1953), p. 11 ff. See D. Flusser, 'Matthew XVII, 24–27 and the Dead Sea Sect', *Tarbiz* 31 (1962), p. 153, n. 10 (Hebrew).

the Essenes—was Sadducean. The assumption that the halakha of the Dead Sea sect was anti-Pharisaic and similar to the Sadducean halakha has already been noted by some scholars, most recently Yadin, who wrote (MHM I, pp. 305–306): 'It appears to me that there can be no further doubt that we have here a Torah whose halakhot are diametrically opposed to the halakhot formulated in rabbinic literature'. 'Moreover . . . there is occasional similarity between some of the halakhot in the Scroll and the halakhot of the Sadducees'—although Yadin subsequently modified his position, without any real reason. In any case, I believe that the new scroll, which itemizes the distinct points of dispute between the sect and its opponents, decisively resolves this issue. Thus, I would venture to say that those of the sect's halakhot which are not explicitly identified by the rabbinic sources as Sadducean may be assumed to be such, since these rulings were followed by the members of the sect, whose halakhic views are otherwise known to be Sadducean.

This assumption that the halakhot in the writings of the Dead Sea sect are actually Sadducean is not at all new. The early Karaites, who apparently had access to some of the sect's writings, already attributed these halakhot to the Sadducees. And some of the halakhot which Qirqisani and others ascribe to the Sadducees (e.g., the prohibition against marrying one's niece) are indeed found in the writings of the sect. The connection between Sadducean halakha and Karaitic halakha has been dealt with frequently in scholarly literature ever since Geiger, although this issue still requires further investigation; I shall not go into greater detail here, and instead refer to H. Ben-Shammai's balanced and cautious summary.[77] In any case, Schechter's 'Sadducean' conjecture—which was based, *inter alia*, on Karaitic tradition—is now fully confirmed by a first-hand source: *Miqṣat Maʿaśe Ha-Torah*.

[4]

If I were to summarise the significance of the Dead Sea scrolls for the study of the history of the halakha in even the most broad general terms, it is clear that these contemporary documents indeed enable us to perceive the facts correctly, clarifying and illuminating them in a new light.[78]

The end of the Second Temple period was a dynamic and effervescent era as far as religious thought and observance were concerned. The Hasmonean victories brought in their wake not only a great national awakening and devotion to the Jews' ancestral land, but also (and perhaps especially) a great religious awakening and revival and devotion to the ancestral traditions. This religious awakening manifested itself, first and foremost, in the scrupulous, meticulous, and exacting observance of the Torah's commandments. Different religious approaches and conflicting interpretations regarding the observance of the ancestral tradition in all its details, among other factors, engendered controversies and led to the division and formation of different sects. It would appear that the basic split occurred between the stringent, inflexible, and uncompromising (Sadducean) approach, which was opposed by the flexible, evolving, and relatively lenient (Pharisaic) approach, which answered the needs of the general public and sought to enable the people to share in the new spirit.[79] Indeed, when the leaders of the sects face off, polemicising directly with one another and raising 'some' of their differences—i.e., the principal ones—they discuss halakhic details, and not theological issues: it was over the halakha that they fought, and because of it that they split. It is clear

---

[77] 'Some Methodological Notes Concerning the Relationship Between the Karaites and Ancient Jewish Sects', *Cathedra* 42 (1987), p. 69 ff (Hebrew).

[78] The general, schematized discussion which follows obviously requires additional documentation, which will hopefully be provided on another occasion.

[79] This lenient Pharisaic approach, which ultimately found its fullest expression in the acceptance of Beit Hillel's view as authoritative, is an important feature of rabbinic halakha. I hope to elaborate on this point in a future study.

that the dispute had theological import and was laden with ethical and religious significance, but the practical manifestation of this conflict was to be found in the observance of the halakha.

Scrupulous observance of the Torah's commandments was not the exclusive heritage of the Pharisees: the members of the Dead Sea sect were no less zealous in the observance of their Sadducean tradition. Quite the contrary, they score their Pharisaic opponents as 'deviates', who 'violated the law' (CD 1:13, 20). Representation of the Sadducees as rebels against religion reflects an essentially Pharisaic and rabbinic outlook, generally a late one. The rabbis, who were aware of the fact that the people were divided into different camps—'twenty-four sects'—knew very well that this was a great religious age, and they remarked of the Jewish people in general during the Second Temple period (and not just of the Pharisees): 'We know that they toiled in the Torah and were meticulous [about observance of the commandments] and tithes [and all good manners were to be found among them] . . .'[80] Nor was such meticulous observance limited to tithes; the rabbis even declared: 'Come and see how far ritual purity has spread in Israel' (t. Šabb. 1:14 and parallels). Purity laws were taken as seriously as incest laws (t. Ki-Fshuṭa ad loc.); 'the impurity of a knife was more distressing to Israel than murder' (t. Yoma 1:12 and parallels)—and, as the Jerusalem Talmud notes ad loc. (Yoma 2:39d): 'Disparagingly so (!)'

Observance of the Torah's laws and the milieu of the halakha were the central factor in Jewish life during this period. The assertion that 'there was no factor, force or event which made so significant an impression on the history of the Jewish people, molded its life and forged its character, as the halakha',[81] is particularly appropriate with regard to the Second Temple period,[82] not only with respect to the Pharisees, but also with regard to their opponents, who scrupulously observed the law according to the Sadducean tradition. Not only observance of the Torah's commandments, but also preoccupation with the proper interpretation of the law in its most minute details, stood in the center of their spiritual world. The halakhic minutiae, concepts, and terms of the talmudic sages that we find in the Mishna of the later Tannaim and which occasionally appear to be the result of late, abstract rabbinic speculation, actually have their roots in this period; they now come alive in front of our eyes as a concrete historical reality, in contemporary documents stemming from Hasmonean times. The people toiled over the halakha and meditated upon it; they clashed over it and divided because of it. Extremists who refrained from joining members of the other camp, refusing to associate with them and 'rely upon them', 'separated from the majority of the people' until they were almost completely forgotten.

As stated above, Geiger already noted, and Lieberman pointed out at greater length and depth, that sectarian halakha in general, and Sadducean halakha in particular, was stringent. This conclusion, originally suggested as a hypothesis on the basis of obscure allusions in rabbinic literature, is now attested clearly and explicitly by the sectarian documents themselves. Not only in their halakhic writings, but even in the Psalms Pesher, the members of the sect explicitly accused the Pharisees: 'For they have chosen leniency'.[83] Indeed, all the halakhot in the Dead Sea scrolls which are at variance with Pharisaic halakha are stricter than the corresponding Pharisaic rulings. However, in contrast to Geiger, the Pharisaic halakha is not a late development, opposed to the 'early' Sadducean halakha. It is now evident that both halakhic systems existed side by side and grappled with each other from ancient times. And it is clear that the Tannaitic halakhot were not merely an artificial creation of the academy

---

[80] T. Menaḥot, end; y. Yoma 1:38c.

[81] Urbach, see above, n. 58, p. 7.

[82] The meticulous observance of religious precepts is attested not only by the literary evidence, but also by archaeological finds; see n. 203 in the Hebrew version.

[83] DJD V, p. 43, as already noted by Flusser (see above, n. 55), pp. 160–161.

(*beit midraš*), or late rabbinic speculation which substituted for the temple and for political independence.

Here too, the rabbinic sources and the Dead Sea scrolls complement and illuminate each other. All the sources which cite the rabbis' claim that 'the Sadducees complain against the Pharisees' apparently refer to Pharisaic leniency. Similarly, in the case of all other sectarian traditions cited in rabbinic literature (wherever it is possible to distinguish between leniency and stringency), the Sadducees and Boethusians are stringent, while the Pharisees are lenient.

However, the principal issue here was not just leniency versus stringency—the Pharisees' primary goal was to enable the general public to participate as extensively as possible in temple life and religious worship,[84] and this issue seems to underlie the dispute as to whether public sacrifices may be brought from individual contributions or only from public donations.[85] This principle apparently accounts for those isolated halakhot where it would appear, *prima facie*, that the Pharisees ruled stringently, e.g., *t. Ḥag.* (end): 'Once they immersed the candelabrum [on the festival], and the Sadducees said: Come and see the Pharisees immersing the moon [Jerusalem Talmud reads: the sun]'.[86] At first sight, it would appear (as explained by most commentators) that the Sadducees are criticising the overly meticulous and exacting Pharisees, who are concerned about ritual impurity everywhere, even in objects insusceptible to ritual uncleanliness, such as the sun and the moon. Indeed, R. David Pardo, followed by Lieberman,[87] explained that the Sadducees maintained that liquids were insusceptible to ritual impurity, and hence their lenient ruling here. But we now know that the members of the sect—whose halakha was Sadducean, as pointed out above—were particularly strict about the impurity of liquids, and they even distinguished between the 'purity of the many' and the more severe 'drink of the many', as noted by scholars.[88]

However, this passage, too, should be explained in accordance with its context. The Mishna in *Ḥagiga* (2:6–7) discusses 'degrees of ritual purity' (*maʿalot ṭohorah*)—for ordinary food, heave-offering (*terumah*), sacrificial food, and the red-heifer (and everything associated with it). Yet, paradoxically, it was in Jerusalem and the temple, of all places, that the rabbis were particularly lenient regarding the purity laws, especially during the holidays, to the extent that they ruled that even the masses (*ʿammei ha-ʾarez*) 'are trusted in Jerusalem regarding sacred food, and during the festival, with regard to heave-offering as well' (*m. Ḥag.* 3:6). The rabbis relied on the masses' scrupulous purification in preparation for the festivals and the pilgrimage to Jerusalem. In the words of the Babylonian Talmud (ibid., 26ᵃ): 'As it is written: "And all the men of Israel gathered to the city as one man, friends [*ḥaverim*]" [Judg 20:11]'—the biblical verse treated them as *ḥaverim* [= people known for observance of the purity laws]—as if the biblical verse itself had endorsed the purification of the Jewish masses, so as to permit them to participate in the divine service. Or, to cite the formulation in the Jerusalem Talmud: '"A city which is joined (*she-hubberah*) together" [Ps 122:3]—a city which renders all Israel *ḥaverim*' (*y. Ḥag.* 3:79ᵈ); 'a city which joins [*she-mehabberet*] [the people of] Israel to one another' (ibid., *b. Qam.* 7:6ᵃ). The general public was considered trustworthy even with regard to the purification waters of the red heifer, and this lenient ruling was also based on rabbinic exegesis of a biblical verse (Num 19:9): 'It shall be for the community of the children of Israel for safekeeping, as water for sprinkling'—'hence all are trusted to watch over them' (*t. Ḥag.* 3:20). All of these concessions were made explicitly and intentionally, to preserve unity among the people and to prevent divisions between lenient and strict factions, as the rabbis stated: 'Why are all trusted

84 See E. E. Urbach, *The Sages—Their Concepts and Beliefs*, trans. I. Abrahams, Jerusalem, 1975, p. 582 ff.

85 See n. 91 in the Hebrew version.

86 See variants in ed. Lieberman and *Tosepta Ki-Fshuṭa, Ḥagigah*, vol. 5, p. 1336.

87 *Tosepta Ki-Fshuṭa*, ibid.

88 J. Licht, *Megillat Ha-Serakhim*, Jerusalem, 1965, p. 294; Yadin, MHM I, p. 241.

regarding the purity of the red heifer . . . so each one will not say: I shall build an altar for myself, I shall burn a red heifer for myself' (ibid., 2:19; *b. Ḥag.* 22ᵃ). In all probability, this statement was directed against the more extreme sects, who, in their stringency and zealousness for observing the Torah's laws according to their own interpretation, 'built altars for themselves' and 'separated from the majority of the people, refraining from coming together with them and relying upon them'.

But caution was obviously necessary before the general public could be allowed mass participation and free contact with the temple and holy articles. Hence the Mishna's declaration (following the reading of the Palestinian tradition, variously interpreted): 'Take heed lest you touch the table and the candelabrum [and render it impure]' (ibid. 3:8). It was in response to such leniency that the Sadducees jeered: See how far Pharisaic liberalism has gone, to the point where the Pharisees abandon the temple to the impurity of people who fail to observe the purity laws properly, until the Pharisees eventually had to immerse the sun! This is not to be taken as derisive mockery, as has been postulated by scholars.[89] Rather, it represents a genuine expression of shock on the part of the Sadducees when they saw how the candelabrum was defiled by the ignorant common people, who were seemingly encouraged by the Pharisees.

The exponents of these two fundamental approaches to the halakha—the Sadducean, the Pharisaic, and their different subtypes—polemicised against each other and fought one another for generations. But just as the Pharisees represented different shades of opinion, the Sadducees were not a monolithic sect. They too had differences of opinion and trying struggles among themselves, to the point where the most stringent extremists—Sadducees with religious and ethical-spiritualistic tendencies, Essenes, *beit sin*, Boethusians, who became alienated from the fossilised temple worship under the leadership of the priestly aristocracy—found themselves compelled to separate both from the temple and the majority of the people.[90] It is quite possible that during the early stages, the Sadducean secessionists viewed the Pharisees as potential partners in their ethical-religious battle against the ruling priesthood. But while the Pharisees were supported by the masses, the secessionists represented an extremist, fanatic sect, and eventually found themselves in isolation. As time passed, the Pharisees succeeded in influencing priestly circles and the temple ritual, and, most important, they imbued the daily life of the masses with holiness and religious faith. The differing halakhic traditions of the Pharisees and Sadducees, which originated in different religious conceptions, eventually led to different solutions, one oriented toward the people, and the other turning to the desert. But this latter solution was temporary and unsatisfactory. The fanatical groups who adopted this approach, unable to adapt to the changing conditions, could not withstand the test of time, and, like their Sadducean brethren—the descendants of the high priests and their adherents in Jerusalem—they vanished from the stage of history. Of all the different groups that flourished before the destruction of the temple, adhering faithfully to their ancestral traditions, customs, and practices and not contenting themselves with a 'New Covenant' based on 'benevolence and faith' (Matt 23:23), only one survived—that group whose sages were able to unify the various factions, impose religious responsibility on the people, renew their hopes and thereby prepare them for the long darkness of exile. In the rabbis' words: 'Before Israel was exiled they were numerous herds . . . after they were exiled they became a single herd' (*Lam. Rab.*, Proem 25 [ed. Buber, p. 30]).

---

[89] See p. 66, n. 214, in the Hebrew version.

[90] These two religious approaches, the priestly-ritualistic approach and the popular-spiritualistic approach, apparently existed since ancient times, from the biblical period onward. To a certain extent, the conflict with the priesthood continued even after the destruction of the temple. See nn. 226 and 234 in the Hebrew version.

Postscript (August 1993)

Over six years have elapsed since this paper was presented. MMT has since been extensively discussed and is now widely acknowledged as a major clue to the identity of the Dead Sea sect. But as we are far from definitive answers, I tried to be cautious, avoiding clearcut conclusions. I take this opportunity to reiterate in brief some major points of my argument:

'. . . it is becoming increasingly clear—and apparently justifiably so—that the Dead Sea sect is to be identified with the Essenes' but, on the other hand, 'the halakha represented by our scroll . . . accords with the halakha explicitly described by the rabbinic sources as Sadducean'; therefore my major problem was: 'How then can these two conclusions be reconciled'? (p. 192).

I thus suggested that 'the usage of these terms' in the varied sources 'requires further investigation'. As a Talmudist I emphasized that 'the fundamental question . . . . in rabbinic literature, is the total absence of the appellation "Essenes". Instead, the sources speak of Boethusians (*baytusim*) . . . which are not mentioned at all in the other sources' (p. 193).

As the single source for the halakha of all the sects are the talmudic sources, I suggested to solve both problems with the simple solution: 'The Sadducean halakha mentioned in rabbinic literature was followed not only by the Sadducean aristocrats . . . but also . . . by fanatical religious sects (e.g. Essenes) . . . Only from the perspective of the Pharisees were all the opponents . . . included in the same category . . . they generally speak only of "Sadducees", an inclusive term apparently referring both to Sadducees and Boethusians'. The Essenes 'waged a dual battle: a religious-*political* struggle . . . against the priestly Sadducean aristocracy, on the one hand, and a religious-*halakhic* struggle against the opponents of the strict Sadducean tradition (i.e., the Pharisees), on the other' (pp. 194–195).

YAʿAKOV SUSSMANN

APPENDIX 2

ADDITIONAL TEXTUAL OBSERVATIONS ON 4QMMT

THERE are certain peculiarities in the numeration of lines in MS[a]. As can be seen on the photographs, the bottom and the upper margins of several columns have been preserved.

Since frg. 8 contains the bottom margin of col. iii and the upper margin of col. iv, Strugnell was able to tell that the scroll had twenty lines in each column and that its height was 16.6 cm (see § 1.2). He believes, however, that some of the columns contained less than twenty lines; this can be inferred from his numbering of the lines. For example, he assumes that col. i in frgs. 3–7 had nineteen lines.

H. Stegemann, in contrast, suggests that this column also contained twenty lines and that the first line has been lost. It is, however, also possible that more than one line has been lost, considering the fact that the twenty lines of the column on frg. 8 are about 12.5 cm in height and the nineteen lines of col. i in frgs. 3–7 are about 10 cm in height; there being room for four to five lines up to the top margin.

A similar problem exists in reconstructing the lines of the calendar at the beginning of this manuscript. It seems impossible to assume that there were as many as twenty lines in any of the columns of the calendar.

Finally, we note that the letters in this manuscript differ somewhat from each other in form and in size. For example, some of the letters in the calendar differ from their counterparts in the halakhic section. The ascription of the calendar written in narrow columns to MMT is based on palaeographical considerations, and on its typological resemblance with the end of the calendar which appears on 4Q394 3–7 i.

The placement of frgs. 11–13 of MS[e] is problematical. According to Strugnell, MS[e] seems to be only about ten lines in height (see § 1.6). Frgs. 14–17 consist of the ultimate and penultimate columns of the work. The ultimate column contains seven lines, and the penultimate one now contains eight lines. Since seven lines have been preserved in frgs. 11–13, these fragments cannot, according to Strugnell, belong to the last two columns but come rather from the column which precedes these two columns.

This is the order given in chap. 1. In chap. 2, the Composite Text, however, a different order was preferred and frgs. 11–13 were taken as part of the penultimate column, coming at its bottom. If this is correct, MS[e] must originally have had some sixteen lines in each column.

It was M. Kister who suggested the order adopted in the Composite Text. His arguments for it are purely contextual. He noticed that the text both of frgs. 11–13 and of the penultimate column discuss the issue of eschatological blessings and curses, and that this discussion is in both cases followed by examples from the conduct of the biblical kings of Israel (end of the text of frgs. 11–13) and of David (beginning of the last column). Each example begins with the formula זכור את.

It is possible that frgs. 11–13 preserve the last line of the penultimate column and its bottom margin and that the ultimate column contains the upper margin. Accordingly, we restored the text as lacking only one word (נשוא[‏] at the beginning of the last column). It is possible that several letters of the last line of MS[d] overlap with the text of the first line of frgs. 11–13 (see the underlining in § 1.6.3.9).

We have asked two experts, B. Porten and H. Stegemann, whether they can support or reject either of these two possibilities on purely material grounds. Each of them had carefully studied the original

manuscript. Porten concluded that the papyrology confirms Kister's suggestion, while Stegemann said that materially the joining of frgs. 11–13 to the bottom of the penultimate column is impossible. We thank both of them for their assistance and hope that they make the further investigations (such as microscopic inspection of the fibers) which are needed in order to prove the correctness of one or other of the two possibilities.

ELISHA QIMRON

APPENDIX 3

ADDITIONAL OBSERVATIONS ON 4QMMT

MOST writers divide MMT into three sections: a calendaric section, a legal section, and a final, hortatory section. Each of these presents difficulties which have not yet been completely explained in the discussion.

Section A: The Calendaric Section

The calendar implied in the first section is the 364-day calendar familiar to scholars from the book of *Jubilees*, the *Temple Scroll*, and several Qumran texts. The listing of Sabbaths in the calendar is easy to understand and reconstruct. The listing of feasts is also easy to understand, though the choice of the feasts is irregular and much harder to understand. The principal question is whether this list belongs to the same work as Sections B and C, i.e., to MMT. The legal and hortatory parts of MMT are addressed by one group to another and have a notably polemic tendency to them. The calendar, however, is clearly only a list, not addressed to anyone, and with no internal indicators of polemical intent. [It would be rash to try to postulate a missing incipit to this list which would convert it into a polemic document. That it could have had its own incipit is not impossible, but to postulate one with precisely such a polemic tendency would be highly unlikely.]

It is hard, then, to relate this calendar to the rest of the work, whether form-critically or even in terms of subject matter. Moreover, additional material indicators render it problematic whether the section belongs to MMT at all. In manuscript 4Q394, the presence of the 364-day calendar-list is certain since it is preserved directly before the first line of Section B (the legal section). However, in the second manuscript of the work, 4Q395, which also contains the beginning of Section B, enough uninscribed leather is preserved before Section B to make it highly probable that no text ever stood before it. Section A thus becomes attested in only half of those manuscripts where we should have found it. To this argument we can add another: if one reconstructs the entire calendar in 4Q394, it would be difficult to postulate anything before it except an incipit of a calendar—scarcely a general title for the whole work (whether this whole work would have been cast in the form of a letter or some other genre) and certainly no room for one, two, or more, separate sections of the work (in whatever subject matter or form) to have preceded. This one can tell by reconstructions, in the style of H. Stegemann, of the diminishing widths of the layers in manuscript A: there was no space for any greater length of scroll at the beginning.

The hesitant consequence of these ambiguous observations is that it is far from certain that the calendar, as found here, belonged to any letter at all, or that it formed any part of the document MMT^{b+c}. At the most it should be conceived as a list, of another genre, prefixed in 4Q394 to Sections B and C for uncertain reasons. The calendar in it may simply have been a non-controversial list, a non-polemic mnemonic like our 'thirty days has September'. It was addressed to no 'opponents' and formed no part of MMT's loftier polemic or hortatory themes.

Section B: The Legal Section

The beginning of the legal section does not provide a sentence easy to supplement completely; the incipit—which would have told us so much about the form of this work and its purpose—remains at least half unreconstructed. At the start of a new paragraph, the text runs (eliminating supplements which are possible but uncertain):

אלה מקצת דבْרינו]   [ל שהם מ[קצת דברי]
[ה]מֿעשים שא אֿ[נ]חֿ[נ]ו חושבים וכו]לֿם על]   [
וטהרת]   [הרֿ
(B 1–3)

The first law follows immediately.

The phrases at the end of this damaged section—'the precepts which we recommend', 'all of them concerning', and, at the end, 'purity'—make, formally and materially, plausible parts of an incipit to a collection of purity laws. Form-critically, it is extremely unlikely that the first words belong to the incipit of a letter (though they could conceivably be the beginning of a section within a letter). However, they look very like the incipit of a collection of laws—indeed, there is a very close parallel to them in another incipit of a collection of laws, the first verse of Deuteronomy: 'These are the words that Moses spoke to all Israel'. Syntactically, the indefinite phrase 'some of our words' could be, in the language of MMT, a variant for Deuteronomy's 'the words'; and it could easily be that the next damaged word in MMT corresponded to the word 'Israel' that comes next also in the verse from Deuteronomy.

There is no obvious supplement for the fragmentary words that follow. The lacunae could be filled in several ways: Qimron's supplements are all plausible, but none of the supplements so far proposed for the beginning bring that feeling of conviction which we expect from a palmary conjecture and which might be confirmed by a good literary parallel. Despite the difficulties of reconstruction, this sentence is scarcely likely to be an incipit of a letter and is more likely to introduce a collection of laws, pronouncements, or the like—that is, after all, the function of the possible parallel in Deuteronomy.

It is hard to maintain that these laws were chosen because of their structural importance for this legal topos. Banal though it may seem at first, a literal translation of the incipit, 'these are some of our precepts', makes a suitable introduction for the following subject matter; such an indefinite title for a collection or a treatise seems formally attested also in Hellenistic book titles and not merely in the rare Oriental parallels that can be found. For the moment, then, the formal indications are that this is just an introduction to a collection of some laws, however chosen.

Another possibility would also explain the presence in Section B of the same mixture of personal pronouns as in the following Section C, each having also the same reference. Rather than a letter, Sections B and C could instead be a treatise. However, the treatise is, at least in Hellenistic literature, a very ill-defined genre, and such a distribution of the personal pronouns could be expected in many other literary contexts too. So the suggestion, mentioned in the main part of this volume, that this was a treatise rather than a letter, should be withdrawn. In its place, we should view these lines as a freestanding introduction to a collection of laws, perhaps consciously modelled on the opening of Deuteronomy.

Section C: The Hortatory Epilogue

Clearly, the subject matter of the final section is very different from that of the collection of laws. The damage to the text, and the loss of over twenty complete lines at the beginning, make it difficult

to establish the point where the text changes from one section and subject-matter, i.e., from Section B, to another, and also to establish whether there was any formal marker of that shift—there could have been a brief, formal incipit of the new section, or an imperceptible glide from the one to the other.

Qimron views this as a homiletic closure to his epistle, after its preceding sections. I have frequently questioned the use of the term 'epistle' for the earlier sections, finding it inappropriate on form-critical grounds. The same uneasiness confronts me as I turn to Section C. The beginning, it is true, is completely missing, but the bulk of the section, and especially the end which is completely preserved, would be formally unlike the conclusion of any letter. Admittedly, many forms can be found in the conclusion of a letter, but this passage seems rather an exhortation on the observance of the previously mentioned laws. Like the legal section, this contained a 'we' for the writers and a 'you' identical to the addressee of the legal section. In section C, the 'you' group is split up into a 'thou' and 'thy people Israel', which suggests the mention of a singular leader or sovereign of Israel. Whoever that may be, the *dramatis personae* of Section C would not be inconsistent with those of Section B. Formally, we would not expect such a conclusion in a legal letter, but one might suggest that such a hortatory conclusion (putting it broadly, a benediction), would well fit at the end of a legal code as it does in covenant formulae. Deuteronomy would thus provide a parallel for the ending of this work, just as it did for the beginning.

This volume does not contain a chapter on the theology and tradition-history of Section C, a counterpart perhaps to Qimron's lengthy treatment of the legal background of the laws. A running commentary on some details in Section C is included, but not a thorough attempt to understand the relations between the language and theological traditions of this section and those of works which we expect to be near it chronologically and in thought, i.e., Daniel, *1 Enoch*, the *Divre Hamme'ôrot*, the *Damascus Document*, and the *Temple Scroll*. Such an important study remains to be done.

One notices that, although the grammar of Section C is similar to that of Section B, with its numerous -ש relative clauses and participles, there is very little in the somewhat biblicizing and commonplace language and thought which we view as characteristic of the Qumran sect, its writings, organization, and special theology (e.g., its two-spirit doctrine). This was true for the far longer *Temple Scroll* as well, where the apparent difference cannot be due to chance alone. One might object that the phrase in MMT, והרחיק ממך מחשבת רעה ועצת בליעל [C 29] shows some of the two-spirit dualism typical of Qumran. Its meaning is ambiguous, however, and not all somewhat dualistic expressions must be considered specifically Qumranic; from Second Isaiah onward, many expressions that might be called 'dualistic' have been quite at home in Judaism. Even before the dualism at Qumran, many less developed antecedent stages existed. In general, the absence from all of MMT of Qumranic sectarian language, organizational or theological, requires some explanation, especially in light of the similarity of the legal part of MMT to the legal traditions of the Qumran sect. One will best explain this by making a distinction between MMT and the standard Qumran texts. MMT may predate them or it may represent another branch of the Sadducean family tree.

The language of this section is somewhat ordinarily biblical, and its intellectual contents rather amorphous. Accordingly, the precise nature of the exhortation is hard to follow, even if it can be generally translated where the text is complete. It should be especially noticed that some eight lines, relatively well preserved, could be placed at either one or the other of two different places. Qimron prefers to place ll. 18–24 at that point, but it is just as plausible on grounds of context and, preferable, considering the material shape of the manuscript (so in the opinion of both myself and H. Stegemann), that they be placed some twenty lines earlier, before line 1.

The disputed paragraph runs as follows:

. . . in the days of Solomon the son of David. And the curses that have befallen us from the days of Jeroboam the son of Nebat and up to when Jerusalem and Zedekiah king of Judah went into captivity . . . And we know that some of the blessings and the curses have been fulfilled as was written in the Book of Moses. And this is the end of days when *they will return to Israel* . . . Think of the kings of Israel and contemplate their deeds, how whoever among them who feared the Torah was delivered from troubles. They were seekers of Torah . . .

All this would, it is true, fit thematically well after lines 15ff where we find a quotation of Deuteronomy's text, 'and it shall come to pass, when all these things befall thee in the end of days, the blessing and the curse, then thou shall take it to heart and return to Him with all thy heart and soul at the end of days, then . . .' followed by further damaged phrases: ' it is written in the Book of Moses and in the Book of the Prophets, that there will come . . . the blessings . . .'. These phrases would lead smoothly to the reference, at the start of our fragment, to further blessings in the days of *incerti loci* Solomon the son of David, and to blessings and curses throughout Israel's history up to the end of days. Such a sequence would certainly be conceivable in its thought even if not clear in all its details. Materially, however, this placing of the fragment would be difficult. One could make as good a case for placing it in the text missing before l. 1, though the poor state of the text in lines 1ff hinders us from seeing how appropriate the sequence of thought would be.

I refrain from discussing the arguments on either side, but merely point out that, when we are unable to establish where a complete paragraph belongs, then we may not yet have reached a precise enough understanding of the document. In any case, I suspect that this problem will not be solved until the missing chapter on the theological background of Section C is written, perhaps to give us an answer to this major difficulty.

JOHN STRUGNELL

CONCORDANCE TO 4QMMT

THE concordance is based on the composite text (with its diacritical signs). The concordance covers all words in the basic manuscript for a given passage plus all words in complementary manuscripts that are not in the basic manuscript. Phrases in the concordance taken from complementary manuscripts are enclosed in square brackets, and an entry-word taken from a complementary manuscript is underlined in the concordance.

א

אבד

qal pf.

בגלל]ה[חמס והזנות אבד[ו] מקצת מקומות   C 5

אָדָם

ועל [טמאת נפש] האדם אנחנו אומרים   B 73

אַהֲרֹן pers.

כי לבני [אהרן] ראואי [להיות מ̇   B 17

ובני אהרון ק[דושי קדושים]   B 79

אוֹ

כמשפט המת או החלל הוֹא   B 74

אֶחָד

א[ת האם ואת הולד ביום אחד   B 36

אַחַר

עליו אחר השבת ו[יו]ם השנ̇י השלישי נוסף   A ii

ע[ל]ו אחר [ה]ש̇[ב]ת ויום השני השלישי נו[ס]ף   A 19

אַחֲרִית

כול הדברים[ה]אלה ב[א]חרי[ת] הימים   C 14

בכל לבב[ך ובכו]ל נפש̇[ו]ל באחריו̇[ת]   C 16

וזה הוא אחרית הימים   C 21

בשל שתשמח באחרית העת   C 30

אַחַת

[ונשים]ל[ו]ל[ק]ח̇[י]ם להיו[ת]ם עצם [אחת   B 41

וה̇מקובל מהמה כהם לחה אחת   B 58

אֵין

[וא̇י]ן לה]ת̇לכם [ו]לעשותם [עצם אחת   B 44

ואף ע[ל] הסומ]י[ן]ם שאינם רואים   B 50

ותערובת [א]שם אינם רואים   B 51

אנח̇נו אומר[ים] שהם שאין בהם [ט]הרה   B 55

אינ̇ם מבדילות בין הטמא [ל]טהור   B 56

ואין להבי למחני הק[ו]ד[ש כלבים   B 58

אִישׁ

זכור [את] דוי̇ד שהיא איש חסדים   C 25

אכל

qal part.

שהם אוכלים מקצת [ע]צ̇מות המק[ד]ש   B 59

nip'al impf.

אנח[נ]ו חושבים ש̇איאכל את הולד]   B 37

nip'al part.

שהמנ[ח]ה נאֶ̇כֶ̇לֶ̇ת על ה̇חלבים והבשר   B 11

hip'il inf.

אין להאכילם מהקו[ד]שים   B 71

אֹכֶל

ועל האוכל̇ אנח[נ]ו חושבים   B 37

אֶל prep.

שהם זובחים] אל ה[ן   B 9

[שא הוֹא [כ]מ̇י שזנ̇ת אליו   B 9

ואף[כתב]נ̇ו אליכה   C 10

והשיבות̇[ה אל ל]בבך   C 15

וש̇ב̇ת̇ה אלו בכל לבבך [ובכו]ל נפש̇[ך   C 15

ואף אנחנו כתבנו אל̇י̇ך מקצת מעשי התורה   C 26

אֵלֶּה

אלה מקצת דברינו   B 1

לכול אלה להערי[בון]ת̇ השמש להיות טהורים   B 15

(אֵלָה see also) כי באלה[ו   C 5

[ו]מהתערב בדברים האלה   C 8

ומלבוא ע[ו]מהם [ו]לגב אלה   C 8

[וכול הדברים] האלה ב[א]חרי[ת] הימים   C 14

הבן בכל אלה   C 28

אֵלָה

(אֵלֶּה see also) כי באלה[ו   C 5

אֵם

א[ת] האם ואת הולד ביום אחד | B 36

אמר

qal part.

ו[א]ף על המוצקות אנחנו אומר[ים] | B 55

ואף על הצרועים א[נחנו א]ומרים | B 65

ועל [טמאת נפש] האדם אנחנו אומרים | B 73

אֲנַחְנוּ

ואנחנו חושבים שהמקדש[| B 29

[ועל העברות אנחנו חושבים] | B 36

ועל האוכל אנח]נו חושבים | B 37

ואף חוש[בים אנחנו | B 42

ו[א]ף על המוצקות אנחנו אומר[ים | B 55

ואף על הצרועים א[נחנו א]ומרים | B 64

ועל [טמאת נפש] האדם אנחנו אומרים | B 73

כי על [אלה א]נחנו נותנים א[ת | C 9

ו]אנחנו מכירים שבאו מקצת הברכות | C 20

ואף אנחנו כתבנו אליך מקצת מעשי התורה | C 26

אסף

qal part.

והאוס[ף] [א]ת אפרה | B 14

אַף particle

ו[א]ף [כתוב]שהמל[א]כה נאכל[ת] | B 10

ואף על טהרת פרת החטאת | B 13

ואף על עור[ו]ת ועצמות הבהמה הטמאה | B 21

וא[ף על העו]ר | B 24

ואף חוש[בים אנחנו | B 42

ו]א[ף על החרשים שלוא שמעו חוק [ומ]שפט | B 52

ו]א[ף על המוצקות אנח]נו אומרים | B 55

ואף המוצקות אינם מבדילות | B 56

ו]א[ף ע]ל מ[טעת עצ]י] המאכל | B 62

ואף על הצרועים א]נחנו א]ומרים | B 64

ו]א[ף כתוב שמעת שיגלח וכבס | B 66

ואף כתוב ש[ותסורו] מהד[רן]ך | C 12

ואף הקללות [ש]באו ב[ימ]י ירו[בעם | C 18

ו]א[ף היא [נ]צל מצרות רבות ונסלוח לו | C 25

ואף אנחנו כתבנו אליך מקצת מעשי התורה | C 26

אֵפֶר

והאוסף [א]ת אפרה | B 14

אֶרֶץ

הנטע ב[א]רץ ישראל | B 63

אִשָׁה

ועל הנש[י]ם | C 4

אָשָׁם

ותערובת [א]שם אינם רואים | B 51

אֲשֶׁר

כי ירושלים]היא המקום אשר [בחר בו | B 32

אֵת particle

ומ..ים א[ות]ה] במרק זבח[ם | B 7

שמניחים אותה מיום ליום | B 10

בשל שלוא י[היו] מסיא[י]ם את העם עוון | B 13

השוח[ט אותה והסורף אותה | B 14

השוח[ט אותה והסורף אותה | B 14

והאוסף [א]ת אפרה | B 14

והמזה א[ת [מי] החטאת | B 14

הנוש[א א[ו]ת(ה) נבלת[ה | B 23

בשל שלוא יהיו] משיאים את העם עוון | B 27

ו[מ]וציאים את דשא [ה]מ[ז]בח | B 31

א[ת האם ואת הולד ביום אחד | B 36

א]ת האם ואת הולד ביום אחד | B 36

אנח]נו חושבים שיאכל את הולד [| B 37

מתוככים ומטמא[י]ם את זרע [הקודש | B 81

ואף את [זרע]ם ע[ם הזונות | B 82

כי על [אלה א]נחנו נותנים א[ת | C 9

זכׄור את מלכי ישרא[ל]	C 23
ובקש מלפנו שׁיׄתקן את עצתך	C 29

אַתֶּם

ואתם יודעים [שעל השוגג	B 68
וא[תׄם] יודעים שמקצת הׄכהׄנים ו[העם	
[ואת]מה] ‏MS^d: ¶ מתערבים ¶	B 80
ואתם יודעים ש[פׄרישנו מרוׄב העׄ]ם	C 7
ואׄתם י[ׄודעים שלוא] [יׄ]מצא בידנו מעל	C 8

ב

ב prep.

בׄעׄשרים ושלושה בו שבׄת	A i
בׄעׄשרים ושלושה בו שבׄת	A i
בעשרים] [ו]א[חׄ]ד בׄו שׄבת	A ii
[ב]עׄשריׄם ושמונה בוׄ שבת	A ii
בארבעה] בוׄ [שבת]	A iii
בע[שתי עשר] בו שבת	A iii
בע[שתי עשר] בו שבת	A iii
בשמונה עשר בו שבת	A iii
בשמונה עשר בו שבת	A iii
בעשרים וחמשה בו שבת	A iii
בעשרים וחמשה בו שבת	A iii
בשנים בחמ[י]ש[י] [ש]ב[ת]	A iii
בשנים בחמ[י]ש[י] [ש]ב[ת]	A iii
בׄשש אׄשר בו שבת	A iv
בׄשש אׄשר בו שבת	A iv
בעשרם ושלושא בׄו שבת	A iv
בעשרם ושלושא בׄו שבת	A iv
בעשרים ואחד] בו שבת	A v
בעשרים ושנים בו מועד השמן	A v
בעשרים ושנים בו מועד השמן	A v
ומׄגיעׄי[ן]ׄ בה א[ׄ]ת [ׄ]הם	B 4
מבׄשלׄים [אות]ׄה בכׄלי [נחושת	B 6
ומ..ים בׄה את [בשר זבחיהם	B 6
וׄמ[ן] [ים בעׄזׄר[ה	B 7
אותׄה] במרק זבחׄם	B 8
עׄל הׄחלבים והבשר ביוׄם זׄוׄב[חם	B 11
לבניׄן] הכוהׄנׄים] ראׄו להׄזׄׄר בדבר הזה	B 12
בשל שלוא יׄ]היו] מסיאׄיׄן]ׄם את העם עוון	B 12
בשל שׄא יהיה הטהר מזה על הטמה	B 16
ראואׄי [להשׄ]מׄׄר בכׄוׄל הדׄׄבׄׄרׄים [האלה	B 26
איׄנׄם שוחטים במקׄׄדׄׄש	B 35
אׄ[ׄת האם ואת הׄולד ביום אחד	B 36
שהם שאין בהם [ט]הרה	B 55
וׄהׄיא המקוׄׄם שבחר בו מכל שבטי יׄ[שראל	B 61
הנטע בׄׄארץ ישראל	B 63
ועתה בהיות טמאתם עמהם	B 67
עד בוא השמש ביום השמיני	B 72
ועל הזונות הנעסה בתוך העם	B 75
[בׄ]גלל שהׄמה קדושים	B 79
כי באלה[	C 5
[ו]מׄהתערב בדברים האלה	C 8
שלוא] י]מׄצא בידנו מעל ושקר ורעׄה	C 9
שתבין בספר מוׄשׄה [ורׄ]בׄספרׄׄי הנׄ[בׄיאים	C 10
שתבין בספר מוׄשׄה [ורׄ]בׄספרׄׄי הנׄבׄיאים	C 10
בספר מוׄשׄה [ורׄ]בׄספרׄׄי הנׄ[בׄיאים ובדוׄׄי]ד	C 10
ובספר כתוב[	C 11
בׄאׄחריׄ[ת] הימים	C 14
ושׄׄבׄׄתׄׄה אלו בכל לבבך [ובׄכׄו]ׄל נפשׄׄ[ך	C 15
ושׄׄבׄׄתׄׄה אלו בכל לבבך [ובׄׄכׄו]ׄל נפשׄׄ[ך	C 16
בׄאׄחריׄ[ת] [	C 16
[כתוב בספר מושה ובׄספרׄׄי הנביאים	C 17
בׄׄ]ימי שלומוה בן דויׄׄד	C 18
ואף הׄקׄללות [ש]באוׄׄ ב[ׄי]ׄמי ירׄׄ]ובעׄם	C 19
שׄכׄׄתׄׄוב בסׄׄ]ׄׄׄׄׄפר מוׄׄ]שׄׄה	C 21
שיישובו ביׄשרא[ל] לתׄׄמׄׄיד	C 21
זׄכׄור את מלכי ישרא[ל] והתבנן במעשיהמׄהׄ	C 23
הבן בכל אלה	C 28
בשל שתשמח באחרית העת	C 30

בשל שתשמח **באחרית** העת	C 30		*hipʿil* inf.	
במצאך מקצת דברינו כן	C 30		ואין **להבי]אם** [למקדש	B 45
בעשותך הישר והטוב לפנו	C 31		ואין **להב]י** למחני הק]ו[דש כלבים	B 58

בִּגְלָל

see גָּלָל

בָּדָד

כי **בדד** [יהיו מחוץ לבית	B 65

בדל

hipʿil part.

אינם **מבד]ילות** בין הטמא [ל]טהור	B 56

בְּהֵמָה

ועל **בה]מתו** הטהור]ה כתוב	B 76

בוא

qal pf.

ואף הקללות [ש]**באו]** בי]מי ירו]ובעם	C 19
שבאו מקצת הברכות והקללות	C 20

qal impf.

שלוא י]**בואו** עם טהרת הקוד]ש	B 65
]וש]**יבוא]ו**	C 2
והיא כי **]יבו]א** עליך [כול הדברים] האלה	C 14
[בספר מושה ובספרי הנביאים **שיבואו**	C 17

qal part.

וכרו]ת השפכת שהם **באים** [בקהל	B 39
והמה **בא]ים** לטה]ר]ת המקדש	B 54

qal inf.

] מדג]ן הג]ו[ים [ואין] **לבוֹא** למקדש	B 5
עד **בוא** השמש ביום השמיני	B 72
ומלבוא ע]ומהם]ולגב אלה	C 8

hipʿil impf.

שלו]א **תב[יא** תועבה א]ל ביתכה	C 6
MS⁴:]]ושיבוא[ו **ש]יב]י]אם** ב]ן	C 20

] ונעלה ממנו **להביא** (ח) [חטאת	B 69		

בזה

qal part.

כת]ו[ב שהואה **בוזה** ומג]ד]ף	B 70

בחר

qal pf.

וה]יא המקום **שבחר** בו מכל שבטי י]שראל	B 61

בין

hipʿil impv.

הבן בכל אלה	C 28

hitpolel impv.

ז]כור את מלכי ישרא]ל[**והתבנן** במעשיהמ]ה	C 23

בֵּין prep.

אינם מבד]ילות **בין** הטמא [ל]טהור	B 56

בַּיִת

הצרועים באים ע]ם טהרת הקודש **לבית**	B 68

בְּלִיַּעַל

והרחיק ממך מחשבת רעה ועצת **בליעל**	C 29

בֵּן

כי **לבני** [אהרן] ראואי	B 16
והמה **ב]ני** זרע] קדש	B 75
ובני אהרון ק]דושי קדושים	B 79
°]°[ ]**ב]ימי** שלומוה **בן** דויד	C 18
ואף הקללות [ש]באו] בי]מי ירו]ובעם **בן** נבט	C 19

בָּקָר

ועל ע]ו]רות **הבק]ר** והצאן	B 18
ומעשר **הבקר** והצאן לכוהנים הוא	B 63

בקש

piʿel impv.

ובקש מלפנו שׁ֯יֿתֿקֿן את עצתך   C 28

piʿel part.

והם מֿבֿ[קֿ]שׁי תורה [נשו]א֯י עונות   C 24

בְּרָכָה

בֿ֯אֿחרי[תֿ] הימים הבֿרכה [וה]קֿללא   C 14

שבאוו מקצֿת הבֿרֿכות והקללֿות   C 20

בשל

piʿel part.

שהם מֿבֿשׁלֿ֯יֿם [אות]֯ה בכֿלי [נחושת   B 6

בְּשֶׁל

see   שֶׁל

בָּשָׂר

בשר זבחיהם   B 7

שהמנ[ח]ה נאכֿלֿ֯ת על הֿחלבים והבשר   B 11

מקצת [ע]צֿ֯מות המקֿ[דש ו]הֿ֯בשר עליהם   B 59

ג

גַּב

ומֿ֯לֿבוא עֿ֯וֿמהם וֿ֯[לֿ]גֿבֿ֯י ¶עֿ֯ו֯[ל גב or ¶ אלֿה   C 8

גֶּבֶר

מֿכֿול תֿ[ע]רובֿת [ה]גֿבר   B 48

גדף

piʿel part.

כת[ו]ב שהואה בוזה ומֿגֿ[דֿ]ף֯   B 70

גוי

ואין לאכול מֿדֿגֿן [הגֿ]וֿ֯יֿ֯ם   B 5

ועל זבֿחֿ הגוים [אנחנו אומרים   B 8

גלה

qal inf.

ועד גֿלֿ[וֿ]ת ירושלם וצדקיה מלך יֿהֿוֿדֿ[ה   C 19

גלח

piʿel impf.

שמעת שׁיגלח וכבס [יֿ]שׁב מחוֿ֯ץ [B 66

גָּלָל

בֿ֯]גלל שהמה קדושים   B 79

ד

דָּבָר

אלֿה מקצת דבֿרינו   B 1

לבני] הכוהנֿ[י]ם רֿ֯אֿו להֿזֿהֿר בדבר הזה   B 12

ראואֿי [להש]מֿ֯וֿר בכֿול הדֿ֯בֿ]רֿ֯ים [האלה   B 26

וֿ֯הֿדבר כתוב עברה   B 38

ו֯]מֿהתערב בדברים האֿלה   C 8

והיא כי [יבו]א עליך [וכול <u>הדברים</u>] הֿאלה   C 14

במצאך מקצֿת דברינו כֿן   C 30

דָּגָן

ועל תרומת ד[ָ]גֿן הֿ[גוים   B 3

[מֿדֿגֿן [הגֿ]וֿיֿם [ואין] לבוא למקדש]   B 5

דָּוִד pers.

[ו]בֿספרֿ֯י הנֿ֯[ב]יאים ובדוֿי֯]ד   C 10

[בֿימי שלומוה בן דויֿד   C 18

זכור [את] דוֿ֯יֿ֯ד שהיא איש חסדים   C 25

דּוֹר

ובדוֿ֯י]ד   במעשיֿ] דור ודור   C 11

ובדוֿ֯י]ד   במעשיֿ] דור ודור   C 11

דֶּרֶךְ

שׁ[תסורו] מהֿדֿ[ר]וֿ֯ך וקרתֿ[ך] הרֿעֿה   C 12

דֶּשֶׁן

וׁי[מ]וציאים את דשא [ה]מׁזבח	B 31

ה

הוּא

יׁ[ה]וׁא מחׁנה ערׁ[י]הׁם	B 30
כראשית הׁוׁא לכוהנים	B 63
ומעשר הבקר והׁצׁאן לכוהנׁיׁם הׁוא	B 64
כת[ו]ב שהׁואה בוזה ומג[ד]ף	B 70
כמשפט המת או החלל הׁוׁא	B 74
וזה הׁוׁא אחרית הימים	C 21

הִיא

ויׁ[רׁו]שׁלׁי[ם] מחנה היא'	
ׁ[י]רושלים [הי]אה מחנה ¶MSᵈ:	B 30
כי ירושלים יׁ[ה]יא המׁקום אשר [בחר בו	B 32
כי ירושלים היאׁה מחנה הקׁדש	B 60
וׁהׁיא המקוׁם שבחר בו מכל שבטׁי יׁ[שראל	B 60
כי יר[ו]שלים היא' ראש [מׁ]חׁנׁות ישראל	
היאה ¶MSᵈ:	B 61
כי] התועבה שנואה הׁיׁאׁה	C 7

הִיָה

qal pf.

וׁהׁיא כי [יבׁו]א עׁליך [וכל הדברים] הׁאׁלה	C 13
שמי מהם שהׁיא ירׁא [ואת התוׁ]רה	C 24
היה מצׁל מצרות	C 24
זכור [את] דוׁיׁד שהׁיא איש חסדים	C 25
וׁ[אׁף] הׁיׁא [נ]צׁל מצׁרות רבות	C 26

qal impf.

בשל שלוא יׁ[היו] מסיאׁ[י]ׁם את העם עוון	B 12
בשל שׁא יהיה הטהר מזה על הטמה	B 16
כי בדד יׁהׁיׁו מחוץ לבית	B 66
ועל לבושׁ[ו] כתב שלוׁא יהיה שעטנז	B 78
וׁ]יׁהיה מתׁ]	C 3

qal inf.

להערי[בו]ׁת השמש לׁהׁיות טהורים	B 15
כי לבני [אהרן] ראואי לׁהׁיות מׁ	B 17
ולהיות יראים מהמקדש	B 49
ועתה בהיות טמאתם עׁמהם	B 67

הֵם

שהם מׁ[קצת דבריׁ] [ה]מׁעשים	B 1
שהם מבשלׁים [אות]ה בכלׁי [נחושת	B 6
ׁ]ׁת שהמׁ[ה]	B 24
וכרוׁ]ׁת השפכת שהם באים [בקהל	B 39
וׁהמה באׁים לטהׁ[רׁ]ת הׁמקדש	B 54
אנחׁנׁו אומרׁ[ים] שהם שאין בהם [ט]הרה	B 55
שהם אוכלים מקצת [עׁצׁ]מׁות המקׁ[דש	B 58
והמה בׁ[נׁי זרע] קדש	B 75
בׁ[גׁ]לל שהׁמׁה קדושים	B 79
והם מׁבׁ[קׁ]שׁי תורה [נשׁוׁ]אׁי עׁונות	C 24

הָעֲרִיבוֹת

see ערב

ו

וָלָד

א]ׁת האם ואת הׁולד ביום אחד	B 36
שאׁיאכל את הׁולד]	B 37

ז

זבח

qal part.

שהם זׁובׁחׁים] אל הׁי[ן	B 8

qal inf.

שהמנׁ[חה נאׁכׁלׁת] עׁל הׁחלבים	
(וׁזֶבַח see also) והבשר ביוׁם זׁ]ׁבׁ]חם	B 11

זֶבַח

את] בשר זבחיהם	B 7

אות֯ה] במרק זבח֯ם   B 8

ועל זב֯ח הגוים [אנחנו חושבים   B 8

ואף על מנחת זבח השל[ו]מים   B 9

שהמנ[חה נא֯כ֯לת] ע֯ל ה֯חלבים והבשר

ביום ז֯[ב]חם (see also זבח, *qal* inf.)   B 11

זֶה

כי לבני] הכוהנ֯[י]ם ר֯או להזהיר בדבר הזה   B 12

וזה ה֯וא אחרית הימים   C 21

זהר

nipʿal inf.

[שאינם רואים להזהר מכל תערובת]   B 50

hipʿil inf.

כי לבני] הכוהנ֯[י]ם ר֯או להזה֯ר' בדבר הזה

ולה[ז]הר ¶MSᵇ: B 12

זכר

qal impv.

זכור [את] דו֯יד שהיא איש חסדים   C 25

זנה

qal pf.

[שא ה֯ו֯א] כ]מ֯י שז֯נ֯ת אליו   B 9

qal part.

ומטמא֯י[ם] את זר֯ע֯ [הקודש ואף]

את [זרע֯]ם֯ ע֯ם הזונות   B 82

זנות

ועל הזונות' הנעסה בתוך העם

והזנות ¶MSᵈ: B 75

בגלל י[ה]חמס והזנות אבד֯[ו מקצת] מקומות   C 5

זרע

qal inf.

ושלוא לזרו֯ע שדו ול[כ]רמו כלאים   B 78

זֶרַע

מ֯תוככים ומטמאי֯[ם] את זר֯ע֯ [הקודש   B 81

ח

חוּץ

או ישחט מ֯חוץ למח֯נה שו֯ר וכשב ועז   B 28

וחו[צה] הוא חוצה לירושלים   B 30

חוץ ממ֯[חנה   B 31

[י]שב מחו֯ץ [לאוהלו שבעת י]מ֯י[ם   B 66

חַטָּאת

ואף על טהרת פרת החטא֯ת   B 13

והמזה את֯ [מי] החטאת   B 15

ו֯[החטא֯ת ו֯[מ]וציאים את דשא [ה]מ֯זבח   B 31

ונעלה ממנו להביא (ה) [ח֯ט֯את   B 70

חֵלֶב

שהמנ[חה נא֯כ֯לת] על ה֯חל֯בים והבשר   B 11

חָלָל

כמשפט המת או החלל הוא   B 74

חֲמִישִׁי

בשנים בחמ֯[י]ש֯[י] [ש֯[ב]֯ת   A iii

חָמָס

בגלל י[ה]חמס והזנות אבד֯[ו מקצת] מקומות   C 5

חֲמִשָּׁה

בעשרים וחמשה בו שבת   A iii

חֶסֶד

זכור [את] דו֯יד שהיא איש חסדים   C 25

חֹק

שלוא שמעו חוק [ומ]שפט וטהרה   B 52

חָרֵשׁ

וא[ף] על החרשים שלוא שמעו חוק   B 52

חשב

qal part.

וּאֲנֹחֹנו חושבים שהמקדש‏[‏‏	B 29
‏[‏ועל העברות אנֹחֹנו חֹוֹשבים שאין	B 36
אנח‏[‏נֹו חושבים שאיאכל את הולד ‏]	B 37
ואף חֹוֹשֹ‏[‏ב‏]‏ים אנחנו ‏[‏שאין	B 42

nip'al pf.

ונחשבה לך לצדקה	C 31

ט

טָהוֹר

להעריֹ‏[‏בו‏]‏ֹת השמש להֹיות טהורים	B 15
בשל שא יהיה הטהר מזה על הטמה	B 16
(see also טהר, *qal* part. *pa'el*)	
ואף על עור נבלת הבהמה‏] הטהורה	B 23
אינם מבֹדֹילות בין הטמא ‏[‏ל‏]‏טהור	B 57

טהר

qal part. *pa'el*

בשל שא יהיה הטהר מזה על הטמה	B 16
(see also טָהוֹר)	

טָהֳרָה

וכוֹ‏[‏לֹֹם על‏]‏ וטהרת ‏[‏הֹ‏]	B 3
ואף על טהרֹת פרת החטאת	B 13
‏[‏לוא יגֹשֹ לטהרת הקודש	B 23
שלוא שמעו חוק ‏[‏ומֹ‏]‏שפט וטהרה	B 52
והמה באֹיֹם לטהֹ‏[‏רֹ‏]‏ֹת הֹמקדש	B 54
שהם שאין בהם ‏[‏ט‏]‏הרה	B 56
שלוא יֹ‏[‏בואו עם טהרת הקֹוֹד‏]‏ש	B 65
הצרועים באֹ‏[‏‏‏ֹֹם ע‏]‏‏ֹ טֹהרת הֹקודש לבית	B 68

טמא

qal part. *pa'el*

בשל שא יהיה הטהר מזה על הטמה	B 16

pi'el part.

ומֹגיעֹ‏[‏‏י‏]‏ֹם בה אֹ‏[‏ת ‏]‏ֹהם ומטֹמאים אותה	B 4
‏[‏ מֹתוככים ומטמאיֹ‏[‏ם‏]‏ את זרעֹ ‏[‏הקודש	B 81

טֻמְאָה

‏[טמאות ‏]	B 42
ועתה בהיות טמאתם עֹמהם	B 67
‏[‏ואף בהיות להֹמֹה טֻמֹאֹוֹת נגע‏]	B 71

י

יָד

ומן עֹ‏[‏‏ו‏]‏‏ֹ‏[‏וֹ‏]‏‏ֹת‏[‏‏‏]‏מה ידות בֹ‏[‏לים	B 22
שלוא‏] יֹ‏[‏מֹצא בידנו מעל ושקר ורעֹה	C 9

ידע

qal impf.

כֹי שלוא ראה ולוא שמע ולוא ‏[‏יֹ‏]‏ֹדֹע לעשות	B 54

qal part.

ואתם יודעים ‏]	B 68
וֹאֹתֹֹם יודעים שמקצת הֹכֹהנים וֹ‏[‏	B 80
וֹאתם יֹ‏[‏‏ו‏]‏דעים שלוא‏] יֹ‏[‏מֹצא בידנו מעל	C 8

יְהוּדָה

ועד גֹל‏[‏ו‏]‏ֹת ירושלם וצדקיה מלך יֹ‏[‏הֹוֹד‏]‏ה	C 19

יוֹם

שלוש מאת וֹשֹ‏[‏שים וארבעה‏] יֹוֹם	A 21
שמניחיֹם אותה מיום ליום	B 10
שמניחים אותה מיום ליום	B 10
עֹֹ הֹחלבים והבשר ביוֹ‏[‏ם זֹבֹ‏]‏חם	B 11
אֹ‏[‏ֹת האם ואת הולד ביום אחד	B 36
יֹ‏[‏שב מחוֹץ ‏[‏לאוהלו שבעת יֹ‏]‏מֹֹם	B 67
עד בוא השמש ביום השמיני	B 72
‏[‏וכול הדברים‏]‏ֹ האלה בֹאֹחריֹ‏[‏ו‏]‏ֹת‏]‏ הימים	C 14
בֹ‏[‏ימי שלומה בן דויֹד	C 18
ואף הֹקללות ‏[‏ש‏]‏באוֹ בֹ‏[‏י‏]‏מיֹֹ ירֹ‏[‏ו‏]‏בעֹֹ	
בן נבט ¶MSᵈ: ¶מיומֹ‏[‏י?¶	C 19

וזה הוא אחרית הימים	C 21

יָסֻף

nip'al part.

ע[ל]ו אחר [ה[שֹ]בת ויום השני השלישי נו[סֻ]ף	A 20

יָצָא

hip'il part.

וי[מֹ]וֹציאים את דשא [הֹ]מֹזבח	B 31

יָצַק

hup'al pass. part.

ו[אֹ]ף על המוצקות אנחֹנֹו אומר[ים]	B 55
ֹואף המוצקות אינם מבדֹּילות	B 56
כי לחת המוצקות והֹמֹקבל מהמה	B 57

יָרֵא

qal part. *pa'el*

[ולהיות יראים מהמקדש	B 49
שמי מהם שהיא ירֹא [ו]את התוֹ[רה	C 24

יָרָבְעָם pers.

ואף הֹקללות [ש]באֹוֹ בֹיֹמי יר[וֹ]ֹבעֹם	C 19

יְרוּשָׁלַיִם

וי[רֹו]שלי[ם] מחנה היא	B 29
כי ירושלים היאה מחנה הקֹדש	B 60
כי יר[ו]שלים היא ראש [מ]חֹנֹות ישראל	B 61
ועד גל[ו]ת ירושלם וצדקיה מלך יֹהֹוֹ]ֹה	C 19

יָשַׁב

qal impf.

[י]שב מחֹוץ [לאוהלו שבעת י]מֹיֹם	B 66

יָשָׁר

בעשותך הישר והטוב לפנֹו	C 31

יִשְׂרָאֵל

ולא [ש]מעו משפטי ישראל	B 53

והֹיא המקוֹם שבחר בו מכל שבטי י[שראל]	B 61
כי יר[ו]שלים היא ראש [מֹ]חֹנֹות ישראל	B 62
הנטע בֹארץ ישראל	B 63
משכתוב קודש ישראל	B 76
שישובו ביש[ראֹל] לתֹ[מיד]	C 21
זֹכֹוֹר את מלכי ישרא[ל] והתבנן במעשיהֹמֹה	C 23
לטוב לך ולישראל	C 32

כ

כ prep.

כי לחת המוצקות והֹמֹקבל מהמה כהֹם	B 57
כראשית הוֹא לכוהנים	B 63
כמשפט המת או החלל הוֹא	B 74
כֹשכתוב' קודש [ישראל] ¶MS'¶	B 76

כבס

pi'el pf.

שמעת שיגלה וכבס [י]שב מחוֹץ	B 66

כהן

qal part.

לבני] הכוהנֹ[י]ם רֹאו להֹזֹהֹר בדבר הזה	B 12
כי לבני] הכֹ[וֹ]הנֹ[י]ם ראוֹי [להש]מֹ[וֹר	B 26
כראשית הוֹא לכוהנים	B 63
ומעשר הבקר והֹצֹון לכוהֹנים הוא	B 64
וא]תֹם יודעים שמקצת הֹכֹהֹנים וֹ]	B 80

כון

qal part. *pa'el*

במצאך מקֹצֹת דברינו כֹן	C 30

see also כֵּן

כִּי

כי לבני [אהרן] ראוֹי [להיות מֹ' [	B 16
כי °[בצפֹ[ו]ן המחנֹה]	B 28
כֹי שלוא ראֹה ולוא שמע לוא [י]ֹדע לעשות	B 53

כי לחת המוצקות והׁמׁקבל מהמה — B 57

כי ירושלים היׁאה מחנה הקדׁש — B 59

כׁי יר[ו]שלים היא ראש [מ]חׁנׁות ישראל — B 61

כי בדד [יהיו מחוץ לבית — B 65

כֹ]י לבני אהרון [— B 82

כי באלה ו — C 5

כי על [אלה א]נחנו נותנים א[ת — C 9

והיא כי [יבו]א עׁליך [וכול הדברים] הׁאלה — C 13

כל

וכו]לׁם על[— B 2

לכול אלה להערי[בו]ׁת השמש להׁיות טהורים — B 15

ראוׁי [להש]מׁ[ר] בׁכׁוׁל הד[ב]רׁ[ים [האלה — B 26

אשר [בחר בו מֹכֹוֹל שֹבֹטי ישראל — B 33

להזהר מֹכֹוֹל תֹ[ערובת [ה]גבר — B 48

להזהר מכל תערו[בת] — B 50

והׁיא המקוׁם שבחר בו מכל שבטי יׁ[שראל — B 61

שכול עצם ש[היא חסרה וׁשלמה — B 73

והיא כי [יבו]א עׁליך [וכׁול הדברים] הׁאלה — C 14

וש[ב]תׁה אלו בכל לבבך [ובכו]ל נפשׁ[ך — C 15

וש[ב]תׁה אלו בכל לבבך [וׁבׁ]כׁו]ל נפשׁ[ך — C 16

הבן בכל אלה — C 28

כִּלְאַיִם

כתוב שלוא לרבעה כלאים — B 77

כֶּלֶב

ואין להׁבׁי למחני הֹקֹ[ו]דׁש כלבים — B 58

כְּלִי

שהם מבׁשׁלׁים [אות]ׁה בכׁלׁי [נחושת — B 6

מן [עורות]יׁהם כלׁי[ם — B 19

כֵּן

ואתם יודעים שהו[א] כן והׁדבר כתוב עברה — B 38

see also כן

כרת

qal pass. part.

והׁממזר ופׁצוע הדכה וכרו]ׁת השפכת — B 39

כֶּשֶׂב

או ישחט] מחוׁץ למחׁנה שוׁר וכשב ועז — B 28

כתב

qal pf.

ואף אנחנו כתבנו אׁליך מקצת מעשי התורה — C 26

qal pass. part.

וע[ל] שא כתוב [איש כי ישחט במחנה — B 27

ואתם יודעים שהו[א] כן והׁדבר כתוב עברה — B 38

ו]אף כתוב שמעת שיגלה וכבס — B 66

כת]וב שהואה בוזה ומג[ד]ףׁ — B 70

משכתוב קודש ישראל — B 76

ועל בה[מתו הטהור]ה כתוב — B 77

ואף] כתוׁב בספר מושה — C 6

ובספר כתוב ו — C 11

ואף כתוב שנ[ותסור]ו מהד[ר]ך — C 12

וׁכׁתׁ[וב] והיא כי [יבו]א עׁליך ו — C 12

הברכות והקללות שׁ[כׁ]תׁוׁב בס[פׁר מו]שׁה — C 21

ל

ל prep.

[ואין] לבׁו]א למקדׁש] — B 5

[ואין] לבוׁא למקדׁש] — B 5

שמניחים אותׁה מיום ליום — B 10

לבני] הכוהׁנׁ[י]ם רׁאׁו להזהׁ[ר בדבר הזה — B 12

לכול אלה להערי[בו]ׁת השמש להׁיות טהורים — B 15

להערי[בו]ׁת השמש להׁיׁות טהורים — B 15

להערי[בו]ׁת השמש להׁיׁות טהורים — B 15

כי לבני [אהרן] ראוׁי [להיות מׁ[— B 16

כי לבני [אהרן] ראוׁי [לְהֱיֹות מׁ[— B 17

אין] [להביא]ם למקד]ש — B 20

מֶלֶךְ

ועד גל[ו]ת ירושלם וצדקיה מלך יהוד[ה]	C 19
זכ[ו]ר את מלכי ישרא[ל]	C 23

מַמְזֵר

והממזר ופצוע הדכה וכרו[ת] השפכת	B 39

מִן prep.

אלה מקצת דברינו [ ]ל	B 1
שהם מ[קצת דברי] ה[מ]עשים	B 1
שמניחים אותה מיום ליום	B 10
[ומ]ן ע[ו]ר[ות]מה ידות כ[לים	B 22
או ישחט מ[חוץ למחנה ש]ור וכשב ועז	B 28
חוץ ממ[חנה]א[ר ו]ל החטאת	B 31
[ו]היא המקום אשר [בחר בו מכול	B 33
ראוי להזהר מכול ת[ערובת ה]גבר	B 48
[ולהיות יראים מהמקדש	B 49
להזהר מכל תערובת]	B 50
כי לחת המוצקות והמ[ק]בל מה[מה כהם	B 57
שהם אוכלים מקצת [ע]צמות המק[דש	B 59
והיא המקום שבחר בו מכל שבטי י[שראל	B 61
שמעת שיגלח וכבס [י]שב מחוץ [לאוהלו	B 66
שמעת שיגלח וכבס [י]שב מחוץ [לאוהלו	B 66
ונעלה ממנו להביא (ח) [ח]טאת	B 69
אין להאכילם מהקו[ד]שים	B 71
משכתוב קודש ישראל	B 76
[וא]ת[ם יודעים שמקצת ה]כהנים ו[	B 80
[ואתם יודעים ש]פ[ר]שנו מרו[ב] הע[ם	C 7
ומ]לבוא ע[ו]מהם ו]לגב אלה	C 8
ואף כתוב ש[ו]תסורו מהד[רו]ך	C 12
מיומ[י] ¶MSᵈ¶	C 19
שבאוו מקצת הברכות והקללות	C 20
שמי מהם שהיא ירא [את התו]רה	C 23
היה מצול מצרות	C 24
[ו]אף הי[א נ]צל מצרות רבות	C 26

מַדָּע

שר[וא]ינו עמך ערמה ומדע תורה	C 28

מוֹאָבִי

[ ]ועל העמוני והמואבי והממזר	B 39

מוֹעֵד

בעשרים ושנים בו מועד השמן	A v

מוּת

qal part. paᶜel

כמשפט המת או החלל הו[א	B 74

מִזְבֵּח

ו[מ]וציאים את דשא [ה]מ[ז]בח	B 32

מַחֲנֶה

או ישחט] מחוץ למ[ח]נה ש[ור וכשב ועז	B 28
כי [ ] בצפון המחנה]	B 28
וי[רושלי]ם] מחנה היא	B 30
וחו[צה] למחנה[ ] הוא חוצה לירושלים	B 30
[הוא מח]נה עד[י]הם	B 30
חוץ ממ[חנה]א[ר ו]ל החטאת	B 31
ואין להבי למחני הק[וד]ש כלבים	B 58
כי ירושלים היאה מחנה הקדש	B 60
כי יר[ו]שלים היא ראש [מ]ח[נ]ות ישראל	B 62

מַחֲשָׁבָה

והרחיק ממך מחשב(ו)ת[י] רעה ועצת בליעל	
[ ]מחשבת :MSᶜ¶	C 29

מַטָּעַת

ואף ע[ל מ]טעת עצ[י]ן המאכל	B 62

מִי

[שא הי]א] כ]מי שזנת אליו	B 9
[ומ]י ישנו]	C 3
שמי מהם שהיא ירא [את התו]רה	C 23

כתבנו אליך מקצת מעשי התורה	C 27
ובקש מלפנו שׁיתקן את עצתך	C 28
והרחיק ממך מחשבת רעה ועצת בליעל	C 29
במצאך מקצת דברינו כן	
¶מדברינו :MSᶜ¶	C 30

מִנְחָה

שהמנ]חה נאבלת] על החלבים והבשר	B 11

מַעַל

החמס והמעל]	[	C 4
שלוא י]מצא בידנו מעל ושקר ורעה	C 9

מַעֲשֶׂה

שהם מ]קצת דברי [ה]מעשים	B 2
זכור את מלכי ישראל[ל] והתבנן במעשיהמה	C 23
כתבנו אליך מקצת מעשי התורה	C 27

מצא

qal inf.

במצאך מקצת דברינו כן	C 30

nip'al impf.

שלוא י]מצא בידנו מעל ושקר ורעה	C 9

מָצוֹל

היה מצול מצרות	C 24

מִקְדָּשׁ

מדגן [הג]ויים [ואין] לבוא למקדש]	B 5
אין] [להביא]ם למקד]ש	B 20
שהמקדש]ו משכן אהל מועד הוא	B 29
אי]ם שוחטים במקד]ש	[	B 35
ולהיות יראים מהמקדש	B 49
והמה באים לטה]ר]ת המקדש	B 54
שהם אוכלים מקצת [ע]צמות המ[ק]דש	B 59

מָקוֹם

כי ירושלים]היא המקום אשר [בחר בו	B 32

והיא המקום שבחר בו מכל שבטי י]שראל	B 60
בגלל]ה]חמס והזנות אבד]ו מקצת] מקומות	C 6

מִקְצָת

see קְצָת

מָרָק

אותה] במרק זבחם	B 8

מֹשֶׁה pers.

שתבין בספר מושה]ובו]בספרו]י הנ]ביאים	C 10
כתוב בספר] מושה ובס]פרי הנביאי]ם	C 17
הברכות והקללות שכתוב בס]פר מו]שה	C 21

מִשְׁפָּט

שלוא שמעו חוק [ומ]שפט וטהרה	B 52
ולא [ש]מעו משפטי ישראל	B 53
כמשפט המת או החלל הו֗א	B 74

נ

נְבָט pers.

ואף ה֗קללות [ש]באו בי]מי ירו]בעם בן נבט	C 19

נָבִיא

בספר מוש֗ה]ובו]בספר]י הנ]ביאים ובדוי]ד	C 10

נְבֵלָה

ואף על עור נבלת הבהמה הטהורה	B 22
הנוש֗א א]ו]ת(ה) נבלת֗ה [לוא יגש לטהרת	B 23

נגע

hip'il part.

ומ֗גיע[י]ם בה א֗ת]ל]הם	B 4

נֶגַע

ואף בהיות להמה ט]מאות נ]גע	B 71

נגש

qal impf.

הנושׁ[ו]א א[ו]ת(ה) נבלתׁ[ה] [לוא יֻגֹשׁ לטהרת　B 23

נוח

hipʿil part.

[השׁל]מים] שׁמניחיׄם אותה מיום ליום　B 10

נזה

hipʿil part.

והמזה את [מי] החטאת　B 14

בשל שׁא יהיה הטהר מזה על הטמא　B 16

נכר

hipʿil part.

ׁואנחנו מכׁירים שֹבאׁוׄ מקצׁת הברׁכות　C 20

נֶפֶשׁ

ושֹבׁתׁה אלו בכל לבבך [ובֹכו]ׁל נֹפשׁך　C 16

נצל

qal part. *mafʿul*

see מַצּוּל

nipʿal part.

וׁ[א]ׁף הׁיׁא [נ]צׁלׄ מׁצׁרות רבות ונסלוח לׁו

]ׁמ[צׁול :MSᶜ]　C 26

נשא

qal part.

<u>הנושׁ</u>[ו]א א[ו]ת(ה) נבלתׁ[ה] [לוא יגש לטהרת　B 23

hipʿil part.

בשל שלוא יׁהׁיׁו] מסיאׁ[י]ׁם את העם עווׁן　B 13

בשל שלוא יהיו] משיאׁים את העׁם עווׁן　B 27

נתן

qal part.

כי על [ואלה א]ׁ[נ]חׁנו נותנים א]ׁת　C 9

ס

סלח

nipʿal inf.

וׁ[א]ׁף הׁיׁא [נ]צׁל מׁצׁרות רבות ונסלוח לׁו　C 26

סמה

qal part.

ואף ע[ל] הסומׁ[י]ׁם [שֹאינם רואים　B 49

סֵפֶר

שתבין בספר מׁושׁה [וׁו]ׁבׁסׁפׁרׁ]ׁי הנׁבׁיׁאים　C 10

שתבין בספר מׁושׁה [וׁו]ׁבׁסׁפׁרׁ]ׁי הנׁבׁיׁאים　C 10

ובספר כתוב]ׁ　C 11

ע

עֲבָרָה

ואתם יודעים שהו]ׁא כן וׁ[הׁדׁבׁר כתוב עברה　B 38

עַד prep.

עד בוא השמש ביום השמיני　B 72

ועד גל[ו]ׁת ירושלם וצדקיה מלך יׁהׁו]ׁה　C 19

עָווֹן

בשל שלוא יׁ[הׁיׁו] מסיאׁ]ׁ[י]ׁם את העם עווׁן　B 13

בשל שלוא יהיו] משיאים את העם עווׁן　B 27

והם מׁבׁ[ק]ׁשׁי תורה [נשו]ׁאׁי עווׁנׁות　C 25

עוֹר

ועל עׁוׁ[ר]ׁרׁות הבקׁ[ר והצאן　B 18

ואף עׁ[ל] עוׁר[ות ועצמות הבהמה הטמאה　B 21

ומן עׁ]ׁ[וׁ]ׁרׁ[וׁת]ׁ]ׁמה ידות כׁלים　B 22

ואף על עׁוׁר נבלת הבהמה] הטהורה　B 22

עֵז

או ישחט למחׁנה מחוץ שׁוׁר וכשב ועז　B 28

עָרְמָה

שר[א]ינו עמך ערמה ומדע תורה   C 28

עשׂה

qal inf.

ואי[ן] לה[י]ל[כ]ם [ו]ל[ע]שׂותם [עצם אחת   B 44

כי שלוא ראה ולוא שמע ולוא [י]דע לעשות   B 54

בעשותך הישר והטוב לפנו   C 31

nip‘al part. fem.

ועל הזונות הנעסה בתוך העם   B 75

עֶשֶׂר

בשמונה עשר בו שבת   A iii

בשש אשר בו שבת   A iv

עֶשְׂרִים

ב[ע]שרים ושלושה בו שבת   A i

[ב]עשרים ושמונה בו שבת   A ii

בעשרים וחמשה בו שבת   A iii

בעשרם ושלושא בו שבת   A iv

בעשרים ושנים בו מועד השמן   A v

עַשְׁתֵּי-עָשָׂר

בע[שתי עשר] בו שבת   A iii

עֵת

שמעת שיגלה וכבס [י]שב מחוץ]   B 66

בשל שתשמח באחרית העת   C 30

עַתָּה

ועתה בהיות טמאתם עמהם]   B 67

פ

פָּנִים

ובקש מלפנו שיתקן את עצתך   C 28

בעשותך הישר והטוב לפנו   C 31

פָּרָה

ואף על טהרת פרת החטאת   B 13

פרש

qal pf.

ואתם יודעים ש[י]פרשנו מרוב הע[ם]   C 7

צ

צאן

ומעשר הבקר והצון לכוהנים הוא   B 64

צְדָקָה

ונחשבה לך לצדקה   C 31

צִדְקִיָּה pers.

ועד גל[ו]ת ירושלם וצדקיה מלך יהוד[ה]   C 19

צוק

see יצק

צָפוֹן

כי ○○ בצפון המחנה]   B 28

צָרָה

היה מצול מצרות   C 24

ו]אף היא [נ]צל מצרות רבות   C 26

צרע

qal pass. part.

ואף על הצרועים אנחנו א[ו]מרים   B 64

הצרועים באים ע[ם] טהרת הקודש לבית   B 68

ק

קבל

pi‘el part.

כי לחת המוצקות והמקבל מהמה   B 57

קָדוֹשׁ

ב[ג]לל שהמה קדושים ובני אהרון ק[B 79

ובני אהרון ק[ד]ושי קדושים   B 79

קֹדֶשׁ

ואין להבי למחני הק[ו]דש כלבים   B 58

כי ירושלים היאה מחנה הקֹדש¹

¶והקודש :MSᵈ¶   B 60

שלוא י]בואו   עם טהרת הקֹוד[ש   B 65

הצרועים באים ע[ם ט]הרת הקֹדש לבית   B 68

אין להאכילם מהקו[ד]שים   B 71

והמה ב[ני זרע] קדש   B 76

משכתוב קודש ישראל   B 76

קָהָל

שהם באים [בקהל   B 40

קְלָלָה

בֹאחרי[ת] הימים הברכה [וה]קללא   C 14

ואף הֹקללות [ש]באוֹ בֹ[י]מי ירֹ[ו]בעם   C 18

שֹבאוו מקצת הברכות והקללוֹת   C 20

קָצָת

אלה מקצת דברינו   B 1

ואתם יודעים שמקצת] העם   B 46

שהם אוכלים מקצת [ע]צֹמות המק[ד]ש   B 59

שמקצת הֹכֹהנים ו]הֹעם מתערבים   B 80

שֹבאו מקצת הברכות והקללות   C 20

כתבנו אליך מקצת מעשי התורה   C 27

במצֹאך מקצֹת דברינו כֹן   C 30

קָרְבָּן

אֹ[ח]ריו קרבֹ[ן]   A v

קרה

qal pf.

ש[ו]תסורֹ] מהֹ[ד]רֹ[ו]ך וקרֹתֹ[ו]ך הרֹעה   C 12

ר

ראה

qal pf.

כי שלוא רֹאה ולוא שמע לוא [י]דֹע לעשות   B 53

שר[א]ינֹו עמך ערמה ומדע תורה   C 27

qal part.

ואף ע[ל] הסומ[י]ם [שאינם רואים להזהר   B 50

ותערובת [א]שֹם אינם רואים   B 51

qal pass. part.

כי לבני] הכוהנ[י]ם רֹאוֹי להזֹה'ר בדבר הזה

¶וראוי :MSᵇ¶   B 12

כי לבני [אהרן] ראואי¹ [להיות מֹ

¶וראוי :MSᵇ¶   B 17

כי לבני] הכֹ[ו]הנ[י]ם ראואֹ¹ [להש]מֹ'ר   B 26

ראש

כי יר]ושלים היא ראש מ[חֹ]נֹות ישראל   B 61

רֵאשִׁית

כראשית הֹוֹא לכוהנים   B 63

רַב

[ו]אֹף הֹיא [נ]צֹל מצֹרות רבוֹת   C 26

רֹב

ואתם יודעים ש[ו]פֹרשנו מרוֹב העֹם   C 7

רבע

piʿel inf.

ועל בהֹ[מתו הטהור]ה כתוב שלוא לרבעה¹

¶ולהרביע]ה :MSᵈ¶   כלאים   B 77

רחק

hipʿil pf.

והרחיק ממך מחשבת רעה ועצת בליעל   C 29

רָעָה

C 9 שלוא [י]מצא בידנו מעל ושקר ורעה

C 12 ש[י]תסורו מהדר[ך] וקרת[ך] הרעה

והרחיק ממך מחשבת רעה ועצת בליעל

C 29 ¶רע :MS^f¶

רשע

hip'il impf.

C 22]והרשעים ירש[יע]ו ואמ[ ]

רָשָׁע

C 22]והרשעים ירש[יע]ו ואמ[ ]

ש

ש particle

B 1 שהם מ[קצת דברי] [ה]מעשים

B 2 [ה]מעשים שא א[נ]ח[נו חושבים

B 9]שא היא[כ]מי שזנת אליו

B 9]שא היא[כ]מי שזנת אליו

B 10 שמניחים אותה מיום ליום

B 11 שהמנ[חה נאכלת] על החלבים והבשר

B 12 בשל שלוא י[היו] מסיא[י]ם את העם עוון

B 16 בשל שא יהיה הטהר מזה על הטמה

B 24]ת שהמ[ה

B 27 [וע]ל שא כתוב [איש כי ישחט במחנה

B 29 ואנחנו חושבים שהמקדש[

B 37 אנח]נו חושבים שאיאכל את הולד

B 39 שהם באים [בקהל

B 50 ואף ע[ל הסומ[י]ם [שאינם רואים

B 52 וא]ף על החרשים שלוא שמעו חוק

B 53 כי שלוא ראה ולוא שמע לוא [י]דע לעשות

B 55 אנחנו אומר[ים] שהם שאין בהם [ט]הרה

B 55 אנחנו אומר[ים] שהם שאין בהם [ט]הרה

B 58 שהם אוכלים מקצת [ע]צמות המק[דש

B 61 והיא המקום שבחר בו מכל שבטי [ישראל

B 66 כתוב שמעת שיגלח וכבס

B 66 כתוב שמעת שיגלח וכבס

B 70 כת]וב שהואה בוזה ומג[ד]ף

B 73 שאנחנו א[ומ]רים שכול[עצם

B 73 שכול עצם ש[היא חסרה] ושלמה

B 73 שכול עצם ש[היא חסרה] ושלמה

B 76 משכתוב קודש ישראל

B 77 כתוב שלוא לרבעה כלאים

B 78 ושלוא לזרוע שדו וכ[רמו כלאים]

B 79 [ב]גלל שהמה קדושים

B 80 [וא]תם יודעים שמקצת הכהנים ו[

C 2]שיבוא[ו]

C 10 שתבין בספר מושה [ו]ב[ספר]י הנ[ב]יאים

C 12 ואף כתוב ש[י]תסורו מהדר[ך

C 17 בספר] מושה וב[ספרי הנביאי]ם שיבוא

C 20 [ש]יב[ו]אם ב[

C 20 ואנחנו מכירים שבאו מקצת הברכות

C 21 שכתוב בס[פר מו]שה

C 21 שישובו בישר[אל] לת[מיד

C 23 שמי מהם שהיא ירא [ו]את התו[רה

C 24 שמי מהם שהיא ירא [ו]את התו[רה

C 25 זכור [את] דויד שהיא איש חסדים

C 27 כתבנו אליך מקצת מעשי התורה שחשבנו

C 27 שר[א]ינו עמך ערמה ומדע תורה

C 28 ובקש מלפנו שיתקן את עצתך

C 30 בשל שתשמח באחרית העת

שֵׁבֶט

B 61 והיא המקום שבחר בו מכל שבטי [ישראל

שַׁבָּת

A i בעשרים ושלושה בו שבת

A ii בעשרים] [ו]אח[ד] בו שבת

A ii [ב]עשרים ושמונה בו שבת

A ii עליו אחר השבת ו[יו]ם השני השלישי נוסף

A iii בע[שתי עשר] בו שבת

A iii בשמונה עשר בו **שבת**

A iii בעשרים וחמשה בו **שבת**

A iv בשש אשר בו **שבת**

A iv בעשרם ושלושא בו **שבת**

A v בעשרים ואחד] בו **שבת**

A 19 [בעשרים ושמונה בו]**שבת**

שָׂדֶה

B 78 ושלוא לזרוע **שדו** וכ[רמו כלאים

שׁוב

qal pf.

C 15 **ושבתה** אלו בכל לבבך [ובכו]ל נפש[ך

qal impf.

C 21 **שישובו** בישר[אל] לת[מיד

C 22 [י ולוא **ישובו** אחו[ר

שׁוֹר

B 28 או ישחט] מחוץ למחנה **שור** וכשב ועז

שׁחט

qal part.

B 14 **השוחט** אותה והסורף אותה

B 35 אי]נם **שוחטים** במקדש

שֶׁל

B 12 **בשל** שלוא י[היו] מסיא[י]ם את העם עוון

B 16 **בשל** שא יהיה הטהר מזה על הטמה

C 30 **בשל** שתשמח באחרית העת

שָׁלוֹשׁ

A 20 **שלוש** מאת וש[שים וארבעה] יום

שְׁלוֹשָׁה

A i בעשרים **ושלושה** בו שבת

A iv בעשרם **ושלושא** בו שבת

שְׁלוֹשִׁים

A i [ב]**של[ושי]ם** [בו שבת

A iv **בש]לושים** [בו שבת

שׁלם

qal part. *paʿel*

A 20 **ושלמה** השנה

B 74 שכול עצם ש[היא חסרה] **ושלמה**

שְׁלֹמֹה pers.

C 18]בימי **שלומוה** בן דויד

שְׁמוֹנָה

A ii [ב]עשרים **ושמונה** בו שבת

A iii **בשמונה** עשר בו שבת

שׂמח

qal impf.

C 30 בשל **שתשמח** באחרית העת

שְׁמִינִי

B 72 עד בוא השמש ביום **השמיני**

שֶׁמֶן

A v בעשרים ושנים בו מועד **השמן**

שׁמע

qal pf.

B 52 וא]ף על החרשים שלוא **שמעו** חוק

B 53 ולא [ש]**מעו** משפטי ישראל

B 53 כי שלוא ראה ולוא **שמע** לוא [י]דע לעשות

שׁמר

nipʿal inf.

B 26 ראוי [**להש]מ[ר** בכול הד[ב]רים

שֶׁמֶשׁ

B 15 להערי[בו]ת **השמש** להיות טהורים

B 72 עד בוא **השמש** ביום השמיני

מֹתוככים ומטמאי[ם] את זרﬠ [הקודש]	B 81

תּוֹךְ

ועל הזונות הנעסה בתוך העם	B 75

תּוֹעֵבָה

שלו]א תבﭏא תועבה אﬥ[ל] ביתכה	C 6
כי] התועבה שנואה הﭏאֹ	C 7

תּוֹרָה

שמי מהם שהיא ירא [ואת התו]רה	C 24
והם מﬡ[ק]שי תורה [נשו]אﬨי עונות	C 24
כתבנו אליך מקצת מעשי התורה	C 27
שר[א]ינו עמך ערמה ומדע תורה	C 28

תָּמִיד

שישובו ביש[ראל] לת[ו]מיד	C 22

תַּעֲרֹבֶת

להזהר מכול תﬡ[ה]ערובת [ה]גבר	B 48
[שאינם רואים להזהר מכל תערוﬡבת]	B 50
ותערובת [א]שם אינם רואים	B 50

תקן

pi'el impf.

ובקש מלפנו שיﬨﬡקﬥ את עצתך	C 28

שֹׂנֵא

qal pass. part.

כי] התועבה שנואה הﭏאﬣ	C 7

שָׁנָה

ושלמה השנה	A 20

שֵׁנִי

עליו אחר השבת ו[יו]ﬦ הש֯נ֯י[י]	A ii

שְׁנַיִם

בשנים בחמ[י]ש[י] [ש]ﬔ[ת]	A iii
בעשרים ושנים בו מועד השמן	A v

שַׁעַטְנֵז

ועל לבוש[ו] כתוב שלוא יהיה שעטנז	B 78

שְׁפֶכֶת

והממזר ופצוע הדכה וכרו[ת] השפכת	B 39

שֶׁקֶר

שלוא [י]ﬦצא בידנו מעל ושקר ורעﬣ	C 9

שָׂרַף

qal part.

השוחﬨ אותה והסורף אותה	B 14
ושור[פ]ים שם את החטאת	B 32

שִׁשָּׁה

ﬡשש אשר בו שבת	A iv

ת

תּוֹךְ

hip'il inf.

ואין לה]תﬥכֹם֯ [ו]לעשותﬦ [עצם אחת	
ﬦ֯להתיכמה¶MSᵈ:¶	B 44

hitpolel part.

מתוכ[כים]	B 47

REVERSE INDEX TO 4QMMT

בוזה	B 70
מזה	B 16
והמזה	B 14
לחה	B 58
שהמנחה	B 11
היה	C 24
יהיה	B 16
יהיה	B 78
יהיה	C 3
וצדקיה	C 19
לבבכה var.	C 22
לבבכה var.	C 22
אליכה	C 10
הברכה	C 14
וקרתכה	C 12
אלה	B 1
אלה	B 15
אלה	C 8
אלה	C 28
באלה	C 5
באלה	C 5
האלה	C 8
האלה	C 14
ונעלה	B 69
והמה	B 54
והמה	B 75
במעשיהמֺה	C 23
שהמה	B 24
שהמה	B 79
הטמה	B 16
להתיכמה var.	B 39
ושלמה	A 20
ושלמה	B 74
ערמה	C 28
עורותמה	B 22
ואתמה var.	B 75
לעשותמה var.	B 35
בשמונה	A III
ושמונה	A II
מחנה	B 30
מחנה	B 30
מחנה	B 60
המחנה	B 28

כתוב	B 27
כתוב	B 38
כתוב	B 66
כתוב	B 70
כתוב	B 77
כתוב	C 6
כתוב	C 11
כתוב	C 12
וכתוב	C 12
שכתוב	C 21
משכתוב	B 76
ומהתערב	C 8
ישב	B 66
וכשב	B 28
בדד	B 65
אחד	B 36
דויד	C 18
דויד	C 25
ובדויד	C 10
לתמיד	C 22
הולד	B 36
הולד	B 37
עד	B 72
ועד	C 19
מועד	A V
שהואה	B 70
שנואה	C 7
היאֹה	B 60
הֹיֹאֹה	C 7
היאה var.	B 25
היאה var.	B 56
ראה	B 53
בה	B 4
בה	B 6
תועבה	C 6
התועבה	C 7
ונחשבה	C 31
יהודה	C 19
שלומוה	C 18
הזה	B 12
וזה	C 21

בוא	B 72
יבוא	C 14
לבוא	B 5
ומלבוא	C 8
הוא	B 30
הוא	B 63
הוא	B 64
הוא	B 74
הוא	C 21
לוא	B 53
לוא	C 11
ולוא	B 53
ולוא	C 22
שלוא	B 12
שלוא	B 52
שלוא	B 53
שלוא	B 77
שלוא	C 6
ושלוא	B 78
להביא	B 69
תביא	C 6
היא	B 30
היא	B 32
היא	B 61
היא	C 26
והיא	B 60
והיא	C 14
שהיא	C 24
שהיא	C 25
ולא	B 52
והקללא	C 14
ימצא	C 9
ירא	C 24
שא	B 2
שא	B 9
שא	B 16
שא	B 27
דשא	B 31
ושלושא	A IV
הנושא	B 23
לגב	C 8
מרוב	C 7

בני	B 75	בקהל	B 40		
ובני	B 79	כול	C 14	האם	B 36
לבני	B 16	בכול	B 26	להביאם	B 45
למחני	B 58	ובכול	C 16	שיביאם	C 20
השמיני	B 72	לכול	B 15	האדם	B 73
והשני	A II	מכול	B 33	בהם	B 55
עצי	B 62	מכול	B 48	והם	C 24
ובספרי	C 10	שכול	B 73	זבחיהם	B 7
קדושי	B 79	מצול	C 24	עליהם	B 43
בחמישי	A III	שאיאכל	B 37	עליהם	B 59
מעשי	C 27	המאכל	B 62	עריהם	B 31
מבקשי	C 24	בכל	C 15	כהם	B 57
		בכל	C 28	מהם	C 23
במצאך	C 30	מכל	B 50	עמהם	B 67
לבבך	C 15	מכל	B 61	עמהם	C 8
לבבך	C 15	בגלל	B 79	שהם	B 1
בתוך	B 75	החלל	B 74	שהם	B 6
אליך	C 26	על	B 2	שהם	B 39
עליך	C 14	על	B 11	שהם	B 55
לך	C 27	על	B 13	שהם	B 58
לך	C 31	על	B 16	יום	A 21
לך	C 31	על	B 21	ביום	B 11
מלך	C 19	על	B 24	ביום	B 36
ממך	C 29	על	B 52	ביום	B 72
עמך	C 28	על	B 55	ליום	B 10
ולעמך	C 27	על	B 62	מיום	B 10
מהדרך	C 12	על	B 64	כתבנום var.	C 10
נפשך	C 16	על	C 9	המקום	B 32
בעשותך	C 31	ועל	B 8	המקום	B 60
עצתך	C 29	ועל	B 27	זבחם	B 8
		ועל	B 39	באים	B 39
אל	B 1	ועל	B 72	באים	B 54
אל	B 9	ועל	B 75	רואים	B 50
אל	C 15	ועל	B 76	רואים	B 51
ישראל	B 53	ועל	B 77	הנביאים	C 10
ישראל	B 61	ועל	C 4	הנביאים	C 17
ישראל	B 62	בליעל	C 29	מסיאים	B 13
ישראל	B 63	מעל	C 9	ומוציאים	B 31
ישראל	B 76	והמעל	C 4	משיאים	B 27
ישראל	C 23	נצל	C 26	כלאים	B 77
בישראל	C 21	בשל	B 12	ומטמאים	B 4
ולישראל	C 32	בשל	B 16	ומטמאים	B 81
והמקבל	B 57	בשל	C 30	יראים	B 49

החלבים	B 11	הדברים	B 26		
כלבים	B 58	הדברים	C 14	בן	C 18
חושבים	B 29	טהורים	B 15	בן	C 19
חושבים	B 36	מכירים	C 20	הבן	C 28
חושבים	B 37	אומרים	B 55	קרבן	A V
חושבים	B 42	אומרים	B 65	דגן	B 3
חסדים	C 25	אומרים	B 73	מדגן	B 5
הגוים	B 5	בעשרים	A I	עוון	B 13
הגוים	B 8	בעשרים	A II	עוון	B 27
זובחים	B 8	בעשרים	A III	בצפון	B 28
שמניחים	B 10	בעשרים	A V	והצון	B 64
לוקחים	B 40	מהקודשים	B 71	אהרון	B 79
שוחטים	B 35	קדושים	B 79	ואין	B 44
מתוככים	B 47	בשלושים	A I	ואין	B 58
מתוככים	B 81	בשלושים	A IV	שאין	B 55
כלים	B 19	הנשים	C 4	בין	B 56
אוכלים	B 59	המעשים	B 2	כן	B 38
מבשלים	B 6	החרשים	B 52	כן	C 30
ירושלים	B 60	להתיכם	B 44	ומן	B 22
ירושלים	B 61	וכולם	B 2	השמן	A V
וירושלים	B 29	להאכילם	B 71	והתבנן	C 23
הסומים	B 49	ירושלם	C 19	שיתקן	C 28
ימים	B 67	אינם	B 51	אהרן	B 17
הימים	C 14	אינם	B 56		
הימים	C 21	שאינם	B 50	וכבס	B 66
הכוהנים	B 12	עם	B 65	החמס	C 5
הכוהנים	B 26	עם	B 82		
לכוהנים	B 63	ירובעם	C 19	נגע	B 71
לכוהנים	B 64	העם	B 13	ידע	B 54
הכהנים	B 80	העם	B 27	ומדע	C 28
בשנים	A III	העם	B 46	לזרוע	B 78
ושנים	A V	העם	B 75	שמע	B 53
נותנים	C 9	העם	C 7	זרע	B 81
יודעים	B 68	עצם	B 40		
יודעים	B 80	עצם	B 73	ואף	B 10
יודעים	C 7	בעשרם	A IV	ואף	B 13
יודעים	C 8	אשם	B 51	ואף	B 21
הצרועים	B 64	ואתם	B 68	ואף	B 24
הצרועים	B 68	ואתם	B 80	ואף	B 42
ומגיעים	B 4	ואתם	C 7	ואף	B 52
והרשעים	C 22	ואתם	C 8	ואף	B 55
ושורפים	B 32	טמאתם	B 67	ואף	B 56
בדברים	C 8	ולעשותם	B 44	ואף	B 62

ואף	B 64	אשר	A IV	ואת	B 36
ואף	B 66	אשר	B 32	חטאת	B 70
ואף	C 12	בשר	B 7	החטאת	B 13
ואף	C 18	והבשר	B 11	החטאת	B 15
ואף	C 25	והבשר	B 59	החטאת	B 31
ואף	C 26	הישר	C 31	מאת	A 20
ומגדף	B 70	עשר	A III	תערובת	B 48
והאוסף	B 14	בעשתי עשר	A III	תערובת	B 50
נוסף	A 20			ותערובת	B 50
והסורף	B 14	ראש	B 61	שבת	A 19
		יגש	B 23	שבת	A I
חוץ	B 31	קודש	B 76	שבת	A II
מחוץ	B 28	הקודש	B 58	שבת	A III
מחוץ	B 66	הקודש	B 65	שבת	A III
בארץ	B 63	הקודש	B 68	שבת	A III
		קדש	B 76	שבת	A II
חוק	B 52	הקדש	B 60	שבת	A IV
והרחיק	C 29	במקדש	B 35	שבת	A IV
במרק	B 8	המקדש	B 54	שבת	A V
		המקדש	B 59	השבת	A II
הגבר	B 48	מהמקדש	B 49	טמאות	B 42
בדבר	B 12	שהמקדש	B 29	טמאות	B 71
והדבר	B 38	למקדש	B 5	להעריבות	B 15
להזהר	B 50	למקדש	B 20	רבות	C 26
הטהר	B 16	שלוש	A 20	מחשבות	C 29
הטהר	B 16	איש	C 25	ידות	B 22
דור	C 11	השמש	B 15	בהיות	B 67
ודור	C 11	השמש	B 72	להיות	B 15
לטהור	B 57	ובקש	C 28	להיות	B 17
זכור	C 25	בשש	A IV	ולהיות	B 49
עור	B 22			הברכות	C 20
שור	B 28	את	B 13	גלות	C 19
והממזר	B 39	את	B 14	מבדילות	B 56
אחר	A 19	את	B 14	הקללות	C 18
אחר	A II	את	B 27	והקללות	C 20
שבחר	B 61	את	B 31	מקומות	C 6
להזהר	B 12	את	B 36	הזונות	B 75
להשמר	B 26	את	B 37	הזונות	B 82
בספר	C 10	את	B 81	עונות	C 25
ובספר	C 11	את	B 82	והזנות	C 5
הבקר	B 18	את	C 9	מחנות	B 62
הבקר	B 63	את	C 23	המוצקות	B 55
ושקר	C 9	את	C 29	המוצקות	B 56

PLATES

PLATE I

2

Cols. iv-v

1

Cols. i-iii

4Q**394** 1-2
PAM 43.521; Mus. Inv. 693

PLATE II

3a

4

5

3b

6

7

Col. i

Col. ii

PLATE III

Col. v

8

Col. iv

4Q**394** 8-10
PAM 43.477; Mus. Inv. 335

Col. iii

9

10

4Q**395** 1
PAM 41.462; Mus. Inv. 187

PLATE IV

2

Col. i

1

Col. ii

4Q396 1
PAM 41.638; Mus. Inv. 520

Col. iv

Col. iii

2

4Q396 2
PAM 42.631; Mus. Inv. 526

PLATE V

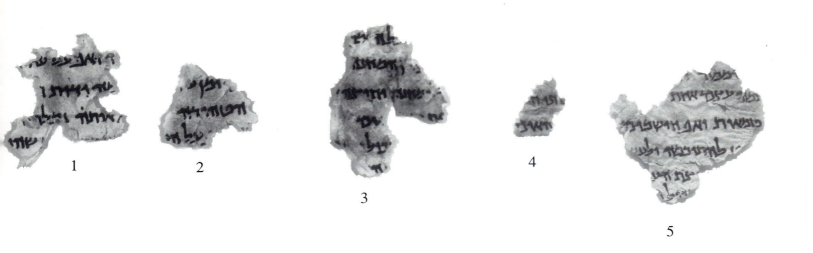

1 2 3 4 5

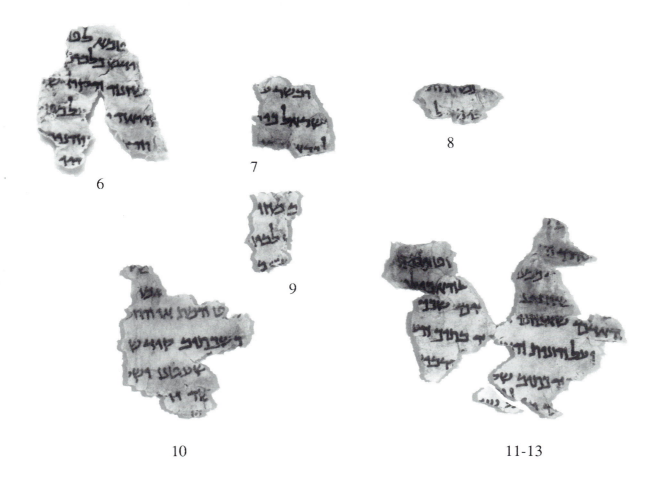

6 7 8 9 10 11-13

4Q**397** 1-13
PAM 42.717; Mus. Inv. 1216

PLATE VI

4Q**397** 14-23
PAM 42.717; Mus. Inv. 157a

PLATE VII

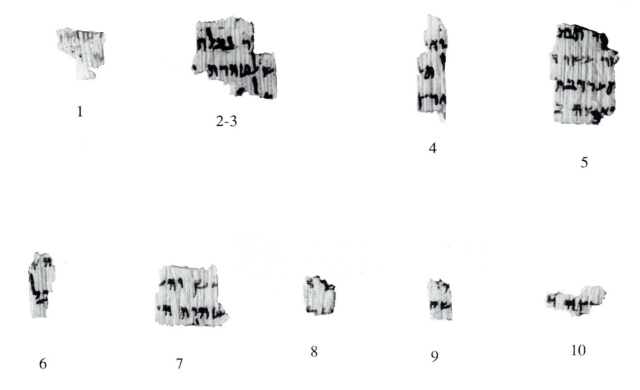

4Q**398** 1-10
PAM 43.489; Mus. Inv. 157b

4Q**398** 11-13
PAM 42.183; Mus. Inv. 157b

PLATE VIII

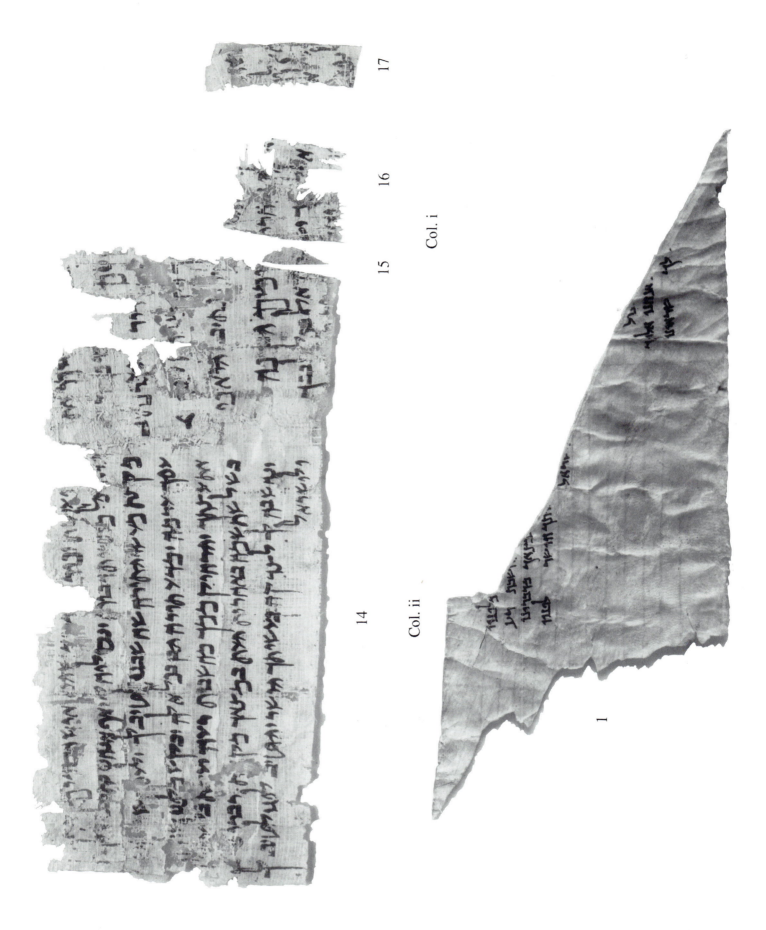

17

16

15

Col. i

14

Col. ii

1

4Q**398** 14-17
PAM 42.368; Mus. Inv. 157c

4Q**399** 1
PAM 41.823; Mus. Inv. 292

D0103178